OS/2 Presentation Manager Programming

Titles in the IBM McGraw-Hill Series

Open Systems and IBM: Integration and Convergence
Pamela Gray   ISBN 0-07-707750-4

OS/2 Presentation Manager Programming: Hints and Tips
Bryan Goodyer   ISBN 0-07-707776-8

IBM RISC System/6000
Clive Harris   ISBN 0-07-707668-0

IBM RISC System/6000 User Guide
Mike Leaver and Hardev Sanghera   ISBN 0-07-707687-7

PC User's Guide: Simple Steps to Powerful Personal Computing
Peter Turner   ISBN 0-07-707421-1

Dynamic Factory Automation: Creating Flexible Systems for Competitive Manufacturing
Alastair Ross   ISBN 0-07-707440-8

MVS Systems Programming
Dave Elder-Vass   ISBN 0-07-707767-9

The New Organization: Growing the Culture of Organizational Networking
Colin Hastings   ISBN 0-07-707784-9

Commonsense Computer Security Second Edition: Your Practical Guide to Information Protection
Martin Smith   ISBN 0-07-707805-5

CICS Concepts and Uses: A Management Guide
Jim Geraghty   ISBN 0-07-707751-2

Risk Management for Software Projects
Alex Down, Michael Coleman and Peter Absolon ISBN 0-07-707816-0

Investing in Information Technology: Managing the decision-making process
Geoff Hogbin and David Thomas   ISBN 0-07-707957-1

The Advanced Programmer's Guide to AIX 3.x
Phil Colledge   ISBN 0-07-707663-X

Details of these titles in the series are available from:

The Product Manager, Professional Books
McGraw-Hill Book Company Europe
Shoppenhangers Road, Maidenhead, Berkshire, SL6 2QL
Telephone: 0628 23432 Fax: 0628 770224

Bryan Goodyer

OS/2 Presentation Manager Programming: Hints and tips

McGRAW-HILL BOOK COMPANY

London · New York · St Louis · San Francisco · Auckland
Bogotá · Caracas · Lisbon · Madrid · Mexico · Milan
Montreal · New Delhi · Panama · Paris · San Juan
São Paulo · Singapore · Sydney · Tokyo · Toronto

Published by
McGRAW-HILL Book Company Europe
Shoppenhangers Road, Maidenhead, Berkshire, SL6 2QL, England
Telephone 0628 23432 Fax 0628 770224

British Library Cataloguing in Publication Data

Goodyer, Bryan
   OS/2 Presentation Manager Programming:
   Hints and Tips. – (IBM McGraw-Hill Series)
   I. Title II. Series
   005.4
   ISBN 0-07-707776-8

Library of Congress Cataloging-in-Publication Data

Goodyer, Bryan
   OS/2 Presentation Manager Programming: Hints and Tips/Bryan Goodyer.
    p. cm. – (The IBM McGraw-Hill series)
   Includes index.
   ISBN 0-07-707776-8:
   1. Operating systems (Computers) 2. OS/2 (Computer file)
   3. Presentation manager. I. Title. II. Series.
   QA76.76.063G6635 1993
   005.4'3–dc20   92-41989
                                                                                                                              CIP

Copyright © 1993 McGraw-Hill International (UK) Limited. All rights reserved. No part of this publication may be reproduced, stored in a retrieval system, or transmitted, in any form or by any means, electronic, mechanical, photocopying, recording, or otherwise, without the prior permission of McGraw-Hill International (UK) Limited, with the exception of material entered and executed on a computer system for the reader's own use.

1234 CUP 9543

Typeset by Alden Multimedia
and printed and bound in Great Britain at the University Press, Cambridge

*This book is dedicated to my wife Susan and children
Joanne and Andrew.
Their support and encouragement have
made it all worth while.*

Contents

	IBM Series Foreword	xi
	Preface	xiii
	Acknowledgements	xvii
	Trademarks	xix
1	**16-bit to 32-bit conversion**	**1**
	1.1 Hungarian notation	1
	1.2 Skeleton program and its conversion to 32-bit	2
	1.3 16-bit to 32-bit conversion summary	13
2	**General window processing**	**17**
	2.1 Some common errors	17
	2.2 Initial display of the client window	19
	2.3 Controlling movement, position and size	23
	2.4 Class names	30
	2.5 Obtaining the process ID of the active window	30
	2.6 System modal window	32
	2.7 Saving your application's current state	32
	2.8 Changing the window title	34
	2.9 EXE name appearing in the title bar	34
	2.10 Removing the title bar	34
	2.11 Sending/posting a message	35
	2.12 Sending a `WM_COMMAND` message	35
	2.13 Sample program	36
3	**A system modal application**	**46**
	3.1 Sample program (32-bit)	47
	3.2 Sample program (16-bit)	53
4	**Presentation parameters**	**57**
	4.1 Changing colour	57
	4.2 Changing font	58
	4.3 Applying presentation parameters to a frame window	59
	4.4 Sample program	59
5	**Dialog boxes and their controls**	**60**
	5.1 Dialog box as a main window	60
	5.2 Minimizing a dialog box	61
	5.3 Starting minimized	62
	5.4 Positioning a dialog box on the desktop	63
	5.5 Mnemonics for controls	63
	5.6 Modeless dialog box	63

5.7	Adding a status bar	64
5.8	Disabling controls	65
5.9	Window ID of a control	65
5.10	Buttons	66
5.11	Entry fields	70
5.12	Focus	76
5.13	Icons	76
5.14	Listboxes	77
5.15	Menus	96
5.16	Multiline entry fields	97
5.17	Styles	98
5.18	Text	99
5.19	Sample programs	101

6 More controls — 139
6.1	The slider control	140
6.2	The value set control	147
6.3	The notebook control	152

7 Standard dialogs — 162
7.1	The file dialog	162
7.2	The font dialog	165
7.3	Sample program	168

8 The atom manager and user messages — 189
8.1	The atom manager	189
8.2	Unique user messages	190
8.3	Sample program	191

9 Window words and initialization data — 199
9.1	Window words for client windows	199
9.2	Window words for dialog boxes	201
9.3	Initialization data for dialog boxes	201
9.4	Sample program	202

10 Window enumeration — 220
10.1	What is enumeration?	220
10.2	Obtaining the handle of a child window	221
10.3	Sample program	222

11 Icons — 223
11.1	Are icons necessary?	223
11.2	Changing icon text	224
11.3	Hiding icon text	224
11.4	Dynamic update of icon	225
11.5	Sample program	226

12 Threads and timers — 240
12.1	Creating a thread	240
12.2	Communicating with the main thread	241

		Contents	ix

	12.3	Killing a thread (32-bit)	244
	12.4	Killing a thread (16-bit and 32-bit)	245
	12.5	Setting a timer for longer than 65 seconds	246
	12.6	Sample program	247
13	**Menus, task management and shutdown**		**259**
	13.1	Menus and menu bars	259
	13.2	Pop-up menus	266
	13.3	Task management	268
	13.4	Shutdown	272
	13.5	Sample program	273
14	**A sample application**		**287**
	14.1	A program to monitor the swap file partition	287
	14.2	Program summary	288
15	**A basic exception handler**		**339**
	15.1	Trapping access violations	339
	15.2	Trapping guard page exceptions	342
	15.3	Running the debugger	343

Appendices

1	Glossary	345
2	Obtaining accompanying software	353

Index	**354**

Foreword

The IBM McGraw-Hill Series

IBM UK and McGraw-Hill Europe have worked together to publish this series of books about information technology and its use in business, industry and the public sector.

The series provides an up-to-date and authoritative insight into the wide range of products and services available, and offers strategic business advice. Some of the books have a technical bias, others are written from a broader business perspective. What they have in common is that their authors—some from IBM, some independent consultants—are experts in their field.

Apart from assisting where possible with the accuracy of the writing, IBM UK has not sought to inhibit the editorial freedom of the series, and therefore the views expressed in the books are those of the authors, and not necessarily those of IBM.

Where IBM has lent its expertise is in assisting McGraw-Hill to identify potential titles whose publication would help advance knowledge and increase awareness of computing topics. Hopefully these titles will also serve to widen the debate about the important information technology issues of today and of the future—such as open systems, networking, and the use of technology to give companies a competitive edge in their market.

IBM UK is pleased to be associated with McGraw-Hill in this series.

Sir Anthony Cleaver
Chairman
IBM United Kingdom Limited

Preface

Before we start, let me explain what this book is about and why it is different from all the other books you may have read about OS/2 and Presentation Manager. Since June 1988 many have taken the road to Presentation Manager programming, and inevitably found that it wasn't as straight as they first thought. It contained many twists and turns, dead-ends and up and downs, but fortunately they found the way in the end. Those programmers in IBM were fortunate to have at their disposal an extremely powerful, comprehensive computer conferencing facility which has been used, and still is today, to solve no end of problems. Even now, many of these problems are still causing trouble, especially among newcomers to Presentation Manager. Every two or three weeks the same questions are being asked, hence the reason for writing this book. It is a compilation of the most commonly asked questions and their solutions. For example, some of the questions repeatedly asked are:

- How can I make a dialog box a main window?
- How do I arrange data in columns in my listbox?
- Why can I not set the focus in my dialog box on initialization?
- How can I prevent users from accessing applications other than mine?

These, and many more questions are answered in this book. Where applicable each solution is backed up with code fragments and, where appropriate, is incorporated into a sample program. These programs do not have any significant function however, they only serve to confirm that the solutions are correct. For this reason I have ignored such things as error checking, except where relevant to the solution. Also, on occasions when it has been necessary to verify that certain values have been returned, I have omitted to display them. Instead, I used the Presentation Manager debugger to check the values. For this reason, all programs have been built for use with the debugger. You will also notice in the sample programs code which has been commented out. This code was used to confirm alternative methods, or just to verify a particular point.

All the problems covered by this book were originally identified whilst using the 16-bit version of OS/2 (OS/2 V1.x), however, the majority still apply to the 32-bit version (OS/2 V2.0) and for these all the code is written for IBM's new 32-bit compiler, C Set/2. Where the problem no longer exists for version 2.0, the code is written for IBM's C/2 version 1.1 compiler and is clearly identified. If a solution is applicable to both 16-bit and 32-bit but the code differs then this will also be identified.

Now a word of warning, this book is *not* intended to teach you *how* to write Presentation Manager programs, there are several very good books on the market today intended for that purpose. No, this book is for those of you who have already written at least one basic Presentation Manager program, *'Hello World'* for example, and need to go that bit further. It's not until you actually start writing your own Presentation Manager programs that you find the simplest things you want to do just are not documented anywhere, or appear not to be. This is the idea behind this book. Hopefully you will find the answer to many of the 'How do I . . .' type of questions.

In order to keep this book down to a manageable size I have made no attempt to explain parameter usage on individual function calls. It is assumed that you have the OS/2 version 2.0 developer's toolkit installed which has all this information on-line. In fact, to get the most out of this book you should take the sample code, and experiment with it by making changes and observing the results. You will also notice, particularly for the chapter on dialog boxes, that I have not included examples for all the controls. The reason for this is that the book is based on the areas that have caused, and still cause, most problems, or raised most questions. The fact that a particular control, or other topic, does not appear is because it has not had the same level of difficulty. This book addresses those questions which arise regularly.

For completeness, you will find at the end of the book a simple utility program. It is a program which monitors the swap file partition and warns when you are low on disk space. It uses many of the hints given throughout the book, and, indeed, it is almost impossible to write any application without using this information in one way or another.

Finally, as a reminder, the sample programs were *not* designed to conform to any standard or provide any major functionality, they are here *only* to verify each solution and to give you the code to extract, and modify where necessary, for your own programs. For this reason, it is strongly recommended that you obtain the accompanying diskettes which contain all the source code, both 16-bit and 32-bit, and the executable modules.

> *Warning:* This book makes reference to some *undocumented* interfaces and features. *You are strongly advised that under no circumstances should you use these, or indeed any such undocumented interface or feature that you may discover, for any software intended for the marketplace.* There are many reasons why they are not documented, most importantly:
>
> - They are liable to change at any time, either through a corrective service diskette (CSD) or a new release.
> - They may be removed.
> - They may only work currently under special conditions.
>
> All such interfaces and features are clearly marked, and *you use them at your own risk*.

Preface

Now let us briefly look at what the book covers.

Chapter 1 takes a very simple 16-bit skeleton program and goes through the process of converting it to 32-bit. This program then forms the basis of most of the other sample programs. After this we look at some of the other areas that have changed with the introduction of OS/2 version 2.0. This is intended to give you an idea of what to look for if you have to convert any of your own 16-bit applications.

Chapter 2 looks at the problems associated with processing windows in general. These are mainly to do with size and position, but the chapter also covers subclassing.

Chapter 3 covers the essentials of a system modal application, this is something that crops up quite regularly. It would appear that many organizations want to restrict their users to one specific application, this chapter shows you how to do just that.

Chapter 4 takes a quick look at presentation parameters, these are used throughout the book whenever we need to change the font or colour of a control.

Chapter 5, by far the largest, covers dialog boxes and their controls. This is the one area that has raised more questions than any other. I have not mentioned all the possible controls here, just those that have given rise to the most questions. Probably the one topic that has caused most concern is the ownerdraw listbox; this is covered in some detail and should be enough to get you started. Another very common question related to dialog boxes is how to use them as the main application window. Again this is covered in detail and in fact, the three sample programs I have written for this chapter use this approach.

Chapter 6 takes a look at some of the new controls for version 2.0: the slider, value set and notebook.

Chapter 7 continues looking at version 2.0 by introducing the two new standard dialogs, file open and font change. All these version 2.0 additions are combined into one sample program.

Chapter 8 looks at the atom manager and user messages. Specifically it deals with the problem of message IDs. If you send a message to another application you need to be sure that the message ID is unique to prevent the receiving application from doing something you had not intended.

Chapter 9 covers the use of window words and the problem of passing initialization data to a dialog box.

Chapter 10 investigates window enumeration, a topic which has not been covered much up to now. We see how to obtain the handle of a window in another application and hence change its appearance.

Chapter 11 looks at icon handling, specifically animated icons and how to change, or hide, the text under an icon. This also uses window enumeration.

Chapter 12 looks at threads and timers. It specifically shows how to create a timer greater than one minute using a separate thread. It also discusses how the DosCreateThread function has changed for version 2.0 as well as the introduction of DosKillThread.

Chapter 13 covers three related topics: menus, task management and shutdown. It shows how to modify the system and application menus, and how to implement pop-up menus. It then goes on to look at the window list and how you can add, or change, your program's entry in that list. Finally, it deals with the shutdown process.

Chapter 14 puts many of the tips covered in this book together to build a complete 32-bit utility program. This program monitors the size of the swap file to give you an early warning of space shortage. As soon as the free space on your swap partition falls below 3Mb a message box is displayed giving you this warning and remains on the desktop until the free space once again rises above 3Mb.

Chapter 15 is a little beyond the scope of this book since it does not explicitly deal with Presentation Manager. However, because memory management is fundamentally different in version 2.0, and exception handling has been greatly enhanced, I have provided an exception handler as an easy way to manage memory for those programs which may need to manipulate large amounts of memory.

Acknowledgements

I would like to thank John Galvez, Mike Parker, Gordon Price, Dave Saunders and Dilbagh Singh, all from the European Personal Systems Centre, IBM Europe, for their comments and criticisms. In particular, I would like to thank John and Mike for meticulously reviewing the book as they were coding their own Presentation Manager programs. Their experiences have helped to make this a better book.

Of course, the book would never have been possible if it had not been for all those programmers in IBM, too many to mention, who had the problems in the first place.

Trademarks

C Set/2, C/2, CUA, IBM, OS/2, Operating System/2, Presentation Manager, Workplace Shell are registered trademarks of International Business Machines Corporation.

1
16-bit to 32-bit conversion

As an introduction, let us start by taking a simple 16-bit OS/2 skeleton program and going through the process of converting it to 32-bit. Once this has been done we will look at some other areas you should be aware of if converting to 32-bit. But first, a quick review of the notation used throughout the book.

1.1 Hungarian notation

Presentation Manager uses a variable naming convention which, at first sight, looks rather strange. Briefly, the method is to prefix each variable with a lower-case tag so that its type is quickly identifiable, for example, the variable `szText` would be a zero-terminated string of text. The variable name itself begins in upper case and uses mixed case from then on. This notation is called the *Hungarian notation* and is so-called because its inventor, Charles Simonyi, is a Hungarian.

The most common prefixes are as follows:

short	s
unsigned short	us
long	l
unsigned long	ul
character	ch
unsigned character	uch
byte	b
zero-terminated string	sz
counter	c
pointer	p
rectangle	rc
window handle	hwnd
other handle	h
flag	f

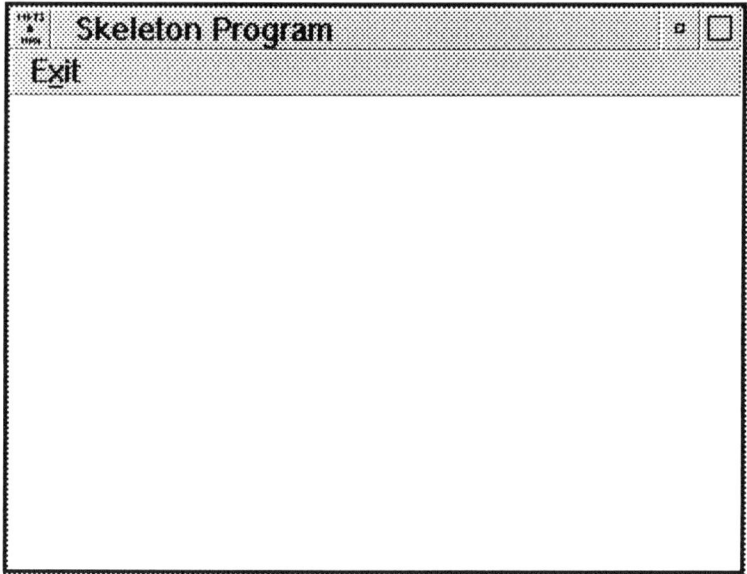

Figure 1.1. Skeleton program output.

These prefixes can also be combined, for example, the variable `pszText` would be a pointer to a string of text.

You will find this notation used extensively throughout the book.

1.2 Skeleton program and its conversion to 32-bit

This skeleton program does nothing more than build a small, sizeable, client window centralized on the desktop. It contains a menu bar with an `Exit` option, minimize and maximize icons and the system menu (Fig 1.1).

The C source for this program is shown in Fig. 1.2. It is used as the base for all the other programs in this book, so let us take a quick look at it.

Obviously, the first thing we must do in any Presentation Manager program is to inform Presentation Manager of our presence by calling `WinInitialize`. This returns us an anchor block handle, through which Presentation Manager keeps track of us. We must then start a message queue and register our window class. Notice that we have used the anchor block handle in both these calls. We can now consider ourselves fully signed-up and ready to go with Presentation Manager; it knows where our queue is, what our window class is and what window procedure it is to use when a message is destined for it. However, before we can do anything useful we must have a window, so that is what we do next. We load the title of the window from the resource file, the source of which is in Fig. 1.3, and set the frame flags for the controls we need and then call `WinCreateStdWindow`. Because we have not specified any window styles, the second parameter, the

```c
#define     INCL_WINWINDOWMGR
#define     INCL_WINFRAMEMGR
#define     INCL_WINSWITCHLIST
#define     INCL_WINSYS

#include    <os2.h>
#include    <string.h>
#include    <stdlib.h>
#include    "skeleton.h"

MRESULT EXPENTRY MainWndProc(HWND, USHORT, MPARAM, MPARAM);

/**************************************************************/

VOID    cdecl main(void)
{
  HAB       hab;
  HMQ       hmq;

  HWND      hwndFrame,
            hwndClient;
  QMSG      qmsg;
  ULONG     flFrameFlags;
  CHAR      szTitle[80];
  SWCNTRL   PgmEntry;
  SHORT     sX_Left,
            sY_Bot,
            sHeight,
            sWidth;
  LONG      lScrHeight,
            lScrWidth;

/**************************************************************/
  hab = WinInitialize(0);
  hmq = WinCreateMsgQueue(hab, 0);

  WinRegisterClass(hab, "Skeleton", MainWndProc, CS_SIZEREDRAW, 0);

  WinLoadString(hab, NULL, ID_TITLE, sizeof(szTitle), szTitle);

  flFrameFlags = FCF_TITLEBAR | FCF_SYSMENU | FCF_MENU |
                 FCF_SIZEBORDER | FCF_MINMAX | FCF_ACCELTABLE |
                 FCF_ICON;
```

Figure 1.2. Skeleton program: C source file (16-bit). Continues.

```c
    hwndFrame = WinCreateStdWindow(HWND_DESKTOP, 0L, &flFrameFlags,
                                   "Skeleton", (PSZ)szTitle, 0L,
                                   NULL, ID_MAINWND, &hwndClient);
    lScrWidth  = WinQuerySysValue(HWND_DESKTOP, SV_CXSCREEN);
    lScrHeight = WinQuerySysValue(HWND_DESKTOP, SV_CYSCREEN);
    sWidth  = 400;
    sHeight = 300;
    sX_Left = ((SHORT)lScrWidth  - sWidth)  / 2;
    sY_Bot  = ((SHORT)lScrHeight - sHeight) / 2;
                                     /*----------------------*/
                                     /* Startup in foreground   */
                                     /*----------------------*/
    WinSetWindowPos(hwndFrame, NULL, sX_Left, sY_Bot, sWidth,
                    sHeight,
                    SWP_SIZE | SWP_MOVE | SWP_SHOW | SWP_ACTIVATE);
    PgmEntry.hwnd          = hwndFrame; /*----------------------*/
    PgmEntry.hwndIcon      = NULL;      /* Add to task list       */
    PgmEntry.hprog         = NULL;      /*----------------------*/
    PgmEntry.idProcess     = NULL;
    PgmEntry.idSession     = NULL;
    PgmEntry.uchVisibility = SWL_VISIBLE;
    PgmEntry.fbJump        = SWL_JUMPABLE;
    strcpy(PgmEntry.szSwtitle, szTitle);

    WinAddSwitchEntry(&PgmEntry);

    while (WinGetMsg(hab, &qmsg, NULL, 0, 0))
       WinDispatchMsg(hab, &qmsg);
                                     /*--------------------------------*/
                                     /*Remove from task list and clean up*/
                                     /*--------------------------------*/
    WinRemoveSwitchEntry(WinQuerySwitchHandle(hwndFrame, 0));
    WinDestroyWindow(hwndFrame);
    WinDestroyMsgQueue(hmq);
    WinTerminate(hab);
}
/*************************************************************/
MRESULT EXPENTRY MainWndProc(HWND hwnd, USHORT msg, MPARAM mp1,
                             MPARAM mp2)
```

Figure 1.2. Skeleton program: C source file (16-bit). Continues.

```
{
  switch (msg)
    {
      case WM_COMMAND:
         switch (SHORT1FROMMP(mp1))
            {
              case MI_EXIT:
                 WinPostMsg(hwnd, WM_QUIT, 0L, 0L);
                 break;
              default:
                 break;
            }
         break;
      case WM_ERASEBACKGROUND:
         return (MRESULT)TRUE;
    }
  return WinDefWindowProc(hwnd, msg, mp1, mp2);
}
```

Figure 1.2. Skeleton program: C source file (16-bit). Concluded.

window will be created *invisible*. We do this so that we can size and position it ourselves; that is the significance of the next few statements. The window is displayed as a result of the `WinSetWindowPos` call. Having finally displayed the window, we add ourselves to the task list, or window list as it is called in OS/2 version 2.0. We then start our message-processing loop and remain in it until a `WM_QUIT` message arrives, when we remove our entry from the task list and destroy the window and message queue. We finally tell Presentation Manager that we have finished by calling `WinTerminate`. The window procedure, `MainWndProc`, is concerned with two messages only, `WM_ERASEBACKGROUND`, from which we return TRUE, which causes our window to be painted with the default window background colour, and `WM_COMMAND` with a command value of `MI_EXIT`, which causes the `WM_QUIT` message to be sent, and hence termination of the program. One last point worth mentioning is the presence of the `#define INCL_*` statements at the start of the program. You need these so that all the function prototypes and other definitions are known to your program. You may sometimes come across programs that just have `#define INCL_PM`. This is not recommended as you will then include all the Presentation Manager function prototypes and definitions that exist, and that is a lot! This will make your compile time much longer and will also make your executable file slightly larger. It is much better to `#define` only those you need. The toolkit documentation specifies which `INCL` you need for any particular function. Failing this, you can always browse the header files in the \TOOLKT20\C\OS2H directory. This is a useful source of information; it is well worth taking a quick look.

```
#include <os2.h>
#include "skeleton.h"

STRINGTABLE PRELOAD
BEGIN
  ID_TITLE, "Skeleton Program"
END

ICON        ID_MAINWND skeleton.ico

ACCELTABLE  ID_MAINWND
BEGIN
  VK_F3,    MI_EXIT,            VIRTUALKEY
END

MENU        ID_MAINWND PRELOAD
BEGIN
  SUBMENU "E~xit",                        IDM_ONE
  BEGIN
    MENUITEM "~Exit Program\tF3",    MI_EXIT,    MIS_TEXT
    MENUITEM "~Resume Program",      MI_RESUME,  MIS_TEXT
  END
END
```

Figure 1.3. Skeleton program: resource file (16/32-bit).

You will find some of the above treated in far greater detail as you work through the book, but before we start looking at Presentation Manager problems, let us convert this simple 16-bit program of Fig. 1.2 to 32-bit. The obvious thing to do first is change the make and link control files, and then just run our 16-bit code through the compiler and let it tell us what needs to be done.

If you already have a 16-bit application that needs converting, you may find that you will not need to do much depending on which APIs you use. The areas that have changed significantly are memory management and semaphores, so if you make little use of these you will find conversion very quick and easy.

First, however, let us look at the 16-bit versions of the make (Fig. 1.4) and link control (Fig. 1.5) files. Before we can compile our skeleton program we must first change these files.

All we need do for the make file, is to change the linker to the 80386 version, LINK386.EXE, and switch to the IBM C Set/2 32-bit compiler, ICC.EXE (Fig 1.6). We also need to change the compile options. These will be used throughout the book:

/c	Compile only
/Gm	Use the multithreaded libraries
/kb	Produce basic diagnostic messages
/n50	End compilation after 50 errors
/Ti	Generate information for the C Set/2 debugger.

Note that the compile options are *case insensitive*, so /Gm = /GM = /gm = /gM.

```
skeleton.exe: skeleton.obj skeleton.def skeleton.res
  link @skeleton.l
  rc skeleton.res

skeleton.obj: skeleton.c skeleton.h
  cl /c /Alfu /W2 /Gs /Gc /Zi /Od skeleton.c

skeleton.res: skeleton.h skeleton.rc skeleton.ico
  rc -r skeleton.rc
```

Figure 1.4. Skeleton program: make file (16-bit).

```
skeleton /A:16 /CO
skeleton.exe
skeleton.map /NOD
llibce.lib+
os2.lib
skeleton.def
```

Figure 1.5. Skeleton program: link control file (16-bit).

```
skeleton.exe: skeleton.obj skeleton.def skeleton.res
  link386 @skeleton.l                    ⇐
  rc skeleton.res

skeleton.obj: skeleton.c skeleton.h
  icc /c /Gm /kb /n50 /Ti skeleton.c     ⇐

skeleton.res: skeleton.h skeleton.rc skeleton.ico
  rc -r skeleton.rc
```

Figure 1.6. Skeleton program: make file (32-bit).

All we need to change in the link control file is the library (Fig. 1.7), by using OS2386.LIB. We also no longer need the /NOD option. In fact, it is recommended that we do omit it, since the C Set/2 compiler passes the correct library names to the linker in the object file, based on the /G option. To keep the EXE size down to a minimum, we have retained the /A:16 option and added the /EXEPACK option. Note that this option is now valid for OS/2.

```
skeleton /A:16 /E /CO         ⇐
skeleton.exe
skeleton.map
os2386.lib                    ⇐
skeleton.def
```

Figure 1.7. Skeleton program link control file (32-bit).

Because OS/2 uses the flat memory model of the 80386 architecture we do not need to worry about models, for example whether they are small, medium or large; all programs may now be considered *small model*.

The other files required for this program are:

- Header (Fig. 1.8)
- Module definition (Fig. 1.9)
- Resource (see Fig. 1.3)

These do not need changing; they are valid for both the 16-bit and 32-bit versions. However, the `HEAPSIZE` statement may be deleted from the module definition file for 32-bit OS/2.

```
#define    ID_MAINWND      200
#define    ID_TITLE        201
#define    IDM_ONE         202
#define    MI_EXIT         203
#define    MI_RESUME       204
```

Figure 1.8. Skeleton program header file (16/32-bit).

```
NAME        skeleton WINDOWAPI

DESCRIPTION 'Skeleton Program'

STUB        'OS2STUB.EXE'

DATA        MULTIPLE

HEAPSIZE  8192  ⇐ Can be removed for version 2.0

STACKSIZE 8192

PROTMODE
```

Figure 1.9. Skeleton program: module definition file (16/32-bit).

16-bit to 32-bit conversion

Note: Because the link control files, module definition files and make files are similar for all the sample programs in this book, they will not be reproduced for each program, since it is normally only the program name and description that differs. However, all program source files are supplied on the diskettes.

Running the program through the compiler produces the listing shown in Fig. 1.10. Note that for each error the compiler reports the line number and the offset within that line where the error has occurred. Note also that the 32-bit make program is now called **NMAKE.EXE**.

```
         icc /c /Gm /kb /n50 /Ti skeleton.c
SKELETON.C(15:9)   : error EDC0187: The declaration or definition of
                     the function is not valid.
SKELETON.C(15:15)  : error EDC0348: Syntax error: possible missing
                     '{'?
SKELETON.C(38:37)  : error EDC0322: Type of the parameter cannot
                     conflict with previous declaration of function.
SKELETON.C(38:37)  : informational EDC0141: Prototype has type
                     unsigned long integer.
SKELETON.C(38:37)  : informational EDC0147: Argument has type
                     unsigned short integer.
SKELETON.C(40:22)  : error EDC0322: Type of the parameter cannot
                     conflict with previous declaration of function.
SKELETON.C(40:22)  : informational EDC0141: Prototype has type
                     unsigned long integer.
SKELETON.C(40:22)  : informational EDC0147: Argument has type pointer
                     to void.
SKELETON.C(46:38)  : error EDC0322: Type of the parameter cannot
                     conflict with previous declaration of function.
SKELETON.C(46:38)  : informational EDC0141: Prototype has type
                     unsigned long integer.
SKELETON.C(46:38)  : informational EDC0147: Argument has type pointer
                     to void.
SKELETON.C(57:30)  : error EDC0322: Type of the parameter cannot
                     conflict with previous declaration of function.
SKELETON.C(57:30)  : informational EDC0141: Prototype has type
                     unsigned long integer.
SKELETON.C(57:30)  : informational EDC0147: Argument has type pointer
                     to void.
SKELETON.C(61:28)  : warning EDC0807: Variable hwndFrame may not have
                     been set before first reference.
SKELETON.C(62:26)  : error EDC0117: The operation between these types
                     is not valid.
```

Figure 1.10. Skeleton program: compiler listing. Continues.

```
SKELETON.C(62:3)   : informational EDC0140: Operand has type unsigned
                     long integer.
SKELETON.C(62:28)  : informational EDC0140: Operand has type pointer
                     to void.
SKELETON.C(63:26)  : error EDC0117: The operation between these types
                     is not valid.
SKELETON.C(63:3)   : informational EDC0140: Operand has type unsigned
                     long integer.
SKELETON.C(63:28)  : informational EDC0140: Operand has type pointer
                     to void.
SKELETON.C(64:26)  : error EDC0117: The operation between these types
                     is not valid.
SKELETON.C(64:3)   : informational EDC0140: Operand has type unsigned
                     long integer.
SKELETON.C(64:28)  : informational EDC0140: Operand has type pointer
                     to void.
SKELETON.C(65:26)  : error EDC0117: The operation between these types
                     is not valid.
SKELETON.C(65:3)   : informational EDC0140: Operand has type unsigned
                     long integer.
SKELETON.C(65:28)  : informational EDC0140: Operand has type pointer
                     to void.
SKELETON.C(72:32)  : error EDC0322: Type of the parameter cannot
                     conflict with previous declaration of function.
SKELETON.C(72:32)  : informational EDC0141: Prototype has type
                     unsigned long integer.
SKELETON.C(72:32)  : informational EDC0147: Argument has type pointer
                     to void.
SKELETON.C(82:1)   : warning EDC0833: Implicit return statement
                     encountered.
SKELETON.C(82:0)   : warning EDC0805: Automatic variable sY_Bot is
                     set but not referenced.
SKELETON.C(82:0)   : warning EDC0805: Automatic variable sX_Left is
                     set but not referenced.
SKELETON.C(82:0)   : warning EDC0805: Automatic variable
                     flFrameFlags is set but not referenced.
SKELETON.C(82:0)   : warning EDC0805: Automatic variable hwndClient
                     is set but not referenced.
```

Figure 1.10. Skeleton program: compiler listing. Concluded.

As you can see, we do not have too many problems to fix. In fact, all we need to do is to change the definition of `main`,—it now returns an `INT`—and pay attention to parameters on our function calls to OS/2 (Fig. 1.11). The main problem encountered here is the redefinition of `NULL`. It is now defined as `((void *)0)`, so you may have to cast it, for example (HMODULE)NULL in line number 46, or replace it with 0. You will also need to change some SHORTs to LONGs, the most common being the definition of all your window procedures, the msg parameter is now defined as a ULONG.

Making these very simple changes converts our skeleton program into a pure 32-bit program. All the changed statements have been marked in Fig. 1.11 with an arrow to make them easily identifiable.

```
#define    INCL_WINWINDOWMGR
#define    INCL_WINFRAMEMGR
#define    INCL_WINSWITCHLIST
#define    INCL_WINSYS

#include   <os2.h>
#include   <string.h>
#include   <stdlib.h>
#include   "skeleton.h"
MRESULT EXPENTRY MainWndProc(HWND, ULONG, MPARAM, MPARAM);       ⇐
/***************************************************************/
INT main(VOID)                                                   ⇐
{
  HAB      hab;
  HMQ      hmq;

  HWND     hwndFrame,
           hwndClient;
  QMSG     qmsg;
  ULONG    flFrameFlags;
  CHAR     szTitle[80];
  SWCNTRL  PgmEntry;
  LONG     lX_Left,                                              ⇐
           lY_Bot,                                               ⇐
           lHeight,                                              ⇐
           lWidth,                                               ⇐
           lScrHeight,
           lScrWidth;
/***************************************************************/
  hab = WinInitialize(0);
  hmq = WinCreateMsgQueue(hab, 0);

  WinRegisterClass(hab, "Skeleton", MainWndProc, CS_SIZEREDRAW, 0);

  WinLoadString(hab, (HMODULE)NULL, ID_TITLE, sizeof(szTitle),   ⇐
                szTitle);
```

Figure 1.11. Skeleton program: C source file (32-bit). Continues.

```
    flFrameFlags =  FCF_TITLEBAR  | FCF_SYSMENU | FCF_MENU |
                    FCF_SIZEBORDER | FCF_MINMAX | FCF_ACCELTABLE |
                    FCF_ICON;
    hwndFrame = WinCreateStdWindow(HWND_DESKTOP, 0L, &flFrameFlags,
                            "Skeleton", (PSZ)szTitle, 0L,
                            (HMODULE)NULL, ID_MAINWND,           ⇐
                            &hwndClient);
    lScrWidth  = WinQuerySysValue(HWND_DESKTOP, SV_CXSCREEN);
    lScrHeight = WinQuerySysValue(HWND_DESKTOP, SV_CYSCREEN);
    lWidth  = 400;                                               ⇐
    lHeight = 300;                                               ⇐
    lX_Left = (lScrWidth  - lWidth)  / 2;                        ⇐
    lY_Bot  = (lScrHeight - lHeight) / 2;                        ⇐
    WinSetWindowPos(hwndFrame, (HWND)NULL, lX_Left, lY_Bot, lWidth,
                    lHeight,                                     ⇐
                    SWP_SIZE | SWP_MOVE | SWP_SHOW | SWP_ACTIVATE);
                                       /*---------------------*/
                                       /* Startup in foreground */
                                       /*---------------------*/
                                       /* Add to window list    */
                                       /*---------------------*/
    PgmEntry.hwnd          = hwndFrame;
    PgmEntry.hwndIcon      = (HWND)NULL;                         ⇐
    PgmEntry.hprog         = (HPROGRAM)NULL;                     ⇐
    PgmEntry.idProcess     = (PID)NULL;                          ⇐
    PgmEntry.idSession     = (ULONG)NULL;                        ⇐
    PgmEntry.uchVisibility = SWL_VISIBLE;
    PgmEntry.fbJump        = SWL_JUMPABLE;
    strcpy(PgmEntry.szSwtitle, szTitle);

    WinAddSwitchEntry(&PgmEntry);
    while (WinGetMsg(hab, &qmsg, (HWND)NULL, 0, 0))              ⇐
      WinDispatchMsg(hab, &qmsg);
                        /*----------------------------------*/
                        /* Remove from window list and clean up */
                        /*----------------------------------*/
    WinRemoveSwitchEntry(WinQuerySwitchHandle(hwndFrame, 0));
    WinDestroyWindow(hwndFrame);
    WinDestroyMsgQueue(hmq);
    WinTerminate(hab);
    return 0;                                                    ⇐
}

/***************************************************************/
```

Figure 1.11. Skeleton program: C source file (32-bit). Continues.

```
MRESULT EXPENTRY MainWndProc(HWND hwnd, ULONG msg, MPARAM mp1,    ⇐
                             MPARAM mp2)
{
  switch (msg)
    {
    case WM_COMMAND:
      switch (SHORT1FROMMP(mp1))
         {
         case MI_EXIT:
           WinPostMsg(hwnd, WM_QUIT, 0L, 0L);
           break;
         default:
           break;
         }
      break;
    case WM_ERASEBACKGROUND:
      return (MRESULT)TRUE;
    }
  return WinDefWindowProc(hwnd, msg, mp1, mp2);
}
```

Figure 1.11. Skeleton program: C source file (32-bit). Concluded.

1.3   16-bit to 32-bit conversion summary

Figure 1.11 is obviously a very trivial program, but does illustrate some of the differences you will most likely encounter when you convert your own applications to 32-bit. Before we move on, let us take a few moments to summarize the main changes that have taken place with the introduction of OS/2 version 2.0.

First, look at Table 1.1 to familiarize yourself with the filenames for the main toolkit components that will be of interest to us in version 2.0.

Table 1.1. Main toolkit components

Product	Filename
32-bit make	NMAKE.EXE
32-bit compiler	ICC.EXE
32-bit linker	LINK386.EXE
32-bit library	OS2386.LIB
32-bit debugger	IPMD.EXE
32-bit dialog box editor	DLGEDIT.EXE
32-bit font editor (name unchanged)	FONTEDIT.EXE
32-bit icon editor (name unchanged)	ICONEDIT.EXE

The first thing you should do after installing the C Set/2 compiler and developer's toolkit is read the READ.ME files in the **IBMC** and **TOOLKT20** directories.

As was mentioned earlier, the easiest way to find out what needs to be converted is to run your code through the compiler. This is probably all right for a small module, but for one of any great size you would be advised to at least consider the following:

1. If you use // for comments then you should either change to /* */ to conform to the ANSI standard, or, if you prefer to keep // then use the /ss compiler option.
2. Change the msg parameter for your window procedures from USHORT to ULONG.
3. Change your **MAIN** statement; it now returns an integer and does not use cdecl, and on exit add a return 0;
4. NULL has been redefined as ((void *)0). This may cause you to receive many diagnostic messages. To overcome them, cast as appropriate or replace with 0. You will see this many times in the sample programs.
5. Window locking, a function of OS/2 version 1.1, was removed with the introduction of OS/2 version 1.2. However, to maintain compatibility, the following functions kept Lock as a parameter, but it was ignored by OS/2. Now, with OS/2 version 2.0 these functions have had the Lock parameter removed so you will need to change the parameter list on any of those that you may have used:

```
WinEnumDlgItem
WinLockWindow                  ⇐ Removed from OS/2 V2
WinQueryActiveWindow
WinQueryCapture
WinQueryClipbrdOwner
WinQueryClipbrdViewer
WinQueryFocus
WinQuerySysModalWindow
WinQueryWindow
WinQueryWindowLockCount        ⇐ Removed from OS/2 V2
WinWindowFromPoint
```

6. All parameters that were defined as USHORT on the Dos... functions have changed to ULONG.
7. All parameters that were defined as USHORT on the Win... functions have changed to ULONG except WinSetWindowUShort and WinSetDlgItem-Short.
8. In order to be consistent in function-naming conventions, that is, verb/object, some Dos... functions have been renamed:

DosBufReset	⟹ DosResetBuffer	DosQFSAttach	⟹ DosQueryFSAttach
DosCaseMap	⟹ DosMapCase	DosQFSInfo	⟹ DosQueryFSInfo
DosChDir	⟹ DosSetCurrentDir	DosQFileInfo	⟹ DosQueryFileInfo
DosChgFilePtr	⟹ DosSetFilePtr	DosQHandType	⟹ DosQueryHType
DosCwait	⟹ DosWaitChild	DosQPathInfo	⟹ DosQueryPathInfo
DosFindFirst2	⟹ DosFindFirst	DosQSysInfo	⟹ DosQuerySysInfo
DosGetCollate	⟹ DosQueryCollate	DosQVerify	⟹ DosQueryVerify
DosGetCp	⟹ DosQueryCp	DosRmDir	⟹ DosDeleteDir
DosGetCtryInfo	⟹ DosQueryCtryInfo	DosSelectDisk	⟹ DosSetDefaultDisk
DosGetDBCSEv	⟹ DosQueryDBCSEnv	DosSetFHandState	⟹ DosSetFHState
DosGetInfoSeg	⟹ DosGetInfoBlocks	DosSetProcCp	⟹ DosSetProcessCp
DosGetResource2	⟹ DosGetResource	DosSetPrty	⟹ DosSetPriority
DosInsMessage	⟹ DosInsertMessage	DosSubAlloc	⟹ DosSubAllocMem
DosMkDir	⟹ DosCreateDir	DosSubFree	⟹ DosSubFreeMem
DosMkDir2	⟹ DosCreateDir	DosSubSet	⟹ DosSubSetMem
DosNewSize	⟹ DosSetFileSize	DosSubUnset	⟹ DosSubUnsetMem
DosOpen2	⟹ DosOpen	DosTimerAsync	⟹ DosAsyncTimer
DosQCurDir	⟹ DosQueryCurrentDir	DosTimerStart	⟹ DosStartTimer
DosQCurDisk	⟹ DosQueryCurrentDisk	DosTimerStop	⟹ DosStopTimer
DosQFHandState	⟹ DosQueryFHState		

9 The set window position structure has changed:

```
typedef struct _SWP
{
    ULONG   fl;                   ⇐
    LONG    cy;                   ⇐
    LONG    cx;                   ⇐
    LONG    y;                    ⇐
    LONG    x;                    ⇐
    HWND    hwndInsertBehind;
    HWND    hwnd;
    ULONG   ulReserved1;          ⇐
    ULONG   ulReserved2;          ⇐
} SWP;
```

10 The switch-list block structure has changed. This structure is a combination of three structures, SWBLOCK, SWENTRY and SWCNTRL, as follows:

```
typedef struct _SWBLOCK
{
    ULONG     cswentry;           ⇐
    SWENTRY   aswentry[1];
} SWBLOCK;

typedef struct _SWENTRY
{
    HSWITCH   hswitch;
    SWCNTRL   swctl;
} SWENTRY;
```

```
typedef struct _SWCNTRL
{
    HWND        hwnd;
    HWND        hwndIcon;
    HPROGRAM    hprog;
    PID         idProcess;              ⇐
    ULONG       idSession;              ⇐
    ULONG       uchVisibility;          ⇐
    ULONG       fbJump;                 ⇐
    CHAR        szSwtitle[MAXNAMEL+1];
    ULONG       bProgType;              ⇐
} SWCNTRL;
```

11 More library extension names now start with an underscore:

```
_alloca         _fcvt       _ltoa       _tzset
_ecvt           _gcvt       _putenv     _ultoa
_fcloseall      _itoa       _rmtmp
```

12 Finally, the two areas which may cause you more conversion effort than any other are memory management and semaphores. As you know, version 2.0 uses a flat memory model and so removes the problems associated with memory segmentation. This has meant a major application programming interface (API) redesign, and so if you made use of the 16-bit memory management API you will need to recode using the following API (their functions are self-explanatory):

```
DosAllocMem             DosGetSharedMem         DosSubAllocMem
DosAllocSharedMem       DosGiveSharedMem        DosSubFreeMem
DosFreeMem              DosQueryMem             DosSubSetMem
DosGetNamedSharedMem    DosSetMem               DosSubUnsetMem
```

The area of semaphores has also been totally redesigned and so, like memory management, will cause some effort to convert. The 32-bit semaphore API comprises the following (again, their functions are self-explanatory):

```
DosCreateEventSem       DosCreateMutexSem       DosCreateMuxWaitSem
DosOpenEventSem         DosOpenMutexSem         DosOpenMuxWaitSem
DosCloseEventSem        DosCloseMutexSem        DosCloseMuxWaitSem
DosResetEventSem        DosRequestMutexSem      DosWaitMuxWaitSem
DosPostEventSem         DosReleaseMutexSem      DosAddMuxWaitSem
DosWaitEventSem         DosQueryMutexSem        DosDeleteMuxWaitSem
DosQueryEventSem                                DosQueryMuxWaitSem
```

Just following these simple steps should ensure that the number of diagnostic messages you receive is reduced to a minimum, making your 16-bit to 32-bit conversion a very quick and easy process.

2
General window processing

This chapter looks at how you can control your application's main client window. It covers topics such as window positioning on start-up, controlling window movement, position and sizing, and subclassing. But, to begin with, let us look at some very common mistakes that most programmers (and that includes me) make when starting to code for Presentation Manager.

2.1 Some common errors

2.1.1 *Don't use* `hwndFrame` *during* `WM_CREATE`

If you define `hwndFrame` as a *global* variable—not good practice—then you cannot use it during your `WM_CREATE` message processing as it is not assigned until that processing is complete. Instead, define it as an *auto*, or *static*, variable and use `WinQueryWindow` to obtain the client's parent window handle. For 32-bit only:

```
hwndFrame = WinQueryWindow(hwnd, QW_PARENT);
```

Do not forget that this is one of those functions that has had its parameter list changed due to the removal of the lock parameter. So if you are still coding for OS/2 V1.x then use:

```
hwndFrame = WinQueryWindow(hwnd, QW_PARENT, FALSE);
```

2.1.2 *Window not being displayed*

Sometimes you may find that when you attempt to create a window it does not display and the return code from `WinCreateStdWindow` is NULL. The most common cause of this problem is that you have used the frame creation flag of `FCF_STANDARD`, which tells Presentation Manager that you are including a menu, icon and accelerator resource. The flags included are:

FCF_TITLEBAR	Title bar
FCF_SYSMENU	System menu
FCF_MINMAX	Minimize and maximize icons
FCF_SIZEBORDER	Sizing border
FCF_TASKLIST	Add program name to task list
FCF_MENU	Menu bar
FCF_ACCELTABLE	Accelerator table
FCF_SHELLPOSITION	Let Presentation Manager position and size window
FCF_ICON	Icon

If you have failed to define any one of these then your window is not created.

If you do require a standard window, but for some reason you do not require a particular resource, such as an accelerator table, then you could set up your own identifier, for example `FCF_STDNOACCEL`, and use that in your call to `WinCreateStdWindow`:

```
#define FCF_STDNOACCEL FCF_STANDARD & ~FCF_ACCELTABLE
```

You should also check that all resources belonging to a frame have the same ID, so check your resource file to ensure, for example, that your menu does not have a different ID to your icon, or else the create will fail. See the following resource file extract where `ID_MAINWND` is the window ID:

```
ACCELTABLE  ID_MAINWND
BEGIN
  VK_F3,    MI_EXIT,   VIRTUALKEY
END

ICON        ID_MAINWND wingen.ico

MENU        ID_MAINWND PRELOAD
BEGIN
    .
    .
    .
END
```

One other area to look at is your `WM_CREATE` message processing. If you return `TRUE` from this then window creation is discontinued. If, however, the create does not fail, that is, you receive a valid handle, then the most likely cause is that you do not have the `WS_VISIBLE` style specified for the window. The default is, in fact, invisible. It is also possible that if you are not using `WinSetWindowPos` to size and position the window yourself, see Sec. 2.2, you may have omitted the frame creation flag `FCF_SHELLPOSITION` for that window.

2.2 Initial display of the client window

2.2.1 *Starting with a predetermined window size and position*

If you do not wish your window size and position to be set by Presentation Manager then in your `WinCreateStdWindow` call do *not* specify the style `WS_VISIBLE`, and do *not* specify the frame creation flag `FCF_SHELLPOSITION`. Instead, follow `WinCreateStdWindow` with a call to `WinSetWindowPos` specifying your own size and position:

```
HWND   hwndFrame,
       hwndClient;
ULONG  flFrameFlags;
LONG   lX_Left = 100, /* Initial window position = (100, 100) */
       lY_Bot  = 100, /* Initial window size     = (400, 300) */
       lWidth  = 400,
       lHeight = 300;
flFrameFlags = FCF_TITLEBAR | FCF_SYSMENU | FCF_MENU |
               FCF_SIZEBORDER | FCF_MINMAX | FCF_ACCELTABLE |
               FCF_ICON;
hwndFrame = WinCreateStdWindow(HWND_DESKTOP, 0,
                               &flFrameFlags, "WinClass",
                               "Window Title", 0,
                               (HMODULE)NULL, ID_MAINWND,
                               &hwndClient);
WinSetWindowPos(hwndFrame, HWND_TOP, lX_Left, lY_Bot,
                lWidth, lHeight, SWP_SIZE | SWP_MOVE |
                SWP_SHOW | SWP_ACTIVATE);
```

If you do use `WS_VISIBLE` and `FCF_SHELLPOSITION` as well as `WinSetWindowPos` then when the application starts Presentation Manager will display your window in the default position and then disappear to be replaced with the window of your choice.

Ensure that you always use `SWP_SIZE | SWP_MOVE` on the `WinSetWindowPos` call otherwise your size and start position will not be honoured. Also, use `SWP_SHOW` to make your window visible, and `SWP_ACTIVATE` to give your window the focus. But beware, this will take the focus away from your users, even if they are typing into another window at the time it becomes active. This can be annoying.

> *Note:* A common mistake in this area is to use `FCF_SHELLPOSITION`, which is included when you specify `FCF_STANDARD`, and to trap the `WM_CREATE` message with the aim of resizing the window. But Presentation Manager acts on the `FCF_SHELLPOSITION` after the `WM_CREATE` message and so your size and position is ignored.

2.2.2 Starting minimized or maximized

To create a window in its minimized or maximized state use `SWP_MINIMIZE` or `SWP_MAXIMIZE` respectively in a call to `WinSetWindowPos`, but make sure you specify a size to which the window will be restored.

To start in the minimized state:

```
SWP swp;

swp.x  = 100;              /*--------------------------*/
swp.y  = 100;              /* Set restored size/position */
swp.cx = 200;              /*--------------------------*/
swp.cy = 200;

WinSetWindowPos(hwndFrame, HWND_TOP, swp.x, swp.y, swp.cx,
                swp.cy, SWP_SIZE | SWP_MOVE | SWP_SHOW |
                SWP_ACTIVATE | SWP_MINIMIZE);
```

To start in the maximized state:

```
swp.x  = 100;              /*--------------------------*/
swp.y  = 100;              /* Set restored size/position */
swp.cx = 200;              /*--------------------------*/
swp.cy = 200;

WinSetWindowPos(hwndFrame, HWND_TOP, swp.x, swp.y, swp.cx,
                swp.cy, SWP_SIZE | SWP_MOVE | SWP_SHOW |
                SWP_ACTIVATE | SWP_MAXIMIZE);
```

2.2.3 Starting in the background

To start with your client window in the background so that it does not take the focus away from your user, use `WinSetWindowPos` with the `Behind` parameter set to `HWND_BOTTOM` and `SWP_ZORDER` as one of the options:

```
WinSetWindowPos(hwndFrame, HWND_BOTTOM, lX_Left, lY_Bot,
                lWidth, lHeight, SWP_SIZE | SWP_MOVE |
                SWP_SHOW | SWP_ZORDER);
```

This is now the recommended way to start applications, especially if they take a while to initialize. The reason is that if the user starts it and then continues to type into another application's window, when your application finally shows it comes to the top and takes the focus. This can cause some annoyance to the user.

2.2.4 Positioning on screens with different resolution

If you use absolute values when initializing the size of your window and then run

General window processing

your application on a machine which has a screen of different resolution, you may find that your window overlaps the screen, or appears in an unexpected position. To overcome this you should not use absolute values but ask the system for the screen dimensions first by using `WinQuerySysValue`. This will give you back the correct number of picture elements (pels) for the screen you are running under. You can then use these values in `WinSetWindowPos` to set your window's size and position correctly.

As an example, if you want your window to occupy the entire screen, use the following sample code.

```
HWND    hwndFrame,
        hwndClient;
ULONG   flFrameFlags;
LONG    lScrHeight,
        lScrWidth;

flFrameFlags = FCF_TITLEBAR | FCF_SYSMENU | FCF_MENU |
               FCF_SIZEBORDER | FCF_MINMAX | FCF_ACCELTABLE |
               FCF_NOBYTEALIGN;

hwndFrame = WinCreateStdWindow(HWND_DESKTOP, 0,
                               &flFrameFlags, "WinClass",
                               "Window Title", 0,
                               (HMODULE)NULL, ID_MAINWND,
                               &hwndClient);

lScrWidth  = WinQuerySysValue(HWND_DESKTOP, SV_CXSCREEN);
                    /* Returns width of screen */
lScrHeight = WinQuerySysValue(HWND_DESKTOP, SV_CYSCREEN);
                    /* Returns height of screen */

WinSetWindowPos(hwndFrame, HWND_TOP, 0, 0, lScrWidth,
                lScrHeight, SWP_SIZE | SWP_MOVE | SWP_SHOW |
                SWP_ACTIVATE);
```

Make sure you include a frame creation flag of `FCF_NOBYTEALIGN` when you create your window, otherwise it will align on eight pel boundaries and will not fit the screen exactly. If you do not wish your window to be this large then, of course, you can set the `lScrWidth` and `lScrHeight` variables to any suitable values and, if necessary, centralize it (see Sec. 2.2.5).

2.2.5 Centralizing your window

To centralize your window on the screen, first use `WinQuerySysValue` to obtain the screen resolution, and then calculate the appropriate coordinates and call `WinSetWindowPos`. For example:

```
HWND    hwndFrame,
        hwndClient;
ULONG   flFrameFlags;
LONG    lX_Left,
        lY_Bot,
        lHeight,
        lWidth,
        lScrHeight,
        lScrWidth;

flFrameFlags = FCF_TITLEBAR | FCF_SYSMENU | FCF_MENU |
               FCF_SIZEBORDER | FCF_MINMAX | FCF_ACCELTABLE |
               FCF_NOBYTEALIGN;

hwndFrame = WinCreateStdWindow(HWND_DESKTOP, 0,
                               &flFrameFlags, "WinClass",
                               "Window Title", 0,
                               (HMODULE)NULL, ID_MAINWND,
                               &hwndClient);

lScrWidth  = WinQuerySysValue(HWND_DESKTOP, SV_CXSCREEN);
                                /* Returns width of screen */
lScrHeight = WinQuerySysValue(HWND_DESKTOP, SV_CYSCREEN);
                                /* Returns height of screen */

lWidth  = 400;
lHeight = 300;

lX_Left = (lScrWidth  - lWidth)  / 2;
lY_Bot  = (lScrHeight - lHeight) / 2;

WinSetWindowPos(hwndFrame, HWND_TOP, lX_Left, lY_Bot,
                lWidth, lHeight, SWP_SIZE | SWP_MOVE |
                SWP_SHOW | SWP_ACTIVATE);
```

By doing this you can be sure that your window will always be centred, no matter what screen device your program is running on.

Depending on your application it may be more appropriate to set the window size as a percentage of the screen size, for example:

```
lWidth  = lScrWidth/3;
lHeight = lScrHeight/2;
```

2.3 Controlling movement, position and size

2.3.1 Prohibiting window movement

There may be occasions when you require the movement of your main window to be prohibited some time during your processing. This could be achieved by subclassing the frame window, but a much easier way is to call `WinEnableWindow` to disable the title bar, which has an ID of `FID_TITLEBAR`. This also has the added advantage of greying out `Move` from the window's system menu.

To prohibit window movement:

```
hwndFrame = WinQueryWindow(hwnd, QW_PARENT);
WinEnableWindow(WinWindowFromID(hwndFrame, FID_TITLEBAR),
            FALSE);
```

To restore window movement:

```
hwndFrame = WinQueryWindow(hwnd, QW_PARENT);
WinEnableWindow(WinWindowFromID(hwndFrame, FID_TITLEBAR),
            TRUE);
```

2.3.2 Keeping your main window on top

If you require to keep your main window in view at all times, that is, on top of all other windows, a very simple way of doing this is to start a timer and in the `WM_TIMER` message processing for your client window make a call to `WinSetWindowPos` using the `SWP_ZORDER` option:

```
#define ID_TIMER_TOP 1

/*--------------------------------------------------*/
/* At a convenient position start a 500 millisecond timer */
/*--------------------------------------------------*/

WinStartTimer(hab, hwndClient, ID_TIMER_TOP, 500);

/****************************************************/

/*------------------------------------------------ */
/* Trap the timer message in your window procedure... */
/*------------------------------------------------ */

case WM_TIMER:
   hwndFrame = WinQueryWindow(hwnd, QW_PARENT);
```

```
WinSetWindowPos(hwndFrame, HWND_TOP, 0, 0, 0, 0,
                SWP_ZORDER);
break;
```

Be careful doing this sort of thing: depending on your application it may be considered to be 'antisocial' behaviour. However, there are times when this may be quite acceptable, for example, for a clock program. Even then it should be offered as a choice.

Use `WinStopTimer` to stop the timer when you close down your application, or before if it is no longer required:

```
WinStopTimer(hab, hwndClient, ID_TIMER_TOP);
```

2.3.3 Keeping a secondary window on top

If you need to keep one of your application windows visible while you use another, maybe in order to keep your application's status in view or for a tool palette, then make the window's parent `HWND_DESKTOP`, and then use `WinSetOwner` to make its owner the application's main window:

```
flTFrameFlags = FCF_TITLEBAR | FCF_SYSMENU | FCF_NOBYTEALIGN |
                FCF_SIZEBORDER | FCF_MINMAX;

hwndTopFrame = WinCreateStdWindow(HWND_DESKTOP, 0,
                                  &flTFrameFlags,
                                  "WinGen2", szTTitle, 0,
                                  (HMODULE)NULL, 0,
                                  &hwndTop);
WinSetOwner(hwndTopFrame, hwndFrame);

WinSetWindowPos(hwndTopFrame, HWND_TOP, 350, 100, 200, 200,
                SWP_SIZE | SWP_MOVE | SWP_SHOW |
                SWP_ACTIVATE);
```

2.3.4 Restoring to a fixed size or position

If you always want your window to be set to a particular size and/or position when it is restored then you can use the `WinSetWindowUShort` function with the relevant `QWS_*RESTORE` value(s) in your `WM_MINMAXFRAME` case statement. For example:

```
case WM_MINMAXFRAME:
  /***********************************************************/
  /* Restore window to (100,100) with a size of (200,200) */
  /***********************************************************/
```

```
hwndFrame = WinQueryWindow(hwnd, QW_PARENT);

WinSetWindowUShort(hwndFrame, QWS_XRESTORE, 100);
WinSetWindowUShort(hwndFrame, QWS_YRESTORE, 100);
WinSetWindowUShort(hwndFrame, QWS_CXRESTORE, 200);
WinSetWindowUShort(hwndFrame, QWS_CYRESTORE, 200);
break;
```

A `WM_MINMAXFRAME` message is sent to your frame window whenever it is minimized, maximized or restored:

- `QWS_XRESTORE`   *x*-coordinate of the position to which the window is restored
- `QWS_YRESTORE`   *y*-coordinate of the position to which the window is restored
- `QWS_CXRESTORE` Width to which the window is restored
- `QWS_CYRESTORE` Height to which the window is restored.

As was mentioned earlier, only do this if there are legitimate reasons for enforcing a restored size or position, to prevent your application from being branded 'antisocial'. It is better to allow the system to restore the window to its previous size and position. However, there may be times when enforcement could be considered the correct action.

2.3.5 Controlling window size

Presentation Manager restricts the minimum size to which a window can be sized. If you have to allow your window size to be less then you must subclass your frame window and process the `WM_QUERYTRACKINFO` message. This message is sent to your window procedure whenever the window is moved or sized.

You can, of course, extend this to ensure that your window is always square, or never smaller or greater than a certain size. In the following example the window is allowed to be sized down to 25 × 25 pels:

```
/*------------------------------------------------------*/
/* Declare your subclassed window procedure and pointer to */
/* the default frame window procedure                   */
/*------------------------------------------------------*/
MRESULT EXPENTRY SubFrameProc(HWND, ULONG, MPARAM, MPARAM);
PFNWP            OldFrameProc;

/*------------------------------------------------------*/
/* Immediately after creating your main window store the */
/* address of the default frame window procedure        */
/*------------------------------------------------------*/

OldFrameProc = WinSubclassWindow(hwndFrame,
                        (PFNWP)SubFrameProc);
```

```
/*---------------------------------------------------------*/
/* The following example procedure allows your window to be */
/* reduced in size to 25 x 25 pels                          */
/*---------------------------------------------------------*/

MRESULT EXPENTRY SubFrameProc(HWND hwnd, ULONG msg,
                              MPARAM mp1, MPARAM mp2)
{
  PTRACKINFO ptrack;

  switch(msg)
  {
    case WM_QUERYTRACKINFO:
    /*---------------------------------------------------------*/
    /* Invoke the default frame window procedure first in      */
    /* order to update the tracking rectangle to the           */
    /* new position                                            */
    /*---------------------------------------------------------*/

      OldFrameProc(hwnd, msg, mp1, mp2);

      ptrack = (PTRACKINFO)mp2;
      ptrack->ptlMinTrackSize.x = 25;
      ptrack->ptlMinTrackSize.y = 25;

      return((MRESULT)TRUE);
    }
    return OldFrameProc(hwnd, msg, mp1, mp2);
                                   /* Pass all other messages to */
}                                  /* the default procedure      */
```

Very briefly, when you subclass a window you have the opportunity to alter the standard processing of that window, as this example shows. Whenever a frame window receives a WM_QUERYTRACKINFO message the default frame procedure does some processing, for example, drawing the tracking rectangle and maintaining its size when you move the mouse pointer. We still need this, so we call the default procedure first and then add our bit of code, in this case reset the minimum track size. For all other messages we pass them straight on to the default procedure for processing.

2.3.6 Detecting when minimize/maximize/restore is occurring

To check if your window is about to be minimized, maximized or restored, trap the WM_MINMAXFRAME message:

```
case WM_MINMAXFRAME:
```

General window processing

```
      if (((PSWP)mp1)->fl & SWP_MINIMIZE)
      {
            /* ------------------ */
            /* About to be minimized */
            /* ------------------ */
      }
      else
         if (((PSWP)mp1)->fl & SWP_MAXIMIZE)
         {
               /* ------------------ */
               /* About to be maximized */
               /* ------------------ */
         }
         else
            if (((PSWP)mp1)->fl & SWP_RESTORE)
            {
                  /* ------------------ */
                  /* About to be restored */
                  /* ------------------ */
            }
   break;
```

Do not forget, the `SWP` structure changed in version 2.0. If you need to do this under version 1.x then `fl` should be `fs`.

2.3.7 *Detecting if your window is minimized/maximized*

To check if your window is already minimized or maximized, use `WinQueryWindowULong` with the `QWL_STYLE` index. This call interrogates the window words for the unsigned long integer value which represents the window style. If this value is ANDed with either `WS_MINIMIZED` or `WS_MAXIMIZED` and the result is true, then the window is minimized or maximized respectively:

```
hwndFrame = WinQueryWindow(hwnd, QW_PARENT);

if (WinQueryWindowULong(hwndFrame, QWL_STYLE) &
                        WS_MINIMIZED)
{
   /* Window is minimized */
}

if (WinQueryWindowULong(hwndFrame, QWL_STYLE) &
                        WS_MAXIMIZED)
{
    /* Window is maximized */
}
```

2.3.8 Minimizing your window

If you need to minimize your window automatically from your client's window procedure, call WinSetWindowPos specifying SWP_MINIMIZE:

```
hwndFrame = WinQueryWindow(hwnd, QW_PARENT);

WinSetWindowPos(hwndFrame, NULL, 0, 0, 0, 0, SWP_MINIMIZE);
```

2.3.9 Obtaining window size

To obtain the size of a window use the WinQueryWindowRect function:

```
RECTL rclWin;

WinQueryWindowRect(hwnd, &rclWin);
```

For top-level windows this will return the values in screen coordinates. For child windows the coordinates will be in parent coordinates. If you need to query the screen coordinates of child windows, which your client area is (child of the frame window), follow WinQueryWindowRect with a call to WinMapWindowPoints:

```
hwndFrame = WinQueryWindow(hwnd, QW_PARENT);

WinQueryWindowRect(hwnd, &rclWin);
WinMapWindowPoints(hwnd, hwndFrame, (PPOINTL)&rclWin, 2);
```

2.3.10 Prohibiting window minimization/maximization

To prevent the user from minimizing or maximizing your window, assuming you have FCF_MINMAX defined for the window, use WinEnableWindow with the handle of the minimize/maximize icon and a value of FALSE for the new enabled state parameter. You can obtain the minimize/maximize handle by using WinWindowFromID specifying the frame ID FID_MINMAX. To restore minimization and maximization call WinEnableWindow with the new enabled state parameter set to TRUE:

```
hwndFrame = WinQueryWindow(hwnd, QW_PARENT);

/* ---------------- */
/* Prohibit min/max */
/* ---------------- */

WinEnableWindow(WinWindowFromID(hwndFrame, FID_MINMAX),
                FALSE);
```

```
/* -------------- */
/* Restore min/max */
/* -------------- */
WinEnableWindow(WinWindowFromID(hwndFrame, FID_MINMAX),
                TRUE);
```

2.3.11 Prohibiting window sizing

There may be occasions when it is necessary to prohibit the sizing of your main window during the course of your processing. This can be achieved by changing the window's style from FS_SIZEBORDER to FS_DLGBORDER using WinSet-WindowULong:

```
hwndFrame = WinQueryWindow(hwnd, QW_PARENT);

WinSetWindowULong(hwndFrame,QWL_STYLE,
                  (WinQueryWindowULong(hwndFrame,
                  QWL_STYLE) & ~FS_SIZEBORDER |
                  FS_DLGBORDER));

WinInvalidateRect(hwndFrame, NULL, TRUE);
```

This also greys out Size from the window's system menu. You will also need a call to WinInvalidateRect to ensure the frame is updated immediately.

To restore sizing using WinSetWindowULong use:

```
hwndFrame = WinQueryWindow(hwnd, QW_PARENT);

WinSetWindowULong(hwndFrame, QWL_STYLE,
                  (WinQueryWindowULong(hwndFrame,
                  QWL_STYLE) & ~FS_DLGBORDER |
                  FS_SIZEBORDER));

WinInvalidateRect(hwndFrame, NULL, TRUE);
```

Another method is to use WinSetWindowBits. To prohibit sizing use:

```
hwndFrame = WinQueryWindow(hwnd, QW_PARENT);

WinSetWindowBits(hwndFrame, QWL_STYLE, (~FS_SIZEBORDER |
                                        FS_DLGBORDER),
                                       (FS_SIZEBORDER |
                                        FS_DLGBORDER));

WinInvalidateRect(hwndFrame, NULL, TRUE);
```

To restore sizing use:

```
hwndFrame = WinQueryWindow(hwnd, QW_PARENT);

WinSetWindowBits(hwndFrame, QWL_STYLE, (FS_SIZEBORDER |
                                        ~FS_DLGBORDER),
                                       (FS_SIZEBORDER |
                                        FS_DLGBORDER));

WinInvalidateRect(hwndFrame, NULL, TRUE);
```

2.4 Class names

When using `WinQueryClassName` to obtain the class name of a window, a necessity when using window enumeration (see Chapter 10), Presentation Manager does not return the string name, for example `WC_BUTTON`, but an integer atom in a string of the form `"#nnnnn"`. You can, of course, obtain the name by querying the system atom table using `WinQueryAtomName` (see the sample program in Chapter 8 for an example). However, the most common are shown as follows:

```
"#1"      WC_FRAME
"#2"      WC_COMBOBOX
"#3"      WC_BUTTON
"#4"      WC_MENU
"#5"      WC_STATIC
"#6"      WC_ENTRYFIELD
"#7"      WC_LISTBOX
"#8"      WC_SCROLLBAR
"#9"      WC_TITLEBAR
"#10"     WC_MLE
"#32"     WC_SPINBUTTON
"#33"     WC_CONTAINER
"#34"     WC_SLIDER
"#35"     WC_VALUESET
"#36"     WC_NOTEBOOK
```

For a complete list look in the header file PMWIN.H supplied with the version 2.0 developer's toolkit. For an example of use see Sec. 10.2.

2.5 Obtaining the process ID of the active window

To determine which window is currently active and to obtain its process ID, first call `WinQueryActiveWindow`. This returns the handle of the active window. Using this we then call `WinQueryWindowProcess` to obtain the process ID of that window. Note that for a video input/output (VIO) window or workplace object this will be the process ID of the shell. The following code fragment obtains the active window's process ID and displays it:

```
MRESULT EXPENTRY MainWndProc(HWND hwnd, ULONG msg, MPARAM mp1,
                             MPARAM mp2)
{
  RECTL rcl;
  HPS   hps;
  HWND  hwndActiveWin;
  PID   pid;
  TID   tid;
  CHAR  szText[20];

  case WM_PAINT:
    hps = WinBeginPaint(hwnd, (HPS)NULL, (PRECTL)NULL);
    hwndActiveWin = WinQueryActiveWindow(HWND_DESKTOP);
    WinQueryWindowProcess(hwndActiveWin, &pid, &tid);
    sprintf(szText, "Process ID = %d", pid);
    WinQueryWindowRect(hwnd, &rcl);
    WinDrawText (hps, strlen(szText), szText, &rcl,
                 SYSCLR_WINDOWTEXT, SYSCLR_WINDOW, DT_LEFT |
                 DT_ERASERECT);
    WinEndPaint(hps);
    break;

  case WM_TIMER:
                                   /* Force a WM_PAINT message */
    WinInvalidateRect(hwnd, NULL, TRUE);
    break;
  ;
  ;
  ;
```

To display the ID we use `WinDrawText`, but first we need the size of the window, which is obtained by calling `WinQueryWindowRect`. To left-justify the text use the option `DT_LEFT`; use the option `DT_ERASERECT` to clear the window before drawing.

To force the window to be painted, and hence update the process ID, we start a half second timer, and in the `WM_TIMER` case statement we invalidate the rectangle by calling `WinInvalidateRect`. Note that you *never* send yourself a `WM_PAINT` message as it is not really possible to determine its parameters— only Presentation Manager can do this. The correct way is to call `WinInvalidateRect` and let the system generate the `WM_PAINT` message for you. *Remember*, you must always use `WinBeginPaint` and `WinEndPaint` in your `WM_PAINT` processing otherwise results may be unpredictable.

2.6 System modal window

A simple way to prevent Alt-Esc and Ctrl-Esc from operating is to make your window system modal, that is, the user can interact with only that window and no other application window in the system. This renders the control key sequences unusable until you remove system modality for that window. To make a window system modal use WinSetSysModalWindow in your WM_CREATE case statement, but do not forget to obtain hwndFrame using WinQueryWindow (see Sec. 2.1):

```
case WM_CREATE:
   /* ---------------- */
   /* Make system modal */
   /* ---------------- */

   hwndFrame = WinQueryWindow(hwnd, QW_PARENT);
   WinSetSysModalWindow(HWND_DESKTOP, hwndFrame);
   break;


case WM_xxx:
   /* --------------------- */
   /* Remove system modality */
   /* --------------------- */

   WinSetSysModalWindow(HWND_DESKTOP, NULL);
   break;
```

For an example of a system modal application see Chapter 3.

2.7 Saving your application's current state

This is an area that has changed with the introduction of the Workplace Shell in OS/2 V2.0, so we will look at the 16-bit and 32-bit implementations separately.

First, the 16-bit. If you have a requirement to save your application's current state of execution then you can make use of the WM_SAVEAPPLICATION message. This message is dispatched to your client window procedure when the user requests Save... from the desktop manager, or requests Shutdown from the desktop manager and checks the Save check box. You may want to save several different types of application data but probably the most common is the window's size and its position on the desktop.

In the 32-bit version, 2.0, there is no facility to do a desktop save except when you shut down the system. However, when an application is just about to close it receives a WM_SAVEAPPLICATION message anyway. Also, in this version a new pair of API functions have been introduced, WinStoreWindowPos and

WinRestoreWindowPos. With a call to WinStoreWindowPos, the window's size, position and presentation parameters are automatically saved in the OS2.INI file. Calling WinRestoreWindowPos and WinShowWindow on initialization will display the window in its previous state. Be aware that if you use the frame creation flag FCF_STANDARD then your window will not be restored to its previous size and position. This is because a standard frame window includes the style FCF_SHELLPOSITION, so the window will be sized and positioned by Presentation Manager instead. See also Sec. 2.2.1.

The following sample code, both 16-bit and 32-bit, shows how to save the application's size and position in OS2.INI and restore next time it starts.

To save size and position (16-bit):

```
SWP    swp;

case WM_SAVEAPPLICATION:
  WinQueryWindowPos(WinQueryWindow(hwnd, QW_PARENT, FALSE),
                    &swp);
  PrfWriteProfileData(HINI_USERPROFILE, "WinGen",
                      "SizePos", &swp, (ULONG)sizeof(swp));
  return NULL;
```

and to restore size and position:

```
/* ----------------------------------------------------*/
/* This would probably go just after your WinCreateStdWindow */
/* call                                                */
/* ----------------------------------------------------*/

ULONG   ulDataLength;

ulDataLength = sizeof(swp);
if (!PrfQueryProfileData(HINI_USERPROFILE, "WinGen",
                         "SizePos", &swp, &ulDataLength))
{
   swp.x = 100;        /* ----------------------------- */
   swp.y = 100;        /* Profile not found so use defaults */
   swp.cx = 200;       /* ----------------------------- */
   swp.cy = 200;
}
WinSetWindowPos(hwndFrame, HWND_TOP, swp.x, swp.y, swp.cx,
                swp.cy, SWP_SIZE | SWP_MOVE | SWP_SHOW |
                SWP_ACTIVATE);
```

To save size and position (32-bit):

```
case WM_SAVEAPPLICATION:
  WinStoreWindowPos("WinGen", "SizePos",
          WinQueryWindow(hwnd, QW_PARENT));
  return NULL;
```

and to restore size and position:

```
/* ----------------------------------------------------*/
/* As in the 16-bit version this would probably go just after */
/* your WinCreateStdWindow call                            */
/* ----------------------------------------------------*/

if (!WinRestoreWindowPos("WinGen", "SizePos", hwndFrame))
  WinSetWindowPos(hwndFrame, HWND_TOP, 100, 100, 200, 200,
                  SWP_SIZE | SWP_MOVE | SWP_SHOW |
                  SWP_ACTIVATE);
else
  WinShowWindow(hwndFrame, TRUE);
```

2.8 Changing the window title

To change the window title use `WinSetWindowText` to set the frame window text:

`hwndFrame = WinQueryWindow(hwnd, QW_PARENT);`

`WinSetWindowText(hwndFrame, "New Title");`

2.9 EXE name appearing in the title bar

You may sometimes notice that your title bar contains the program name as part of the title. This happens because you specified `FCF_TASKLIST` for the window. To overcome this, omit this style and add the program to the window list yourself. See Sec. 13.3.1 for details.

2.10 Removing the title bar

To remove the title bar from a window, change its parent to `HWND_OBJECT`. To replace it again set its parentage back to the original. After making any changes you must send a `WM_UPDATEFRAME` message to the frame window.

```
static  HWND  hwndFrame,
              hTitleBar;
```

```
/* --------------- */
/* Remove title bar */
/* --------------- */

hwndFrame = WinQueryWindow(hwnd, QW_PARENT);
hTitleBar = WinWindowFromID(hwndFrame, FID_TITLEBAR);
WinSetParent(hTitleBar, HWND_OBJECT, FALSE);
WinSendMsg(hwndFrame, WM_UPDATEFRAME,
           MPFROMLONG(FCF_TITLEBAR), 0);

/* ---------------- */
/* Replace title bar */
/* ---------------- */

WinSetParent(hTitleBar, hwndFrame, FALSE);
WinSendMsg(hwndFrame, WM_UPDATEFRAME,
           MPFROMLONG(FCF_TITLEBAR), 0);
```

Note that if you have a system menu, menu bar and minimize/maximize icons you will have to set their parent to `HWND_OBJECT` also. See the SWAPMON program in Chapter 14 for an example.

2.11 Sending/posting a message

When you send a message to a window using `WinSendMsg`, it does not go into a message queue, but makes a synchronous call to the window procedure associated with that window, and does *not* return until that window procedure returns.

When you post a message using `WinPostMsg`, the message is placed in the queue in the form of a QMSG structure and processing continues. This structure comprises the familiar window handle, message ID and message parameters along with a timestamp and the mouse pointer position. `WinGetMsg` then removes the QMSG structure from the queue and `WinDispatchMsg` takes it and extracts the `(hwnd, msg, mp1, mp2)` values. It then effectively does a `WinSendMsg` with these parameters and, just like `WinSendMsg`, does not return until the window procedure it called returns.

If you wish to communicate with another thread and you use `WinPostMsg` in the sending thread then that thread does *not* require a message queue. If, on the other hand, you use `WinSendMsg` then the sending thread *must* have a message queue. See Sec. 12.2 for more information.

2.12 Sending a WM_COMMAND message

To send a `WM_COMMAND` message to your window procedure, for example to simulate the pressing of a button or selecting a menu option, use `WinSendMsg` with `mp1` set to the relevant command value. In the following example we simulate

the pressing of a delete pushbutton which has been defined with the value
ID_DELETE:

WinSendMsg(hwnd, WM_COMMAND, MPFROMSHORT(ID_DELETE), 0);

2.13 Sample program

This program opens two windows (Fig. 2.1), a main client window, and to its right, another top-level window. The initial size and position of the main window are either obtained from the OS2.INI file if previously saved, or set explicitly. The secondary window's size and position are always set explicitly. The main window's frame is subclassed so that its size can be reduced to as small as 25 × 25 pels. Because an icon has not been supplied with this program the system's standard application icon has been used.

The main window displays the process ID of the active window and the other window just displays a text string and stays on top of all other windows, including the main window. In order to keep these windows on top of the desktop, and to ensure that the active process ID is updated regularly, we start a half-second timer. This causes a WM_TIMER message to be sent to our client window every half-second which we trap to force our windows to the top. We then invalidate the client window which in turn causes a WM_PAINT message to be sent, during which we update the process ID.

If you press mouse button 1 when the pointer is over the main window, the window's size and position are fixed, the minimize and maximize buttons are disabled and the title text is changed. Pressing mouse button 2 returns the window to its normal state.

When the main window is minimized, maximized or restored it sounds a short beep to verify that a WM_MINMAXFRAME has been sent. You can also minimize it by selecting Minimize from the menu bar. Because the other top-level window has its *owner*

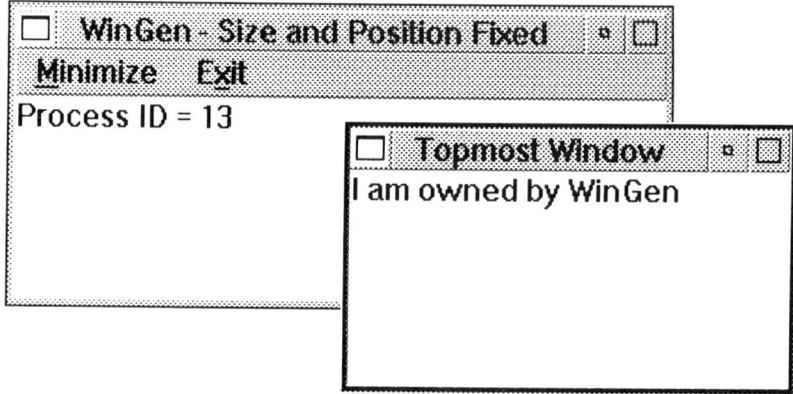

Figure 2.1. General window control output.

set to the main window, it is also minimized when the main window is minimized. When the windows are restored, the main window is forced to position (100, 100) with a size of (200, 200). The other window assumes its previous size and position.

Whenever you quit from this program, or shut the system down when it is running, it will receive a `WM_SAVEAPPLICATION` message. We then save the current state of the application. In this case only the size and position are relevant, but in a real application there may be many other attributes that you may wish to save so that next time it starts it can be restored to the same state.

As mentioned in Chapter 1, the make file, link control file and the module definition file are similar for all the programs in this book, except the sample application in Chapter 14, and so we only show here the program's header file, see Fig. 2.2, the resource file, see Fig. 2.3, and the C source file, see Fig. 2.4.

```
#define    ID_MAINWND    200
#define    ID_TOPWND     201
#define    ID_TITLE      202
#define    ID_TTITLE     203
#define    MI_EXIT       300
#define    MI_RESUME     301
#define    MI_MIN        302
```

Figure 2.2. General window control: header file.

```
#include <os2.h>
#include "wingen.h"

STRINGTABLE PRELOAD
BEGIN
   ID_TITLE,  "General Window Control"
   ID_TTITLE, "Topmost Window"
END

ACCELTABLE ID_MAINWND
BEGIN
   VK_F3,    MI_EXIT,            VIRTUALKEY
END

MENU       ID_MAINWND PRELOAD
BEGIN
   MENUITEM "~Minimize",                MI_MIN,     MIS_TEXT
   SUBMENU  "E~xit",                    1
   BEGIN
      MENUITEM "~Exit Program\tF3",     MI_EXIT,    MIS_TEXT
      MENUITEM "~Resume Program",       MI_RESUME,  MIS_TEXT
   END
END
```

Figure 2.3. General window control: resource file.

```c
#define   INCL_WINWINDOWMGR
#define   INCL_WINFRAMEMGR
#define   INCL_WINSWITCHLIST
#define   INCL_WINSYS
#define   INCL_WINSHELLDATA
#define   INCL_WINTIMER
#define   INCL_WINPOINTERS
#define   INCL_WININPUT
#define   INCL_WINTRACKRECT
#define   INCL_WINWORKPLACE

#include  <os2.h>
#include  <string.h>
#include  <stdio.h>
#include  "wingen.h"

PFNWP     OldFrameProc;

MRESULT   EXPENTRY MainWndProc(HWND, ULONG, MPARAM, MPARAM);
MRESULT   EXPENTRY TopWndProc (HWND, ULONG, MPARAM, MPARAM);
MRESULT   EXPENTRY NewFrame   (HWND, ULONG, MPARAM, MPARAM);

/*************************************************************/
INT main(void)
{
   HAB     hab;
   HMQ     hmq;
   HWND    hwndClient,
           hwndTop,
           hwndFrame,
           hwndTopFrame;
   QMSG    qmsg;
   ULONG   flFrameFlags,
           flTFrameFlags;
   CHAR    szTitle[80],
           szTTitle[80];
   SWCNTRL PgmEntry;

/*************************************************************/

   hab = WinInitialize(0);
   hmq = WinCreateMsgQueue(hab, 0);
```

Figure 2.4. General window control: C source file. Continues.

```
WinRegisterClass(hab, "WinGen", MainWndProc,
                 CS_SIZEREDRAW, 0);
WinRegisterClass(hab, "WinGen2", TopWndProc,
                 CS_SIZEREDRAW, 0);
WinLoadString(hab, (HMODULE)NULL, ID_TITLE,
              sizeof(szTitle), szTitle );
WinLoadString(hab, (HMODULE)NULL, ID_TTITLE,
              sizeof(szTTitle), szTTitle );
flTFrameFlags = FCF_TITLEBAR | FCF_SYSMENU |
                FCF_NOBYTEALIGN | FCF_SIZEBORDER | FCF_MINMAX;
flFrameFlags = FCF_TITLEBAR | FCF_SYSMENU | FCF_MENU |
               FCF_SIZEBORDER | FCF_MINMAX | FCF_ACCELTABLE |
               FCF_NOBYTEALIGN;

hwndFrame = WinCreateStdWindow(HWND_DESKTOP, 0,
                               &flFrameFlags, "WinGen",
                               szTitle, 0, (HMODULE)NULL,
                               ID_MAINWND, &hwndClient);

OldFrameProc = WinSubclassWindow(hwndFrame,
                                 (PFNWP)NewFrame);

if (!WinRestoreWindowPos("WinGen", "WinPos", hwndFrame))
   WinSetWindowPos(hwndFrame, HWND_TOP, 100, 100, 200, 200,
                   SWP_SIZE | SWP_MOVE | SWP_SHOW | SWP_ACTIVATE);
else
   WinShowWindow(hwndFrame, TRUE);
/* -----------------------------------------------------------*/
/*                    To start full-screen                    */
/* -----------------------------------------------------------*/
/* {                                                          */
/*    SWP swp;                                                */
/*                                                            */
/*                                                            */
/*    swp.x = 0;                                              */
/*    swp.y = 0;                                              */
/*    swp.cx = WinQuerySysValue(HWND_DESKTOP,                 */
/*                              SV_CXSCREEN);                 */
/*    swp.cy = WinQuerySysValue(HWND_DESKTOP,                 */
/*                              SV_CYSCREEN);                 */
/*                                                            */
```

Figure 2.4. General window control: C source file. Continues.

```
/*      WinSetWindowPos(hwndFrame, HWND_TOP, swp.x, swp.y,       */
/*                      swp.cx, swp.cy,                          */
/*                      SWP_SIZE | SWP_MOVE | SWP_SHOW |         */
/*                      SWP_ACTIVATE);                           */
/* }                                                             */
/* ------------------------------------------------------------- */

hwndTopFrame = WinCreateStdWindow(HWND_DESKTOP, 0,
                                  &flTFrameFlags,
                                  "WinGen2", szTTitle, 0,
                                  (HMODULE)NULL, 0,
                                  &hwndTop);

WinSetOwner(hwndTopFrame, hwndFrame);

WinSetWindowPos(hwndTopFrame, HWND_TOP, 350, 100, 300,
                200, SWP_SIZE | SWP_MOVE | SWP_SHOW |
                SWP_ACTIVATE);

PgmEntry.hwnd           = hwndFrame;
PgmEntry.hwndIcon       = (HWND)NULL;
PgmEntry.hprog          = (HPROGRAM)NULL;
PgmEntry.idProcess      = (PID)NULL;
PgmEntry.idSession      = (ULONG)NULL;
PgmEntry.uchVisibility  = SWL_VISIBLE;
PgmEntry.fbJump         = SWL_JUMPABLE;
strcpy(PgmEntry.szSwtitle, szTitle);
WinAddSwitchEntry(&PgmEntry);
WinStartTimer(hab, hwndClient, 1, 500);

WinSendMsg(hwndFrame, WM_SETICON,
           (MPARAM)WinQuerySysPointer(HWND_DESKTOP,
           SPTR_APPICON, FALSE), 0);
WinSendMsg(hwndTopFrame, WM_SETICON,
           (MPARAM)WinQuerySysPointer(HWND_DESKTOP,
           SPTR_APPICON, FALSE), 0);

while(WinGetMsg(hab, &qmsg, (HWND)NULL, 0, 0))
   WinDispatchMsg(hab, &qmsg);

WinStopTimer(hab, hwndClient, 1);
WinDestroyWindow(hwndFrame);
WinRemoveSwitchEntry(WinQuerySwitchHandle(hwndFrame, 0));
```

Figure 2.4. General window control: C source file. Continues.

```
  WinDestroyMsgQueue(hmq);
  WinTerminate(hab);
  return 0;
}

/********************************************************/

MRESULT EXPENTRY MainWndProc(HWND hwnd, ULONG msg, MPARAM mp1,
                              MPARAM mp2)
{
  RECTL  rcl;
  HPS    hps;
  HWND   hwndActiveWin,
         hwndFrame;
  PID    pid;
  TID    tid;
  CHAR   szText[20];

  switch (msg)
    {
      case WM_PAINT:
        hps = WinBeginPaint(hwnd, (HPS)NULL, (PRECTL)NULL);
        hwndActiveWin = WinQueryActiveWindow(HWND_DESKTOP);
        WinQueryWindowProcess(hwndActiveWin, &pid, &tid);
        sprintf(szText, "Process ID = %d", pid);

        WinQueryWindowRect(hwnd, &rcl);

        /*----------------------------------------*/
        /* WinMapWindowPoints(hwnd, WinQueryWindow   */
        /* (hwnd, QW_PARENT), (PPOINTL)&rcl, 2);     */
        /*----------------------------------------*/

        WinDrawText (hps, strlen(szText), szText, &rcl,
                     SYSCLR_WINDOWTEXT, SYSCLR_WINDOW,
                     DT_LEFT | DT_ERASERECT);
        WinEndPaint(hps);
        break;

      case WM_TIMER:
        hwndFrame = WinQueryWindow(hwnd, QW_PARENT);
        WinSetWindowPos(hwndFrame, HWND_TOP, 0, 0, 0, 0,
                        SWP_ZORDER);
```

Figure 2.4. General window control: C source file. Continues.

```
                                          /* Cause PID to be displayed */
      WinInvalidateRect(hwnd, NULL, TRUE);
      break;

   case WM_BUTTON1DOWN:
      hwndFrame = WinQueryWindow(hwnd, QW_PARENT);
      WinSetWindowText(hwndFrame,
         "WinGen - Size and Position Fixed");
      WinEnableWindow (WinWindowFromID (hwndFrame,
                     FID_TITLEBAR), FALSE);
      WinEnableWindow (WinWindowFromID (hwndFrame,
                     FID_MINMAX), FALSE);

      WinSetWindowBits(hwndFrame, QWL_STYLE,
                     (~FS_SIZEBORDER | FS_DLGBORDER),
                     (FS_SIZEBORDER | FS_DLGBORDER));
      /*----------------------------------------*/
      /* WinSetWindowULong(hwndFrame, QWL_STYLE,    */
      /*                  (WinQueryWindowULong      */
      /*                  (hwndFrame, QWL_STYLE) &  */
      /*                  ~FS_SIZEBORDER |          */
      /*                  FS_DLGBORDER));           */
      /*----------------------------------------*/

      WinInvalidateRect(hwndFrame, NULL, TRUE);
      break;

   case WM_BUTTON2DOWN:
      hwndFrame = WinQueryWindow(hwnd, QW_PARENT);
      WinSetWindowText(hwndFrame, "WinGen");
      WinEnableWindow (WinWindowFromID (hwndFrame,
                     FID_TITLEBAR), TRUE);
      WinEnableWindow (WinWindowFromID (hwndFrame,
                     FID_MINMAX), TRUE);

      WinSetWindowBits(hwndFrame, QWL_STYLE,
                     (FS_SIZEBORDER | ~FS_DLGBORDER),
                     (FS_SIZEBORDER | FS_DLGBORDER));
      /*----------------------------------------- */
      /* WinSetWindowULong(hwndFrame, QWL_STYLE,    */
      /*                  (WinQueryWindowULong      */
```

Figure 2.4. General window control: C source file. Continues.

```
      /*                   (hwndFrame, QWL_STYLE) &     */
      /*                    ~FS_DLGBORDER |              */
      /*                     FS_SIZEBORDER));            */
      /* ----------------------------------------*/

      WinInvalidateRect(hwndFrame, NULL, TRUE);
      break;

   case WM_MINMAXFRAME:
      hwndFrame = WinQueryWindow(hwnd, QW_PARENT);
      if (((PSWP)mp1)->fl & SWP_MINIMIZE)
      {
         DosBeep(100, 100);
      }
      else
         if (((PSWP)mp1)->fl & SWP_MAXIMIZE)
         {
            DosBeep(1000, 100);
         }
         else
            if (((PSWP)mp1)->fl & SWP_RESTORE)
            {
               DosBeep(500, 100);
            }

      WinSetWindowUShort(hwndFrame, QWS_XRESTORE, 100);
      WinSetWindowUShort(hwndFrame, QWS_YRESTORE, 100);
      WinSetWindowUShort(hwndFrame, QWS_CXRESTORE, 200);
      WinSetWindowUShort(hwndFrame, QWS_CYRESTORE, 200);
      break;

   case WM_SAVEAPPLICATION:
      WinStoreWindowPos("WinGen", "WinPos",
         WinQueryWindow(hwnd, QW_PARENT));
      return NULL;

   case WM_COMMAND:
      switch (SHORT1FROMMP(mp1))
         {
            case MI_MIN:
               hwndFrame = WinQueryWindow(hwnd, QW_PARENT);
               WinSetWindowPos(hwndFrame, 0, 0, 0, 0, 0,
```

Figure 2.4. General window control: C source file. Continues.

```
                        SWP_MINIMIZE);
                    break;
                 case MI_EXIT:
                    WinPostMsg(hwnd, WM_QUIT, 0, 0);
                    break;
            }
            break;
      }
   return WinDefWindowProc(hwnd, msg, mp1, mp2);
}

MRESULT EXPENTRY NewFrame(HWND hwnd, ULONG msg, MPARAM mp1,
                         MPARAM mp2)
{
   PTRACKINFO   ptrack;

   switch(msg)
   {
      case WM_QUERYTRACKINFO:
         /*---------------------------------------------*/
         /* Invoke the default frame window procedure first  */
         /* in order to update the tracking rectangle to the */
         /* new position.                                   */
         /*---------------------------------------------*/
         OldFrameProc(hwnd, msg, mp1, mp2);

         ptrack = (PTRACKINFO)mp2;
         ptrack->ptlMinTrackSize.x = 25;
         ptrack->ptlMinTrackSize.y = 25;

         return((MRESULT)TRUE);
    }
    return OldFrameProc(hwnd, msg, mp1, mp2);
}

/************************************************************/

MRESULT EXPENTRY TopWndProc(HWND hwnd, ULONG msg, MPARAM mp1,
                            MPARAM mp2)
{
   RECTL   rcl;
   HPS     hps;
```

Figure 2.4. General window control: C source file. Continues.

```
  CHAR    szText[22];
  HWND    hwndTopFrame;

  switch(msg)
    {
      case WM_PAINT:
        hps = WinBeginPaint(hwnd, (HPS)NULL, (PRECTL)NULL);
        strcpy(szText, "I am owned by WinGen");
        WinQueryWindowRect(hwnd, &rcl);
        WinDrawText (hps, strlen(szText), szText, &rcl,
                     SYSCLR_WINDOWTEXT, SYSCLR_WINDOW,
                     DT_LEFT | DT_ERASERECT);
        WinEndPaint(hps);
        break;

      case WM_ERASEBACKGROUND:
        return (MRESULT)TRUE;

      case WM_CLOSE:
        hwndTopFrame = WinQueryWindow(hwnd, QW_PARENT);
        WinDestroyWindow(hwndTopFrame);
        break;
    }
  return WinDefWindowProc(hwnd, msg, mp1, mp2);
}
```

Figure 2.4. General window control: C source file. Concluded.

3
A system modal application

An increasingly common requirement is for an application to be the *only* one that a user can interact with. In other words, it is undesirable that the application users be permitted to switch to other parts of OS/2, for example the drives folder, or to any other application.

One possible solution to this problem is to make your application system modal. You do this by calling `WinSetSysModalWindow`, specifying your frame window handle. This ensures that the user can only input, via the mouse or keyboard, into this window, or indeed any of its child windows or windows owned by it, and has the added advantage of preventing the window list from being displayed when Ctrl-Esc is pressed. Alt-Esc and Alt-Tab also have no effect.

It is possible, and for this type of application probably essential, to prohibit closing of the application, except for shutdown. A word of warning here: you must allow the user to shut the system down on completion since it is vital that the file system be closed properly. You can provide this facility by calling the `Dos-Shutdown` function. The sample program in this chapter does not do this because there is an `Exit` option on the menu bar.

There may also be a further requirement to allow a user to switch to DOS at some point in the application processing. Now, this is where there is a difference between 16-bit and 32-bit OS/2. In the 16-bit version it was only possible to have one DOS full-screen session running, and it was always in the task list as DOS. By selecting it, OS/2 would either start DOS or just switch to it if already started. This obviously makes things easy for us, since to switch to DOS we need its switch handle, and since we know its title is DOS it is a simple matter of searching the task list for it, hence obtaining its window handle. Now, with the 32-bit version everything has changed; the task list has become the window list and DOS sessions do not show until they are started. The window titles can be changed to anything the user wishes so we just do not know what to look for anymore. So, to overcome this we must use `DosStartSession` to start a full-screen DOS session and give it a unique program title. Once started, the user can switch back to Presentation Manager by pressing Ctrl-Esc or Alt-Esc. To allow the user to return to the DOS session we can then search the window list for our unique program title, obtain its switch handle, and issue the WinSwitchToProgram call.

Another possibility is to replace the workplace shell with your application by changing the statement:

SET RUNWORKPLACE=C:\OS2\PMSHELL.EXE

in your CONFIG.SYS to:

SET RUNWORKPLACE=myappname

Your program will then become the shell and you have complete control. As an experiment try the statement:

SET RUNWORKPLACE=C:\OS2\CMD.EXE

This will cause your system to start with just a windowed command prompt as the shell, and you will be able to start any Presentation Manager program or full-screen application from the command line. You can even restart the shell by typing START PMSHELL.

3.1 Sample program (32-bit)

Once you have started this program you will only have two options (Fig. 3.1):

Figure 3.1. System modal output.

- Jump to DOS
- Exit

Ctrl-Esc will not display the window list and so you will not be able to switch to any other program you may have running until you exit.

We start by creating the window full-screen with a dialog border rather than a size border. We also use the `FCF_NOBYTEALIGN` flag to ensure that the window occupies the entire screen. Without this, the window will be aligned on eight-pel boundaries and so a gap will be evident on the desktop. To prevent the window from being moved, and hence exposing the desktop, we disable the title bar. We do this at window creation time along with the call to `WinSetSysModalWindow`. At this point, access to any other part of the system is denied; interaction can only take place within this window.

When the `DOS` button is pushed we check if it is the first time the user has done so, and, if so, set up the `STARTDATA` structure and call `DosStartSession` to start a full-screen DOS session. After starting it we query the window list to obtain, and save, the window handle of the DOS session so that we can jump to it next time by calling `WinSwitchToProgram`. See also Sec. 13.3.4.

Figure 3.2 lists the source for the 32-bit version. Note that the header file (Fig. 3.3) and resource file (Fig. 3.4) are the same for both 16-bit and 32-bit versions.

```
#define  INCL_WINWINDOWMGR
#define  INCL_WINFRAMEMGR
#define  INCL_WINSWITCHLIST
#define  INCL_WINSYS
#define  INCL_WINBUTTONS
#define  INCL_DOSSESMGR

#include <os2.h>
#include <string.h>
#include <stdlib.h>
#include "sysmodal.h"

MRESULT EXPENTRY MainWndProc(HWND, ULONG, MPARAM, MPARAM);
HWND    GetDOSHwnd(HWND);

/***************************************************************/
INT main(void)
{
  HAB   hab;
  HMQ   hmq;
  HWND  hwndFrame,
        hwndClient;
```

Figure 3.2. A system modal application (32-bit): C source file. Continues.

```
    QMSG    qmsg;
    ULONG   flFrameFlags;
    CHAR    szTitle[80];
    LONG    lScrHeight,
            lScrWidth;

/****************************************************************/

    hab = WinInitialize(0);
    hmq = WinCreateMsgQueue(hab, 0);

    WinRegisterClass(hab, "Sysmodal", MainWndProc, CS_SIZEREDRAW, 0);

    WinLoadString(hab, (HMODULE)NULL, ID_TITLE, sizeof(szTitle),
                  szTitle);

    flFrameFlags = FCF_TITLEBAR | FCF_MENU | FCF_ACCELTABLE |
                   FCF_NOBYTEALIGN | FCF_DLGBORDER;

    hwndFrame = WinCreateStdWindow(HWND_DESKTOP, 0, &flFrameFlags,
                                   "Sysmodal", szTitle, 0,
                                   (HMODULE)NULL, ID_MAINWND,
                                   &hwndClient);

    lScrWidth  = WinQuerySysValue(HWND_DESKTOP, SV_CXSCREEN);
    lScrHeight = WinQuerySysValue(HWND_DESKTOP, SV_CYSCREEN);
                                            /*--------------------*/
    WinSetWindowPos(hwndFrame, 0, 0, 0,     /*Startup in foreground*/
                    lScrWidth, lScrHeight, /*--------------------*/
                    SWP_SIZE | SWP_MOVE | SWP_SHOW | SWP_ACTIVATE);

    WinCreateWindow(hwndClient, WC_BUTTON, "Jump to DOS", WS_VISIBLE,
                    (lScrWidth/2 - 90), (lScrHeight/2 - 15), 180, 30,
                    hwndClient, HWND_TOP, ID_DOS, 0, 0);

    while (WinGetMsg(hab, &qmsg, (HWND)NULL, 0, 0))
       WinDispatchMsg(hab, &qmsg);

    WinDestroyWindow(hwndFrame);
    WinDestroyMsgQueue(hmq);
    WinTerminate(hab);
    return 0;
}

/****************************************************************/
```

Figure 3.2. A system modal application (32-bit): C source file. Continues.

```c
MRESULT EXPENTRY MainWndProc(HWND hwnd, ULONG msg, MPARAM mp1,
                             MPARAM mp2)
{
  HWND         hwndFrame;
  static HWND  hwndSwitchDOS;
  static BOOL  fSessionStarted = FALSE;
  STARTDATA    StartData;         /* Start session data structure */
  ULONG        ulSessID;          /* Session ID                   */
  PID          pid;               /* Process ID                   */
  CHAR         szPgmTitle[40],    /* Program title string         */
               szPgmName[100],    /* Program to start in DOS      */
               szPgmIp[10],       /* Program parameters           */
               szObjBuf[100];     /* Object buffer                */
  switch (msg)
    {
    case WM_CREATE:
      /*----------------------------------------------------*/
      /* Make system modal and disable the title bar to prevent */
      /* user from moving the window                        */
      /*----------------------------------------------------*/

      hwndFrame = WinQueryWindow(hwnd, QW_PARENT);
      WinSetSysModalWindow(HWND_DESKTOP, hwndFrame);
      WinEnableWindow(WinWindowFromID(hwndFrame,
                      FID_TITLEBAR), FALSE);
      break;

    case WM_COMMAND:
      switch (SHORT1FROMMP(mp1))
         {
         case ID_DOS:
           if (!fSessionStarted)
           {
             fSessionStarted = TRUE;
             strcpy(szPgmTitle,"DOS Session");
                            /* Path to your DOS application */
             strcpy(szPgmName,"D:\\DOSUTIL\\applname");
                            /* Application parameters       */
             strcpy(szPgmIp,"applparm");
             StartData.Length    = sizeof(STARTDATA);
             StartData.Related   = SSF_RELATED_INDEPENDENT;
             StartData.FgBg      = SSF_FGBG_FORE;
             StartData.TraceOpt  = SSF_TRACEOPT_NONE;
             StartData.PgmTitle  = szPgmTitle;
```

Figure 3.2. A system modal application (32-bit): C source file. Continues.

```
                StartData.PgmName       = szPgmName;
                StartData.PgmInputs     = szPgmIp;
                StartData.TermQ         = 0;
                StartData.Environment   = 0;
                StartData.InheritOpt    = SSF_INHERITOPT_SHELL;
                StartData.SessionType   = SSF_TYPE_VDM;
                StartData.IconFile      = 0;
                StartData.PgmHandle     = 0;
                StartData.PgmControl    = 0;
                StartData.InitXPos      = 0;
                StartData.InitYPos      = 0;
                StartData.InitXSize     = 0;
                StartData.InitYSize     = 0;
                StartData.Reserved      = 0;
                StartData.ObjectBuffer  = szObjBuf;
                StartData.ObjectBuffLen = 100;

                DosStartSession(&StartData, &ulSessID, &pid);
                hwndSwitchDOS = GetDOSHwnd(hwnd);
            }
            else
               WinSwitchToProgram(hwndSwitchDOS);
            break;

          case MI_EXIT:
            WinPostMsg(hwnd, WM_QUIT, 0, 0);
            break;

          default:
            break;
        }
      break;

    case WM_ERASEBACKGROUND:
       return (MRESULT)TRUE;
    }
  return  WinDefWindowProc(hwnd, msg, mp1, mp2);
}

HWND   GetDOSHwnd(HWND hwnd)
{
  HAB       hab;
  SWENTRY   swentry;
  SWCNTRL   swcntrl;
  USHORT    usNumTasks, usBufSize, I;
  PSWBLOCK  pswblk;
```

Figure 3.2. A system modal application (32-bit): C source file. Continues.

```
   HWND        hwndDOS;
   PVOID       BaseMem;

/*------------------------------------------------------------*/
/* Get number of task entries so that space can be allocated to store */
/* the switch list block.                                     */
/*------------------------------------------------------------*/

   hab = WinQueryAnchorBlock(hwnd);
   usNumTasks = WinQuerySwitchList(hab, NULL, 0);
   usBufSize = sizeof(SWBLOCK) * usNumTasks;
   DosAllocMem(&BaseMem, usBufSize, PAG_READ | PAG_WRITE |
               PAG_COMMIT);
   pswblk = BaseMem;
   WinQuerySwitchList(hab, pswblk, usBufSize);

   for (I = 0; I < usNumTasks; I++)
   {
      swcntrl = *(PSWCNTRL)((char *)&(pswblk[I].aswentry[0].swctl) -
                sizeof(ULONG)*I);
      if (!strcmp(swcntrl.szSwtitle, "DOS Session"))
      {
         swentry = *(PSWENTRY)((char *)&(pswblk[I].aswentry[0]
                   .hswitch) - sizeof(ULONG)*I);
         hwndDOS = swentry.hswitch;
      }
   }
   DosFreeMem(BaseMem);
   return hwndDOS;
}
```

Figure 3.2. A system modal application (32-bit): C source file. Concluded.

```
#define  ID_MAINWND   200
#define  ID_TITLE     201
#define  IDM_ONE      202
#define  MI_EXIT      203
#define  MI_RESUME    204
#define  ID_DOS       205
```

Figure 3.3. A system modal application (16/32-bit): header file.

```
#include <os2.h>
#include "sysmodal.h"

STRINGTABLE   PRELOAD
BEGIN
   ID_TITLE, "You're Stuck with this Program!!"
END

ACCELTABLE ID_MAINWND
BEGIN
  VK_F3,  MI_EXIT,         VIRTUALKEY
END

MENU        ID_MAINWND PRELOAD
BEGIN
   SUBMENU "E~xit",                     IDM_ONE
   BEGIN
     MENUITEM "~Exit Program\tF3",      MI_EXIT,    MIS_TEXT
     MENUITEM "~Resume Program",        MI_RESUME,  MIS_TEXT
   END
END
```

Figure 3.4 A system modal application (16/32-bit): resource file.

3.2   Sample program (16-bit)

The main difference between this version and the 32-bit version is that we do not need to use `DosStartSession` to start our DOS session. It is already present because we define it in the CONFIG.SYS by specifying `PROTECTONLY=NO`. All we need to do is scan the task list to obtain the window handle of the DOS session and use `WinSwitchToProgram` to switch to it. Figure 3.5 lists the 16-bit source file.

```
#define    INCL_WINWINDOWMGR
#define    INCL_WINFRAMEMGR
#define    INCL_WINSWITCHLIST
#define    INCL_WINSYS
#define    INCL_WINBUTTONS

#include <os2.h>
#include <string.h>
#include <stdlib.h>
#include "sysmodal.h"
```

Figure 3.5. A system modal application (16-bit): C source file. Continues.

```c
MRESULT  EXPENTRY MainWndProc(HWND, USHORT, MPARAM, MPARAM);
HWND     GetDOSHwnd(HWND);
/*****************************************************************/
VOID     cdecl main (void)
{
  HAB    hab;
  HMQ    hmq;
  HWND   hwndFrame,
         hwndClient;
  QMSG   qmsg;
  ULONG  flFrameFlags;
  CHAR   szTitle[80];
  LONG   lScrHeight,
         lScrWidth;
/*****************************************************************/
  hab = WinInitialize(0);
  hmq = WinCreateMsgQueue(hab, 0);

  WinRegisterClass(hab, "Sysmodal", MainWndProc, CS_SIZEREDRAW, 0);

  WinLoadString(hab, NULL, ID_TITLE, sizeof(szTitle), szTitle);

  flFrameFlags = FCF_TITLEBAR | FCF_MENU | FCF_ACCELTABLE |
                 FCF_NOBYTEALIGN | FCF_DLGBORDER;

  hwndFrame = WinCreateStdWindow(HWND_DESKTOP, 0L, &flFrameFlags,
                                 "Sysmodal", (PSZ)szTitle, 0L,
                                 NULL, ID_MAINWND, &hwndClient);

  lScrWidth  = WinQuerySysValue(HWND_DESKTOP, SV_CXSCREEN);
  lScrHeight = WinQuerySysValue(HWND_DESKTOP, SV_CYSCREEN);
                                             /*--------------------*/
  WinSetWindowPos(hwndFrame, NULL, 0, 0, /* Startup in foreground */
                  (SHORT)lScrWidth,    /*--------------------*/
                  (SHORT)lScrHeight,
                  SWP_SIZE | SWP_MOVE | SWP_SHOW | SWP_ACTIVATE);

  WinCreateWindow(hwndClient, WC_BUTTON, "Jump to DOS", WS_VISIBLE,
                  (SHORT)(lScrWidth/2 - 90),
                  (SHORT)(lScrHeight/2 - 15),
                  180, 30, hwndClient, HWND_TOP, ID_DOS, 0, 0);

  while (WinGetMsg(hab, &qmsg, NULL, 0, 0))
    WinDispatchMsg(hab, &qmsg);
```

Figure 3.5. A system modal application (16-bit): C source file. Continues.

```
  WinDestroyWindow(hwndFrame);
  WinDestroyMsgQueue(hmq);
  WinTerminate(hab);
}
/****************************************************************/
MRESULT EXPENTRY MainWndProc(HWND hwnd, USHORT msg, MPARAM mp1,
                             MPARAM mp2)
{
  HWND         hwndFrame;
  static HWND  hwndSwitchDOS;
  switch (msg)
    {
    case WM_CREATE:
      /*----------------------------------------------------*/
      /* Make system modal and disable the title bar to prevent  */
      /* user from moving the window                             */
      /*----------------------------------------------------*/

        hwndFrame = WinQueryWindow(hwnd, QW_PARENT, FALSE);
        WinSetSysModalWindow(HWND_DESKTOP, hwndFrame);
        WinEnableWindow(WinWindowFromID(hwndFrame,
                        FID_TITLEBAR), FALSE);
        hwndSwitchDOS = GetDOSHwnd(hwnd);
        break;

            case WM_COMMAND:
        switch (SHORT1FROMMP(mp1))
          {
          case ID_DOS:
             WinSwitchToProgram(hwndSwitchDOS);
                break;
          case MI_EXIT:
             WinPostMsg(hwnd, WM_QUIT, 0L, 0L);
          default:
             break;
          }
        break;

    case WM_ERASEBACKGROUND:
        return (MRESULT)TRUE;
    }
  return WinDefWindowProc(hwnd, msg, mp1, mp2);
}
/****************************************************************/
```

Figure 3.5. A system modal application (16-bit): C source file. Continues.

```
HWND GetDOShwnd(HWND hwnd)
{
  HAB      hab;
  SWENTRY  swentry;
  SWCNTRL  swcntrl;
  USHORT   usNumTasks,
           usBufSize,
           I;
  PSWBLOCK pswblk;
  HWND     hwndDOS;

  /*----------------------------------------------------------*/
  /* Get number of task entries so that space can be allocated to  */
  /* store the switch list block                                   */
  /*----------------------------------------------------------*/

  hab = WinQueryAnchorBlock(hwnd);
  usNumTasks = WinQuerySwitchList(hab, NULL, 0);
  usBufSize  = sizeof(SWBLOCK) * usNumTasks;
  pswblk     = malloc(usBufSize);
  WinQuerySwitchList(hab, pswblk, usBufSize);

  for (I = 0; I < usNumTasks; I++)
  {
    swcntrl = *(PSWCNTRL)((char *)&(pswblk[I].aswentry[0].swctl)
              - sizeof(USHORT)*I);

    if (!strcmp(swcntrl.szSwtitle, "DOS"))
    {
      swentry = *(PSWENTRY)((char *)&(pswblk[I].aswentry[0]
                .hswitch) - sizeof(USHORT)*I);
      hwndDOS = swentry.hswitch;
    }
  }
  free(pswblk);
  return hwndDOS;
}
```

Figure 3.5. A system modal application (16-bit): C source file. Concluded.

4
Presentation parameters

To change the colour or font of a dialog control or window, you can either do it at runtime using `WinSetPresParam` or, for a dialog control, preset it in your dialog template using the `PRESPARAMS` statement.

One of the most common problems in using `WinSetPresParam` occurs when changing the font. The size parameter, `AttrValueLen`, must include the null terminator for the font string; the best way to do this is to use `sizeof` rather than `strlen`. You can, of course, use the latter but make sure you add 1 to it for the terminator.

4.1 Changing colour

The following sample code changes the foreground and background colours of a multiline entry field in a dialog box using `WinSetPresParam`:

```
LONG    lColour;

lColour = CLR_RED;
WinSetPresParam(WinWindowFromID(hwndDlg, ID_MULTILINE),
                PP_BACKGROUNDCOLORINDEX,
                sizeof(lColour), &lColour);
lColour = CLR_YELLOW;
WinSetPresParam(WinWindowFromID(hwndDlg, ID_MULTILINE),
                PP_FOREGROUNDCOLORINDEX,
                sizeof(lColour), &lColour);
```

If you are using OS/2 V1.x then the `PRESPARAMS` statement can be added manually to the dialog template to add colour for a control:

```
PUSHBUTTON      "Clear MLE", ID_CLEAR, 85, 5, 70, 13
                PRESPARAMS PP_BACKGROUNDCOLORINDEX, CLR_RED
```

```
              PRESPARAMS PP_FOREGROUNDCOLORINDEX,
              CLR_YELLOW
```

The dialog box editor for this version does not support presentation parameters. However, with the introduction of OS/2 version 2.0, the dialog box editor does support presentation parameters, so if you had previously added them manually, as shown, then you must remove them, otherwise when you set them using the editor the new values will be appended *after* your colour settings and so will be ignored. In addition, the editor uses **RGB** values rather than index values and so will add statements of the form:

```
              PRESPARAMS PP_FOREGROUNDCOLOR, 0x000000FFL
              PRESPARAMS PP_BACKGROUNDCOLOR, 0x0000FF00L
```

which represents a blue foreground on a green background.

Obviously, if you are still using OS/2 V1.x then you must add these statements manually.

4.2   Changing font

As in Sec. 4.1, we use both methods to change the font for a dialog control. First, using `WinSetPresParam`:

```
CHAR    szfont[11];

/*----------------------------------------------------------*/
/* The length parameter must include the NULL terminator,   */
/* so use SIZEOF and not STRLEN                             */
/*----------------------------------------------------------*/

strcpy(szfont, "10.Courier");
WinSetPresParam(WinWindowFromID(hwndDlg, ID_CLEAR),
                PP_FONTNAMESIZE, sizeof(szfont), szfont);
```

or using the `PRESPARAMS` statement, as before:

```
PUSHBUTTON    "Clear MLE", ID_CLEAR, 85, 5, 70, 13
              PRESPARAMS PP_FONTNAMESIZE, "10.Tms Rmn"
```

As stated in Sec. 4.1, the dialog box editor for OS/2 version 2.0 supports presentation parameters. This includes the setting of fonts as well as colour. Again, if you had inserted a `PRESPARAMS` statement manually in the dialog box template for a different font, as shown above, and then subsequently edited it with the dialog box editor, the `10.Tms Rmn` would be replaced by its numeric equivalent, that is:

```
PRESPARAMS PP_FONTNAMESIZE, "10.Tms Rmn"
```

would become

```
PRESPARAMS PP_FONTNAMESIZE, 0x542E3031L, 0x5220736DL,
           0x00006E6DL
```

Although this is a very simple way of changing the font, care must be exercised when using this method for multiline entry fields, as some fonts cannot be set this way. Similarly, if you are using an ownerdraw listbox care should be taken where you place the `WinSetPresParam` call. See Sec. 5.14.12 for details.

Note: You can now use this method to change the font style, for example, italic or bold. The following will set the font to 12 point Times New Roman Bold Italic:

```
CHAR    szfont[40];
strcpy(szFont, "12.Times New Roman Bold Italic");
WinSetPresParam(hwnd, PP_FONTNAMESIZE, sizeof(szFont),
                szFont);
```

4.3 Applying presentation parameters to a frame window

If you specify a frame window handle when using `WinSetPresParam` then it will affect all the controls within that frame, since presentation parameters are passed on to any owned windows. However, you may still find that the font for any multi-line entry fields may not be changed.

4.4 Sample Program

See the sample program in Fig. 5.10 for uses of `WinSetPresParam`.

5
Dialog boxes and their controls

This area causes many problems, notably when minimizing a dialog box and ownerdraw listboxes. However, there are also many common problems associated with the controls, and we also look at these here. Some of the problems encountered relate to setting the focus on a particular control, how to set up a user button, the use of entry fields, including multiline, pop-up menus and menu bars, and how to change the style of a particular control. Because there have been many problems attributed to dialog boxes three sample programs have been included to illustrate the solutions. The first looks at general dialog box issues like minimizing and menus, plus various problems associated with entry fields, user buttons, styles and focus. The second concentrates on MLEs and radio buttons, and the final program deals solely with listboxes and mnemonics.

To start with, let us look at dialog boxes in general.

5.1 Dialog box as a main window

It is sometimes very convenient to use the dialog box editor to create a window and then to use this window as your main, or only, window. The easiest way to do this is to create a modal dialog box in your main routine:

```
INT main(VOID)
{
  HAB    hab;
  HMQ    hmq;
  hab = WinInitialize(0);
  hmq = WinCreateMsgQueue(hab, 0);
  WinDlgBox(HWND_DESKTOP, HWND_DESKTOP, DlgProc,
            (HMODULE)NULL, DLG_BOX, 0);
  WinDestroyMsgQueue(hmq);
  WinTerminate(hab);
  return 0;
}
```

You will not need a message loop as this is part of the `WinDlgBox` call. When this call returns it means your dialog box no longer exists and you can terminate your application.

Instead of using `WinDlgBox` you can use the following sequence, which is identical:

```
hDlg = WinLoadDlg(HWND_DESKTOP, HWND_DESKTOP, DlgProc,
                  (HMODULE)NULL, DLG_BOX, 0);
WinProcessDlg(hDlg);
WinDestroyWindow(hDlg);
```

5.2 Minimizing a dialog box

Dialog boxes were never intended to be minimized and so the most common problem encountered when minimizing them is the non-appearance of its icon. Instead, Presentation Manager paints the icon with the bottom-left corner of the dialog box. So, to minimize your dialog box and ensure the icon is displayed correctly, load the icon using `WinLoadPointer` and then send a `WM_SETICON` message to the dialog box. You should do this in your `WM_INITDLG` code. You must then trap the `WM_ADJUSTWINDOWPOS` message and, if minimizing, hide the control(s) at the bottom-left corner of the box. Conversely, when restoring, you must show the control(s) again. Finally, pass control back to the default dialog procedure so that it can do any default processing. In the following code there is a pushbutton, with an ID of ID_OK, that must be hidden/reshown:

```
static   HWND    hDlgBoxIcon;

case WM_INITDLG:
  hDlgBoxIcon = WinLoadPointer(HWND_DESKTOP, (HMODULE)NULL,
                               ID_ICON);
  WinSendMsg(hwndDlg, WM_SETICON, (MPARAM)hDlgBoxIcon, 0);
  ;
  ;
  return (MRESULT)TRUE;   /* Needed if we have changed focus */

case WM_ADJUSTWINDOWPOS:
  if (((PSWP)mp1)->fl & SWP_MINIMIZE)     /* Being minimized */
  {
    WinShowWindow(WinWindowFromID(hwndDlg, ID_OK), FALSE);
  }
  else
    if (((PSWP)mp1)->fl & SWP_RESTORE)     /* Being restored */
    {
      WinShowWindow(WinWindowFromID(hwndDlg, ID_OK), TRUE);
```

```
          }
       return WinDefDlgProc(hwndDlg, msg, mp1, mp2);

    case ID_EXIT:
       WinDestroyPointer(hDlgBoxIcon);
        ;
        ;
       break;
```

You should also add a `WinDestroyPointer` call during your exit processing.

5.3   Starting minimized

To create a dialog in its minimized state use `SWP_MINIMIZE` in a call to `WinSetWindowPos`:

```
LONG   lX_Left,
       lY_Bot,
       lScreenHeight,
       lScreenWidth;
RECTL rcl;

case WM_INITDLG:

                 /*---------------------------------------*/
                 /* This code will ensure that your dialog  */
                 /* box is centred on the desktop when      */
                 /* restored from its minimized state.      */
                 /*---------------------------------------*/

   lScreenWidth  = WinQuerySysValue(HWND_DESKTOP,
                                    SV_CXSCREEN);
   lScreenHeight = WinQuerySysValue(HWND_DESKTOP,
                                    SV_CYSCREEN);

   WinQueryWindowRect(hwndDlg, &rcl);
   lX_Left = (lScreenWidth  - rcl.xRight) / 2;
   lY_Bot  = (lScreenHeight - rcl.yTop)   / 2;

   WinSetWindowPos(hwndDlg, HWND_TOP, lX_Left, lY_Bot, 0, 0,
          SWP_MOVE | SWP_SHOW | SWP_ACTIVATE | SWP_MINIMIZE);
    ;
    ;
   break;
```

5.4 Positioning a dialog box on the desktop

To position a dialog box on the desktop call `WinSetWindowPos` *without* the `SWP_SIZE` option in your `WM_INITDLG` case statement. Section 5.3 is really a special case of this; just omit the `SWP_MINIMIZE` option to give the desired result.

5.5 Mnemonics for controls

If you want to use mnemonics in a dialog box then define a static text field with the `DT_MNEMONIC` style, either manually or by using the dialog box editor, and place this immediately *before* the control you want the mnemonic to act upon. This creates a mnemonic based on the position of the static text control in the resource, and underlines the letter with the tilde.

In the following example, when the user presses Alt-S from anywhere in the dialog, or S if the focus is not on an entry field or another listbox , it will automatically set the focus to the listbox control:

```
CTEXT              "~Single Selection", 101, 8, 155, 80, 8,
                   DT_MNEMONIC
LISTBOX            ID_LISTBOX, 8, 71, 80, 80
```

5.6 Modeless dialog box

Sometimes you may need to allow users to access your application's main client window while a dialog box is displayed. To do this you must make the dialog box modeless. This is done by calling `WinLoadDlg` to load the dialog box and `WinShowWindow` to make it visible:

```
hDlg = WinLoadDlg(HWND_DESKTOP, HWND_DESKTOP, DlgProc,
                  (HMODULE)NULL, DLG_BOX, 0);
WinShowWindow(hDlg, TRUE);
```

Briefly, the difference between a modal and a modeless dialog box is that with a modal dialog you cannot interact with the main client window until you have dismissed it, whereas with a modeless dialog you can. For example, you would use a modal dialog if you needed information before you could continue processing the application, and a modeless dialog if you wanted to keep information in view at all times.

The important point to note here is that when you dismiss the dialog it is only hidden, not destroyed like a modal dialog box, and so the data is still accessible using `WinQueryWindowText`, etc. You can also use window words (see Chapter 9), to pass the data back to the main window procedure. To remove the dialog box you must use `WinDestroyWindow`:

```
WinDestroyWindow(hDlg);
```

For an example of a modeless dialog see Sec. 9.4, where you will find the source listing in Fig. 9.3.

5.7 Adding a status bar

If you have used the enhanced Presentation Manager editor, supplied with the 32-bit version of OS/2, you will have noticed that it has a status bar. This bar gives you the current application status, for example whether you are in Insert or Replace mode. This feature can also be added to dialog boxes very simply. All you have to do is define a static text field in the dialog box, using the dialog box editor:

```
CTEXT                "", ID_STATUS, 0, 0, 195, 8
```

The above defines a static text field, with centred text, at the dialog box's origin (0, 0) with a length of 195 dialog units and a height of 8 units.

You then use WinSetPresParam in the WM_INITDLG case statement to initialize the colours (alternatively, you can set the presentation parameters using the dialog box editor if you are using OS/2 V2.0):

```
LONG   lColour;

case WM_INITDLG:
  lColour = CLR_DARKGREEN;
  WinSetPresParam(WinWindowFromID(hwndDlg, ID_STATUS),
              PP_BACKGROUNDCOLORINDEX,
              sizeof(lColour), &lColour);

  lColour = CLR_YELLOW;
  WinSetPresParam(WinWindowFromID(hwndDlg, ID_STATUS),
              PP_FOREGROUNDCOLORINDEX,
              sizeof(lColour), &lColour);
  ;
  ;
  ;
  break;
```

You will then need to call WinSetWindowText to display, or change, the status as and when necessary:

```
strcpy(szStatus, "New Status");
WinSetWindowText(WinWindowFromID(hwndDlg, ID_STATUS),
              szStatus);
```

5.8 Disabling controls

To disable a control, call `WinEnableWindow` with the second parameter, `NewEnabled`, set to FALSE, and to enable it again set the parameter to TRUE. To obtain the window handle of the control use `WinWindowFromID`. The following code shows how to disable, and enable, a control in a dialog box with an ID of `ID_DELETE`:

```
/*--------------*/
/* To disable... */
/*--------------*/

WinEnableWindow(WinWindowFromID(hwndDlg, ID_DELETE),
                                FALSE);

/*--------------*/
/* To enable...  */
/*--------------*/

WinEnableWindow(WinWindowFromID(hwndDlg, ID_DELETE),
                                TRUE);
```

This is a useful technique to use when you do not want a user activating a control until any prerequisites have been completed. For example, if you have a delete pushbutton in your dialog you do not want it pressed until the user has selected an item to delete. Using this technique can reduce the size, and complexity, of your program, since the amount of validation code will be greatly reduced.

5.8.1 Entry fields

If you need to disable an entry field which is the *first* control in a dialog box then use `WinEnableWindow` as usual in your `WM_INITDLG` case statement, but alter the focus to another control. Failure to do this if you are coding for version 1.x will allow users to enter data into the field until they tab out to another control. It will only be then that the entry field will become disabled. However, under version 2.0 the field will be disabled, but unless you alter the focus, the cursor will still be positioned on it.

It is also important when changing focus during a `WM_INITDLG` message to return TRUE, otherwise it will not be changed, see also Sec. 5.12.

5.9 Window ID of a control

To retrieve the window identity of a control within a dialog box or client window use `WinQueryWindowUShort` with a value of `QWS_ID`:

```
SHORT    sId;
/*---------------------------------------*/
/*  To find the ID of the control ID_ENTRY    */
/*---------------------------------------*/
sId = WinQueryWindowUShort(WinWindowFromID(hwndDlg,
                                ID_ENTRY), QWS_ID);
```

Now that we have looked at dialog boxes in general, let us take a look at the individual controls which have given rise to numerous questions.

5.10   Buttons

5.10.1 *Default pushbutton*

To determine which pushbutton is the default use `WinQueryWindowULong` with a value of `QWL_STYLE`. If the returned style has the `BS_DEFAULT` bit set then it is the default button:

```
ULONG    ulStyle;

ulStyle = WinQueryWindowULong(WinWindowFromID(hwndDlg,
                                 ID_OK), QWL_STYLE);

if (ulStyle & BS_DEFAULT)
{
/*-----------------------*/
/*  Button is the default  */
/*-----------------------*/
}
```

To remove the default style send the button a `BM_SETDEFAULT` message with mp1 set to **FALSE**. To make it the default again send the same message with mp1 set to **TRUE**:

```
/*---------------------*/
/*  Remove default style  */
/*---------------------*/
WinSendMsg(WinWindowFromID(hwndDlg, ID_OK), BM_SETDEFAULT,
           (MPARAM)FALSE, 0);

/*------------------*/
/*  Set default style  */
/*------------------*/
WinSendMsg(WinWindowFromID(hwndDlg, ID_OK), BM_SETDEFAULT,
```

```
                          (MPARAM)TRUE, 0);
```

Alternatively, to set/remove the default state you can use `WinSetWindow-Bits`, but you must call `WinInvalidateRect` to force a repaint of the button afterwards to ensure the default border is added/removed as appropriate:

```
/*----------------------*/
/*  Remove default style  */
/*----------------------*/
WinSetWindowBits(WinWindowFromID(hwndDlg, ID_OK),
                 QWL_STYLE, 0, BS_DEFAULT);
WinInvalidateRect(WinWindowFromID(hwndDlg, ID_OK), NULL,
                  FALSE);

/*-------------------*/
/*  Set default style  */
/*-------------------*/
WinSetWindowBits(WinWindowFromID(hwndDlg, ID_OK),
                 QWL_STYLE, BS_DEFAULT, BS_DEFAULT);
WinInvalidateRect(WinWindowFromID(hwndDlg, ID_OK), NULL,
                  FALSE);
```

Note: From OS/2 version 1.3 onwards, setting another pushbutton to be the default will cause the current default button to lose its default state.

5.10.2 User pushbutton

If you need to display a bitmap in a pushbutton, for example the system bitmap for a drive, then you must use a pushbutton with the style `BS_USERBUTTON`. Using this causes a `WM_CONTROL` message, with a notification code of `BN_PAINT`, to be sent to your dialog procedure whenever the button needs to be painted. The second parameter of this message contains a pointer to a `USERBUTTON` structure, as follows:

```
typedef struct _USERBUTTON
{
   HWND    hwnd;          /* Window handle              */
   HPS     hps;           /* Presentation space handle */
   ULONG   fsState;       /* New state of user button   */
   ULONG   fsStateOld;    /* Old state of user button   */
} USERBUTTON;
```

Note that this is yet another structure which has changed for version 2.0; the two state variables have changed from `USHORT` to `ULONG`, but at the time of writing their names remain unchanged.

To handle a user button, all we need do is supply a button paint procedure, and in the dialog box procedure process the WM_CONTROL message. The actual button ID will be passed in the low SHORT of the message's first parameter, mp1, so we can check this if we have more than one button. In the following code we only have one user button and so there is really no need for this check. However, the first thing we need to do when we receive this message is to pass the pointer, mp2, to our button procedure. Remember that mp2 contains a pointer to the USER-BUTTON structure.

```
/*----------------------------------*/
/*  Define the button paint procedure   */
/*----------------------------------*/

VOID   Button_Paint(PUSERBUTTON);

/*--------------------------------------------------------*/
/* In the dialog box procedure handle the WM_CONTROL      */
/* message...                                             */
/*--------------------------------------------------------*/

   case WM_CONTROL:
     switch(SHORT2FROMMP(mp1))
      {                              /* Check notification code */
        case BN_PAINT:
          switch(SHORT1FROMMP(mp1))
           {                         /* Check button control ID */
             case ID_USERBUTTON:
               Button_Paint(mp2);
               return (MRESULT)TRUE;

             default:
               break;
           }
      }
     break;

/*-----------------------*/
/*  Handle the button push  */
/*-----------------------*/

   case WM_COMMAND:
     switch(SHORT1FROMMP(mp1))
      {
        ;
        ;
```

Dialog boxes and their controls

```
          ;
        case ID_USERBUTTON:
          DosBeep(500, 100);
          return FALSE;
          ;
          ;
          ;
      }
      return FALSE;
```

All the paint procedure does is to load the bitmap and draw it. In the button's normal state, the value of `fsState` is zero and so we use the `DBM_NORMAL` flag. When the button is pressed, `fsState` is non-zero so we invert the image by using `DBM_INVERT`. The commented section loads the Drives system bitmap:

```
VOID Button_Paint(USERBUTTON *ubtn)
{
  RECTL    DestPt;
  HBITMAP hbm;

  /* ----------------------------------------------------*/
  /* hbm = WinGetSysBitmap(HWND_DESKTOP, SBMP_DRIVE);    */
  /* WinQueryWindowRect(ubtn->hwnd, &DestPt);            */
  /* WinDrawBitmap(ubtn->hps, hbm, NULL, (PPOINTL)       */
  /*               &DestPt, CLR_YELLOW, CLR_BLACK,       */
  /*               ((USHORT)ubtn->fsState ? DBM_INVERT : */
  /*               DBM_NORMAL) | DBM_STRETCH);           */
  /* ----------------------------------------------------*/
  hbm = GpiLoadBitmap(ubtn->hps, (HMODULE)NULL,
                    ID_LOCK, 0, 0);
  WinQueryWindowRect(ubtn->hwnd, &DestPt);
  WinDrawBitmap(ubtn->hps, hbm, NULL, (PPOINTL)&DestPt,
                0, 0, ((USHORT)ubtn->fsState ? DBM_INVERT :
                DBM_NORMAL) | DBM_STRETCH);
  return;
}
```

This paint procedure makes use of the `DBM_STRETCH` flag so that the bitmap is stretched to the full size of the button. If you wish to display a non-system bitmap in a pushbutton then you must define it in your resource file and load it in your paint procedure prior to display:

```
BITMAP  ID_LOCK   lock.bmp
```

You could modify the button paint procedure easily to look at all the system bitmaps by adding the following code:

```
static   USHORT usBitmap = 1;

hbm = WinGetSysBitmap(HWND_DESKTOP, usBitmap++);
if (usBitmap == 49)                /* Currently only 48 bitmaps */
   usBitmap = 1;

WinQueryWindowRect(ubtn->hwnd, &DestPt);
WinDrawBitmap(ubtn->hps, hbm, NULL, (PPOINTL)&DestPt,
              CLR_YELLOW, CLR_BLACK,
              ((USHORT)ubtn->fsState ? DBM_INVERT :
              DBM_NORMAL) | DBM_STRETCH);
```

Note the cast to USHORT for ubtn->fsState. In OS/2 V1.x this field, and fsStateOld were USHORTs but were redefined to ULONG for version 2.0 in readiness for the conversion of the Presentation Manager code to 32-bit. However, since this was not implemented in V2.0 we must still use USHORT, otherwise the image will never be redrawn in its normal colours once the button has been pressed.

5.10.3 *Initializing radio buttons*

This is probably the most common problem for radio buttons. If you have a group of radio buttons and you want to check one other than the first when starting your dialog, then the following will usually work:

```
case WM_INITDLG:
  WinSendDlgItemMsg(hwnd, BUTTON_ID, BM_SETCHECK,
                    MPFROM2SHORT(TRUE, 0), 0);
  ;
  ;
```

However, if the group of buttons is the *first* control in the dialog box then the first button will be checked, irrespective of whatever button ID you specified on the WinSendDlgItemMsg. To overcome this, check the required button as shown, but make sure you return TRUE from the WM_INITDLG as you would when setting the focus.

5.11   Entry fields

5.11.1 *Changing the default length*

To change the default length of 32 for a text entry field send it an EM_SETTEXTLIMIT message. You would normally put this in the

WM_INITDLG case statement:

```
/*----------------------------------------------*/
/* This code sets the password length to 8 bytes    */
/*----------------------------------------------*/

WinSendMsg(WinWindowFromID(hwndDlg, ID_PASSWORD),
           EM_SETTEXTLIMIT, MRFROMSHORT(8), 0);
```

Alternatively, you can modify your dialog box template, the DLG file, by adding control data to the control(s) on which you want the length set. The following example shows how to set the length of an entry field to five bytes:

```
ENTRYFIELD        "", ID_ENTRY, 67, 57, 36, 8,
                  NOT ES_AUTOSCROLL | ES_MARGIN
                  CTLDATA 8, 5, 0, 0
```

The format of CTLDATA for an entry field is:

```
CTLDATA size, length, minsel, maxsel
```

where:
   size   = 8 for 8 bytes of control data
   length = number of characters allowed to be entered
   minsel = 0 (minsel defines the first character to be initially selected)
   maxsel = 0 (maxsel defines the last character to be initially selected)

> *Note:* If you use this latter approach, beware if you use the dialog box editor as you may lose any changes you have made manually to the DLG file.

5.11.2 Cursor not appearing at edge of field

This problem has caused some programmers to spend many hours searching for a cure. Its effect is that the system pointer does not change into the I-beam cursor when it moves into an entry field, but as it is moved to the right it does change.

The cause of this is a static field being defined immediately to the left of the entry field and overlapping it. Hence, when the user moves the pointer into the left side of the entry field, it is effectively pointing to the static text rather than the entry field, and so the pointer does not change until it reaches the end of the static field. Fix this by realigning the fields in the dialog box.

5.11.3 Cursor position

To position the cursor in an entry field send it an EM_SETSEL message. The first parameter of this message, MPFROM2SHORT(m, n), specifies where the cursor is to be positioned and what part of the field needs to be selected, if any.

m specifies the zero-based offset of the first character in the selection
n specifies the zero-based offset of the first character after the selection

If *m* = *n*, there is no selection but the cursor is positioned at offset *m*. If *m* = 0 and *n* ⩾ text limit, the entire text is selected. For example:

```
/*----------------------------------------------------*/
/* Position cursor between 1st and 2nd characters of a     */
/* 5-byte entry field - ID_ENTRY                           */
/*----------------------------------------------------*/

WinSendMsg(WinWindowFromID(hwndDlg, ID_ENTRY), EM_SETSEL,
           MPFROM2SHORT(1, 1), 0);

/*----------------------------------------------------*/
/* Position cursor between 1st and 2nd characters but mark */
/* 2nd and 3rd characters only                             */
/*----------------------------------------------------*/

WinSendMsg(WinWindowFromID(hwndDlg, ID_ENTRY), EM_SETSEL,
           MPFROM2SHORT(1, 3), 0);

/*----------------------------------------------------*/
/* Position cursor at start of field but mark entire field */
/*----------------------------------------------------*/

WinSendMsg(WinWindowFromID(hwndDlg, ID_ENTRY), EM_SETSEL,
           MPFROM2SHORT(0, 5), 0);
```

5.11.4 Reading data

To read data from an entry field use `WinQueryWindowText` or `WinQueryDlgItemText` for character data, or `WinQueryDlgItemShort` to convert the text to an integer value:

```
/*---------------------------------------*/
/*   Get password and store it in szPswd...  */
/*---------------------------------------*/

WinQueryWindowText(WinWindowFromID(hwndDlg, ID_PASSWORD),
                   sizeof(szPswd), szPswd);

/*-------*/
/* Or... */
/*-------*/

WinQueryDlgItemText(hwndDlg, ID_PASSWORD, sizeof(szPswd),
                    szPswd);
```

Dialog boxes and their controls

```
/*------------------------------------------------------*/
/* Get unsigned SHORT value and store it in sValue...   */
/*   The Signed parameter is FALSE for an unsigned value */
/*                  and TRUE for a possible signed value */
/*------------------------------------------------------*/
WinQueryDlgItemShort(hwndDlg, ID_ENTRY, &sValue, FALSE);
```

5.11.5 Numeric data only

To limit an entry field to numeric data you must subclass the entry field window and throw away those keystrokes not required. Do not forget that you will probably need to keep some non-numeric keystrokes, for example, backspace, tab, minus sign and enter. For example:

```
/*------------------------------------------------------*/
/* First define your numeric procedure and a pointer to the */
/* public entry field procedure                         */
/*------------------------------------------------------*/
MRESULT EXPENTRY NumericProc(HWND, ULONG, MPARAM, MPARAM);

PFNWP   EntryFieldProc;    /* Public Entry Field procedure */

/*------------------------------------------------------*/
/* In your WM_INITDLG case statement save the address of */
/* the public entry field procedure                     */
/*------------------------------------------------------*/
case WM_INITDLG:
   EntryFieldProc = WinSubclassWindow (WinWindow FromID
              (hwndDlg, ID_ENTRY), (PFNWP)NumericProc);

/*------------------------------------------------------*/
/* The following is the subclassed window procedure     */
/*------------------------------------------------------*/
MRESULT EXPENTRY   NumericProc(HWND hwnd, ULONG msg,
                               MPARAM mp1, MPARAM mp2)
{
   SHORT     fsKeyFlags,
             sChr;

   if (msg == WM_CHAR)                /* If this is a char msg */
   {
      fsKeyFlags = SHORT1FROMMP(mp1);
      sChr       = SHORT1FROMMP(mp2);
```

```
      if (!(fsKeyFlags & KC_KEYUP))    /* Only act on key down */
      {
        if ((sChr < 0x30 || sChr > 0x39) &&    /* Not numeric    */
            (sChr != 8) &&                      /* Not backspace */
            (sChr != 9) &&                      /* Not tab        */
            (sChr != 0x2D) &&                   /* Not -          */
            (sChr != 0xD))                      /* Not enter      */
        {
          WinAlarm(HWND_DESKTOP, WA_WARNING);
          return (MRESULT)TRUE;       /* Throw away keystroke */
        }
      }
    }                       /* Call public entry field procedure */
    return (* EntryFieldProc)(hwnd, msg, mp1, mp2);
  }
```

5.11.6 Read-only entry field

If you require a read-only entry field then send the control an EM_SETREADONLY message or add the style ES_READONLY to the control in your dialog template either by using the dialog box editor or manually:

```
WinSendMsg(WinWindowFromID(hwndDlg, ID_ENTRY),
           EM_SETREADONLY, (MPARAM)TRUE, 0);

/*-------*/
/* Or... */
/*-------*/

ENTRYFIELD       "", ID_ENTRY, 77, 25, 100, 16, ES_CENTER |
                 ES_MARGIN | ES_READONLY | WS_GROUP |
                 NOT WS_TABSTOP
```

Alternatively, use a static control instead of an entry field and use WinSetWindowText or WinSetDlgItemText to change the text:

```
WinSetWindowText(hwndDlg, "New Title");

/*-------*/
/* Or... */
/*-------*/

WinSetDlgItemText(hwndDlg, FID_TITLEBAR, "New Title");
```

5.11.7 Unreadable entry field

To make an entry field unreadable so that it can be used for entering passwords, use the style `ES_UNREADABLE`. This causes each entered character to be displayed as an asterisk (*). You can either enter it manually in your dialog box template as shown:

```
ENTRYFIELD        "", ID_PASSWORD, 77, 37, 45, 8,
                  NOT ES_AUTOSCROLL | ES_MARGIN |
                  ES_UNREADABLE
```

or you can use the dialog box editor and check the `Unreadable` checkbox for that entry field's styles. In fact, the 16-bit dialog box editor does *not* support this style so you must enter it manually. If you do this, however, and then make further changes to the dialog box using the editor you will lose the `ES_UNREADABLE` style and must enter it again, so beware.

You *cannot* change this style for an entry field dynamically. For example, the code:

```
hPwd = WinWindowFromID(hwndDlg, ID_PASSWORD);

WinSetWindowULong(hPwd, QWL_STYLE,
    (WinQueryWindowULong(hPwd, QWL_STYLE)
     | ES_UNREADABLE));
```

will not work. The reason is that if changing this style flag meant that the window changed from being unreadable to readable, it would be possible to write a program to change the state of password entry fields and read them, thereby removing the password protection.

5.11.8 Writing data

To write character data to an entry field use `WinSetWindowText` or `WinSetDlgItemText`:

```
WinSetWindowText(WinWindowFromID(hwndDlg, ID_ENTRY),
                 "Text");
/*-------*/
/* Or... */
/*-------*/
WinSetDlgItemText(hwndDlg, ID_ENTRY, "Text");
```

If you need to write an integer value to an entry field then use `WinSetDlgItemShort`. This converts the integer value directly to text for you; there is no need to do any conversion yourself. If it is an unsigned value then set the `Signed` parameter to FALSE, otherwise set it to TRUE. The following statement writes the unsigned integer `sID` to an entry field:

```
WinSetDlgItemShort(hwndDlg, ID_ENTRY, sID, FALSE);
```

To clear data from an entry field just write null to it:

```
WinSetDlgItemText(hwndDlg, ID_ENTRY, "");
```

5.12   Focus

The default dialog procedure sets the focus to the first control defined in the dialog box template. To override this call `WinSetFocus` in your `WM_INITDLG` case statement. However, you must return TRUE from `WM_INITDLG` to tell Presentation Manager that the focus has changed, otherwise it will revert to the first control:

```
/*-------------------------------------*/
/* Set the focus to entry field ID_ENTRY    */
/*-------------------------------------*/
case WM_INITDLG:
  WinSetFocus(HWND_DESKTOP, WinWindowFromID(hwndDlg,
           ID_ENTRY));
  ;
  ;
  ;
  return (MRESULT)TRUE;                  /* Focus has changed */
```

5.13   Icons

5.13.1   *System icon in a dialog box*

To include a system icon in a dialog box just add a CONTROL statement directly to your DLG file. But be careful if you use the dialog box editor afterwards; it does not support this so you will lose it. You will also receive a warning message when you start the dialog box editor if it encounters such a statement.

```
/*--------------------------*/
/*  For the information icon  */
/*--------------------------*/
CONTROL "#11", SPTR_ICONINFORMATION, 100, 15, 22, 16,
       WC_STATIC, SS_SYSICON | WS_VISIBLE

/*----------------------*/
/*  For the warning icon  */
/*----------------------*/
```

Dialog boxes and their controls 77

```
CONTROL "#14", SPTR_ICONWARNING, 100, 15, 22, 16, WC_STATIC,
        SS_SYSICON | WS_VISIBLE
```

For all the `"#n"` and `SPTR_*` values see the **PMWIN.H** include file in the OS/2 version 2.0 developer's toolkit.

5.13.2 User icon in a dialog box

To include your own icon in a dialog box use the dialog box editor to define and position the icon on the window and then add an `ICON` statement to your resource file, specifying which icon filename you want associated with the icon ID. In your `WM_INITDLG` statement simply call `WinLoadPointer` and send a `WM_SETICON` message to the dialog box:

```
ICON   ID_ICON   dlggen.ico
```

The associated control statement in the dialog template is:

```
ICON     ID_ICON, ID_ICON, 5, 35, 20, 16, WS_GROUP
```

and in the `WM_INITDLG` code:

```
hDlgBoxIcon = WinLoadPointer(HWND_DESKTOP, (HMODULE)NULL,
                             ID_ICON);
WinSendMsg(hwndDlg, WM_SETICON, (MPARAM)hDlgBoxIcon, 0);
```

5.14 Listboxes

5.14.1 Inserting items

To insert items into a listbox, send it an `LM_INSERTITEM` message. The first parameter of this message indicates where the item is to be inserted. It can be at the end, `LIT_END`, in ascending, `LIT_SORTASCENDING`, or descending, `LIT_SORTDESCENDING`, sequence, or at any position:

```
static SHORT   sIdx;

static PSZ    szCountry[] = {"Austria", "Belgium", "Canada",
                             "Denmark", "Egypt", "Finland",
                             "Greece", "Hungary", "India",
                             "Japan", "Kenya", "Libya",
                             "Morocco", "Nigeria", "Oman",
                             "Peru", "Qatar", "Romania",
                             "Spain", "Turkey", "Uruguay",
                             "Venezuela", "Wales", "Xanxere",
                             "Yemen", "Zambia"};
```

```
for (sIdx = 0; sIdx < 26; sIdx++)
{
  WinSendDlgItemMsg(hwndDlg, ID_LISTBOX, LM_INSERTITEM,
                    MPFROMSHORT(LIT_END),
                    MPFROMP(szCountry[sIdx]));
}
```

5.14.2 Selecting items

To select an item in a listbox, send it an `LM_SELECTITEM` message. Remember that the item's index is zero-based, so to select the first item in a listbox set the first parameter of the message to zero:

```
WinSendDlgItemMsg(hwndDlg, ID_LISTBOX, LM_SELECTITEM,
                  MPFROMSHORT(0), (MPARAM)TRUE);
```

5.14.3 Deselecting items

To deselect an item from a listbox, send it an `LM_SELECTITEM` message with the second parameter set to **FALSE**. The first parameter may either be the actual index of the selected item or `LIT_NONE`:

```
WinSendDlgItemMsg(hwndDlg, ID_LISTBOX, LM_SELECTITEM,
                  (MPARAM)LIT_NONE, (MPARAM)FALSE);
```

If you wish to deselect *all* items in a multiple selection listbox then you must loop through the listbox, deselecting each one separately. The value `LIT_NONE` for the first parameter in this type of listbox is ignored, since selecting another item in a multiple selection listbox does *not* deselect any previously selected item.

5.14.4 Deleting items

To delete an item from a listbox send it an `LM_DELETEITEM` message:

```
static SHORT    sIdx;

WinSendDlgItemMsg(hwndDlg, ID_LISTBOX, LM_DELETEITEM,
                  MPFROMSHORT(sIdx), 0);
```

If you need to delete *all* items then send it an `LM_DELETEALL` message:

```
WinSendDlgItemMsg(hwndDlg, ID_LISTBOX, LM_DELETEALL, 0, 0);
```

5.14.5 Retrieving the text of a selected item

Listboxes generate a WM_CONTROL message whenever an event, such as selecting an item, occurs for a listbox. To process it, check the low word of the mp1 parameter, using the SHORT1FROMMP macro, for the listbox ID, and then the high word of the mp1 parameter, using the SHORT2FROMMP macro, for the LN_* notification code (in this instance LN_SELECT).

To read the text of the selected item you must first send the listbox an LM_QUERYSELECTION message to get the index of the selected item, taking care to note that the first entry in a listbox has an index of zero. Once you have this value send it an LM_QUERYITEMTEXT message to retrieve the actual text:

```
SHORT sIdx;
CHAR  szCtry[10];
case WM_CONTROL:
  switch(SHORT1FROMMP(mp1))
  {
    case ID_LISTBOX:
      switch(SHORT2FROMMP(mp1))
      {
        case LN_SELECT:
          sIdx = (SHORT)WinSendDlgItemMsg(hwndDlg,
                     ID_LISTBOX, LM_QUERYSELECTION,
                     0, 0);
          WinSendDlgItemMsg(hwndDlg, ID_LISTBOX,
                     LM_QUERYITEMTEXT,
                     MPFROM2SHORT(sIdx,
                     sizeof(szCtry)),
                     MPFROMP(szCtry));
          ;
          ;
          ;
          break;
        default:
          break;
      }
      break;
  }
```

5.14.6 Processing multiple items

To process the selected items in a multiple selection listbox, first send an LM_QUERYSELECTION message with the first parameter set to LIT_FIRST, this will return the index of the first selected item. You can then process this item and then send another `LM_QUERYSELECTION` message with the first parameter set to the index previously returned. Continue this until `LIT_NONE` is returned:

```
SHORT    sIdx;
case ID_PROCMULT:                             /* Get first selection */
  sIdx = (SHORT)WinSendDlgItemMsg(hwndDlg, ID_LISTBOX,
            LM_QUERYSELECTION, (MPARAM)LIT_FIRST, 0);
  while(sIdx != LIT_NONE)
  {                                            /* Get its text */
    WinSendDlgItemMsg(hwndDlg, ID_LISTBOX,
                  LM_QUERYITEMTEXT, MPFROM2SHORT(sIdx,
                  sizeof(szCtry)), MPFROMP(szCtry));
                                               /* Display it */
    WinSetDlgItemText(hwndDlg, ID_ENTRY, szCtry);
                  /*-----------------------------*/
                  /* Slow down so we can see it happen */
                  /*                                   */
    DosSleep(1000);   /* DO NOT DO THIS IN PM PROGRAMS    */
                  /* AFFECTS PERFORMANCE SEVERELY      */
                  /*-----------------------------*/
                                               /* Deselect it */
    WinSendDlgItemMsg(hwndDlg, ID_LISTBOX,
                  LM_SELECTITEM, MPFROMSHORT(sIdx),
                  (MPARAM)FALSE);
                                               /* Get next */
    sIdx = (SHORT)WinSendDlgItemMsg(hwndDlg,
                  ID_LISTBOX, LM_QUERYSELECTION,
                  (MPARAM)sIdx, 0);
  }
  WinSetDlgItemText(hwndDlg, ID_ENTRY, "Done");
  return FALSE;                                /* All done */
```

If this process is going to take some time, and it may well do, since many items could be processed, then you should consider putting it in another thread. If you do not want the user interacting with your application while this thread is running then you can disable any relevant controls until the thread has completed (see Sec. 5.8).

> *Note:* a `DosSleep` call has been used in this code. Whatever you do, *do not* do this in your own code. The next message will not be taken off the system queue until this procedure returns control to Presentation Manager, and that will not be at least until the `DosSleep` time period is up. It has only been done here so that you can see what is happening when the multiple selections are being processed and for no other reason.

5.14.7 Saving data associated with items

When inserting items into a listbox it is often useful to save data associated with each item, for example the key field of a database row. To do this, after inserting the item send the listbox an `LM_SETITEMHANDLE` message specifying the zero-based index of the item and its data:

```
ULONG   ulKeyValue;
        SHORT sIdx;

for (sIdx = 0; sIdx < 26; sIdx++)
{
  WinSendDlgItemMsg(hwndDlg, ID_LISTBOX,
                    LM_INSERTITEM, MPFROMSHORT(LIT_END),
                    MPFROMP(szCountry[sIdx]));

                    /*-------------------------------*/
  ulKeyValue = sIdx + 1; /* szCountry and ulKeyValue would */
                    /* probably be obtained from a   */
                    /* database. In this case just   */
                    /* give a key value of 1->26.    */
                    /*-------------------------------*/

  WinSendDlgItemMsg(hwndDlg, ID_LISTBOX, LM_SETITEMHANDLE,
                    (MPARAM)sIdx, (MPARAM)ulKeyValue);
}
```

At its simplest we have just saved the key field of a database row. In reality, you would probably need to store more data, in which case you define the necessary structure and store a pointer to it in the item handle, as follows, for 16-bit:

```
static SHORT sIdx;
SEL          sel;

typedef struct _DBDATA
{
  USHORT usKey;
  CHAR   szCapital[20];
} DBDATA, *PDBDATA;

PDBDATA pDB_Data;

case WM_INITDLG:
  for (sIdx = 0; sIdx < 26; sIdx++)
  {
    WinSendDlgItemMsg(hwndDlg, ID_LISTBOX, LM_INSERTITEM,
                      MPFROMSHORT(LIT_END),
                      MPFROMP(szCountry[sIdx]));
```

```
        DosAllocSeg(sizeof(DBDATA), &sel, 0);
        pDB_Data = MAKEP(sel, 0);
        pDB_Data->usKey = sIdx + 1;
        strcpy(pDB_Data->szCapital, szCapital[sIdx]);
        WinSendDlgItemMsg(hwndDlg, ID_LISTBOX,
                          LM_SETITEMHANDLE, (MPARAM)sIdx,
                          MPFROMP(pDB_Data));
     }
     ;
     ;
     break;
  case ID_DELETE:
     pDB_Data = (PDBDATA)WinSendDlgItemMsg(hwndDlg,
                        ID_LISTBOX, LM_QUERYITEMHANDLE,
                        MPFROMSHORT(sIdx), NULL);
     DosFreeSeg(SELECTOROF(pDB_Data));
     ;
     ;
     return FALSE;
```

Here we store just a couple of fields, the key field and one other—the capital city. Before we can store the data, however, we need to allocate storage for the structure, 22 bytes in this case. Now, a very important point to note here is that whenever storage is allocated in OS/2 version 2.0 it is allocated in multiples of 4 kb pages only, and so a request for 22 bytes will actually allocate 4 kb and so if we are not careful we could consume far more memory than is required. This is one area which needs careful consideration when converting from 16-bit OS/2. The importance of converting this area with care cannot be overstressed. If you were to just change `DosAllocSeg` to `DosAllocMem` then your program would consume far more memory than it needed, so allocate a suitable number of pages and, if necessary, suballocate it for your own particular needs. That said, let us return to look at the code.

Although this is rather a trivial example it does serve to show what needs to be done when either converting to 32-bit or writing for 32-bit for the first time. In the code shown, we know that we are only going to display 26 items in the listbox. However, in reality we may not know how many items we will be displaying, and so our 32-bit memory management may need to be more complex. Here we just allocate a 22-byte segment for each item and store a pointer to it in the item handle. We must remember, though, when we delete an item from the listbox we should free the memory associated with it. Similarly, on exit we should free any remaining memory.

Now, looking at the following 32-bit version, if we just issued a `DosAllocMem` for 22 bytes for each item, as we did with `DosAllocSeg` above, we would in fact allocate 26 × 4096 bytes, or 104 kb. Instead, we allocate a 4 kb page and suballocate memory within that. In this particular case we know we only have 26 items to insert, so we only require 26 × 22 bytes, or 572 bytes, and so one 4 kb page will be more than sufficient. It is worth mentioning here that when you initialize a memory object for suballocation, 64 bytes of this memory are used for control information, and when actually suballocating the memory using `DosSubAlloc-Mem` the allocation size should be a multiple of eight otherwise it will be rounded up. So, in our example, whenever we suballocate a 22 byte portion of memory, 24 bytes are actually allocated each time.

So, for our 32-bit version we first allocate a page of memory and initialize it for suballocation. We can then actually suballocate the memory object and store the returned pointer in the item handle. As we did for the 16-bit version, every time we delete an item from the listbox we free the relevant suballocated memory using `DosSubFreeMem`, and when exiting free all memory using `DosSubUnsetMem` and `DosFreeMem`:

```
typedef struct _DBDATA
{
  USHORT usKey;
  CHAR   szCapital[20];
} DBDATA, *PDBDATA;
PDBDATA         pDB_Data;
static PVOID    BaseMem,
                MemOffset;

case WM_INITDLG:
  DosAllocMem(&BaseMem, 4096, PAG_READ | PAG_WRITE |
              PAG_COMMIT);
  DosSubSetMem(BaseMem, DOSSUB_INIT, 4096);
  for (sIdx = 0; sIdx < 26; sIdx++)
  {
    WinSendDlgItemMsg(hwndDlg, ID_LISTBOX, LM_INSERTITEM,
                      MPFROMSHORT(LIT_END),
                      MPFROMP(szCountry[sIdx]));
    DosSubAllocMem(BaseMem, &MemOffset, sizeof(DBDATA));
    pDB_Data = MemOffset;
    pDB_Data->usKey = sIdx + 1;
    strcpy(pDB_Data->szCapital, szCapital[sIdx]);


    WinSendDlgItemMsg(hwndDlg, ID_LISTBOX,
                      LM_SETITEMHANDLE, (MPARAM)sIdx,
                      MPFROMP(pDB_Data));
```

```
        }
    ;
    ;
    ;
    break;
case ID_DELETE:
    pDB_Data = (PDBDATA)WinSendDlgItemMsg(hwndDlg,
                        ID_LISTBOX, LM_QUERYITEMHANDLE,
                        MPFROMSHORT(sIdx), 0);
    DosSubFreeMem(BaseMem, pDB_Data, sizeof(DBDATA));
    ;
    ;
    ;
    return FALSE;
;
;
;
case ID_EXIT:
    DosSubUnsetMem(BaseMem);
    DosFreeMem(BaseMem);
    ;
    ;
    ;
    break;
```

5.14.8 Retrieving data associated with items

After saving data in an item handle, you can retrieve it again by sending the listbox an LM_QUERYITEMHANDLE message:

```
static SHORT   sIdx,
ULONG          ulKeyValue;

/*---------------------------------------*/
/* If we are just retrieving a ULONG value... */
/*---------------------------------------*/

case LN_SELECT:
    sIdx = (SHORT)WinSendDlgItemMsg(hwndDlg, ID_LISTBOX,
                                LM_QUERYSELECTION, 0, 0);

                        /*------------------------------ */
    if (sIdx != LIT_NONE)   /* If nothing selected then ignore */
    {                       /*------------------------------*/
```

Dialog boxes and their controls

```
    ulKeyValue = (ULONG)WinSendDlgItemMsg(hwndDlg,
                    ID_LISTBOX, LM_QUERYITEMHANDLE,
                    MPFROMSHORT(sIdx), 0);
    WinSetDlgItemShort(hwndDlg, ID_ENTRY,
                    (SHORT)ulKeyValue, FALSE);
    ;
    ;
    ;
  }
  break;
/*--------------------------------------------------------*/
/* Or, to retrieve any data associated with a listbox item... */
/*--------------------------------------------------------*/
case LN_SELECT:
  sIdx = (SHORT)WinSendDlgItemMsg(hwndDlg, ID_LISTBOX,
                    LM_QUERYSELECTION, 0, 0);

                    /*------------------------------*/
  if (sIdx != LIT_NONE)  /* If nothing selected then ignore */
  {                    /*------------------------------*/

    pDB_Data = (PDBDATA)WinSendDlgItemMsg(hwndDlg,
                    ID_LISTBOX, LM_QUERYITEMHANDLE,
                    MPFROMSHORT(sIdx), 0);
    WinSetDlgItemText(hwndDlg, ID_ENTRY1,
                    pDB_Data->szCapital);
    WinSetDlgItemShort(hwndDlg, ID_ENTRY2,
                    (SHORT)pDB_Data->usKey, FALSE);
    ;
    ;
    ;
  }
  break;
```

Note that this code does not show the WM_CONTROL case statement but just the LN_SELECT statement. (See Fig. 5.15 for the full listing.)

5.14.9 *Listbox style*

    LS_NOADJUSTPOS

If you use this style for a listbox it is drawn at the size specified and can cause parts of an item to be clipped at the bottom of the box. This is very evident if you change to a large font in a listbox after it has been initialized. By omitting this style the listbox is sized according to whatever font will be used initially so that only complete lines will be drawn.

LS_EXTENDEDSEL

This is a variation of the LS_MULTIPLESEL style. It allows items to be selected by swiping the pointer over them without releasing the mouse button. It also supports multiple selection by pressing and holding down the Shift or Ctrl key and selecting with the mouse button. With the Shift key pressed down when the mouse button is pressed, the item pointed to, plus all other items above it, up to the previously selected item are marked. With the Ctrl key pressed down when the mouse button is pressed, just that item is selected leaving any previously selected item selected. Also, pressing Ctrl-/ marks all and Ctrl-\ unmarks all.

LS_NOVERTSCROLL

This style, which causes a listbox not to have a vertical scroll bar, is documented in the *Presentation Manager Programming Reference Manual* (volume 2, version 1.2, page 16-1). However, it was never implemented in the product and so is *not* available for use.

If you do not want a vertical scroll bar in your listbox then see Sec. 5.14.10.

5.14.10 Removing scroll bars

There is no clean method for removing a scroll bar from a listbox. The best that can be done is to get the handle of the scroll bar and use WinDestroyWindow to destroy it:

```
/*-----------------------------------------------------*/
/* The scroll bar ID for a listbox's vertical scroll bar is   */
/* 0xC001 and for a horizontal scroll bar is 0xC002.          */
/* This is, however, undocumented, so use with caution,       */
/* it could change in a later version.                        */
/*-----------------------------------------------------*/
hwndListbox = WinWindowFromID(hwndDlg, ID_LISTBOX);

hwndVbar = WinWindowFromID(hwndListbox, 0xC001);
hwndHbar = WinWindowFromID(hwndListbox, 0xC002);

WinDestroyWindow(hwndVbar);
WinDestroyWindow(hwndHbar);
```

However, this leaves a blank space, which looks untidy. Note that removing a vertical scroll bar *does not* prevent scrolling up and down using the arrow keys on the keyboard, whereas removing a horizontal scroll bar *does* prevent sideways scrolling.

The preferred approach, and one that is documented and does not depend on the scroll bar IDs, is to enumerate the listbox's windows for the scroll bars, and then destroy them:

```
hwndListbox = WinWindowFromID(hwndDlg, ID_LISTBOX);

hEnum = WinBeginEnumWindows(hwndListbox);
while (hwndChild = WinGetNextWindow(hEnum))
{
   if (WinQueryWindowULong(hwndChild, QWL_STYLE) & SBS_VERT)
      hwndVbar = hwndChild;      /* ----------------------*/
                                 /* SBS_VERT = 1, SBS_HORZ = 0 */
   else                          /* ----------------------*/
      hwndHbar = hwndChild;
}
WinEndEnumWindows(hEnum);

WinDestroyWindow(hwndVbar);
WinDestroyWindow(hwndHbar);
```

5.14.11 Listbox columns

Using presentation parameters

The easiest way to arrange data in columns in listboxes is to use presentation parameters to change the font to a non-proportional type, for example Courier. See Chapter 4 for more details.

Using proportional fonts

If your columns hold purely numeric data, and that also means no leading blanks, then it does not matter what font you use. Numbers take up the same space, so they will line up even using a non-proportional font. See Fig. 5.10 which has a listbox with the first three rows containing numbers only.

However, if you need to display text in columns then you need to use an `ownerdraw listbox` and do the drawing of items yourself.

5.14.12 Ownerdraw

This topic has probably caused more problems than any other in Presentation Manager. Briefly, if you want to do anything out of the ordinary with a listbox, the chances are you will have to resort to an ownerdraw listbox. What this means is that *you* are responsible for drawing the items in the box, so it gives you complete freedom to do as you please. Probably the most common use of ownerdraw listboxes is to arrange data in columns, but their use is really unlimited.

As a simple introduction we will look at a listbox that centralizes the data in a single column and uses its own colours for highlighting. Although this is a very simple example, it does show the basic steps that can be built on to produce something more complex. We will then enhance this to include columnar data, and then finally to add horizontal scrolling.

So, to start with, you must define your listbox with the style LS_OWNERDRAW. Now, when you have an ownerdraw listbox your application receives two special messages, WM_MEASUREITEM and WM_DRAWITEM. The purpose of the WM_MEASUREITEM message is to establish the height and width of the item to be drawn in the listbox, and the WM_DRAWITEM message is sent whenever the item needs to be drawn.

Looking at the WM_MEASUREITEM message first, all we need to do here is query the font metrics to get the maximum vertical distance from one character baseline to the next character baseline, lMaxBaselineExt, for the current logical font. Once we have this value we return it to the system. Since we do not have a horizontal scroll bar at the moment we are not interested in the width, so we return zero for its value:

```
HPS          hps;
FONTMETRICS  fm;
SHORT        cxText,
             cyText;

case WM_MEASUREITEM:
  hps = WinGetPS(WinWindowFromID(hwndDlg, ID_LISTBOX));
  GpiQueryFontMetrics(hps, sizeof(FONTMETRICS), &fm);
  cyText = (SHORT)fm.lMaxBaselineExt;
  cxText = 0;
  WinReleasePS(hps);
  return MRFROM2SHORT(cyText, cxText);
```

Whenever an ownerdraw listbox needs to be redrawn, for example when an item is inserted or selected, a WM_DRAWITEM message is sent to its owner. On entry, the second parameter, mp2, is a pointer to an OWNERITEM structure, which gives us information about the item to be drawn, such as the size of the rectangle in which it is to be drawn, its select state, a handle to its presentation space and others, but for this simple example that's all we are interested in:

```
typedef struct _OWNERITEM
{
  HWND   hwnd;
  HPS    hps;
  ULONG  fsState;
```

```
  ULONG    fsAttribute;
  ULONG    fsStateOld;
  ULONG    fsAttributeOld;
  RECTL    rclItem;
  LONG     idItem;
  ULONG    hItem;
} OWNERITEM;
```

If `fsState` is 0 then the item is not selected, so we set the normal colours, in the following case yellow on dark green; if it is 1 then it is selected, so we reverse the colours. All that needs to be done now is to draw the text and exit:

```
POWNERITEM   pOwner;
RECTL        rcl;

case WM_DRAWITEM:
  pOwner = (POWNERITEM)mp2;
  rcl.xRight = pOwner->rclItem.xRight;
  rcl.xLeft = pOwner->rclItem.xLeft;
  rcl.yTop = pOwner->rclItem.yTop;
  rcl.yBottom = pOwner->rclItem.yBottom;

  GpiSetBackMix(pOwner->hps, BM_OVERPAINT);

  if (!pOwner->fsState)                         /* Unselected */
  {
    GpiSetBackColor(pOwner->hps, CLR_DARKGREEN);
    GpiSetColor(pOwner->hps, CLR_YELLOW);
  }
  else                                          /* Selected */
  {
    GpiSetBackColor(pOwner->hps, CLR_YELLOW);
    GpiSetColor(pOwner->hps, CLR_DARKGREEN);
  }
  WinSendDlgItemMsg(hwndDlg, ID_LISTBOX, LM_QUERYITEMTEXT,
               MPFROM2SHORT(pOwner->idItem,
               sizeof(szListBuff)),
               MPFROMP(szListBuff));

  WinDrawText(pOwner->hps, strlen(szListBuff), szListBuff,
              &rcl, 0, 0, DT_CENTER | DT_TEXTATTRS |
              DT_ERASERECT);

                                  /* Do not let PM highlight */
  pOwner->fsStateOld = pOwner->fsState = 0;
  return (MRESULT)TRUE;            /* Do not let PM draw     */
```

The important points to note here are:

1 Current and old states must be set to 0 or else Presentation Manager will take over highlighting and change what we have done.
2 We must return TRUE to prevent Presentation Manager from doing the drawing. If we do not then the text will be left justified and in system colours.

If all you want to do with your listbox is to change the font or foreground and background colours then there is no need to resort to an ownerdraw listbox as you can do it with presentation parameters (see Chapter 4). However, if you use presentation parameters to change the font in an ownerdraw listbox then you must put the call to `WinSetPresParam` in your `WM_MEASUREITEM` statement, otherwise the item height will not be set correctly, and if you use a font larger than the system font, it will be clipped. Not only that, but it must only be executed *once*, otherwise the program will receive an exception due to insufficient stack space and terminate. You therefore need a first-time flag to overcome this, as follows:

```
static BOOL fFirst = TRUE;

case WM_MEASUREITEM:
  if (fFirst)
  {
    strcpy(szFont, "24.Helv");
    WinSetPresParam(WinWindowFromID(hwndDlg, ID_LISTBOX),
                    PP_FONTNAMESIZE, sizeof(szFont),
                    szFont);
    fFirst = FALSE;
  }
  hps = WinGetPS(WinWindowFromID(hwndDlg, ID_LISTBOX));
  ;
  ;
  WinReleasePS(hps);
  return MRFROM2SHORT(cyText, cxText);
```

Suppose we now wish to display data in columns, for example a country name in the left-hand column and its capital city in the right-hand column. A very quick and easy way to do this is to split the item rectangle into separate rectangles, treating each rectangle as a column. The country would be drawn in the left-hand column and its capital in the right-hand column. To make it easy to identify which text is to go in which column, a tab character is inserted between each string prior to inserting it into the listbox.

When an item is about to be drawn, the second parameter of the `WM_DRAWITEM` contains the size of the rectangle that is to be used to draw the item, and since we do not have a horizontal scroll bar we must make sure that we have enough room in the listbox to display the data, otherwise it will be clipped.

Dialog boxes and their controls

Since we only need two columns, we divide the rectangle by two and draw the country in the left-hand rectangle. We then adjust the coordinates for the right-hand rectangle and draw the capital in that, as follows:

```
static PSZ    szCountry[] = {"Austria", "Belgium", "Canada",
                    "Denmark", "Egypt", "Finland",
                    "Greece", "Hungary", "India",
                    "Japan", "Kenya", "Libya",
                    "Morocco", "Nigeria", "Oman",
                    "Peru", "Qatar", "Romania",
                    "Spain", "Turkey", "Uruguay",
                    "Venezuela", "Wales", "Xanxere",
                    "Yemen", "Zambia"};

static PSZ    szCapital[] = {
                    "Vienna", "Brussels", "Ottawa",
                    "Copenhagen", "Cairo", "Helsinki",
                    "Athens", "Budapest", "Delhi",
                    "Tokyo", "Nairobi", "Tripoli",
                    "Rabat", "Lagos", "Muscat",
                    "Lima", "Doha", "Bucharest",
                    "Madrid", "Ankara", "Montevideo",
                    "Caracas", "Cardiff", "None",
                    "Sana'a", "Lusaka"};

CHAR          szListBuff[50],
              *pszCountry,
              *pszCapital;

case WM_INITDLG:
  for (sIdx = 0; sIdx < 26; sIdx++)
  {
    sprintf(szListBuff, "%s\t%s", szCountry[sIdx],
            szCapital[sIdx]);
    WinSendDlgItemMsg(hwndDlg, ID_LISTBOX, LM_INSERTITEM,
                    MPFROMSHORT(LIT_END),
                    MPFROMP(szListBuff));
  }
  ;
  ;
  break;

case WM_DRAWITEM:
  pOwner = (POWNERITEM)mp2;
                                    /* Split into two and draw */
                                    /* item in left rectangle  */
```

```
  rcl.xRight  = pOwner->rclItem.xRight/2;
  rcl.xLeft   = pOwner->rclItem.xLeft;
  rcl.yTop    = pOwner->rclItem.yTop;
  rcl.yBottom = pOwner->rclItem.yBottom;

  GpiSetBackMix(pOwner->hps, BM_OVERPAINT);

  if (!pOwner->fsState)              /* Unselected            */
  {
    GpiSetBackColor(pOwner->hps, CLR_DARKGREEN);
    GpiSetColor(pOwner->hps, CLR_YELLOW);
  }
  else                               /* Selected              */
  {
    GpiSetBackColor(pOwner->hps, CLR_YELLOW);
    GpiSetColor(pOwner->hps, CLR_DARKGREEN);
  }

  WinSendDlgItemMsg(hwndDlg, ID_LISTBOX, LM_QUERYITEMTEXT,
                    MPFROM2SHORT(pOwner->idItem,
                    sizeof(szListBuff)),
                    MPFROMP(szListBuff));
  pszCountry = strtok(szListBuff, "\t");
  pszCapital = strtok(NULL, "\t");

  WinDrawText(pOwner->hps, strlen(pszCountry), pszCountry,
          &rcl, 0, 0, DT_LEFT | DT_TEXTATTRS | DT_ERASERECT);

                     /* Draw next item in right rectangle */
  rcl.xLeft = rcl.xRight;
  rcl.xRight = pOwner->rclItem.xRight;

  WinDrawText(pOwner->hps, strlen(pszCapital), pszCapital,
          &rcl, 0, 0, DT_LEFT | DT_TEXTATTRS
          | DT_ERASERECT);
;
;                                   /* Do not let PM highlight */
  pOwner->fsStateOld = pOwner->fsState = 0;
  return (MRESULT)TRUE;              /* Do not let PM draw    */
```

Let us now consider what needs to be done to handle horizontal scrolling. You will remember that with an ownerdraw listbox we get two special messages, and one of these, WM_MEASUREITEM, is used to establish the height and width of the item to be drawn. Up to now we have not been concerned with the item width, we just returned zero since we did not implement horizontal scrolling. However, now that we wish to use horizontal scrolling we need to calculate the item width and return it to the system. We do this by first retrieving the item text and then calling `GpiQueryTextBox`, as follows:

```
POINTL   points[TXTBOX_COUNT];

case WM_MEASUREITEM:
  hps = WinGetPS(WinWindowFromID(hwndDlg, ID_LISTBOX));
  ;
  ;
  WinSendDlgItemMsg(hwndDlg, ID_LISTBOX, LM_QUERYITEMTEXT,
                 MPFROM2SHORT(sIdx,
                 sizeof(szListBuff)),
                 MPFROMP(szListBuff));
  GpiQueryTextBox(hps, (LONG)strlen(szListBuff),
              szListBuff, TXTBOX_COUNT, points);
  cxText = (USHORT)points[TXTBOX_TOPRIGHT].x + 20;
  ;
  ;
  WinReleasePS(hps);
  return MRFROM2SHORT(cyText, cxText);
```

This returns the relative coordinates of the rectangle required in which to draw the text. Unfortunately, we have an added complication here, and that is the tab character we inserted to denote where the next column starts. This is treated just like any other character rather than the space we want. So, if we use this value you will find that not all the text will be scrollable once it has been formatted into columns. As an example consider the following, the tab character being denoted by 'T':

> Item text: DenmarkTCopenhagen
> Width returned from GpiQueryTextBox: 182
> Approximate width when formatted: 200

So, when fully scrolled, not all the text will be visible. For this reason we extend the width a certain amount; 20 is sufficient for this example but you may find you will need a different value depending on your data. You can, of course, just return a constant value that will ensure that your item text will always be fully scrollable. It is really just a matter of what you intend to display.

> *Note:* This only applies where you have columnar data. If the text is to be displayed as a single 'column' then the value returned by `GpiQueryText-Box` will be accurate.

Having retrieved the item width, we now need to process the `WM_DRAWITEM` message actually to draw the text in the listbox. Now, on entry to this message, `mp2` contains the size of the rectangle into which the item is to be drawn. This rectangle, `rclItem`, represents the physical space in the listbox in which the text is to be drawn by default. We can change this if we wish, and indeed we will because we want to split this rectangle into two parts for our columns, so we change the right-hand coordinate to be half its original value and draw the text as before. Now, because we have horizontal scrolling we may need to change the start position of the second column, depending on whether scrolling has taken place or not. We will know if the text has been scrolled because `rclItem.xLeft` will be negative on entry. If this is the case then all we need do is adjust the left-hand coordinate of our second rectangle by the scroll amount:

```
CHAR   szListBuff[50],
       *pszCountry,
       *pszCapital;

case WM_DRAWITEM:
  pOwner       = (POWNERITEM)mp2;
  rcl.xRight   = pOwner->rclItem.xRight/2;
  rcl.xLeft    = pOwner->rclItem.xLeft;
  rcl.yTop     = pOwner->rclItem.yTop;
  rcl.yBottom  = pOwner->rclItem.yBottom;
  ;
  ;
  ;
  WinSendDlgItemMsg(hwndDlg, ID_LISTBOX, LM_QUERYITEMTEXT,
                    MPFROM2SHORT(pOwner->idItem,
                    sizeof(szListBuff)),
                    MPFROMP(szListBuff));

  pszCountry = strtok(szListBuff, "\t");
  pszCapital = strtok(NULL, "\t");

  WinDrawText(pOwner->hps, strlen(pszCountry), pszCountry,
          &rcl, 0, 0, DT_LEFT | DT_TEXTATTRS | DT_ERASERECT);

              /*----------------------------------------*/
              /* Draw next item in the right-hand rectangle */
              /* allowing for horizontal scrolling        */
              /*----------------------------------------*/
  if (pOwner->rclItem.xLeft < 0)
                              /* i.e. we have been scrolled */
    rcl.xLeft = rcl.xRight + pOwner->rclItem.xLeft;
  else
    rcl.xLeft = rcl.xRight;
```

Dialog boxes and their controls

```
    rcl.xRight = pOwner->rclItem.xRight;
    WinDrawText(pOwner->hps, strlen(pszCapital), pszCapital,
                &rcl, 0, 0, DT_LEFT | DT_TEXTATTRS
                | DT_ERASERECT);
                                      /* Do not let PM highlight */
    pOwner->fsStateOld = pOwner->fsState = 0;
    return (MRESULT)TRUE;             /* Do not let PM draw      */
```

When an item has been selected in an ownerdraw listbox with columnar data, it can easily be decoded because we inserted tab characters between the columns. We do this in the `LN_SELECT` case statement, as follows:

```
static SHORT   sIdx;
CHAR    szListBuff[50],
        *pszCountry,
        *pszCapital;
case WM_CONTROL:
  switch(SHORT1FROMMP(mp1))
  {
    case ID_LISTBOX:
      switch(SHORT2FROMMP(mp1))
      {
        case LN_SELECT:
          sIdx = (SHORT)WinSendDlgItemMsg(hwndDlg,
                       ID_LISTBOX, LM_QUERYSELECTION,
                       0, 0);
          WinSendDlgItemMsg(hwndDlg, ID_LISTBOX,
                       LM_QUERYITEMTEXT,
                       MPFROM2SHORT(sIdx,
                       sizeof(szListBuff)),
                       MPFROMP(szListBuff));
          pszCountry = strtok(szListBuff, "\t");
          pszCapital = strtok(NULL, "\t");
          ;
          ;
          ;
          break;
        default:
          break;
      }
    break;
}
```

5.14.13 Non-selectable items

If you need to prohibit selection of certain items in a listbox then you must use an ownerdraw listbox and handle the selection yourself, as discussed in the previous section. In the code for the sample program of Fig. 5.15, you will notice that Finland is not selectable; this is handled in the WM_DRAWITEM case statement where the highlighting is handled, as shown in the following example:

```
case WM_DRAWITEM:
  ;
  ;
  if ((!pOwner->fsState) ||          /* Unselected              */
      (pOwner->idItem == 5))         /* Do not allow Finland    */
  {
    GpiSetBackColor(pOwner->hps, CLR_DARKGREEN);
    GpiSetColor(pOwner->hps, CLR_YELLOW);
  }
  else                               /* Selected                */
  {
    GpiSetBackColor(pOwner->hps, CLR_YELLOW);
    GpiSetColor(pOwner->hps, CLR_DARKGREEN);
  }
  ;
  ;                                  /* Do not let PM highlight */
  pOwner->fsStateOld = pOwner->fsState = 0;
  return (MRESULT)TRUE;              /* Do not let PM draw      */
```

You must, however, still code a trap for it in the LN_SELECT statement. In this program a warning beep is sounded.

This can easily be extended to exclude all entries if desired. You could use WinEnableWindow to disable the listbox, but this would also prohibit scrolling and so is not much use here.

5.15 Menus

Pop-up menus are discussed in detail in Chapter 13.

5.15.1 Menu bar in a dialog box

To add a menu bar to your dialog box, first define the menu layout in your resource file:

```
MENU    ID_MENU PRELOAD
BEGIN
```

Dialog boxes and their controls

```
    SUBMENU    "~Options",   ID_OPTIONS
    BEGIN
        MENUITEM    "Test ~1", ID_TEST1
        MENUITEM    "Test ~2", ID_TEST2
        MENUITEM    "Test ~3", ID_TEST3
    END
END
```

Then add a call to `WinLoadMenu` and send a `WM_UPDATEFRAME` message to the frame to tell it to update. If you omit to update the frame then the menu will not appear until you minimize and restore the box. You should put this in your `WM_INITDLG` case statement:

```
case WM_INITDLG:
  WinLoadMenu(hwndDlg, (HMODULE)NULL, ID_MENU);
  WinSendMsg(hwndDlg, WM_UPDATEFRAME, (MPARAM)FID_MENU, 0);
  ;
  ;
  ;
  break;
```

Do not forget to leave space for the menu bar when using the dialog box editor to create the dialog box. Failure to do so will cause some of your controls to be covered when the menu bar is displayed.

5.16 Multiline entry fields

5.16.1 Clearing an MLE

To clear the text from an MLE use `WinSetDlgItemText` or `WinSetWindowText` to write a null to it:

```
WinSetDlgItemText(hwndDlg, ID_MULTILINE, "");
/*-------*/
/* Or... */
/*-------*/
WinSetWindowText(WinWindowFromID(hwndDlg,
                                 ID_MULTILINE), "");
```

5.16.2 Importing a file

To import a file to an MLE you must first allocate a buffer into which you read the file, or part of the file, and then set this buffer as the current transfer buffer for the

MLE. You can then import the file. If you require the file to be inserted at the current cursor position then set the insertion point to -1.

The following sample code reads in the CONFIG.SYS file and imports it at the current cursor position. Note that it assumes you have installed OS/2 on the C: drive which, for version 2.0, is no longer mandatory:

```
PVOID   BaseMem;
IPT     ipt;
HFILE   hFile;
ULONG   ulAction,
        ulBytesRead;

                                        /* Allocate one page - 4KB */
DosAllocMem(&BaseMem, 4096, PAG_READ | PAG_WRITE |
        PAG_COMMIT);

DosOpen("C:\\CONFIG.SYS", &hFile, &ulAction, (ULONG)NULL,
        (ULONG)NULL,
        OPEN_ACTION_OPEN_IF_EXISTS,
        OPEN_FLAGS_SEQUENTIAL |
        OPEN_SHARE_DENYNONE |
        OPEN_ACCESS_READONLY,
        (ULONG)NULL);

DosRead(hFile, BaseMem, 4096, &ulBytesRead);
DosClose(hFile);

WinSendMsg(WinWindowFromID(hwndDlg, ID_MULTILINE),
        MLM_SETIMPORTEXPORT,
        (MPARAM)BaseMem, MPFROMLONG(4096));

ipt = -1; /* Set insertion point for current cursor position */

WinSendMsg(WinWindowFromID(hwndDlg, ID_MULTILINE),
        MLM_IMPORT, (MPARAM)&ipt,
        MPFROMLONG(ulBytesRead));

DosFreeMem(BaseMem);
```

5.17 Styles

5.17.1 Changing a control's style

To change a control's style, for example to change an entry field's style of left align to centred, use `WinSetWindowULong`:

Dialog boxes and their controls

```
HWND    hEntry;
/*-------------------------------*/
/* Get the handle of the entry field  */
/*-------------------------------*/
hEntry = WinWindowFromID(hwndDlg, ID_ENTRY);

/*--------------------------*/
/* Change its style to centred */
/*--------------------------*/
WinSetWindowULong(hEntry, QWL_STYLE,
                 WinQueryWindowULong(hEntry, QWL_STYLE )
                 | ES_CENTER);
```

5.17.2 Removing and adding tab stops

You also use `WinSetWindowULong` to remove, or add, the tab stop from a dialog box control, for example a pushbutton:

```
HWND    hButton;
/*--------------------*/
/* To remove WS_TABSTOP */
/*--------------------*/
hButton = WinWindowFromID(hwndDlg, ID_EXIT);

WinSetWindowULong(hButton, QWL_STYLE,
                 WinQueryWindowULong(hButton, QWL_STYLE )
                 & ~WS_TABSTOP);
/*----------------*/
/* To add WS_TABSTOP */
/*----------------*/
hButton = WinWindowFromID(hwndDlg, ID_EXIT);
WinSetWindowULong(hButton, QWL_STYLE,
                 WinQueryWindowULong(hButton, QWL_STYLE )
                 | WS_TABSTOP);
```

5.18   Text

5.18.1 Backslash in a static text window

If you require a backslash (\) in a static text window then, as in the C language, you must code a double backslash, \\.

5.18.2 Changing a dialog box title

To change the title of a dialog box use `WinSetWindowText` with the window handle set to the actual dialog box handle:

```
WinSetWindowText(hwndDlg, "New Title");
```

Alternatively, use `WinSetDlgItemText`:

```
WinSetDlgItemText(hwndDlg, FID_TITLEBAR, "New Title");
```

5.18.3 Changing the text in a dialog box control

To change the text in a dialog box control use `WinSetWindowText` with the window handle set to the handle of the control you wish to change. Use `WinWindowFromID` to get this value:

```
/*-------------------------------------*/
/* Change the text of pushbutton ID_EXIT */
/*-------------------------------------*/

WinSetWindowText(WinWindowFromID(hwndDlg, ID_EXIT),
                 "Quit");
```

As before, you can also use `WinSetDlgItemText`:

```
WinSetDlgItemText(hwndDlg, ID_EXIT, "Quit");
```

5.18.4 Forcing a line break in static text windows

If you have a static text window with *word wrap* defined in your dialog box, style `DT_WORDBREAK`, and you wish to force a line break, then manually insert \012 at the point in the text you wish the break to occur as shown:

```
CTEXT            "Line one\012Line two\012Line three",
                 ID_LBREAK, 140, 50, 47, 31, DT_WORDBREAK
```

will produce the following three lines centralized in the window:

```
            Line one
            Line two
            Line three
```

The `CTEXT` aligns the text centrally.

You can also do this by using `WinSetWindowText` within your program:

```
WinSetWindowText(WinWindowFromID(hwndDlg, ID_LBREAK),
                 "Line 1\012Line 2\012Line 3");
```

Unfortunately, this is not supported by the dialog box editor so the `\012`s are ignored and the text is treated as one long string, so be careful if you use it to change other controls.

5.19 Sample programs

5.19.1 *Miscellaneous controls and activities*

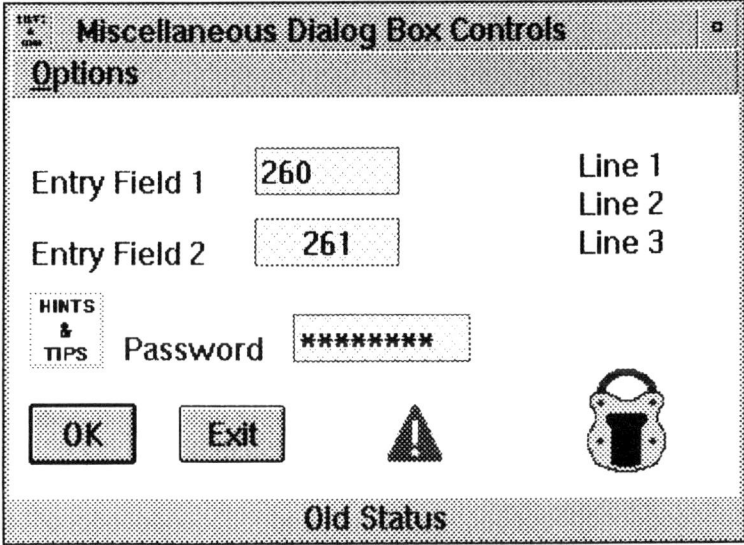

Figure 5.1. Miscellaneous controls and activities output.

This program (Fig. 5.1) illustrates many of the topics covered in this chapter, including:

- Dialog box as a main window
- Minimizing a dialog box
- Menu bar
- Pop-up menu
- Status bar
- Numeric-only entry field
- Centralizing the text in an entry field

- Making an entry field unreadable
- Making an entry field read-only
- Icons in a dialog box
- User button
- Removing/adding default pushbutton
- Removing/adding tab stops
- Changing text in controls
- Forcing line breaks in a text field
- Changing focus at initialization
- Window IDs

The program comprises a dialog box as the main window (Fig. 5.1). Initially, the three entry fields are blank, the status shows some initial text and the static 'word break' text field contains three lines. The default pushbutton is OK so if you press Enter, or click the mouse button on OK the following happens:

- Entry fields 1 and 2 display their respective IDs
- The dialog box title changes
- The Exit pushbutton text changes to Quit
- The status changes
- The 'word break' text field changes
- The default status of OK is removed

Pressing OK again toggles the dialog box title, status and the Exit pushbutton text, and the default status is returned to OK.

Notice that the text in Entry Field 2 is centralized and that you cannot enter any alphabetic characters. Entry Field 1 is read only, while typing anything in the Password field results in an asterisk being displayed for each character entered.

If you position the mouse pointer over the dialog box and press button 2 you will activate the pop-up menu. Pressing button 1 on any menu item will cause a beep and the closure of the menu. Similarly, selecting any item from Options on the menu bar causes a beep. For a description of pop-up menus see Chapter 13.

Finally, if you press the user button it is redisplayed inverted and sounds a beep.

The following listings show the program's header file, Fig. 5.2, resource file, Fig. 5.3, dialog template, Fig. 5.4, and C source file, Fig. 5.5.

```
#define DLG_GEN      256
#define ID_OK        257
#define ID_EXIT      258
#define ID_ICON      259
#define ID_ENTRY1    260
#define ID_ENTRY2    261
```

Figure 5.2. Miscellaneous controls and activities: header file. Continues.

```
#define ID_MENU          262
#define ID_OPTIONS       263
#define ID_TEST1         264
#define ID_TEST2         265
#define ID_TEST3         266
#define ID_MENU2         267
#define ID_ITEM1         268
#define ID_ITEM2         269
#define ID_ITEM3         270
#define ID_ITEM4         271
#define ID_ITEM5         272
#define ID_ITEM6         273
#define ID_STATUS        274
#define ID_LBREAK        275
#define ID_PASSWORD      276
#define ID_USERBUTTON    277
#define ID_LOCK          278
```

Figure 5.2. Miscellaneous controls and activities: Header file. Concluded.

```
#include <os2.h>
#include "dlggen.h"

ICON    ID_ICON dlggen.ico
BITMAP  ID_LOCK lock.bmp

MENU    ID_MENU   PRELOAD
BEGIN
  SUBMENU    "~Options",   ID_OPTIONS
  BEGIN
    MENUITEM    "Test ~1", ID_TEST1
    MENUITEM    "Test ~2", ID_TEST2
    MENUITEM    "Test ~3", ID_TEST3
  END
END

MENU    ID_MENU2  PRELOAD
BEGIN
  MENUITEM    "Menu Item ~1", ID_ITEM1
  MENUITEM    "Menu Item ~2", ID_ITEM2
  MENUITEM    "Menu Item ~3", ID_ITEM3
```

Figure 5.3. Miscellaneous controls and activities: resource file. Continues

```
    MENUITEM    SEPARATOR
    MENUITEM    "Menu Item ~4", ID_ITEM4
    MENUITEM    "Menu Item ~5", ID_ITEM5
    MENUITEM    "Menu Item ~6", ID_ITEM6
END
rcinclude dlggen.dlg
```

Figure 5.3. Miscellaneous controls and activities: resource file. Concluded.

```
DLGINCLUDE 1 "DLGGEN.H"
DLGTEMPLATE DLG_GEN LOADONCALL MOVEABLE DISCARDABLE
BEGIN
  DIALOG "Miscellaneous Dialog Box Controls", DLG_GEN, 105,
         56, 195, 101, FS_NOBYTEALIGN | WS_VISIBLE,
         FCF_SYSMENU | FCF_TITLEBAR | FCF_MINBUTTON
  BEGIN
    ENTRYFIELD    "", ID_ENTRY1, 67, 72, 36, 8,
                  NOT ES_AUTOSCROLL | ES_MARGIN
    ENTRYFIELD    "", ID_ENTRY2, 67, 57, 36, 8,
                  NOT ES_AUTOSCROLL | ES_MARGIN
                  CTLDATA 8, 5, 0, 0
    ENTRYFIELD    "", ID_PASSWORD, 77, 37, 45, 8,
                  NOT ES_AUTOSCROLL | ES_MARGIN |
                  ES_UNREADABLE
    DEFPUSHBUTTON "OK", ID_OK, 5, 15, 29, 13
    PUSHBUTTON    "Exit", ID_EXIT, 45, 15, 29, 13
    CONTROL       "", ID_USERBUTTON, 150, 12, 32, 25,
                  WC_BUTTON, BS_USERBUTTON | WS_TABSTOP |
                  WS_VISIBLE
    LTEXT         "Entry Field 1", 100, 5, 70, 55, 8
    LTEXT         "Entry Field 2", 101, 5, 55, 55, 8
    ICON          ID_ICON, ID_ICON, 5, 35, 20, 16, WS_GROUP
    LTEXT         "Password", 102, 30, 35, 44, 8
    CTEXT         "", ID_STATUS, 0, 0, 195, 8
    CTEXT         "Line one\012Line two\012Line three",
                  ID_LBREAK, 140, 50, 47, 31, DT_WORDBREAK
    CONTROL       "#14", SPTR_ICONWARNING, 100, 15, 22, 16,
                  WC_STATIC, SS_SYSICON | WS_VISIBLE
  END
END
```

Figure 5.4. Miscellaneous controls and activities: dialog template.

```c
#define  INCL_WINWINDOWMGR
#define  INCL_WINFRAMEMGR
#define  INCL_WINSWITCHLIST
#define  INCL_WINSYS
#define  INCL_WINDIALOGS
#define  INCL_WINBUTTONS
#define  INCL_WINPOINTERS
#define  INCL_WINENTRYFIELDS
#define  INCL_WINMENUS
#define  INCL_WININPUT
#define  INCL_GPIBITMAPS

#include <os2.h>
#include <string.h>
#include "dlggen.h"

MRESULT EXPENTRY DlgProc     (HWND, ULONG, MPARAM, MPARAM);
MRESULT EXPENTRY NumericProc (HWND, ULONG, MPARAM, MPARAM);
VOID    Button_Paint         (PUSERBUTTON);

PFNWP   EntryFieldProc;   /* Public Entry Field procedure */
/***************************************************/
INT main(VOID)
{
  HAB  hab;
  HMQ  hmq;
  HWND hDlg;

  hab = WinInitialize(0);
  hmq = WinCreateMsgQueue(hab, 0);

  WinDlgBox(HWND_DESKTOP, HWND_DESKTOP, DlgProc,
            (HMODULE)NULL, DLG_GEN, 0);

  /*-------------------------------------------------------*/
  /* hDlg = WinLoadDlg(HWND_DESKTOP, HWND_DESKTOP,         */
  /*                   DlgProc, (HMODULE)NULL, DLG_GEN, 0); */
  /* WinProcessDlg(hDlg);                                  */
  /* WinDestroyWindow(hDlg);                               */
  /*-------------------------------------------------------*/

  WinDestroyMsgQueue(hmq);
  WinTerminate(hab);
  return 0;
}
```

Figure 5.5. Miscellaneous controls and activities: C source file. Continues.

```
MRESULT EXPENTRY DlgProc(HWND hwndDlg, ULONG msg, MPARAM mp1,
                        MPARAM mp2)
{
  static HWND hDlgBoxIcon,
              hMenu;
  HWND        hButton,
              hEntry;
  static BOOL fNewTitle = FALSE;
  ULONG       ulStyle;
  SWCNTRL     PgmEntry;
  POINTL      Pt;
  HPS         hps;
  RECTL       rcl;
  SHORT       sID;
  LONG        lColour,
              lX_Left,
              lY_Bot,
              lScreenHeight,
              lScreenWidth;
  CHAR        szPswd[9];
  static CHAR szStatus[50] = "This is a status line";

/***************************************************/

  switch (msg)
  {
    case WM_INITDLG:
      EntryFieldProc = WinSubclassWindow
                    (WinWindowFromID(hwndDlg,
                     ID_ENTRY2), (PFNWP)NumericProc);

      WinSendMsg(WinWindowFromID(hwndDlg, ID_PASSWORD),
                 EM_SETTEXTLIMIT, MRFROMSHORT(8), 0);
      WinSendMsg(WinWindowFromID(hwndDlg, ID_ENTRY1),
                 EM_SETREADONLY, (MPARAM)TRUE, 0);

      hDlgBoxIcon = WinLoadPointer(HWND_DESKTOP,
                                   (HMODULE)NULL, ID_ICON);
      WinSendMsg(hwndDlg, WM_SETICON,
                 (MPARAM)hDlgBoxIcon, 0);

      WinSetFocus(HWND_DESKTOP,
                  WinWindowFromID(hwndDlg, ID_ENTRY2));
```

Figure 5.5. Miscellaneous controls and activities: C source file. Continues.

```
hMenu = WinLoadMenu(hwndDlg, (HMODULE)NULL, ID_MENU2);
WinLoadMenu(hwndDlg, (HMODULE)NULL, ID_MENU);
WinSendMsg(hwndDlg, WM_UPDATEFRAME,
           (MPARAM)FID_MENU, 0);

lColour = CLR_DARKGREEN;
WinSetPresParam(WinWindowFromID(hwndDlg, ID_STATUS),
                PP_BACKGROUNDCOLORINDEX,
                sizeof(lColour), &lColour);
lColour = CLR_YELLOW;
WinSetPresParam(WinWindowFromID(hwndDlg, ID_STATUS),
                PP_FOREGROUNDCOLORINDEX,
                sizeof(lColour), &lColour);

WinSetWindowText(WinWindowFromID(hwndDlg,
                 ID_STATUS), szStatus);

lScreenWidth = WinQuerySysValue (HWND_DESKTOP,
                                 SV_CXSCREEN);
lScreenHeight = WinQuerySysValue(HWND_DESKTOP,
                                 SV_CYSCREEN);

                                  /*---------------*/
                                  /* Centre window */
                                  /*---------------*/
WinQueryWindowRect(hwndDlg, &rcl);
lX_Left = (lScreenWidth - rcl.xRight) / 2;
lY_Bot = (lScreenHeight - rcl.yTop) / 2;
WinSetWindowPos(hwndDlg, HWND_TOP, lX_Left, lY_Bot,
                0, 0, SWP_MOVE | SWP_SHOW |
                SWP_ACTIVATE);

PgmEntry.hwnd          = hwndDlg;
PgmEntry.hwndIcon      = hDlgBoxIcon;
PgmEntry.hprog         = (HPROGRAM)NULL;
PgmEntry.idProcess     = (PID)NULL;
PgmEntry.idSession     = (ULONG)NULL;
PgmEntry.uchVisibility = SWL_VISIBLE;
PgmEntry.fbJump        = SWL_JUMPABLE;
strcpy(PgmEntry.szSwtitle,
       "Miscellaneous Dialog Box Controls");
WinAddSwitchEntry(&PgmEntry);
return (MRESULT)TRUE;
```

Figure 5.5. Miscellaneous controls and activities: C source file. Continues.

```
    case WM_BUTTON2DOWN:
      WinQueryPointerPos(HWND_DESKTOP, &Pt);
      WinMapWindowPoints(HWND_DESKTOP, hwndDlg, &Pt, 1);
      WinPopupMenu(hwndDlg, hwndDlg, hMenu, Pt.x, Pt.y, 0,
                   PU_KEYBOARD | PU_MOUSEBUTTON1);
      return (MRESULT)TRUE;

    case WM_NEXTMENU:
      return (MRESULT)NULL;

    case WM_ADJUSTWINDOWPOS:
      if (((PSWP)mp1)->fl & SWP_MINIMIZE)
      {
        WinShowWindow(WinWindowFromID(hwndDlg, ID_OK),
                      FALSE);
        WinShowWindow(WinWindowFromID(hwndDlg, ID_STATUS),
                      FALSE);
      }
      else
        if (((PSWP)mp1)->fl & SWP_RESTORE)
        {
          WinShowWindow(WinWindowFromID(hwndDlg, ID_OK),
                        TRUE);
          WinShowWindow(WinWindowFromID(hwndDlg,
                        ID_STATUS), TRUE);
        }
      return WinDefDlgProc(hwndDlg, msg, mp1, mp2);
    case WM_CONTROL:
      switch(SHORT2FROMMP(mp1))  /* Check notification code */
      {
        case BN_PAINT:
                                  /* Check button control ID */
          switch(SHORT1FROMMP(mp1))
          {
            case ID_USERBUTTON:
              Button_Paint(mp2);
              return (MRESULT)TRUE;

            default:
              break;
          }
      }
      break;
```

Figure 5.5. Miscellaneous controls and activities: C source file. Continues.

```
case WM_COMMAND:
  switch(SHORT1FROMMP(mp1))
  {
    case ID_TEST1:
      DosBeep(500, 100);
      return FALSE;

    case ID_TEST2:
      DosBeep(1000, 100);
      return FALSE;

    case ID_TEST3:
      DosBeep(1500, 100);
      return FALSE;

    case ID_ITEM1:
      DosBeep(500, 100);
      return FALSE;

    case ID_ITEM2:
      DosBeep(1000, 100);
      return FALSE;

    case ID_ITEM3:
      DosBeep(1500, 100);
      return FALSE;

    case ID_ITEM4:
      DosBeep(2000, 100);
      return FALSE;

    case ID_ITEM5:
      DosBeep(2500, 100);
       return FALSE;

    case ID_ITEM6:
      DosBeep(3000, 100);
      return FALSE;

    case ID_USERBUTTON:
      DosBeep(1000, 100);
      DosBeep(500, 100);
      return FALSE;

    case ID_OK:
      WinSetWindowText(WinWindowFromID(hwndDlg,
```

Figure 5.5. Miscellaneous controls and activities: C source file. Continues.

```
                            ID_LBREAK),
                       "Line 1\012Line 2\012Line 3");
     if (fNewTitle)
       fNewTitle = FALSE;
     else
       fNewTitle = TRUE;

     if (fNewTitle)
     {
       WinSetWindowText(hwndDlg,
                       "Dialog Box with New Title");


       /*----------------------------------------*/
       /* WinSetDlgItemText(hwndDlg, FID_TITLEBAR, */
       /*                   "New Title");           */
       /*----------------------------------------*/

       strcpy(szStatus, "New Status");
       WinSetWindowText(WinWindowFromID(hwndDlg,
                       ID_EXIT), "Quit");
       WinSetWindowText(WinWindowFromID(hwndDlg,
                       ID_STATUS), szStatus);
       hButton = WinWindowFromID(hwndDlg, ID_EXIT);
       WinSetWindowULong(hButton, QWL_STYLE,
                        WinQueryWindowULong
                        (hButton, QWL_STYLE )
                        & ~WS_TABSTOP);
     }
     else
     {
       WinSetWindowText(hwndDlg,
           "Miscellaneous Dialog Box Controls");
       strcpy(szStatus, "Old Status");
       WinSetWindowText(WinWindowFromID(hwndDlg,
                       ID_EXIT), "Exit");
       WinSetWindowText(WinWindowFromID(hwndDlg,
                       ID_STATUS), szStatus);
       hButton = WinWindowFromID(hwndDlg, ID_EXIT);
       WinSetWindowULong(hButton, QWL_STYLE,
                        WinQueryWindowULong
                        (hButton, QWL_STYLE ) |
                        WS_TABSTOP);
     }
```

Figure 5.5. Miscellaneous controls and activities: C source file. Continues.

```
hEntry = WinWindowFromID(hwndDlg, ID_ENTRY2);
WinSetWindowULong(hEntry, QWL_STYLE,
                  WinQueryWindowULong(hEntry,
                  QWL_STYLE ) | ES_CENTER);
sID = WINQueryWindowUShort
    (WinWindowFromID(hwndDlg,
     ID_ENTRY1), QWS_ID);
WinSetDlgItemShort(hwndDlg, ID_ENTRY1, sID,
                   FALSE);
sID = WinQueryWindowUShort
    (WinWindowFromID(hwndDlg,
     ID_ENTRY2), QWS_ID);
WinSetDlgItemShort(hwndDlg, ID_ENTRY2, sID,
                   FALSE);
WinQueryWindowText(WinWindowFromID(hwndDlg,
                   ID_PASSWORD),
                   sizeof(szPswd), szPswd);
WinQueryDlgItemText(hwndDlg, ID_PASSWORD,
                    sizeof(szPswd), szPswd);
WinQueryDlgItemShort(hwndDlg, ID_ENTRY1, &sID,
                     FALSE);         /* Unsigned */
WinSetFocus(HWND_DESKTOP,
            WinWindowFromID(hwndDlg,
            ID_ENTRY2));

/*---------------------------------------- */
/* Position cursor at start of field and mark    */
/* entire field                                  */
/*---------------------------------------- */

WinSendMsg(WinWindowFromID(hwndDlg, ID_ENTRY2),
           EM_SETSEL, MPFROM2SHORT(0, 5), 0);
ulStyle = WinQueryWindowULong(WinWindowFromID
           (hwndDlg, ID_OK), QWL_STYLE);
if (ulStyle & BS_DEFAULT)             /* Default */
{
  DosBeep(100, 200);

/*---------------------------------------- */
/* WinSendMsg(WinWindowFromID(hwndDlg, ID_OK), */
/*            BM_SETDEFAULT, (MPARAM)FALSE, 0);*/
/*---------------------------------------- */
```

Figure 5.5. Miscellaneous controls and activities: C source file. Continues.

```
                WinSetWindowBits(WinWindowFromID(hwndDlg,
                                ID_OK), QWL_STYLE, 0,
                                BS_DEFAULT);
                WinInvalidateRect(WinWindowFromID(hwndDlg,
                                  ID_OK), NULL, FALSE);
            }
            else                              /* Not default */
            {
              DosBeep(1000, 200);

                /*----------------------------------------*/
                /* WinSendMsg(WinWindowFromID(hwndDlg,    */
                /*   ID_OK), BM_SETDEFAULT, (MPARAM)TRUE, 0);*/
                /*----------------------------------------*/

                WinSetWindowBits(WinWindowFromID(hwndDlg,
                                ID_OK), QWL_STYLE,
                                BS_DEFAULT, BS_DEFAULT);
                WinInvalidateRect(WinWindowFromID(hwndDlg,
                                  ID_OK), NULL, FALSE);
            }
            return FALSE;
         case ID_EXIT:
            WinDestroyPointer(hDlgBoxIcon);
            WinRemoveSwitchEntry(WinQuerySwitchHandle
                                 (hwndDlg, 0));
            WinPostMsg(hwndDlg, WM_QUIT, 0, 0);
            break;
         default:
            return FALSE;
      }                             /* Remove the dialog box */
      WinDismissDlg(hwndDlg, TRUE);
      break;

   default:
      return WinDefDlgProc(hwndDlg, msg, mp1, mp2);
   }
   return FALSE;

}
MRESULT EXPENTRY   NumericProc(HWND hwnd, ULONG msg,
                               MPARAM mp1, MPARAM mp2)
{
```

Figure 5.5. Miscellaneous controls and activities: C source file. Continues.

```
  SHORT     fsKeyFlags,
            sChr;
  if (msg == WM_CHAR)
  {
    fsKeyFlags = SHORT1FROMMP(mp1);
    sChr       = SHORT1FROMMP(mp2);
    if (!(fsKeyFlags & KC_KEYUP))     /* Only act on key down */
    {
      if ((sChr < 0x30 || sChr > 0x39) &&   /* Not numeric   */
          (sChr != 8) &&                    /* Not backspace */
          (sChr != 9) &&                    /* Not tab       */
          (sChr != 0x2D) &&                 /* Not -         */
          (sChr != 0xD))                    /* Not enter     */
      {
        WinAlarm(HWND_DESKTOP, WA_WARNING);
        return (MRESULT)TRUE;
      }
    }
  }                      /* Call public entry field procedure */
  return (* EntryFieldProc)(hwnd, msg, mp1, mp2);
}
/**********************************************************/
VOID Button_Paint(USERBUTTON *ubtn)
{
  RECTL DestPt;
  HBITMAP hbm;
  /*------------------------------------------------------*/
  /* hbm = WinGetSysBitmap(HWND_DESKTOP, SBMP_DRIVE);     */
  /* WinQueryWindowRect(ubtn->hwnd, &DestPt);             */
  /* WinDrawBitmap(ubtn->hps, hbm, NULL,                  */
  /*               (PPOINTL)&DestPt, CLR_YELLOW,          */
  /*               CLR_BLACK,                             */
  /*               ((USHORT)ubtn->fsState ? DBM_INVERT :  */
  /*               DBM_NORMAL) |                          */
  /*               DBM_STRETCH);                          */
  /*------------------------------------------------------*/
  hbm = GpiLoadBitmap(ubtn->hps, (HMODULE)NULL, ID_LOCK,
                      0, 0);
  WinQueryWindowRect(ubtn->hwnd, &DestPt);
  WinDrawBitmap(ubtn->hps, hbm, NULL, (PPOINTL)&DestPt,
                0, 0, ((USHORT)ubtn->fsState ? DBM_INVERT :
                DBM_NORMAL) | DBM_STRETCH);
  return;
}
```

Figure 5.5. Miscellaneous controls and activities: C source file. Concluded.

5.19.2 MLE and radio buttons

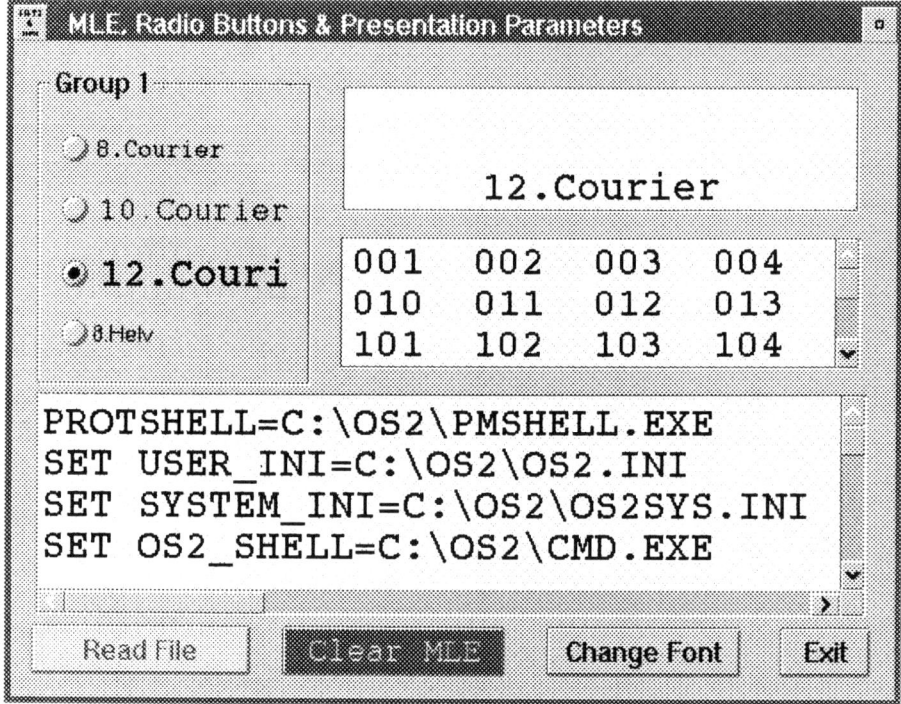

Figure 5.6. MLE and radio buttons output.

This program (Fig. 5.6) illustrates those problems associated with multiline entry fields, radio buttons and presentation parameters. The topics covered include:

- Initializing radio buttons
- Changing fonts
- Importing a file into a multiline entry field
- Verification that numbers in columns are independent of font

In this program we use presentation parameters to change the font in an entry field, listbox and multiline entry field (MLE), though not all fonts can be set in an MLE as this program shows. Initially, the radio button for 12.Courier is selected (Fig. 5.6), and the text in the entry field, listbox and MLE uses this font. Also, the foreground and background colours of the Read File and Clear MLE pushbuttons have been changed from the default colours. The font and colour changes for the buttons are achieved by setting their presentation parameters using the dialog box editor, whereas the font for the three main controls, entry field, listbox and MLE, are set initially using WinSetPresParam in the WM_INITDLG case statement in the program.

If you press the 8.Courier radio button then the font changes in the three main controls, and the colours for the MLE change to yellow on red. Again, this is done using WinSetPresParam. You can also change the font by double-clicking a font item in the listbox.

The Change Font pushbutton will alter the font to 8.Courier and successive presses will cause each font defined in the program to be used and, as you will see, not all will be accepted in the MLE. If you select a font from the listbox and then press Change Font, the next font in the list will be used rather than starting again with 8.Courier.

The Read File pushbutton will cause your CONFIG.SYS file to be imported into the MLE at the cursor position. Note that the program assumes you have installed OS/2 on the C: drive.

The following listings show the program's header file, Fig. 5.7, resource file, Fig. 5.8, dialog template, Fig. 5.9, and C source file, Fig. 5.10.

```
#define DLG_MLE        256
#define ID_OK          257
#define ID_EXIT        258
#define ID_ICON        259
#define ID_MULTILINE   260
#define ID_RADIO1      261
#define ID_RADIO2      262
#define ID_RADIO3      263
#define ID_RADIO4      264
#define ID_ENTRY1      265
#define ID_CLEAR       266
#define ID_FONT        267
#define ID_LISTBOX     268
```

Figure 5.7. MLE and radio buttons: header file.

```
#include <os2.h>
#include "dlgmle.h"

ICON    ID_ICON     dlgmle.ico

rcinclude dlgmle.dlg
```

Figure 5.8. MLE and radio buttons: resource file.

```
DLGINCLUDE 1 "DLGMLE.H"

DLGTEMPLATE DLG_MLE LOADONCALL MOVEABLE DISCARDABLE
BEGIN
  DIALOG "MLE, Radio Buttons & Presentation Parameters",
         DLG_MLE, 68, 30, 276, 159, FS_NOBYTEALIGN |
         WS_VISIBLE, FCF_SYSMENU | FCF_TITLEBAR |
         FCF_MINBUTTON
  BEGIN
    GROUPBOX         "Group 1", 100, 8, 76, 86, 77
    AUTORADIOBUTTON  "8.Courier", ID_RADIO1, 16, 128, 73, 10,
                     WS_TABSTOP
                     PRESPARAMS PP_FONTNAMESIZE,
                     0x6F432E38L, 0x65697275L, 0x00000072L
    AUTORADIOBUTTON  "10.Courier", ID_RADIO2, 16, 113, 72, 10,
                     WS_TABSTOP
                     PRESPARAMS PP_FONTNAMESIZE,
                     0x432E3031L, 0x6972756FL, 0x00007265L
    AUTORADIOBUTTON  "12.Courier", ID_RADIO3, 16, 98, 72, 10,
                     WS_TABSTOP
                     PRESPARAMS PP_FONTNAMESIZE,
                     0x432E3231L, 0x6972756FL, 0x00007265L
    AUTORADIOBUTTON  "8.Helv", ID_RADIO4, 16, 83, 72, 10,
                     WS_TABSTOP
                     PRESPARAMS PP_FONTNAMESIZE,
                     0x65482E38L, 0x0000766CL
    ENTRYFIELD       "", ID_ENTRY1, 105, 119, 158, 28,
                     ES_CENTER | NOT ES_AUTOSCROLL |
                     ES_MARGIN | WS_GROUP
    LISTBOX          ID_LISTBOX, 103, 80, 162, 32,
                     LS_NOADJUSTPOS
    MLE              "", ID_MULTILINE, 8, 20, 259, 54,
                     MLS_HSCROLL | MLS_VSCROLL
    PUSHBUTTON       "Read File", ID_OK, 6, 5, 70, 13
                     PRESPARAMS PP_FOREGROUNDCOLOR,
                     0x0000C800L
                     PRESPARAMS PP_BACKGROUNDCOLOR,
                     0x00640000L
    PUSHBUTTON       "Clear MLE", ID_CLEAR, 85, 5, 70, 13
                     PRESPARAMS PP_FOREGROUNDCOLOR,
                     0x00FFFF00L
                     PRESPARAMS PP_BACKGROUNDCOLOR,
                     0x00000064L
                     PRESPARAMS PP_FONTNAMESIZE,
```

Figure 5.9. MLE and radio buttons: dialog template. Continues.

```
                           0x432E3031L, 0x6972756FL, 0x00007265L
      PUSHBUTTON           "Change Font", ID_FONT, 167, 5, 62, 13
      PUSHBUTTON           "Exit", ID_EXIT, 240, 5, 29, 13
    END
END
```

Figure 5.9. MLE and radio buttons: dialog template. Concluded.

```
#define   INCL_WINWINDOWMGR
#define   INCL_WINFRAMEMGR
#define   INCL_WINSWITCHLIST
#define   INCL_WINSYS
#define   INCL_WINPOINTERS
#define   INCL_WINBUTTONS
#define   INCL_WINDIALOGS
#define   INCL_WINLISTBOXES
#define   INCL_WINMLE

#include <os2.h>
#include <string.h>
#include "dlgmle.h"

MRESULT EXPENTRY DlgProc(HWND, ULONG, MPARAM, MPARAM);

/**********************************************************/
INT main(VOID)
{
  HAB    hab;
  HMQ    hmq;

  hab = WinInitialize(0);
  hmq = WinCreateMsgQueue(hab, 0);

  WinDlgBox(HWND_DESKTOP, HWND_DESKTOP, DlgProc,
            (HMODULE)NULL, DLG_MLE, 0);
  WinDestroyMsgQueue(hmq);
  WinTerminate(hab);
  return 0;
}
/**********************************************************/
MRESULT EXPENTRY DlgProc(HWND hwndDlg, ULONG msg, MPARAM mp1,
                        MPARAM mp2)
{
  static    HWND    hDlgBoxIcon;
```

Figure 5.10. MLE and radio buttons: C source file. Continues.

```
   SWCNTRL           PgmEntry;
   RECTL             rcl;
   LONG              lColour,
                     lX_Left,
                     lY_Bot,
                     lScreenHeight,
                     lScreenWidth;
   CHAR              szFont[25];
   PVOID             BaseMem;
   IPT               ipt;
   HFILE             hFile;
   ULONG             ulAction,
                     ulBytesRead;
   static SHORT      sIdx = 0,
                     sNoFonts = 27;
   static CHAR       szMLEText[] =
                     "This is a Multi-line Entry Field";

   static PSZ        szColumns[] = {"001 002 003 004 005 006",
                                    "010 011 012 013 014 015",
                                    "101 102 103 104 105 106"};

   static PSZ        szFontTable[] =
                     {"8.Courier", "10.Courier", "12.Courier",
                     "14.Courier", "15.Courier", "18.Courier",
                     "24.Courier", "8.Helv", "10.Helv",
                     "12.Helv", "14.Helv", "18.Helv",
                     "24.Helv", "8.Helvetica", "10.Helvetica",
                     "12.Helvetica", "14.Symbol Set",
                     "18.Symbol Set", "24.Symbol Set",
                     "10.System Monospaced",
                     "10.System Proportional",
                     "8.Times New Roman", "10.Times New Roman",
                     "12.Times New Roman", "14.Tms Rmn",
                     "18.Tms Rmn", "24.Tms Rmn"};

 switch (msg)
 {
   case WM_INITDLG:
     hDlgBoxIcon = WinLoadPointer(HWND_DESKTOP,
                                  (HMODULE)NULL, ID_ICON);
     WinSendMsg(hwndDlg, WM_SETICON,
```

Figure 5.10. MLE and radio buttons: C source file. Continues.

```
                    (MPARAM)hDlgBoxIcon, 0);

  lScreenWidth = WinQuerySysValue(HWND_DESKTOP,
                                  SV_CXSCREEN);
  lScreenHeight = WinQuerySysValue(HWND_DESKTOP,
                                   SV_CYSCREEN);
  WinQueryWindowRect(hwndDlg, &rcl);

                                    /*--------------*/
                                    /* Centre window */
                                    /*--------------*/

  lX_Left = (lScreenWidth - rcl.xRight) / 2;
  lY_Bot  = (lScreenHeight - rcl.yTop) / 2;
  WinSetWindowPos(hwndDlg, HWND_TOP, lX_Left, lY_Bot,
                  0, 0, SWP_MOVE | SWP_SHOW |
                  SWP_ACTIVATE);

  PgmEntry.hwnd          = hwndDlg;
  PgmEntry.hwndIcon      = hDlgBoxIcon;
  PgmEntry.hprog         = (HPROGRAM)NULL;
  PgmEntry.idProcess     = (PID)NULL;
  PgmEntry.idSession     = (ULONG)NULL;
  PgmEntry.uchVisibility = SWL_VISIBLE;
  PgmEntry.fbJump        = SWL_JUMPABLE;
  strcpy(PgmEntry.szSwtitle,
         "MLE, Radio Buttons & Presentation Parameters");
  WinAddSwitchEntry(&PgmEntry);

  WinSendDlgItemMsg(hwndDlg, ID_RADIO3, BM_SETCHECK,
                    MPFROM2SHORT(TRUE, 0), 0);

  strcpy(szFont, szFontTable[2]);    /* "12.Courier" */
  WinSetPresParam(WinWindowFromID(hwndDlg, ID_ENTRY1),
                  PP_FONTNAMESIZE, sizeof(szFont),
                  szFont);
  WinSetPresParam(WinWindowFromID(hwndDlg,
                  ID_MULTILINE), PP_FONTNAMESIZE,
                  sizeof(szFont), szFont);
  WinSetPresParam(WinWindowFromID(hwndDlg,
                  ID_LISTBOX), PP_FONTNAMESIZE,
                  sizeof(szFont), szFont);
  WinSetDlgItemText(hwndDlg, ID_ENTRY1, szFont);
  WinSetDlgItemText(hwndDlg, ID_MULTILINE, szMLEText);
```

Figure 5.10. MLE and radio buttons: C source file. Continues.

```
    for (sIdx = 0; sIdx < 3; sIdx++)
    {
      WinSendMsg(WinWindowFromID(hwndDlg, ID_LISTBOX),
               LM_INSERTITEM, MRFROMSHORT(LIT_END),
               MRFROMP(szColumns[sIdx]));
    }
    for (sIdx = 0; sIdx < sNoFonts; sIdx++)
    {
      WinSendMsg(WinWindowFromID(hwndDlg, ID_LISTBOX),
               LM_INSERTITEM, MRFROMSHORT(LIT_END),
               MRFROMP(szFontTable[sIdx]));
    }
    sIdx = 0;

    return (MRESULT)TRUE;

  case WM_ADJUSTWINDOWPOS:
    if (((PSWP)mp1)->fl & SWP_MINIMIZE)
    {
      WinShowWindow(WinWindowFromID(hwndDlg, ID_OK),
                 FALSE);
    }
    else
      if (((PSWP)mp1)->fl & SWP_RESTORE)
      {
        WinShowWindow(WinWindowFromID(hwndDlg, ID_OK),
                   TRUE);
      }
    return WinDefDlgProc(hwndDlg, msg, mp1, mp2);

  case WM_CONTROL:
    switch(SHORT1FROMMP(mp1))
    {
      case ID_LISTBOX:
        switch(SHORT2FROMMP(mp1))
        {                          /*----------------------*/
          case LN_ENTER:           /* Ignore the first 3 rows */
                                   /*----------------------*/
            sIdx = (SHORT)WinSendDlgItemMsg(hwndDlg,
                         ID_LISTBOX,
                         LM_QUERYSELECTION, 0, 0);
            if (sIdx > 2)
```

Figure 5.10. MLE and radio buttons: C source file. Continues.

```
            {
              sIdx -= 3;
              strcpy(szFont, szFontTable[sIdx]);
              WinSetPresParam(WinWindowFromID(hwndDlg,
                          ID_LISTBOX),
                          PP_FONTNAMESIZE,
                          sizeof(szFont), szFont);
              WinSetPresParam(WinWindowFromID(hwndDlg,
                          ID_ENTRY1),
                          PP_FONTNAMESIZE,
                          sizeof(szFont), szFont);
              WinSetPresParam(WinWindowFromID(hwndDlg,
                          ID_MULTILINE),
                          PP_FONTNAMESIZE,
                          sizeof(szFont), szFont);
              WinSetWindowText(WinWindowFromID(hwndDlg,
                            ID_ENTRY1), "");
              WinSetWindowText(WinWindowFromID(hwndDlg,
                          ID_ENTRY1),
                          szFontTable[sIdx++]);
            }
            break;
         default:
            break;
         }
         break;

      case ID_RADIO1:
      case ID_RADIO2:
      case ID_RADIO3:
      case ID_RADIO4:
         switch(SHORT2FROMMP(mp1))
         {
            case BN_CLICKED:
              if (SHORT1FROMMP(mp1) == ID_RADIO1)
              {
                 strcpy(szFont, szFontTable[0]);
                                        /* "8.Courier" */
                 lColour = CLR_RED;
                 WinSetPresParam(WinWindowFromID(hwndDlg,
                      ID_MULTILINE), PP_BACKGROUNDCOLORINDEX,
                      sizeof(lColour), &lColour);
```

Figure 5.10. MLE and radio buttons: C source file. Continues.

```
                    lColour = CLR_YELLOW;
                    WinSetPresParam(WinWindowFromID(hwndDlg,
                       ID_MULTILINE), PP_FOREGROUNDCOLORINDEX,
                       sizeof(lColour), &lColour);
                  }
                  if (SHORT1FROMMP(mp1) == ID_RADIO2)
                    strcpy(szFont, szFontTable[1]);
                                            /* "10.Courier" */
                  if (SHORT1FROMMP(mp1) == ID_RADIO3)
                    strcpy(szFont, szFontTable[2]);
                                            /* "12.Courier" */
                  if (SHORT1FROMMP(mp1) == ID_RADIO4)
                    strcpy(szFont, szFontTable[7]);
                                            /* "8.Helv"    */

                  WinSetDlgItemText(hwndDlg, ID_ENTRY1,
                             szFont);
                  WinSetDlgItemText(hwndDlg, ID_MULTILINE,
                             szMLEText);
                  WinSetPresParam(WinWindowFromID(hwndDlg,
                             ID_ENTRY1), PP_FONTNAMESIZE,
                             sizeof(szFont), szFont);
                  WinSetPresParam(WinWindowFromID(hwndDlg,
                             ID_MULTILINE),
                             PP_FONTNAMESIZE,
                             sizeof(szFont), szFont);
                  WinSetPresParam(WinWindowFromID(hwndDlg,
                             ID_LISTBOX),
                             PP_FONTNAMESIZE,
                             sizeof(szFont), szFont);
                  break;

            default:
               break;
         }
         break;

      }
      break;

   case WM_COMMAND:
      switch(SHORT1FROMMP(mp1))
```

Figure 5.10. MLE and radio buttons: C source file. Continues.

```
{
  case ID_OK:
                            /* Allocate one page - 4KB */
    DosAllocMem(&BaseMem, 4096, PAG_READ | PAG_WRITE |
            PAG_COMMIT);
    DosOpen("C:\\CONFIG.SYS", &hFile, &ulAction,
            (ULONG)NULL,
            (ULONG)NULL,
            OPEN_ACTION_OPEN_IF_EXISTS,
            OPEN_FLAGS_SEQUENTIAL |
            OPEN_SHARE_DENYNONE |
            OPEN_ACCESS_READONLY,
            (ULONG)NULL);
    DosRead(hFile, BaseMem, 4096, &ulBytesRead);
    DosClose(hFile);

    WinSendMsg(WinWindowFromID(hwndDlg,
            ID_MULTILINE), MLM_SETIMPORTEXPORT,
            (MPARAM)BaseMem, MPFROMLONG(4096));
    ipt = -1;
    WinSendMsg(WinWindowFromID(hwndDlg,
            ID_MULTILINE), MLM_IMPORT,
            (MPARAM)&ipt,
            MPFROMLONG(ulBytesRead));
    DosFreeMem(BaseMem);
    return FALSE;

  case ID_CLEAR:

    /*----------------------------------------*/
    /* WinSetDlgItemText(hwndDlg,             */
    /*                ID_MULTILINE, "");      */
    /*----------------------------------------*/

    WinSetWindowText(WinWindowFromID(hwndDlg,
                ID_MULTILINE), "");

    return FALSE;
  case ID_FONT:
    strcpy(szFont, szFontTable[sIdx]);
    WinSetPresParam(WinWindowFromID(hwndDlg,
        ID_LISTBOX), PP_FONTNAMESIZE, sizeof(szFont),
        szFont);
    WinSetPresParam(WinWindowFromID(hwndDlg,
```

Figure 5.10. MLE and radio buttons: C source file. Continues.

```
                    ID_ENTRY1), PP_FONTNAMESIZE, sizeof(szFont),
                    szFont);
                 WinSetPresParam(WinWindowFromID(hwndDlg,
                    ID_MULTILINE), PP_FONTNAMESIZE,
                    sizeof(szFont), szFont);
                 WinSetWindowText(WinWindowFromID(hwndDlg,
                              ID_ENTRY1), "");
                 WinSetWindowText(WinWindowFromID(hwndDlg,
                              ID_ENTRY1),
                              szFontTable[sIdx++]);
              if (sIdx == sNoFonts)
                 sIdx = 0;
              return FALSE;
           case ID_EXIT:
              WinDestroyPointer(hDlgBoxIcon);
              WinRemoveSwitchEntry(WinQuerySwitchHandle
                              (hwndDlg, 0));
              WinPostMsg(hwndDlg, WM_QUIT, 0, 0);
              break;
           default:
              return FALSE;
        }
                                 /* Remove the dialog box */
        WinDismissDlg(hwndDlg, TRUE);
        break;
     default:
        return WinDefDlgProc(hwndDlg, msg, mp1, mp2);
   }
   return FALSE;
}
```

Figure 5.10. MLE and radio buttons: C source file. Concluded.

5.19.3 *Listboxes*

Although the processing of listboxes is, in general, quite straightforward, ownerdraw listboxes have caused several problems. In this program we look at a simple implementation of an ownerdraw listbox as well as a single and multiple selection listbox. The topics covered include:

- Selecting/deselecting listbox items
- Processing an ownerdraw listbox
- Processing a multiple selection listbox
- Processing of listbox item handles
- Mnemonics

The program displays three listboxes (Fig. 5.11): a single selection with the first item initially selected, multiple selection, and an ownerdraw. Items can be deselected from the single and ownerdraw boxes by pressing `Deselect`, and can be deleted from the single selection box by pressing `Delete`. If you select items in the multiple selection box and press `Process MultSel` then each one is processed sequentially and beeps when complete. Notice that this option uses `DosSleep`, which is *not recommended* in practice. It is done here merely to slow down the process so that you can see what is happening. The ownerdraw box is a simple implementation of columnar data with `Finland` non-selectable. If you select a country in the single selection listbox then the value of its key and its capital, stored in the item handle, are displayed.

You will notice that the first letter in the title over each listbox is underlined to show the presence of a mnemonic. Pressing Alt-S, Alt-M or Alt-O will switch focus to the relevant listbox.

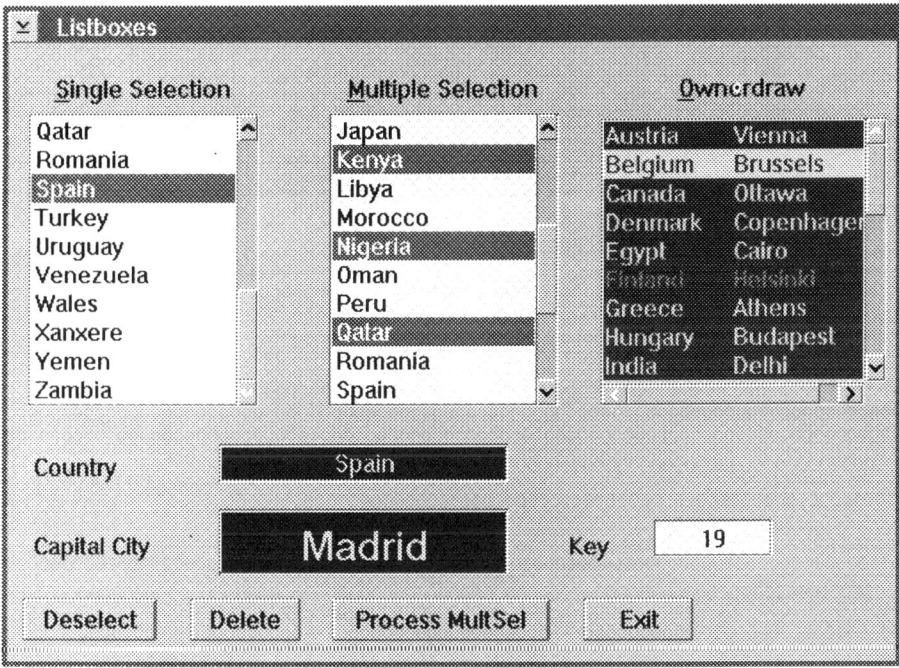

Figure 5.11. Listboxes output.

The following listings show the program's header file, Fig. 5.12, resource file, Fig. 5.13, dialog template, Fig. 5.14, and C source file, Fig. 5.15.

```
#define DLG_LBOX      256
#define ID_DESELECT   257
#define ID_EXIT       258
#define ID_SLISTBOX   259
#define ID_MLISTBOX   260
#define ID_OLISTBOX   261
#define ID_ENTRY1     262
#define ID_DELETE     263
#define ID_ENTRY2     264
#define ID_ENTRY3     265
#define ID_PROCMULT   266
```

Figure 5.12. Listboxes: header file.

```
#include <os2.h>
#include "listbox.h"
rcinclude listbox.dlg
```

Figure 5.13. Listboxes: resource file.

```
DLGINCLUDE 1 "LISTBOX.H"
DLGTEMPLATE DLG_LBOX LOADONCALL MOVEABLE DISCARDABLE
BEGIN
  DIALOG "Listboxes", DLG_LBOX, 30, 24, 317, 172,
         FS_NOBYTEALIGN | WS_VISIBLE, FCF_SYSMENU |
         FCF_TITLEBAR
  BEGIN
    CTEXT      "~Single Selection", 101, 8, 155, 80, 8,
               DT_MNEMONIC
    LISTBOX    ID_SLISTBOX, 8, 71, 80, 80
    CTEXT      "~Multiple Selection", 102, 115, 155, 80, 8,
               DT_MNEMONIC | NOT WS_GROUP
    LISTBOX    ID_MLISTBOX, 115, 71, 80, 80, LS_MULTIPLESEL
    CTEXT      "~Ownerdraw", 103, 216, 155, 91, 8,
               DT_MNEMONIC | NOT WS_GROUP
    LISTBOX    ID_OLISTBOX, 212, 71, 100, 83, LS_OWNERDRAW |
               LS_HORZSCROLL
    PUSHBUTTON "Deselect", ID_DESELECT, 5, 5, 49, 13
    PUSHBUTTON "Delete", ID_DELETE, 65, 5, 40, 13
    PUSHBUTTON "Process MultSel", ID_PROCMULT, 115, 5, 79, 13
    PUSHBUTTON "Exit", ID_EXIT, 205, 5, 40, 13
```

Figure 5.14. Listboxes: dialog template. Continues.

```
    ENTRYFIELD   "", ID_ENTRY1, 77, 25, 100, 16, ES_CENTER |
                 ES_MARGIN | ES_READONLY | WS_GROUP |
                 NOT WS_TABSTOP
    LTEXT        "Capital City", 104, 9, 28, 54, 8,
                 NOT WS_GROUP
    LTEXT        "Key", 105, 200, 28, 21, 8, NOT WS_GROUP
    ENTRYFIELD   "", ID_ENTRY2, 232, 30, 39, 8, ES_CENTER |
                 NOT ES_AUTOSCROLL | ES_MARGIN | ES_READONLY |
                 NOT WS_TABSTOP
    LTEXT        "Country", 106, 9, 50, 48, 8, NOT WS_GROUP
    ENTRYFIELD   "", ID_ENTRY3, 77, 51, 100, 8, ES_CENTER |
                 NOT ES_AUTOSCROLL | ES_MARGIN | ES_READONLY |
                 NOT WS_TABSTOP
  END
END
```

Figure 5.14. Listboxes: dialog template. Concluded.

```
#define    INCL_WINWINDOWMGR
#define    INCL_WINFRAMEMGR
#define    INCL_WINSWITCHLIST
#define    INCL_WINSYS
#define    INCL_WINLISTBOXES
#define    INCL_WINMENUS
#define    INCL_WINDIALOGS
#define    INCL_DOSPROCESS
#define    INCL_DOSMEMMGR
#define    INCL_GPILCIDS
#define    INCL_GPIPRIMITIVES

#include <os2.h>
#include <string.h>
#include <stdio.h>
#include "listbox.h"

MRESULT EXPENTRY DlgProc(HWND, ULONG, MPARAM, MPARAM);

/*********************************************************/

INT main(VOID)
{
  HAB     hab;
```

Figure 5.15. Listboxes: C source file. Continues.

```
  HMQ     hmq;

  hab = WinInitialize(0);
  hmq = WinCreateMsgQueue(hab, 0);

  WinDlgBox(HWND_DESKTOP, HWND_DESKTOP, DlgProc,
            (HMODULE)NULL, DLG_LBOX, 0);

  WinDestroyMsgQueue(hmq);
  WinTerminate(hab);
  return 0;
}

/**********************************************************/

MRESULT EXPENTRY DlgProc(HWND hwndDlg, ULONG msg, MPARAM mp1,
                         MPARAM mp2)
{
  SWCNTRL       PgmEntry;
  RECTL         rcl;
  SHORT         sMidx;
  static SHORT  sIdx,
                sOidx,
                sSavedIdx;
  LONG          lColour,
                lX_Left,
                lY_Bot,
                lScreenHeight,
                lScreenWidth;
  CHAR          szFont[15];
  typedef struct _DBDATA
  {
    USHORT usKey;
    CHAR   szCapital[20];
  } DBDATA, *PDBDATA;

  PDBDATA       pDB_Data;

  static PVOID  BaseMem,
                MemOffset;

  static PSZ    szCountry[] = {
```

Figure 5.15. Listboxes: C source file. Continues.

```
                       "Austria", "Belgium", "Canada",
                       "Denmark", "Egypt", "Finland",
                       "Greece", "Hungary", "India", "Japan",
                       "Kenya", "Libya", "Morocco", "Nigeria",
                       "Oman", "Peru", "Qatar", "Romania",
                       "Spain", "Turkey", "Uruguay",
                       "Venezuela", "Wales", "Xanxere",
                       "Yemen", "Zambia"};
   static PSZ        szCapital[] = {
                       "Vienna", "Brussels", "Ottawa",
                       "Copenhagen", "Cairo", "Helsinki",
                       "Athens", "Budapest", "Delhi", "Tokyo",
                       "Nairobi", "Tripoli", "Rabat", "Lagos",
                       "Muscat", "Lima", "Doha", "Bucharest",
                       "Madrid", "Ankara", "Montevideo",
                       "Caracas", "Cardiff", "None", "Sana'a",
                       "Lusaka"};
   CHAR              szCtry[10],
                     szListBuff[50],
                     *pszCountry,
                     *pszCapital;
   ULONG             ulKeyValue;
   POWNERITEM        pOwner;
   SHORT             cxText,
                     cyText;
   HPS               hps;
   FONTMETRICS       fm;
   POINTL            points[TXTBOX_COUNT];

/*******************************************************/

   switch (msg)
   {
     case WM_INITDLG:
       WinEnableWindow(WinWindowFromID(hwndDlg,
                  ID_PROCMULT), FALSE);
       strcpy(szFont, "18.Helv");
       WinSetPresParam(WinWindowFromID(hwndDlg,
                  ID_ENTRY1), PP_FONTNAMESIZE,
                  sizeof(szFont), szFont);

       lColour = CLR_RED;
```

Figure 5.15. Listboxes: C source fule. Continues.

```
          WinSetPresParam(WinWindowFromID(hwndDlg, ID_ENTRY1),
                     PP_BACKGROUNDCOLORINDEX,
                     sizeof(lColour), &lColour);
          WinSetPresParam(WinWindowFromID(hwndDlg, ID_ENTRY3),
                     PP_BACKGROUNDCOLORINDEX,
                     sizeof(lColour), &lColour);
          lColour = CLR_YELLOW;
          WinSetPresParam(WinWindowFromID(hwndDlg, ID_ENTRY1),
                     PP_FOREGROUNDCOLORINDEX,
                     sizeof(lColour), &lColour);
          WinSetPresParam(WinWindowFromID(hwndDlg, ID_ENTRY3),
                     PP_FOREGROUNDCOLORINDEX,
                     sizeof(lColour), &lColour);

          lScreenWidth  = WinQuerySysValue(HWND_DESKTOP,
                                      SV_CXSCREEN);
          lScreenHeight = WinQuerySysValue(HWND_DESKTOP,
                                      SV_CYSCREEN);

                                      /*---------------*/
                                      /* Centre window */
                                      /*---------------*/
          WinQueryWindowRect(hwndDlg, &rcl);
          lX_Left = (lScreenWidth - rcl.xRight) / 2;
          lY_Bot  = (lScreenHeight - rcl.yTop)  / 2;
          WinSetWindowPos(hwndDlg, HWND_TOP, lX_Left, lY_Bot,
                     0, 0, SWP_MOVE | SWP_SHOW |
                     SWP_ACTIVATE);

          PgmEntry.hwnd          = hwndDlg;
          PgmEntry.hwndIcon      = (HWND)NULL;
          PgmEntry.hprog         = (HPROGRAM)NULL;
          PgmEntry.idProcess     = (PID)NULL;
          PgmEntry.idSession     = (ULONG)NULL;
          PgmEntry.uchVisibility = SWL_VISIBLE;
          PgmEntry.fbJump        = SWL_JUMPABLE;
          strcpy(PgmEntry.szSwtitle, "Listboxes");
          WinAddSwitchEntry(&PgmEntry);

          DosAllocMem(&BaseMem, 4096, PAG_READ | PAG_WRITE |
                     PAG_COMMIT);
          DosSubSetMem(BaseMem, DOSSUB_INIT, 4096);
```

Figure 5.15. Listboxes: C source file. Continues.

```
for (sIdx = 0; sIdx < 26; sIdx++)
{
    /*-------------------------------------------*/
    /* If all we want to do is store the key value... */
    /*                                           */
    /* WinSendDlgItemMsg(hwndDlg, ID_SLISTBOX,   */
    /*     LM_INSERTITEM, MPFROMSHORT(LIT_END),  */
    /*     MPFROMP(szCountry[sIdx]));            */
    /* ulKeyValue = sIdx + 1;                    */
    /* WinSendDlgItemMsg(hwndDlg, ID_SLISTBOX,   */
    /*     LM_SETITEMHANDLE, (MPARAM)sIdx,       */
    /*     (MPARAM)ulKeyValue);                  */
    /*-------------------------------------------*/

    /*-------------------------------------------*/
    /* Otherwise we need to save a pointer to our */
    /* structure...                              */
    /*-------------------------------------------*/

    WinSendDlgItemMsg(hwndDlg, ID_SLISTBOX,
                      LM_INSERTITEM,
                      MPFROMSHORT(LIT_END),
                      MPFROMP(szCountry[sIdx]));

    DosSubAllocMem(BaseMem, &MemOffset,
                   sizeof(DBDATA));
    pDB_Data = MemOffset;
    pDB_Data->usKey = sIdx + 1;
    strcpy(pDB_Data->szCapital, szCapital[sIdx]);
    WinSendDlgItemMsg(hwndDlg, ID_SLISTBOX,
                      LM_SETITEMHANDLE, (MPARAM)sIdx,
                      MPFROMP(pDB_Data));
    WinSendDlgItemMsg(hwndDlg, ID_MLISTBOX,
                      LM_INSERTITEM,
                      MPFROMSHORT(LIT_END),
                      MPFROMP(szCountry[sIdx]));
    sprintf(szListBuff, "%s\t%s", szCountry[sIdx],
            szCapital[sIdx]);
    WinSendDlgItemMsg(hwndDlg, ID_OLISTBOX,
                      LM_INSERTITEM,
                      MPFROMSHORT(LIT_END),
                      MPFROMP(szListBuff));
```

Figure 5.15. Listboxes: C source file. Continues.

```
            }
            WinSendDlgItemMsg(hwndDlg, ID_SLISTBOX,
                              LM_SELECTITEM, MPFROMSHORT(0),
                              (MPARAM)TRUE);
            break;

        case WM_MEASUREITEM:
          hps = WinGetPS(WinWindowFromID(hwndDlg,
                         ID_OLISTBOX));
          WinSendDlgItemMsg(hwndDlg, ID_OLISTBOX,
                            LM_QUERYITEMTEXT,
                            MPFROM2SHORT(sIdx,
                            sizeof(szListBuff)),
                            MPFROMP(szListBuff));
          GpiQueryFontMetrics(hps, sizeof(FONTMETRICS), &fm);
          cyText = (SHORT)fm.lMaxBaselineExt;
          GpiQueryTextBox(hps, strlen(szListBuff), szListBuff,
                          TXTBOX_COUNT, points);

          /*--------------------------------------------*/
          /* Add a small amount to cxText to ensure the entire */
          /* item can be read when fully scrolled. Necessary   */
          /* because we need to allow for the 'tab' character  */
          /* between columns.                                  */
          /*--------------------------------------------*/

          cxText = (USHORT)points[TXTBOX_TOPRIGHT].x + 20;
          WinReleasePS(hps);
          return MRFROM2SHORT(cyText, cxText);

        case WM_DRAWITEM:
          pOwner      = (POWNERITEM)mp2;
          rcl.xRight  = pOwner->rclItem.xRight/2;
          rcl.xLeft   = pOwner->rclItem.xLeft;
          rcl.yTop    = pOwner->rclItem.yTop;
          rcl.yBottom = pOwner->rclItem.yBottom;

          GpiSetBackMix(pOwner->hps, BM_OVERPAINT);

          if ((!pOwner->fsState) ||      /* Unselected */
              (pOwner->idItem == 5))     /* Do not allow Finland */
          {
            GpiSetBackColor(pOwner->hps, CLR_DARKGREEN);
            GpiSetColor(pOwner->hps, CLR_YELLOW);
```

Figure 5.15. Listboxes: C source file. Continues.

Dialog boxes and their controls 133

```
  }
  else                                        /* Selected */
  {
    GpiSetBackColor(pOwner->hps, CLR_YELLOW);
    GpiSetColor(pOwner->hps, CLR_DARKGREEN);
  }
  WinSendDlgItemMsg(hwndDlg, ID_OLISTBOX,
                    LM_QUERYITEMTEXT, MPFROM2SHORT
                    (pOwner->idItem,
                    sizeof(szListBuff)),
                    MPFROMP(szListBuff));

  pszCountry = strtok(szListBuff, "\t");
  pszCapital = strtok(NULL, "\t");

  if (pOwner->idItem == 5)                    /* Finland */
    WinDrawText(pOwner->hps, strlen(pszCountry),
                pszCountry, &rcl, 0, 0,
                DT_LEFT | DT_TEXTATTRS |
                DT_ERASERECT | DT_HALFTONE);
  else
    WinDrawText(pOwner->hps, strlen(pszCountry),
                pszCountry, &rcl, 0, 0,
                DT_LEFT | DT_TEXTATTRS | DT_ERASERECT);

          /*--------------------------------------*/
          /* Draw next item in the right-hand rectangle */
          /* allowing for horizontal scrolling         */
          /*--------------------------------------*/

  if (pOwner->rclItem.xLeft < 0)
                            /* i.e. we have been scrolled */
    rcl.xLeft = rcl.xRight + pOwner->rclItem.xLeft;
  else
    rcl.xLeft = rcl.xRight;

  rcl.xRight = pOwner >rclItem.xRight;

  if (pOwner->idItem == 5)                    /* Finland */
    WinDrawText(pOwner->hps, strlen(pszCapital),
                pszCapital, &rcl, 0, 0,
                DT_LEFT | DT_TEXTATTRS |
                DT_ERASERECT | DT_HALFTONE);
```

Figure 5.15. Listboxes: C source file. Continues.

```
              else
                 WinDrawText(pOwner->hps, strlen(pszCapital),
                            pszCapital, &rcl, 0, 0,
                            DT_LEFT | DT_TEXTATTRS | DT_ERASERECT);
                                     /* Do not let PM highlight */
              pOwner->fsStateOld = pOwner->fsState = 0;
              return (MRESULT)TRUE;      /* Do not let PM draw    */

           case WM_CONTROL:
              switch(SHORT1FROMMP(mp1))
              {
                 case ID_SLISTBOX:
                    switch(SHORT2FROMMP(mp1))
                    {
                       case LN_SELECT:
                          sIdx = (SHORT)WinSendDlgItemMsg(hwndDlg,
                                        ID_SLISTBOX, LM_QUERYSELECTION,
                                        0, 0);
                          if (sIdx != LIT_NONE)
                          {
                             WinEnableWindow(WinWindowFromID(hwndDlg,
                                             ID_DELETE), TRUE);
                             WinSendDlgItemMsg(hwndDlg, ID_SLISTBOX,
                                             LM_QUERYITEMTEXT,
                                             MPFROM2SHORT(sIdx,
                                             sizeof(szCtry)),
                                             MPFROMP(szCtry));
                             WinSetDlgItemText(hwndDlg, ID_ENTRY3,
                                             szCtry);

                             /*-------------------------------------*/
                             /* Retrieve the key value, if that is all we */
                             /* have saved...                       */
                             /*                                     */
                             /* ulKeyValue = (ULONG)WinSendDlgItemMsg */
                             /*              (hwndDlg, ID_SLISTBOX,  */
                             /*               LM_QUERYITEMHANDLE,    */
                             /*               MPFROMSHORT(sIdx), 0); */
                             /* WinSetDlgItemShort(hwndDlg,ID_ENTRY2, */
                             /*    (SHORT)ulKeyValue, FALSE);        */
                             /* ----------------------------------- */
```

Figure 5.15. Listboxes: C source file. Continues.

```
              /*------------------------------------*/
              /* Or, retrieve all data associated with  */
              /* the listbox item...                */
              /*------------------------------------*/

              pDB_Data = (PDBDATA)WinSendDlgItemMsg
                              (hwndDlg, ID_SLISTBOX,
                               LM_QUERYITEMHANDLE,
                               MPFROMSHORT(sIdx), 0);
              WinSetDlgItemText(hwndDlg, ID_ENTRY1,
                              pDB_Data->szCapital);
              WinSetDlgItemShort(hwndDlg, ID_ENTRY2,
                  (SHORT)pDB_Data->usKey, FALSE);
            }
            break;

          default:
            break;
        }
        break;

      case ID_MLISTBOX:
        switch(SHORT2FROMMP(mp1))
        {
          case LN_SELECT:
            WinEnableWindow(WinWindowFromID(hwndDlg,
                        ID_PROCMULT), TRUE);
            break;

          default:
            break;
        }
        break;

      case ID_OLISTBOX:
        switch(SHORT2FROMMP(mp1))
        {
          case LN_SELECT:
            sOidx = (SHORT)WinSendDlgItemMsg(hwndDlg,
                        ID_OLISTBOX,
                        LM_QUERYSELECTION, 0, 0);
            if (sOidx == 5)        /* Do not allow Finland */
```

Figure 5.15. Listboxes: C source file. Continues.

```
                    {
                      DosBeep(1000, 100);
                      WinSendDlgItemMsg(hwndDlg, ID_OLISTBOX,
                         LM_SELECTITEM, MPFROMSHORT(sSavedIdx),
                         (MPARAM)TRUE);
                      break;
                    }
                    sSavedIdx = sOidx;
                    WinSendDlgItemMsg(hwndDlg, ID_OLISTBOX,
                       LM_QUERYITEMTEXT, MPFROM2SHORT(sOidx,
                       sizeof(szListBuff)),
                       MPFROMP(szListBuff));

                    pszCountry = strtok(szListBuff, "\t");
                    pszCapital = strtok(NULL, "\t");
                    WinSetDlgItemText(hwndDlg, ID_ENTRY1,
                                  pszCapital);
                    WinSetDlgItemText(hwndDlg, ID_ENTRY2, "");
                    WinSetDlgItemText(hwndDlg, ID_ENTRY3,
                                  pszCountry);
                    break;

                 default:
                    break;
               }
               break;
         }
         break;

      case WM_COMMAND:
         switch(SHORT1FROMMP(mp1))
         {
            case ID_DESELECT:
               WinSendDlgItemMsg(hwndDlg, ID_SLISTBOX,
                  LM_SELECTITEM, MPFROMSHORT(sIdx),
                  (MPARAM)FALSE);
               WinSendDlgItemMsg(hwndDlg, ID_OLISTBOX,
                  LM_SELECTITEM, MPFROMSHORT(sOidx),
                  (MPARAM)FALSE);
               WinEnableWindow(WinWindowFromID(hwndDlg,
                           ID_DELETE), FALSE);
               WinSetDlgItemText(hwndDlg, ID_ENTRY1, "");
```

Figure 5.15. Listboxes: C source file. Continues.

```
          WinSetDlgItemText(hwndDlg, ID_ENTRY2, "");
          WinSetDlgItemText(hwndDlg, ID_ENTRY3, "");
          return FALSE;

       case ID_DELETE:
          pDB_Data = (PDBDATA)WinSendDlgItemMsg(hwndDlg,
                              ID_SLISTBOX,
                              LM_QUERYITEMHANDLE,
                              MPFROMSHORT(sIdx), 0);
          DosSubFreeMem(BaseMem, pDB_Data,
                        sizeof(DBDATA));
          WinSendDlgItemMsg(hwndDlg, ID_SLISTBOX,
             LM_DELETEITEM, MPFROMSHORT(sIdx), 0);
          WinSetDlgItemText(hwndDlg, ID_ENTRY1, "");
          WinSetDlgItemText(hwndDlg, ID_ENTRY2, "");
          WinSetDlgItemText(hwndDlg, ID_ENTRY3, "");
          WinSendDlgItemMsg(hwndDlg, ID_SLISTBOX,
             LM_SELECTITEM, MPFROMSHORT(0), (MPARAM)TRUE);
          return FALSE;

       case ID_PROCMULT:
          WinSendMsg(hwndDlg, WM_COMMAND,
                     MPFROMSHORT(ID_DESELECT), 0);
          sMidx = (SHORT)WinSendDlgItemMsg(hwndDlg,
                         ID_MLISTBOX, LM_QUERYSELECTION,
                         (MPARAM)LIT_FIRST, 0);
          while(sMidx != LIT_NONE)
          {
             WinSendDlgItemMsg(hwndDlg, ID_MLISTBOX,
                LM_QUERYITEMTEXT, MPFROM2SHORT(sMidx,
                sizeof(szCtry)), MPFROMP(szCtry));

             WinSetDlgItemText(hwndDlg, ID_ENTRY3, szCtry);

                      /*---------------------------*/
                      /* DO NOT DO THIS IN PM PROGRAMS, */
                      /* AFFECTS PERFORMANCE SEVERELY */
                      /*---------------------------*/

             DosSleep(1000);
             WinSendDlgItemMsg(hwndDlg, ID_MLISTBOX,
                LM_SELECTITEM, MPFROMSHORT(sMidx),
                (MPARAM)FALSE);
```

Figure 5.15. Listboxes: C source file. Continues.

```
                sMidx = (SHORT)WinSendDlgItemMsg(hwndDlg,
                            ID_MLISTBOX,
                            LM_QUERYSELECTION,
                            (MPARAM)sMidx, 0);
            }
            WinSetDlgItemText(hwndDlg, ID_ENTRY3, "Done");
            DosBeep(500, 200);
            WinEnableWindow(WinWindowFromID(hwndDlg,
                            ID_PROCMULT), FALSE);
            return FALSE;
          case ID_EXIT:
            DosSubUnsetMem(BaseMem);
            DosFreeMem(BaseMem);
            WinRemoveSwitchEntry(WinQuerySwitchHandle
                            (hwndDlg, 0));
            WinPostMsg(hwndDlg, WM_QUIT, 0, 0);
            break;
          default:
            return FALSE;
        }
                                    /* Remove the dialog box */
        WinDismissDlg(hwndDlg, TRUE);
        break;
      default:
        return WinDefDlgProc(hwndDlg, msg, mp1, mp2);
   }
   return FALSE;
}
```

Figure 5.15. Listboxes: C source file. Concluded.

6
More controls

The introduction of OS/2 version 2.0 has brought about four new controls which will make program development easier and, at the same time, assist in conforming to the common user access (CUA) architecture. They are:

1. The slider
This control has two uses. The first enables the user to vary the value of a particular object, for example frequency, volume, temperature, etc. The other, which is readonly, is used as an indicator, for example a progress indicator. The first function was previously accomplished using the scroll-bar control, which was not what it was intended for, and up until now, there has been no control to facilitate the coding of an indicator.

2. The value set
The value set control is like a graphical radio button, that is, the user can select only one choice from a set of mutually exclusive choices. For example, a common use here would be a colour palette. Instead of a series of radio buttons, each with a description, the user would be presented with a series of colour bitmaps from which to choose, and since no text is needed, valuable screen space is saved.

3. The notebook
This control looks just like a real notebook, complete with binding, tabs and a 3D appearance. It is used to organize related data into pages, which makes it easier for the user to find. Its main use in OS/2 is to present the object settings to the user, for example the desktop settings.

4. The container
The container control is just that, a container. It holds objects and allows them to be viewed in different ways:

- *Icon*   Icons with text underneath.
- *Name*   Icons with text to the right.
- *Text*   Plain textual list.

- *Tree* Hierarchical list.
- *Details* Shows detailed information, for example, this view in `Drives` displays file attributes, last modification date and other information.

Since the container control belongs more to the object-oriented approach to programming, and is thus beyond the scope of this book, it will not be discussed further.

There is a sample program in the next chapter, Fig. 7.7, covering all the following controls in this chapter and the new dialogs discussed in Chapter 7. You should refer to this, as well as the sample code here, while reading the following. So, let us take a look at the first three of these controls in more detail.

6.1 The slider control

Before we start creating a slider let us just define a few terms:
- *Slider shaft* The area in which the slider arm moves.
- *Slider arm* The part the user moves within the shaft to vary the value.
- *Slider buttons* The slider arm can also be moved by clicking on these. They are positioned at one end of the shaft.
- *Tick mark* These indicate the incremental values. When a slider button is pressed the arm moves to the next value.
- *Detent* Like a tick mark but can be placed anywhere along the shaft, not just at incremental values. The slider arm can be positioned to a detent by clicking on it.
- *Ribbon strip* As the slider is moved the shaft is filled with a different colour between the home position, or base value, and the slider arm.

Now that we know the various components that go to make up a slider, let us create a couple. Assume we have an application that controls the filling of a large tank. Obviously, we need some means whereby we can control the flow of liquid into the tank, and at the same time observe the state of the tank. This is an ideal situation in which to use the slider, two of them in fact: one for the user to control the flow and the other, read only, to display the status, see Fig. 6.1.

Let us assume that the maximum flow rate is 100 gallons/second and the tank volume is 3000 gallons. These numbers were chosen just to keep it simple and make it possible to fill the tank in 30 seconds only.

Let us look at the control slider first. Before we can create any slider we need to fill a slider control data structure:

```
typedef struct _SLDCDATA
{
   ULONG    cbSize;                 /* Control block size                   */
   USHORT   usScale1Increments;     /* Number of divisions on scale         */
   USHORT   usScale1Spacing;        /* Space in pels between increments */
   USHORT   usScale2Increments;     /* Number of divisions on scale         */
   USHORT   usScale2Spacing;        /* Space in pels between increments */
} SLDCDATA;
```

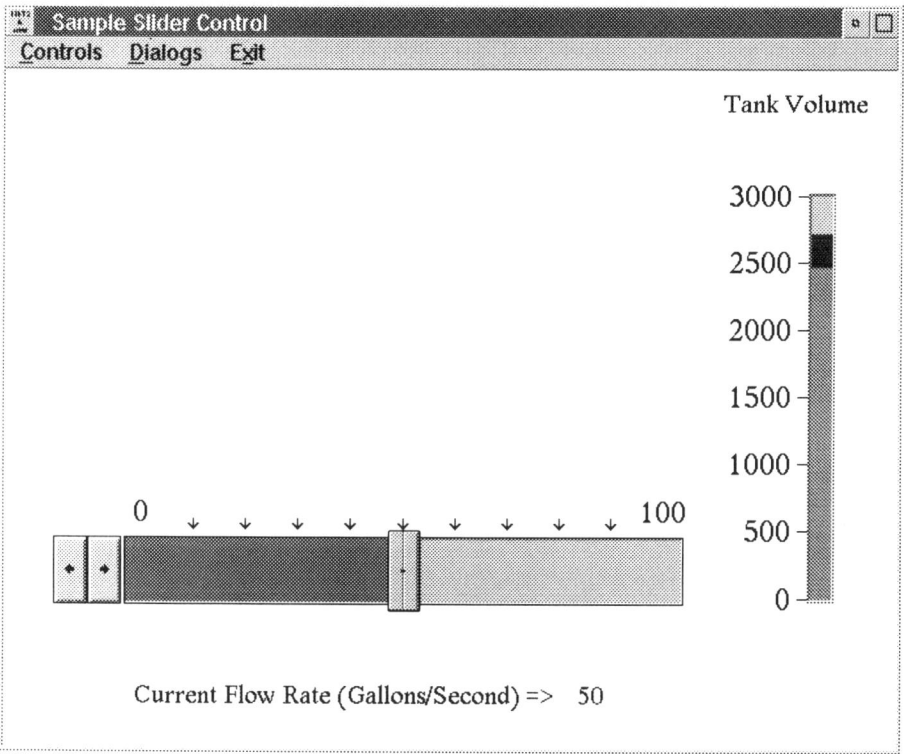

Figure 6.1. Controlling the rate of flow using a slider.

This structure defines the scale information and we specify here whether we want one or both scales. Scale 1 is drawn above a horizontal slider and to the right of a vertical slider. Scale 2 is drawn below a horizontal slider and to the left of a vertical slider. In our example we use scale 1 for the controller and scale 2 for the monitor. Now, our flow rate can vary from 0 to 100, and so if we set our incremental value to 10 this gives us a usScale1Increments value of 11; do not forget to allow for the zero. The next thing to define is the spacing; 40 pels/increment have been allowed, giving us a slider shaft of 400 pels. It is worth mentioning here that this has been assumed to run on a high-resolution screen, rather than overcomplicating the program to size itself according to window size or screen resolution. If you are using a VGA screen then you may want to change this value. However, it does fit on a VGA screen. Since we are only using one scale we set the final two variables in the structure to zero.

We now need to define the style for our control slider. The list of available styles is shown in Table 6.1. We will use a horizontal slider, complete with ribbon strip, buttons on the left and the shaft positioned at the bottom of the slider window. We therefore need to use the styles:

```
SLS_HORIZONTAL | SLS_BOTTOM | SLS_BUTTONSLEFT |
SLS_RIBBONSTRIP | SLS_OWNERDRAW
```

Table 6.1. Slider control styles

Style	Description
SLS_HORIZONTAL	Horizontal slider
SLS_VERTICAL	Vertical slider
SLS_CENTER	Centralize the shaft in the slider window
SLS_BOTTOM	Place the shaft at the bottom of the slider window (horizontal)
SLS_TOP	Place the shaft at the top of the slider window (horizontal)
SLS_LEFT	Place the shaft to the left of the slider window (vertical)
SLS_RIGHT	Place the shaft to the right of the slider window (vertical)
SLS_BUTTONSBOTTOM	Add buttons to the bottom of the shaft (vertical)
SLS_BUTTONSTOP	Add buttons to the top of the shaft (vertical)
SLS_BUTTONSLEFT	Add buttons to the left of the shaft (horizontal)
SLS_BUTTONSRIGHT	Add buttons to the right of the shaft (horizontal)
SLS_HOMEBOTTOM	Set the home position at the bottom of the shaft
SLS_HOMETOP	Set the home position at the top of the shaft
SLS_HOMELEFT	Set the home position at the left of the shaft
SLS_HOMERIGHT	Set the home position at the right of the shaft
SLS_PRIMARYSCALE1	Use scale 1 as the primary scale
SLS_PRIMARYSCALE2	Use scale 2 as the primary scale
SLS_OWNERDRAW	Ownerdraw for the ribbon strip, shaft, arm and background
SLS_READONLY	Read-only slider
SLS_SNAPTOINCREMENT	Snap the slider arm to the nearest increment
SLS_RIBBONSTRIP	Provide a ribbon strip

We have made it ownerdraw because when the slider window is painted it uses the default slider background colour, which is probably different from your background colour. So to make it blend in with our own colour scheme we can either create the slider ownerdraw and paint the background ourselves with our own background colour, `CLR_BACKGROUND`, or use `WinSetPresParam` to set it. Whenever any part of the slider needs to be drawn, we receive a `WM_DRAWITEM` message with `mp2` pointing to an `OWNERITEM` structure, just as we did for the ownerdraw listbox. The field `idItem` tells us which part needs to be drawn, so if it is the background we draw it, otherwise we pass it on to Presentation Manager for drawing:

```
POWNERITEM   pOwner;

case WM_DRAWITEM:
  pOwner = (POWNERITEM)mp2;
  if (pOwner->idItem == SDA_BACKGROUND)
  {
    WinFillRect(pOwner->hps, &pOwner->rclItem,
             CLR_BACKGROUND);
    return (MRESULT)TRUE;
  }
  return (MRESULT)FALSE;
```

We can now create our slider window and change its font if required using `WinSetPresParam`. The next thing to do is 'dress' it, that is, add any tick marks, detents, text or change the slider dimensions. For our control slider we use detents at each 10 gallon/second interval from 10 to 90 inclusively, and just add the home and maximum values as text. We also change the slider dimensions to make it much larger than the default. However, before we look at the code for this, look at the messages and their attributes that we can expect to use with this new control (Tables 6.2–6.4).

Table 6.2. Slider control messages and notification codes

Message	Description
SLM_ADDDETENT	Add a detent
SLM_QUERYDETENTPOS	Query the position of a detent
SLM_QUERYSCALETEXT	Query the text at a tick number
SLM_QUERYSLIDERINFO	Query the slider information
SLM_QUERYTICKPOS	Query the position of a tick
SLM_QUERYTICKSIZE	Query the size of a tick
SLM_REMOVEDETENT	Remove a detent
SLM_SETSCALETEXT	Set the text above a tick
SLM_SETSLIDERINFO	Set the slider parameters
SLM_SETTICKSIZE	Set the size of a tick
SLN_CHANGE	Slider position has changed
SLN_SLIDERTRACK	Slider has been dragged by the user
SLN_SETFOCUS	Slider is gaining the focus
SLN_KILLFOCUS	Slider is losing the focus

Table 6.3. Slider control message attributes

Attribute	Description
SMA_INCREMENTVALUE	Use increment values for slider arm positioning. Used in conjunction with SMA_SLIDERARMPOSITION
SMA_RANGEVALUE	Use pels for slider arm positioning. Used in conjunction with SMA_SLIDERARMPOSITION
SMA_SETALLTICKS	Set all tick marks to the specified size
SMA_SHAFTDIMENSIONS	Sets the height of a horizontal, or width of a vertical, slider shaft
SMA_SHAFTPOSITION	Sets the coordinates of the lower-left corner of the shaft in the slider window
SMA_SLIDERARMDIMENSIONS	Sets the height and width of the slider arm
SMA_SLIDERARMPOSITION	Sets the slider arm position

Table 6.4. Ownerdraw flag definitions

Definition	Description
SDA_BACKGROUND	Background about to be drawn
SDA_RIBBONSTRIP	Ribbon strip about to be drawn
SDA_SLIDERARM	Slider arm about to be drawn
SDA_SLIDERSHAFT	Slider shaft about to be drawn

Using all this information we can create our actual slider:

```
HWND CreateSlider(HWND hwnd)
{
  SLDCDATA   sldcData;
  ULONG      ulSliderStyle;
  HWND       hSlider;
  USHORT     I;
  CHAR       szText[5],
             szFont[15];

  sldcData.cbSize = sizeof(SLDCDATA);
                                  /* 0 -> 100 Gallons/Second */
  sldcData.usScale1Increments = 11;
  sldcData.usScale1Spacing    = 40;
  sldcData.usScale2Increment  = 0;
  sldcData.usScale2Spacing    = 0;
  ulSliderStyle = SLS_HORIZONTAL | SLS_BOTTOM |
                  SLS_BUTTONSLEFT | SLS_RIBBONSTRIP |
                  SLS_OWNERDRAW;
  hSlider = WinCreateWindow(hwnd, WC_SLIDER, "",
                            ulSliderStyle,
                            30, 100, 500, 100,
                            hwnd, HWND_TOP, ID_SLIDER,
                            &sldcData, 0);
  strcpy(szFont, "14.Tms Rmn");
  WinSetPresParam(hSlider, PP_FONTNAMESIZE,
                  sizeof(szFont), szFont);
  for (I = 40; I <= 360; I+=40)
    WinSendMsg(hSlider, SLM_ADDDETENT, MPFROMSHORT(I), 0);
  WinSendMsg(hSlider, SLM_SETSLIDERINFO,
             MPFROM2SHORT(SMA_SHAFTDIMENSIONS, 0),
             (MPARAM)50);
  WinSendMsg(hSlider, SLM_SETSLIDERINFO,
             MPFROM2SHORT(SMA_SLIDERARMDIMENSIONS, 0),
             MPFROM2SHORT(25,60));
  strcpy(szText, "0");
  WinSendMsg(hSlider, SLM_SETSCALETEXT, MPFROMSHORT(0),
             szText);
  strcpy(szText, "100");
  WinSendMsg(hSlider, SLM_SETSCALETEXT,
     MPFROMSHORT(sldcData.usScale1Increments - 1), szText);
  return hSlider;
}
```

We now have our finished slider, and all that needs to be done is show it, since it was created *invisible*:

```
WinShowWindow(hSlider, TRUE);
```

Now that we have drawn our control slider, we need to look at the monitor. Because we do not want the user interacting with this one, we make it read only. Again, we make it ownerdraw, but this time, as well as ensuring that the background matches the user's background colour, we also trap the drawing of the ribbon strip so that as long as the tank contents remain below 2500 gallons the strip is coloured green, but once this is exceeded it changes to red, conveying a visible warning. For this slider, which is vertical, we use scale 2, that is, the left-hand scale, and add tick marks, each with its own value:

```
HWND CreateMonitor(HWND hwnd)
{
  SLDCDATA   sldcData;
  HWND       hMonitor;
  ULONG      ulSliderStyle;
  USHORT     I;
  CHAR       szText[5],
             szFont[15];

  sldcData.cbSize = sizeof(SLDCDATA);
  sldcData.usScale1Increments = 0;
  sldcData.usScale1Spacing    = 0;
                  /* 0 -> 3000 Gallons (500/increment) */
  sldcData.usScale2Increments = 7;
  sldcData.usScale2Spacing    = 50;
  ulSliderStyle = SLS_VERTICAL | SLS_READONLY |
                  SLS_RIBBONSTRIP | SLS_OWNERDRAW |
                  SLS_PRIMARYSCALE2;
  hMonitor = WinCreateWindow(hwnd, WC_SLIDER, "",
                             ulSliderStyle,
                             550, 50, 150, 420,
                             hwnd, HWND_TOP, ID_MONITOR,
                             &sldcData, 0);
  strcpy(szFont, "14.Tms Rmn");
  WinSetPresParam(hMonitor, PP_FONTNAMESIZE,
                  sizeof(szFont), szFont);
  WinSendMsg(hMonitor, SLM_SETSLIDERINFO,
```

```
                MPFROM2SHORT(SMA_SHAFTDIMENSIONS, 0),
                (MPARAM)20);
   for (I = 0; I <= sldcData.usScale2Increments; I++)
   {
     _itoa(I*500, szText, 10);
     WinSendMsg(hMonitor, SLM_SETSCALETEXT, MPFROMSHORT(I),
              szText);
     WinSendMsg(hMonitor, SLM_SETTICKSIZE,
                MPFROM2SHORT(I, 8), 0);
   }
   return hMonitor;
}
```

Now that our sliders have been created, we need to be able to detect when the user has made a change to the control slider, thus altering the flow rate. This is done quite simply by checking the WM_CONTROL message for notification codes of SLN_CHANGE and SLN_SLIDERTRACK for our slider ID. The new slider position is obtained from mp2; it is then a matter of simple arithmetic to convert this figure to our real flow rate:

```
case WM_CONTROL:
  switch(SHORT1FROMMP(mp1))
  {
    case ID_SLIDER:
      switch(SHORT2FROMMP(mp1))
      {
        case SLN_CHANGE:
        case SLN_SLIDERTRACK:
          lNewPos = LONGFROMMP(mp2);
                    /* 40 pels represent 10 gallons/sec */
          lFlowRate = lNewPos/4;
          _ltoa(lFlowRate, szFlowRate, 10);
          WinSetWindowText(hFlowRate, szFlowRate);
          break;
        default:
          break;
      }
      break;
  }
  break;
```

Finally, we need to update the monitor with the new value. We do this by starting a one-second timer and in the processing of the WM_TIMER message we update the tank's capacity and convert it back to pels and update the slider arm:

```
case WM_TIMER:
  lVolume+= lFlowRate;

  if (lVolume > 2500)                       /* Sound warning */
    DosBeep(100,100);

  if (lVolume >= 3000)                      /* Empty tank    */
    lVolume = 0;

  lNewPos = lVolume/10;
  WinSendMsg(hMonitor, SLM_SETSLIDERINFO,
             MPFROM2SHORT(SMA_SLIDERARMPOSITION,
             SMA_RANGEVALUE), (MPARAM)lNewPos);
  break;
```

6.1.1 The user's view of a slider

To complete this section let us just take a look at how the user can operate the slider. The most obvious method is to select the slider arm with the mouse pointer and drag it to the relevant value. It can also be moved by clicking on the slider buttons, when the arm will move by increments in either direction according to which button is pressed. Clicking in the shaft area with mouse button 1 also has the same effect, whereas if mouse button 2 is used to click in this area the arm moves to that position. Last, but by no means least, if the slider has detents then by clicking on one the arm will move to that point.

As you can see, this control has great potential, and its programming simplicity is likely to ensure that it will be very widely used.

6.2 The value set control

Like the slider, before we can create a value set we must set up a control structure. This is called the value set control data structure:

```
typedef struct _VSCDATA
{
  ULONG   cbSize;              /* Control block size   */
  USHORT  usRowCount;          /* Number of rows       */
  USHORT  usColumnCount;       /* Number of columns    */
} VSCDATA;
```

This structure defines the number of rows and columns to use for a control. In our sample program we create two value sets, one displaying colour indices and the other displaying system bitmaps, see Fig. 6.2. For the colour value set we use two rows of eight columns to represent the 16 colours, and the bitmap value set has just two rows of two columns. Other items in a value set can be icons, text, or colour values and can be defined by using any of the styles shown in Table 6.5. Our sample

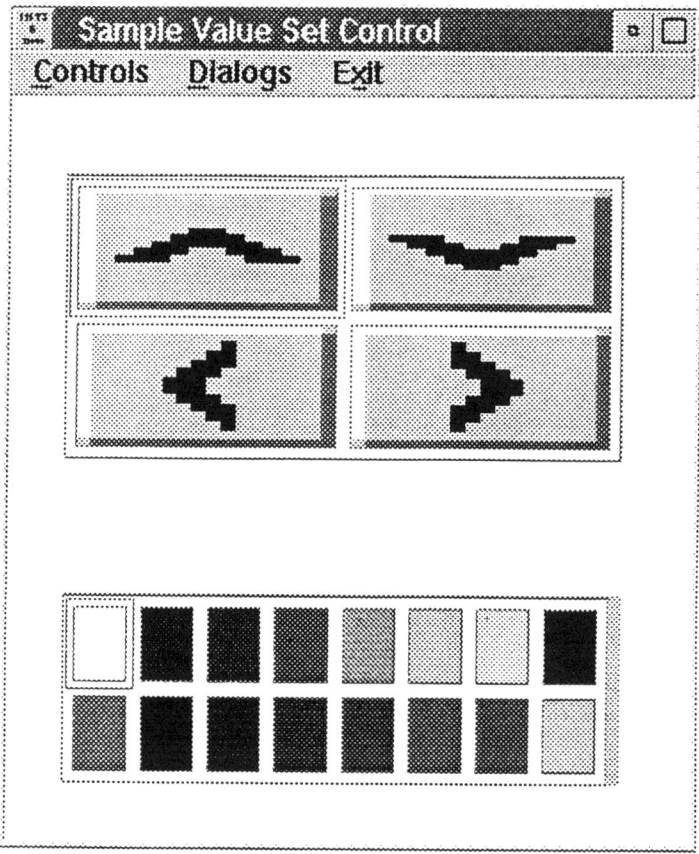

Figure 6.2. Two value sets.

Table 6.5. Value set control styles

Style	Description
VS_BITMAP	Default all items to bitmaps
VS_ICON	Default all items to icons
VS_TEXT	Default all items to text strings
VS_RGB	Default all items to colour information
VS_COLORINDEX	Default all items to colour indices
VS_BORDER	Add a border around the control
VS_ITEMBORDER	Add a border around each item
VS_SCALEBITMAPS	Scale bitmaps to cell size
VS_RIGHTTOLEFT	Support right to left ordering

program uses a value set to represent the 16 colour indices, so we use the styles:

VS_COLORINDEX | VS_BORDER | VS_ITEMBORDER

To improve the appearance of the items and the control we also use the border styles. Having decided on the style of our value set we simply load it by sending it VM_SETITEM messages:

```
HWND CreateVSet(HWND hwnd)
{
  VSCDATA   vscData;
  HWND      hVSet;
  ULONG     ulVSetStyle,
            ulColIdx;
  USHORT    usRow,
            usCol;

  vscData.cbSize = sizeof(VSCDATA);
  vscData.usRowCount    = 2;
  vscData.usColumnCount = 8;

  ulVSetStyle = VS_COLORINDEX | VS_BORDER | VS_ITEMBORDER;

  hVSet = WinCreateWindow(hwnd, WC_VALUESET, "",
                    ulVSetStyle,
                    30, 30, 300, 100,
                    hwnd, HWND_TOP, ID_VSET,
                    &vscData, 0);
  ulColIdx = 0;

  for (usRow = 1; usRow <= vscData.usRowCount; usRow++)
    for (usCol = 1; usCol <= vscData.usColumnCount; usCol++)
    {
      WinSendMsg(hVSet, VM_SETITEM,
                 MPFROM2SHORT(usRow, usCol),
                 MPFROMLONG(ulColIdx++));
    }
  return hVSet;
}
```

Now let us take a quick look at our bitmap value set. All we do here is load four system bitmaps, the up, down, left and right arrows, and use the style VS_SCALEBITMAPS so that they are scaled to the cell size when displayed. To load the bitmaps we use WinGetSysBitmap starting with the up arrow, that is, SBMP_SBUPARROW and store their handles in the array ahBitmap:

```
HWND CreateVSet2(HWND hwnd)
{
  VSCDATA   vscData;
  HWND      hVSet;
  HBITMAP   hbm,
            ahBitmap[3];
  ULONG     ulVSetStyle;
  USHORT    usRow,
            usCol,
            I;

  vscData.cbSize = sizeof(VSCDATA);
  vscData.usRowCount    = 2;
  vscData.usColumnCount = 2;

  ulVSetStyle = VS_BITMAP | VS_BORDER | VS_ITEMBORDER |
                VS_SCALEBITMAPS;
  hVSet = WinCreateWindow(hwnd, WC_VALUESET, "",
                          ulVSetStyle,
                          30, 200, 300, 150,
                          hwnd, HWND_TOP, ID_VSET2,
                          &vscData, 0);
  for (I = 0; I <= 3; I++)
  {
    hbm = WinGetSysBitmap(HWND_DESKTOP, I+SBMP_SBUPARROW);
    ahBitmap[I] = hbm;
  }
  I = 0;
  for (usRow = 1; usRow <= vscData.usRowCount; usRow++)
     for (usCol = 1; usCol <= vscData.usColumnCount; usCol++)
     {
       WinSendMsg(hVSet, VM_SETITEM,
                  MPFROM2SHORT(usRow, usCol),
                  MPFROMLONG(ahBitmap[I++]));
     }
  return hVSet;
}
```

Before we continue to process a value set selection, let us look at the messages and attributes that have been defined for this control (Tables 6.6 and 6.7).

When the user selects an item from a value set, a WM_CONTROL message is sent with a notification code of VN_SELECT. We can then send the control a

Table 6.6. Value set messages and notification codes

Message	Description
VM_QUERYITEM	Query the item at a location
VM_QUERYITEMATTR	Query the attributes of an item
VM_QUERYMETRICS	Query the metrics of a control
VM_QUERYSELECTEDITEM	Query the selected item
VM_SELECTITEM	Set the selected item
VM_SETCOLORMASK	Set the colour mask of an item
VM_SETITEM	Set the item at a location
VM_SETITEMATTR	Set the item attributes
VM_SETMETRICS	Set the metrics of a control
VN_DRAGLEAVE	Drag operation has left the control
VN_DRAGOVER	Drag operation is over the item
VN_DROP	Drop has occurred on an item
VN_DROPHELP	Request help for drop
VN_ENTER	Item has been entered by the user
VN_HELP	Help has been requested by the user
VN_INITDRAG	Drag has been initiated on an item
VN_KILLFOCUS	Value set is losing the focus
VN_SELECT	Item has been selected by the user
VN_SETFOCUS	Value set is gaining the focus

Table 6.7. Value set item attributes

Attribute	Description
VIA_BITMAP	Item contains a bitmap
VIA_ICON	Item contains an icon
VIA_TEXT	Item contains a text string
VIA_RGB	Item contains a colour value
VIA_COLORINDEX	Item contains a colour index
VIA_OWNERDRAW	Item is ownerdraw
VIA_DISABLED	Item is unselectable
VIA_DRAGGABLE	Item can be the source of a drag operation
VIA_DROPONABLE	Item can be the target of a drop operation

VM_QUERYSELECTEDITEM message to obtain the selected item; this returns the row and column numbers as two **SHORT** values. In the case of the colour value set, we can then send it a VM_QUERYITEM message to get the value of the selected item. Using this we force a repaint to change the client window background colour:

```
case WM_CONTROL:
  switch(SHORT1FROMMP(mp1))
  {
    case ID_VSET:
      switch(SHORT2FROMMP(mp1))
      {
        case VN_SELECT:
          ulSelItem = (ULONG)WinSendMsg(hVSet,
                          VM_QUERYSELECTEDITEM, 0, 0);
```

```
            ulWinCol  = (ULONG)WinSendMsg(hVSet,
                               VM_QUERYITEM, MPFROMLONG
                               (ulSelItem), 0);
            WinInvalidateRect(hwnd, NULL, FALSE);
            break;
          default:
            break;
        }
      }
      break;
```

Now, in the case of the other value set, we do not need to obtain a specific value, we just need to know what bitmap was selected. As was said earlier, VM_QUERYSELECTEDITEM returns two SHORTs, the first is the row number and the other is the column, so to obtain the selected bitmap number, assuming number 1 is the top-left bitmap we can use the following:

```
usBitmap = vscData.usColumnCount *
  (SHORT1FROMMR(ulSelItem) - 1) + SHORT2FROMMR(ulSelItem);
```

that is:

```
  Number of columns * (Selected Row - 1) + Selected Column
```

6.3   The notebook control

As was mentioned earlier, this control is used to group together related data. It is an extremely powerful control with many uses, and is very flexible, both in appearance and use. Certainly, its main use by OS/2 is to present to the user the enormous range of settings for each workplace object. It can be used by the application developer to group together several related dialog boxes and avoid any necessity for scrolling dialog boxes (something which they were never designed for), or multiple dialogs. Another use could be for holding static data, such as the OS/2 glossary.

Before we start building a notebook, let us define a few terms and look at the various styles, messages and attributes available. The notebook control is just like a real notebook, complete with a binding and 3D appearance. This appearance is achieved by partial showing of the back pages, and, assuming the binding is on the left, the default, you will see these to the right and bottom, intersecting at the bottom right where there are two pushbuttons for turning the pages. There are also tabs available, major and minor. The major tabs are always immediately opposite the binding, so the positioning of these tabs dictate the orientation of the notebook. At right angles to the major tabs are the minor tabs and, as expected, a major tab indicates a subject and the minor tab a subset of that subject. The minor tabs only show when their associated major tab has been selected to make it the top page, that is, the page in view. Finally, you can add a status line on each page which can be used to display any relevant information.

Tables 6.8–6.10 show the styles, messages, notification codes and attributes associated with this control.

Table 6.8. Notebook control styles

Style	Description
BKS_BACKPAGESBL	Back page intersection at the bottom left
BKS_BACKPAGESBR	Back page intersection at the bottom right
BKS_BACKPAGESTL	Back page intersection at the top left
BKS_BACKPAGESTR	Back page intersection at the top right
BKS_MAJORTABBOTTOM	Major tabs positioned at the bottom
BKS_MAJORTABLEFT	Major tabs positioned to the left
BKS_MAJORTABRIGHT	Major tabs positioned to the right
BKS_MAJORTABTOP	Major tabs positioned at the top
BKS_POLYGONTABS	Polygon-edged tabs
BKS_ROUNDEDTABS	Round-edged tabs
BKS_SOLIDBIND	Solid binding
BKS_SPIRALBIND	Spiral binding
BKS_SQUARETABS	Square-edged tabs
BKS_STATUSTEXTCENTER	Centralize status text
BKS_STATUSTEXTLEFT	Left justify status text
BKS_STATUSTEXTRIGHT	Right justify status text
BKS_TABTEXTCENTER	Centralize tab text
BKS_TABTEXTLEFT	Left justify tab text
BKS_TABTEXTRIGHT	Right justify tab text

Table 6.9. Notebook control messages and notification codes

Message	Description
BKM_CALCPAGERECT	Calculate page rectangle
BKM_DELETEPAGE	Delete a page
BKM_INSERTPAGE	Insert a page
BKM_INVALIDATETABS	Invalidate the tab area
BKM_QUERYPAGECOUNT	Query the number of pages
BKM_QUERYPAGEDATA	Query the page user data
BKM_QUERYPAGEID	Query the page identifier
BKM_QUERYPAGESTYLE	Query the page style
BKM_QUERYPAGEWINDOWHWND	Query the page window handle
BKM_QUERYSTATUSLINETEXT	Query the status line text
BKM_QUERYTABBITMAP	Query the tab bitmap handle
BKM_QUERYTABTEXT	Query the tab text pointer
BKM_SETDIMENSIONS	Set the tab dimensions
BKM_SETNOTEBOOKCOLORS	Set the notebook colours
BKM_SETPAGEDATA	Set the page user data
BKM_SETPAGEWINDOWHWND	Set the page window handle
BKM_SETSTATUSLINETEXT	Set the status line text
BKM_SETTABBITMAP	Set the tab bitmap
BKM_SETTABTEXT	Set the tab text
BKM_TURNTOPAGE	Turn to page
BKN_HELP	Help requested
BKN_NEWPAGESIZE	Page size has changed
BKN_PAGEDELETED	Page has been deleted
BKN_PAGESELECTED	New page has been selected

Table 6.10. Notebook control message attributes

Attribute	Description
BKA_ALL	Delete all pages
BKA_SINGLE	Delete a single page
BKA_TAB	Delete a tab section
BKA_LAST	Insert or query the last page
BKA_FIRST	Insert or query the first page
BKA_NEXT	Insert or query after the current page
BKA_PREV	Insert or query before the current page
BKA_TOP	Query the top page
BKA_MAJORTAB	Major tab
BKA_MINORTAB	Minor tab
BKA_PAGEBUTTON	Page turning button
BKA_STATUSTEXTON	Permit status area text
BKA_MAJOR	Insert a major tab
BKA_MINOR	Insert a minor tab
BKA_AUTOPAGESIZE	Automatically size the page window
BKA_END	Query to the end of the book
BKA_TEXT	Tab contains text data
BKA_BITMAP	Tab contains a bitmap
BKA_BACKGROUNDPAGECOLORINDEX	Page background colour
BKA_BACKGROUNDPAGECOLOR	Page background colour (RGB)
BKA_BACKGROUNDMAJORCOLORINDEX	Major tab background colour
BKA_BACKGROUNDMAJORCOLOR	Major tab background colour (RGB)
BKA_BACKGROUNDMINORCOLORINDEX	Minor tab background colour
BKA_BACKGROUNDMINORCOLOR	Minor tab background colour (RGB)
BKA_FOREGROUNDMAJORCOLORINDEX	Major tab text colour
BKA_FOREGROUNDMAJORCOLOR	Major tab text colour (RGB)
BKA_FOREGROUNDMINORCOLORINDEX	Minor tab text colour
BKA_FOREGROUNDMINORCOLOR	Minor tab text colour (RGB)

In order to illustrate how to create a notebook we will build a very simple address book (Fig. 6.3 (a) and (b)). To do this we read a text file of names and addresses, and for each initial letter of the surname we insert a major tab page, and for all the names starting with this letter we add minor tab pages. Now, since this is an exercise in creating a notebook only, no error-checking on input is included, and so the format is assumed correct, that is, of the form:

Name,House Number and Street,Town,County

For example:

Fred Smith,48 High Street,Anytown,Somecounty

Now, because we want to be able to move the notebook around and change its size, a standard window has been created into which the notebook is drawn. It is during the creation of this window that the notebook is created. Because we will use a spiral binding and major tabs (rounded) on the right with the back pages intersecting at the bottom right, we need the creation flags:

```
BKS_BACKPAGESBR | BKS_MAJORTABRIGHT | BKS_ROUNDEDTABS |
BKS_SPIRALBIND
```

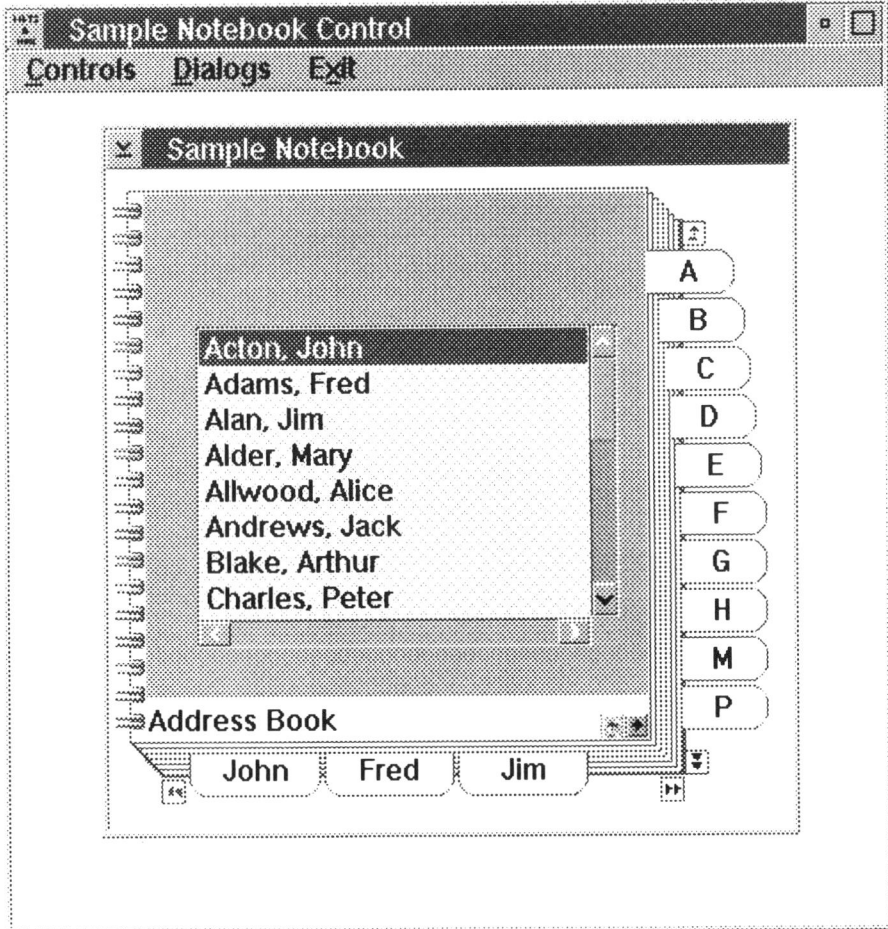

Figure 6.3. (a) Using a notebook control as an address book.

We also need larger tabs, especially for the minor tabs, since we will use these tabs to display the first name of each person. To do this we send the control a BKM_SETDIMENSIONS message for each tab:

```
WinSendMsg(hNotebook, BKM_SETDIMENSIONS,
         MPFROM2SHORT(50, 25),
         MPFROMSHORT(BKA_MAJORTAB));
WinSendMsg(hNotebook, BKM_SETDIMENSIONS,
         MPFROM2SHORT(75, 25),
         MPFROMSHORT(BKA_MINORTAB));
```

We are now ready to insert pages, but before we can do this we need to decide how to associate the page window with our application data. We can either use a dialog box or create our own window, just like any other Presentation Manager window,

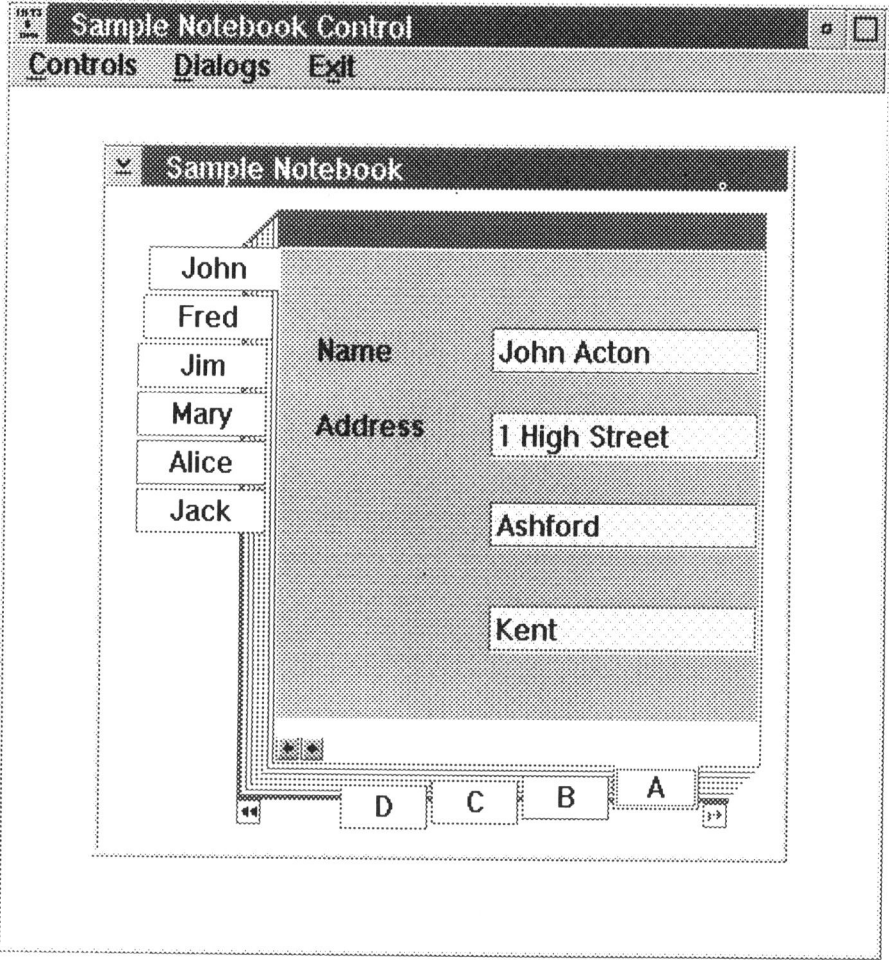

Figure 6.3. (b) Address page.

and associate that. However, for this example we will use a dialog box. In fact, we will use two dialog boxes, one for the major tab pages and the other for the actual names and addresses. Now each page has its own handle, but you can associate a handle with more than one page if desired, and, in fact, we will do just that here. Each major page will contain a listbox displaying all the names, this is the dialog box DLG_LISTPAGE and contains nothing but the listbox. So, each time a major tab is selected you will see the listbox. Another dialog box, DLG_PAGE, containing four read-only entry fields is associated with each page, and so each time we insert a page we must load another copy of the dialog box to associate with it. To associate a window handle with a page we send it a BKM_SETPAGEWINDOWHWND message.

Now let us look at the pseudo-code necessary for loading the notebook:

```
Open the data file
```

```
Load the major dialog box
While we still have records in the data file
{
   Parse input line (first name, last name, street,
                     town and county)
   If initial letter of last name has changed
      {
        Insert major tab page
        Set major tab text
        Associate dialog box window handle with major page
      }
   Insert minor tab page
   Set minor tab text
   Load the minor dialog box
   Fill dialog box with data
   Associate dialog box window handle with minor page
   Insert name into listbox in major dialog box
}
Close file
Show notebook
```

This translates to the following code:

```
bInit = '0';
szInit[1] = '\0';

if ((Names = fopen("NAMES.TXT", "r")) == NULL)
{
   DosBeep(100, 200);
   return (HWND)NULL;
}

hListPage = WinLoadDlg(hNotebook, hNotebook,
                       0, 0, DLG_LISTPAGE, 0);

while (fgets(szNameAddrBuf, 80, Names))
{
   strcpy(szName, strtok(szNameAddrBuf, ","));
   strcpy(szStreet, strtok(NULL, ","));
   strcpy(szTown, strtok(NULL, ","));
   strcpy(szCounty, strtok(NULL, ","));
                          /* Extract first and last names */
   strcpy(szFirstName, strtok(szName, " "));
   strcpy(szLastName, strtok(NULL, " "));
   if (bInit != szLastName[0])   /* Change of surname initial */
```

```c
    {
      bInit = szLastName[0];
      ulPageID = (ULONG)WinSendMsg(hNotebook,
                                   BKM_INSERTPAGE, 0,
                                   MPFROM2SHORT
                                   (BKA_MAJOR |
                                   BKA_AUTOPAGESIZE |
                                   BKA_STATUSTEXTON,
                                   BKA_LAST));
      szInit[0] = bInit;
      WinSendMsg(hNotebook, BKM_SETTABTEXT,
                 MPFROMP(ulPageID), szInit);
      WinSendMsg(hNotebook, BKM_SETSTATUSLINETEXT,
                 MPFROMP(ulPageID),
                 MPFROMP("Address Book"));
      WinSendMsg(hNotebook, BKM_SETPAGEWINDOWHWND,
                 MPFROMP(ulPageID), MPFROMHWND(hListPage));
    }
    ulPageID = (ULONG)WinSendMsg(hNotebook,
                                 BKM_INSERTPAGE, 0,
                                 MPFROM2SHORT(BKA_MINOR |
                                 BKA_AUTOPAGESIZE,
                                 BKA_LAST));
    strcpy(szMinorTab, szFirstName);
    WinSendMsg(hNotebook, BKM_SETTABTEXT,
               MPFROMP(ulPageID), szMinorTab);
    hPage = WinLoadDlg(hNotebook, hNotebook, 0, 0,
                       DLG_PAGE, 0);
    sprintf(szName, "%s %s", szFirstName, szLastName);
    if (szCounty[strlen(szCounty)-1] == '\n')
      szCounty[strlen(szCounty)-1] = '\0';
    WinSetDlgItemText(hPage, ID_NAME, szName);
    WinSetDlgItemText(hPage, ID_ADDR1, szStreet);
    WinSetDlgItemText(hPage, ID_ADDR2, szTown);
    WinSetDlgItemText(hPage, ID_ADDR3, szCounty);
    WinSendMsg(hNotebook, BKM_SETPAGEWINDOWHWND,
               MPFROMP(ulPageID), MPFROMHWND(hPage));
    sprintf(szName, "%s, %s", szLastName, szFirstName);
    WinSendDlgItemMsg(hListPage, ID_LISTBOX, LM_INSERTITEM,
                      MPFROMSHORT(LIT_END),
                      MPFROMP(szName));
```

```
}
fclose(Names);
WinShowWindow(hNotebook, TRUE);
```

Now we have loaded our notebook, let us look at how we process it. If you remember, we were going to make the notebook sizeable and movable, so we created a window in which to place it. This window's procedure then, traps the WM_SIZE message so that every time it is sized we can obtain its coordinates and redraw the notebook accordingly:

```
RECTL    rcl;
static   HWND    hNotebook;
 ;
 ;
case WM_SIZE:
  WinQueryWindowRect(hwnd, &rcl);
  WinMapWindowPoints(hwnd, WinQueryWindow(hwnd,
                   QW_PARENT), (PPOINTL)&rcl, 2);
  WinSetWindowPos(hNotebook, 0, rcl.xLeft, rcl.yBottom,
                   rcl.xRight-20, rcl.yTop-20, SWP_SIZE |
                   SWP_MOVE);
  break;
 ;
 ;
```

The only other thing we need to do is to ensure that, whenever the user presses a major tab, the items will be repositioned in the listbox such that the first item of the selected initial is displayed at the top of the listbox. Now, whenever a new page is selected, either by pressing a major or minor tab, a WM_CONTROL message is sent with a notification code of BKN_PAGESELECTED. We need to trap this and extract the tab text, and if this contains only one byte then we assume it is the major tab that has been requested and send that letter to the listbox control. This causes the next item starting with that letter to be selected, and we can then send the listbox an LM_SETTOPINDEX message to place that entry at the top. To avoid unnecessary flicker in the listbox, we call WinEnableWindowUpdate to switch off drawing to the listbox until we are ready to redisplay it, when we call WinShowWindow.

When a new page is selected, the second parameter in the WM_CONTROL message contains a pointer to a PAGESELECTNOTIFY structure, as follows, which contains information about the selected page:

```
typedef struct _PAGESELECTNOTIFY
{
  HWND     hwndBook;       /* Notebook window handle      */
  ULONG    ulPageIdCur;    /* Current top page identifier */
  ULONG    ulPageIdNew;    /* New top page identifier     */
} PAGESELECTNOTIFY;
```

The variable we are interested in is the new top-page identifier, since we need this to extract the tab text for that page. To do this we send the notebook a BKM_QUERYTABTEXT message specifying our page ID, and in return we obtain a pointer to a BOOKTEXT structure, as follows:

```
typedef struct _BOOKTEXT
{
  PSZ       pString;      /* Text string buffer      */
  USHORT    textLen;      /* Length of the text string */
} BOOKTEXT;
```

but before using this structure we must first initialize the pointer pString. We can then send the BKM_QUERYTABTEXT message:

```
PAGESELECTNOTIFY *pSelectedPage;
BOOKTEXT BookText;
HWND     hPage;
CHAR     szTabText[20],
         *TabText;
SHORT    sItem;
USHORT   usTabTextLength;
static   HWND hNotebook;
;
;
case WM_CONTROL:
  switch(SHORT1FROMMP(mp1))
  {
    case ID_NOTEBOOK:
      switch(SHORT2FROMMP(mp1))
      {
        case BKN_PAGESELECTED:
          pSelectedPage = (PAGESELECTNOTIFY *)mp2;
          TabText = szTabText;
          BookText.pString = TabText;
          usTabTextLength = (USHORT)WinSendMsg(hNotebook,
                                   BKM_QUERYTABTEXT,
                                   MPFROMLONG
                                   (pSelectedPage->
                                   ulPageIdNew),
                                   &BookText);

          if (usTabTextLength == 1)
                                /* Initial letter only in tab? */
```

```
                {
                  hPage = (HWND)WinSendMsg(hNotebook,
                                    BKM_QUERYPAGEWINDOWHWND,
                                    MPFROMLONG(pSelectedPage
                                    ->ulPageIdNew), 0);
                  WinEnableWindowUpdate(WinWindowFromID(hPage,
                                    ID_LISTBOX), FALSE);
                  WinSendDlgItemMsg(hPage, ID_LISTBOX, WM_CHAR,
                                    MPFROMSH2CH(KC_CHAR, 0, 0),
                                    MPFROM2SHORT((USHORT)
                                    szTabText[0], 0));
                  sItem = (SHORT)WinSendDlgItemMsg(hPage,
                            ID_LISTBOX, LM_QUERYSELECTION, 0, 0);
                  WinSendDlgItemMsg(hPage, ID_LISTBOX,
                            LM_SETTOPINDEX, MPFROMSHORT(sItem), 0);
                  WinShowWindow(WinWindowFromID(hPage,
                            ID_LISTBOX), TRUE);
                }
                break;
              default:
                break;
            }
            break;
        }
        break;
  ;
  ;
```

All these controls have been combined into a single program along with the new dialogs covered in the next chapter (see Fig. 7.7).

7
Standard dialogs

In Chapter 6 we briefly looked at some of the new controls introduced in version 2.0. In addition to these, two new dialogs were added, which will undoubtedly ease and standardize the tasks of file and font handling. They are:

1. The file dialog
This dialog has probably been written many times over in varying ways, until now. At last OS/2 has provided a standard way for the user to select, open and save files, making the programmer's job much easier.

2. The font dialog
Similarly, this dialog provides a standard approach to selecting fonts. It contains a sample area so that the user can see exactly what is being selected before making the final choice.

Let us look at these in turn.

7.1 The file dialog

With very little code on your part, this dialog lets you select one or more files to open from any drive or directory on your system. In addition, a filename can be entered directly—useful if creating a new file. The dialog can be tailored to limit which drives are to be displayed. Filenames can be filtered; for example, you may only want the user to see files with an extension of TXT. The dialog can also be implemented as a `Save As...` dialog.

Implementing a basic open dialog (Fig. 7.1) is quite straightforward provided you follow a few simple rules:

- Initialize a `FILEDLG` structure to `NULL`.
- Set the structure length field `cbSize`.
- Decide on the type of dialog you want by setting the fl flag field using a combination of `FDS_*` definitions. For example, if you want a centred, file open

Standard dialogs

![Sample Open Dialog screenshot showing Open filename PMSTDDLG.H, Type of file <All Files>, Drive E:, File list with PMSHL.H, PMSPL.H, PMSTDDLG.H (selected), PMTYPES.H, PMWIN.H, Directory list with E:\, TOOLKT20, C, OS2H, DASD, and Open and Cancel buttons.]

Figure 7.1 A file open dialog.

Table 7.1 File dialog styles

Style	Description
FDS_CENTER	Centre the dialog
FDS_CUSTOM	Use custom user template
FDS_FILTERUNION	Use union of filters
FDS_HELPBUTTON	Display Help button
FDS_APPLYBUTTON	Display Apply button
FDS_PRELOAD_VOLINFO	Preload volume information
FDS_MODELESS	Make dialog modeless
FDS_INCLUDE_EAS	Always load EA information
FDS_OPEN_DIALOG	Select Open dialog
FDS_SAVEAS_DIALOG	Select SaveAs dialog
FDS_MULTIPLESEL	Enable multiple selection
FDS_ENABLEFILELB	Enable SaveAs Listbox

dialog then use FDS_OPEN_DIALOG and FDS_CENTER. All the styles are shown in Table 7.1.

You can then optionally set other fields in the structure such as the dialog title, text for the OK pushbutton, an initial drive and directory. For convenience, the FILEDLG structure follows. When you exit from the dialog this structure is updated with your choice, the selected path and filename being returned in the field szFullFile. You can then call DosOpen and proceed. You can also tailor the dialog by providing your own dialog procedure and template, see the fields pfnDlgProc and hMod in the following structure:

```
typedef struct _FILEDLG
{
    ULONG     cbSize;                    /* Structure size             */
    ULONG     fl;                        /* FDS_* flags                */
    ULONG     ulUser;                    /* User defined               */
    LONG      lReturn;                   /* Return code from dialog    */
    LONG      lSRC;                      /* System return code         */
    PSZ       pszTitle;                  /* Dialog title               */
    PSZ       pszOKButton;               /* OK button text             */
    PFNWP     pfnDlgProc;                /* Entry point to custom      */
                                         /*   dialog procedure         */
    PSZ       pszIType;                  /* Pointer to string          */
                                         /*   containing initial       */
                                         /*   EA type filter           */
    PAPSZ     papszITypeList;            /* Pointer to table of        */
                                         /*   pointers that point      */
                                         /*   to null-terminated       */
                                         /*   Type strings             */
    PSZ       pszIDrive;                 /* Pointer to string          */
                                         /*   containing initial       */
                                         /*   drive                    */
    PAPSZ     papszIDriveList;           /* Pointer to table of        */
                                         /*   pointers that point      */
                                         /*   to null-terminated       */
                                         /*   Drive strings            */
    HMODULE   hMod;                      /* Custom file dialog         */
                                         /*   template                 */
    CHAR      szFullFile[CCHMAXPATH];    /* Initial or selected        */
                                         /*   fully qualified path     */
                                         /*   and file                 */
    PAPSZ     papszFQFilename;           /* Pointer to table of        */
                                         /*   pointers that point      */
                                         /*   to null-terminated       */
                                         /*   FQFname strings          */
    ULONG     ulFQFCount;                /* Number of files selected   */
    USHORT    usDlgId;                   /* Custom dialog ID           */
    SHORT     x;                         /* X coordinate of the        */
                                         /*   dialog                   */
    SHORT     y;                         /* Y coordinate of the        */
                                         /*   dialog                   */
    SHORT     sEAType;                   /* Selected file's EA Type    */
} FILEDLG;
```

Let us see what this translates to when we code it:

```
VOID OpenFile(HWND hwnd)
{
 FILEDLG OpenDlg;
 CHAR szText[CCHMAXPATH];

 memset(&OpenDlg, 0, sizeof(FILEDLG));
                                  /* Initialize FILEDLG to NULL */
 OpenDlg.cbSize = sizeof(FILEDLG); /* Set size                  */
 OpenDlg.fl = FDS_OPEN_DIALOG | FDS_CENTER;
                                  /* Open dialog and centred    */
 OpenDlg.pszTitle = "Sample Open Dialog";
                                  /* Dialog title               */
 OpenDlg.pszOKButton = "Open";    /* OK button text             */
 OpenDlg.pszIDrive = "D:";        /* Start with the D drive     */
                                  /* Display dialog             */

 WinFileDlg(HWND_DESKTOP, hwnd, &OpenDlg);
 if (OpenDlg.lReturn == DID_OK)   /* User pressed "Open"        */
 {
    sprintf(szText, "Selected File:\n%s", OpenDlg.szFullFile);
 }
 else                             /* User cancelled             */
    sprintf(szText, "Open Dialog Cancelled");

 WinMessageBox(HWND_DESKTOP, hwnd, szText, OpenDlg.pszTitle, 0,
               MB_INFORMATION | MB_OK | MB_MOVEABLE);
 return;
}
```

As you can see, a little effort goes a long way. Now let us look at the font dialog.

7.2 The font dialog

This dialog gives you a standard method whereby you can select a font, its style and its size. Whenever a font is selected, a sample is immediately displayed in a preview window (Fig. 7.2). Programming it is very similar to the file dialog, with just a few simple rules to follow:

- Initialize a FONTDLG structure to NULL.
- Set the structure length field cbSize.
- Assign the hpsScreen and/or the hpsPrinter fields.
- Pass a pointer to a buffer into which the selected font will be returned.
- Assign the font buffer's length.

You can optionally pass the dialog title, change the preview text, abcdABCD by default, and generally customize it as you can with the file dialog. Like the file

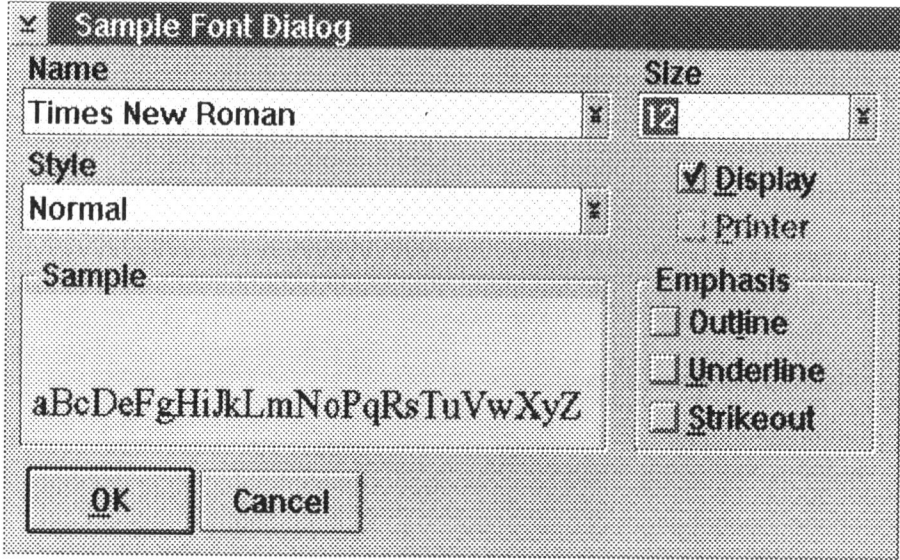

Figure 7.2. A font change dialog.

dialog, you can also provide your own dialog procedure and template. The font dialog styles are listed in Table 7.2.

Table 7.2. Font dialog styles

Style	Description
FNTS_CENTER	Centre the dialog
FNTS_CUSTOM	Use custom template
FNTS_OWNERDRAWPREVIEW	Application to draw the preview window
FNTS_HELPBUTTON	Display Help button
FNTS_APPLYBUTTON	Display Apply button
FNTS_RESETBUTTON	Display Reset button
FNTS_MODELESS	Make dialog modeless
FNTS_INITFROMFATTRS	Initialize from font attributes
FNTS_BITMAPONLY	Bitmap font only
FNTS_VECTORONLY	Vector font only
FNTS_FIXEDWIDTHONLY	Monospaced only
FNTS_PROPORTIONALONLY	Proportional font only
FNTS_NOSYNTHESIZEDFONTS	Do not synthesize fonts

The FONTDLG structure is as follows:

```
typedef struct _FONTDLG
{
  ULONG    cbSize;         /* Structure size                      */
  HPS      hpsScreen;      /* Screen presentation space           */
  HPS      hpsPrinter;     /* Printer presentation space          */
  PSZ      pszTitle;       /* Dialog title                        */
  PSZ      pszPreview;     /* Preview text                        */
  PSZ      pszPtSizeList;  /* Application provided size list      */
```

Standard dialogs

```
   PFNWP     pfnDlgProc;              /* Dialog subclass procedure    */
   PSZ       pszFamilyname;           /* Family name of font          */
   FIXED     fxPointSize;             /* Selected point size          */
   ULONG     fl;                      /* FNTS_* flags                 */
   ULONG     flFlags;                 /* FNTF_* state flags           */
   ULONG     flType;                  /* Font type option bits        */
   ULONG     flTypeMask;              /* Font types mask              */
   ULONG     flStyle;                 /* Selected style bits          */
   ULONG     flStyleMask;             /* Style bits mask              */
   LONG      clrFore;                 /* Selected foreground colour   */
   LONG      clrBack;                 /* Selected background colour   */
   ULONG     ulUser;                  /* Application use              */
   LONG      lReturn;                 /* Return code from the dialog  */
   LONG      lSRC;                    /* System return code           */
   LONG      lEmHeight;               /* Em height of the current font */
   LONG      lXHeight;                /* X height of the current font */
   LONG      lExternalLeading;        /* External leading of the font */
   HMODULE   hMod;                    /* Module to load custom template*/
   FATTRS    fAttrs;                  /* Font attribute structure     */
   SHORT     sNominalPointSize;       /* Nominal point size of the font */
   USHORT    usWeight;                /* Boldness of the font         */
   USHORT    usWidth;                 /* Width of the font            */
   SHORT     x;                       /* X coordinate of the dialog   */
   SHORT     y;                       /* Y coordinate of the dialog   */
   USHORT    usDlgId;                 /* ID of a custom dialog template */
   USHORT    usFamilyBufLen;          /* Buffer length                */
   USHORT    usReserved;              /* Reserved                     */
} FONTDLG;
```

So to generate a basic font dialog all we need to do is the following:

```
VOID ChgFont(HWND hwnd)
{
   FONTDLG   FontDlg;
   CHAR      szFamilyName[FACESIZE],
             szText[CCHMAXPATH];
   HPS       hps;

   szFamilyName[0] = '\0';              /* Initialize buffer             */
   hps = WinGetPS(hwnd);                /* Get presentation space        */
   memset(&FontDlg, 0, sizeof(FONTDLG));
                                        /* Initialize FONTDLG to NULL */
   FontDlg.fl = FNTS_CENTER;            /* Centre dialog                 */
   FontDlg.cbSize = sizeof(FONTDLG);    /* Set size                      */
   FontDlg.hpsScreen = hps;             /* Set presentation space        */
   FontDlg.usFamilyBufLen = FACESIZE;   /* Set buffer length             */
   FontDlg.pszFamilyname = szFamilyName;
                                        /* Pass pointer to buffer        */
```

```
    FontDlg.pszTitle = "Sample Font Dialog";
                                       /* Dialog title                */
    FontDlg.clrFore = CLR_RED;         /* Preview foreground colour */
    FontDlg.clrBack = CLR_YELLOW;      /* Preview background colour */
    FontDlg.pszPreview = "aBcDeFgHiJkLmNoPqRsTuVwXyZ";
                                       /* Preview text                */
    WinFontDlg(HWND_DESKTOP, hwnd, &FontDlg); /*Display dialog       */
    WinReleasePS(hwnd);                /* Return presentation space */
    if (FontDlg.lReturn == DID_OK)     /* User pressed OK             */
    {
       sprintf(szText, "Selected Font:\n%u.%s",
               FIXEDINT(FontDlg.fxPointSize),
    FontDlg.fAttrs.szFacename);
    }
    else                               /* User cancelled              */
       sprintf(szText, "Font Dialog Cancelled");
    WinMessageBox(HWND_DESKTOP, hwnd, szText, FontDlg.pszTitle, 0,
                  MB_INFORMATION | MB_OK | MB_MOVEABLE);
    return;
}
```

7.3 Sample program

This program demonstrates the use of sliders, value sets, notebooks, the file dialog and the font dialog.

The sliders, value sets and dialogs use the main window as their client areas, whereas the notebook uses a separate child window in which to be displayed. This allows it to be moved and sized. The main window has three menu options, Controls, Dialogs and Exit. The slider option simulates a simple control system depicting two sliders, one to control the water flow into a tank and the other to monitor the tank level. The value set option displays two controls, one for colour, which alters the client window colour, and the other showing four arrow bitmaps. Selecting any of these causes a warning beep to be sounded.

The notebook option displays a basic address book, the names and addresses being read from a file called NAMES.TXT. If you press mouse button 2, the notebook style is changed to a solid binding with the major tabs placed at the bottom. Pressing it again toggles the style back to the original. The two dialogs do not open the selected file or change the font, but when they are dismissed a message box pops up displaying your selection, as shown in Fig.7.3 for the font dialog.

All the controls and dialogs are created invisibly when the program starts. Selecting any one from the menu will show it and hide the previous choice.

The following listings show the program's header file, Fig. 7.4, resource file, Fig. 7.5, dialog template, Fig. 7.6, and C source file, Fig. 7.7.

Standard dialogs

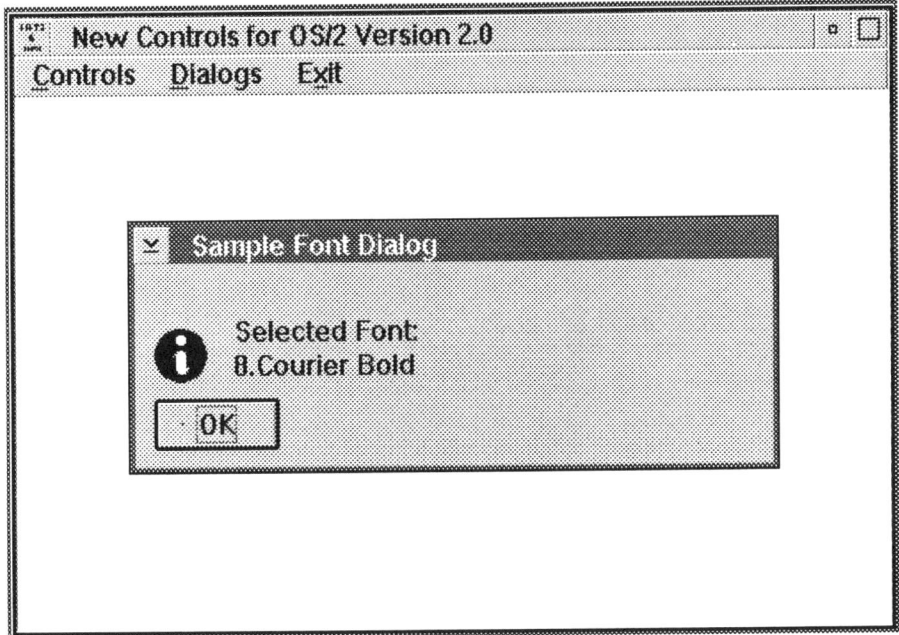

Figure 7.3. New font selected.

```
#define DLG_PAGE          100
#define ID_NAME           102
#define ID_ADDR1          104
#define ID_ADDR2          105
#define ID_ADDR3          106
#define ID_LISTBOX        107
#define DLG_LISTPAGE      200
#define ID_SLIDER         256
#define ID_MAINWND        257
#define ID_TITLE          258
#define ID_ICON           259
#define ID_TEXT1          260
#define ID_TEXT2          261
#define ID_FLOWRATE       262
#define ID_MONITOR        263
#define ID_VSET           264
#define ID_VSET2          265
#define ID_NOTECLIENT     266
#define ID_NOTEBOOK       267
#define MI_EXIT           300
#define MI_RESUME         301
#define MI_SLIDER         302
#define MI_VALUESET       303
#define MI_NOTEBOOK       304
#define MI_OPEN           305
#define MI_FONT           306
```

Figure 7.4. Version 2.0 controls and dialogs: header file.

```
#include <os2.h>
#include "newctrls.h"


STRINGTABLE PRELOAD
BEGIN
  ID_TITLE, "New Controls for OS/2 Version 2.0"
END

ICON          ID_MAINWND newctrls.ico

ACCELTABLE    ID_MAINWND
BEGIN
  VK_F3,      MI_EXIT,           VIRTUALKEY
END


MENU          ID_MAINWND PRELOAD
BEGIN
  SUBMENU "~Controls",                 1
  BEGIN
    MENUITEM "~Slider",              MI_SLIDER,      MIS_TEXT
    MENUITEM "~Value Set",           MI_VALUESET,    MIS_TEXT
    MENUITEM "~Notebook",            MI_NOTEBOOK,    MIS_TEXT
  END
  SUBMENU "~Dialogs",                  2
  BEGIN
    MENUITEM "~Open File",           MI_OPEN,        MIS_TEXT
    MENUITEM "~Change Font",         MI_FONT,        MIS_TEXT
  END
  SUBMENU "E~xit",                     3
  BEGIN
    MENUITEM "~Exit Program\tF3",    MI_EXIT,        MIS_TEXT
    MENUITEM "~Resume Program",      MI_RESUME,      MIS_TEXT
  END
END


rcinclude newctrls.dlg
```

Fig. 7.5. Version 2.0 controls and dialogs: resource file.

```
DLGINCLUDE 1 "NEWCTRLS.H"

DLGTEMPLATE DLG_PAGE LOADONCALL MOVEABLE DISCARDABLE
BEGIN
   DIALOG "", DLG_PAGE, 168, 59, 151, 96, NOT FS_DLGBORDER |
           WS_VISIBLE
   BEGIN
      LTEXT             "Name", 101, 10, 78, 36, 8
      ENTRYFIELD        "", ID_NAME, 62, 78, 74, 8, ES_MARGIN |
                        ES_READONLY | NOT WS_TABSTOP
      LTEXT             "Address", 103, 10, 61, 43, 8
      ENTRYFIELD        "", ID_ADDR1, 62, 59, 74, 8, ES_MARGIN |
                        ES_READONLY | NOT WS_TABSTOP
      ENTRYFIELD        "", ID_ADDR2, 62, 39, 74, 8, ES_MARGIN |
                        ES_READONLY | NOT WS_TABSTOP
      ENTRYFIELD        "", ID_ADDR3, 62, 16, 74, 8, ES_MARGIN |
                        ES_READONLY | NOT WS_TABSTOP
   END
END

DLGTEMPLATE DLG_LISTPAGE LOADONCALL MOVEABLE DISCARDABLE
BEGIN
   DIALOG    "", DLG_LISTPAGE, 168, 59, 151, 96, NOT FS_DLGBORDER |
             WS_VISIBLE
   BEGIN
      LISTBOX           ID_LISTBOX, 15, 11, 119, 76, LS_HORZSCROLL |
                        NOT WS_TABSTOP
   END
END
```

Figure 7.6. Version 2.0 controls and dialogs: dialog template.

```
#define     INCL_WINWINDOWMGR
#define     INCL_WINFRAMEMGR
#define     INCL_WINSWITCHLIST
#define     INCL_WINSYS
#define     INCL_WINSTATICS
#define     INCL_WINSTDSLIDER
#define     INCL_WINSTDVALSET
#define     INCL_WINSTDBOOK
#define     INCL_WINSTDFILE
#define     INCL_WINSTDFONT
#define     INCL_WINMENUS
```

Figure 7.7. Version 2.0 controls and dialogs: C source file. Continues.

```
#define     INCL_WINTIMER
#define     INCL_WINPOINTERS
#define     INCL_WINDIALOGS
#define     INCL_WINLISTBOXES
#define     INCL_WININPUT
#define     INCL_GPICONTROL

#define     UM_CLEAR        WM_USER

#include    <os2.h>
#include    <string.h>
#include    <stdlib.h>
#include    <stdio.h>
#include    "newctrls.h"

MRESULT     EXPENTRY MainWndProc (HWND, ULONG, MPARAM, MPARAM);
MRESULT     EXPENTRY NbookWndProc(HWND, ULONG, MPARAM, MPARAM);

HWND        CreateSlider(HWND);
HWND        CreateMonitor(HWND);
HWND        CreateVSet(HWND);
HWND        CreateVSet2(HWND);
HWND        CreateNotebook(HWND);
VOID        OpenFile(HWND);
VOID        ChgFont(HWND);

FILE        *Names;
/**************************************************************/
INT main(VOID)
{
  HAB       hab;
  HMQ       hmq;
  HWND      hwndFrame,
            hwndClient;
  QMSG      qmsg;
  ULONG     flFrameFlags;
  CHAR      szTitle[80];
  SWCNTRL   PgmEntry;
  LONG      lX_Left,
            lY_Bot,
            lHeight,
            lWidth,
            lScrHeight,
```

Figure 7.7. Version 2.0 controls and dialogs: C source file. Continues.

Standard dialogs

```
                lScrWidth;
/*************************************************************/
  hab = WinInitialize(0);
  hmq = WinCreateMsgQueue(hab, 0);
  WinRegisterClass(hab, "NewCtrls", MainWndProc, CS_SIZEREDRAW |
                   CS_CLIPCHILDREN, 0);
  WinRegisterClass(hab, "Notebook", NbookWndProc, CS_SIZEREDRAW,
                   0);
  WinLoadString(hab, (HMODULE)NULL, ID_TITLE, sizeof(szTitle),
                szTitle);
  flFrameFlags  = FCF_TITLEBAR | FCF_SYSMENU | FCF_MENU |
                  FCF_MINMAX | FCF_SIZEBORDER | FCF_ACCELTABLE |
                  FCF_ICON;
  hwndFrame = WinCreateStdWindow(HWND_DESKTOP, 0, &flFrameFlags,
                                 "NewCtrls", szTitle, 0,
                                 (HMODULE)NULL, ID_MAINWND,
                                 &hwndClient);
  lScrWidth  = WinQuerySysValue(HWND_DESKTOP, SV_CXSCREEN);
  lScrHeight = WinQuerySysValue(HWND_DESKTOP, SV_CYSCREEN);
  lWidth   = lScrWidth/4 * 3;
  lHeight  = lScrHeight/4 * 3;
  lX_Left  = (lScrWidth - lWidth) / 2;
  lY_Bot   = (lScrHeight - lHeight) / 2;
                                         /*--------------------*/
                                         /*  Start in foreground */
                                         /*--------------------*/
  WinSetWindowPos(hwndFrame, (HWND)NULL, lX_Left, lY_Bot, lWidth,
                  lHeight, SWP_SIZE | SWP_MOVE | SWP_SHOW |
                  SWP_ACTIVATE);
  PgmEntry.hwnd           = hwndFrame;     /*-------------------*/
  PgmEntry.hwndIcon       = (HWND)NULL;    /* Add to window list */
  PgmEntry.hprog          = (HPROGRAM)NULL;/*-------------------*/
  PgmEntry.idProcess      = (PID)NULL;
  PgmEntry.idSession      = (ULONG)NULL;
  PgmEntry.uchVisibility  = SWL_VISIBLE;
  PgmEntry.fbJump         = SWL_JUMPABLE;
  strcpy(PgmEntry.szSwtitle, szTitle);

  WinAddSwitchEntry(&PgmEntry);

  while (WinGetMsg(hab, &qmsg, (HWND)NULL, 0, 0))
     WinDispatchMsg(hab, &qmsg);
```

Figure 7.7. Version 2.0 controls and dialogs: C source file. Continues.

```
/*-----------------------------------*/
/* Remove from window list and clean up   */
/*-----------------------------------*/

  WinRemoveSwitchEntry(WinQuerySwitchHandle(hwndFrame, 0));
  WinDestroyWindow(hwndFrame);
  WinDestroyMsgQueue(hmq);
  WinTerminate(hab);
  return 0;
}

/****************************************************************/

MRESULT EXPENTRY MainWndProc(HWND hwnd, ULONG msg, MPARAM mp1,
                             MPARAM mp2)
{
  static    HWND  hFlowRate,
                  hFlowText,
                  hTankText,
                  hSlider,
                  hMonitor,
                  hVSet,
                  hVSet2,
                  hNoteFrame,
                  hNoteClient;
  static    LONG  lFlowRate,
                  lVolume,
                  lWinCol = CLR_BACKGROUND;
  HPS             hps;
  RECTL           rcl;
  LONG            lNewPos;
  ULONG           ulSelItem,
                  flFrameFlags;
  USHORT          usBitmap;
  CHAR            szFlowRate[5],
                  szFont[15];
  POWNERITEM      pOwner;
  switch (msg)
     {
       case WM_CREATE:
          flFrameFlags = FCF_TITLEBAR | FCF_SYSMENU | FCF_SIZEBORDER;

          hSlider   = CreateSlider(hwnd);
```

Figure 7.7. Version 2.0 controls and dialogs: C source file. Continues.

Standard dialogs 175

```
        hMonitor   = CreateMonitor(hwnd);
        hVSet      = CreateVSet(hwnd);
        hVSet2     = CreateVSet2(hwnd);

        hNoteFrame = WinCreateStdWindow(hwnd, 0, &flFrameFlags,
                                        "Notebook",
                                        "Sample Notebook",
                                         0, (HMODULE)NULL,
                                         ID_NOTECLIENT,
                                        &hNoteClient);

        hTankText = WinCreateWindow(hwnd, WC_STATIC,
                                    "Tank Volume",
                                     SS_TEXT, 550, 450, 150, 40,
                                     hwnd, HWND_TOP, ID_TEXT1, 0,
                                     0);
        hFlowText = WinCreateWindow(hwnd, WC_STATIC,
                                "Current Flow Rate (Gallons/Second) => ",
                                 SS_TEXT, 100, 10, 330, 40, hwnd, HWND_TOP,
                                 ID_TEXT2, 0, 0);
        hFlowRate = WinCreateWindow(hwnd, WC_STATIC, "0",
                                    SS_TEXT, 440, 10, 40, 40,
                                    hwnd, HWND_TOP, ID_FLOWRATE,
                                    0, 0);
        strcpy(szFont, "12.Tms Rmn");
        WinSetPresParam(hFlowText, PP_FONTNAMESIZE,
                        sizeof(szFont), szFont);
        WinSetPresParam(hTankText, PP_FONTNAMESIZE,
                        sizeof(szFont),szFont);
        WinSetPresParam(hFlowRate, PP_FONTNAMESIZE,
                        sizeof(szFont), szFont);
        break;

    case WM_PAINT:
        hps = WinBeginPaint(hwnd, (HPS)NULL, &rcl);
        WinQueryWindowRect(hps, &rcl);
        WinFillRect(hps, &rcl, lWinCol);
        WinEndPaint(hps);
        break;

    case WM_TIMER:
        lVolume+= lFlowRate;
```

Figure 7.7. Version 2.0 controls and dialogs: C source file. Continues.

```
        if (lVolume > 2500)                         /* Sound warning */
          DosBeep(100,100);

        if (lVolume >= 3000)                        /* Empty tank    */
          lVolume = 0;

        lNewPos = lVolume/10;
        WinSendMsg(hMonitor, SLM_SETSLIDERINFO,
                   MPFROM2SHORT(SMA_SLIDERARMPOSITION,
                   SMA_RANGEVALUE), (MPARAM)lNewPos);
        break;

      case WM_DRAWITEM:
        pOwner = (POWNERITEM)mp2;
        if (pOwner->idItem == SDA_BACKGROUND)
        {
          WinFillRect(pOwner->hps, &pOwner->rclItem, lWinCol);
          return (MRESULT)TRUE;
        }
        if (pOwner->idItem == SDA_RIBBONSTRIP &&
            SHORT1FROMMP(mp1) == ID_MONITOR)
        {
          if (lVolume <= 2500)
            WinFillRect(pOwner->hps, &pOwner->rclItem, CLR_GREEN);
          else
            WinFillRect(pOwner->hps, &pOwner->rclItem, CLR_RED);
          return (MRESULT)TRUE;
        }
        return (MRESULT)FALSE;

      case WM_CONTROL:
        switch(SHORT1FROMMP(mp1))
        {
          case ID_SLIDER:
            switch(SHORT2FROMMP(mp1))
            {
              case SLN_CHANGE:
              case SLN_SLIDERTRACK:
                lNewPos = LONGFROMMP(mp2);
                lFlowRate = lNewPos/4;
                               /* 40 pels represent 10 gallons/sec */
                _ltoa(lFlowRate, szFlowRate, 10);
                WinSetWindowText(hFlowRate, szFlowRate);
                break;

              default:
```

Figure 7.7. Version 2.0 controls and dialogs: C source file. Continues.

```
          break;
      }
      break;
  case ID_VSET:
    switch(SHORT2FROMMP(mp1))
    {
      case VN_SELECT:
        ulSelItem = (ULONG)WinSendMsg(hVSet,
                          VM_QUERYSELECTEDITEM, 0, 0);
        lWinCol = (ULONG)WinSendMsg(hVSet, VM_QUERYITEM,
                         MPFROMLONG(ulSelItem), 0);
        WinSetPresParam(hFlowRate, PP_BACKGROUNDCOLORINDEX,
                     sizeof(lWinCol), &lWinCol);
        WinSetPresParam(hFlowText, PP_BACKGROUNDCOLORINDEX,
                     sizeof(lWinCol), &lWinCol);
        WinSetPresParam(hTankText, PP_BACKGROUNDCOLORINDEX,
                     sizeof(lWinCol), &lWinCol);
        WinSetPresParam(hVSet, PP_BACKGROUNDCOLORINDEX,
                     sizeof(lWinCol), &lWinCol);
        WinSetPresParam(hVSet2, PP_BACKGROUNDCOLORINDEX,
                     sizeof(lWinCol), &lWinCol);
        WinInvalidateRect(hwnd, NULL, FALSE);
         break;

      default:
         break;
    }
    break;
  case ID_VSET2:
    switch(SHORT2FROMMP(mp1))
    {
      case VN_SELECT:
        ulSelItem = (ULONG)WinSendMsg(hVSet2,
                          VM_QUERYSELECTEDITEM, 0, 0);
        usBitmap = 2 * (SHORT1FROMMR(ulSelItem) - 1) +
                   SHORT2FROMMR(ulSelItem);
        DosBeep(1000*usBitmap, 100);
        break;

      default:
        break;
    }
    break;
```

Figure 7.7. Version 2.0 controls and dialogs: C source file. Continues.

```
      }
      break;
    case UM_CLEAR:
      WinStopTimer(WinQueryAnchorBlock(hwnd), hwnd, 1);
      WinShowWindow(hSlider, FALSE);
      WinShowWindow(hMonitor, FALSE);
      WinShowWindow(hFlowText, FALSE);
      WinShowWindow(hTankText, FALSE);
      WinShowWindow(hFlowRate, FALSE);
      WinShowWindow(hVSet, FALSE);
      WinShowWindow(hVSet2, FALSE);
      WinShowWindow(hNoteFrame, FALSE);
      WinInvalidateRect(hwnd, NULL, FALSE);
      break;
    case WM_COMMAND:
      switch (SHORT1FROMMP(mp1))
        {
        case MI_SLIDER:
          lVolume = 0;
          WinSetWindowText(WinQueryWindow(hwnd, QW_PARENT),
                           "Sample Slider Control");
          WinSendMsg(hwnd, UM_CLEAR, 0, 0);
                                                       /* 1 second timer */
          WinStartTimer(WinQueryAnchorBlock(hwnd), hwnd, 1, 1000);
          WinShowWindow(hSlider, TRUE);
          WinShowWindow(hMonitor, TRUE);
          WinShowWindow(hFlowText, TRUE);
          WinShowWindow(hTankText, TRUE);
          WinShowWindow(hFlowRate, TRUE);
          break;
        case MI_VALUESET:
          WinSetWindowText(WinQueryWindow(hwnd, QW_PARENT),
                           "Sample Value Set Control");
          WinSendMsg(hwnd, UM_CLEAR, 0, 0);
          WinShowWindow(hVSet, TRUE);
          WinShowWindow(hVSet2, TRUE);
          break;
        case MI_NOTEBOOK:
          WinSetWindowText(WinQueryWindow(hwnd, QW_PARENT),
                           "Sample Notebook Control");
          WinSendMsg(hwnd, UM_CLEAR, 0, 0);
          WinSetWindowPos(hNoteFrame, 0, 50, 50, 400, 400,
                          SWP_SIZE | SWP_MOVE);
```

Figure 7.7. Version 2.0 controls and dialogs: C source file. Continues.

```
          WinShowWindow(hNoteFrame, TRUE);
          break;
        case MI_OPEN:
          WinSendMsg(hwnd, UM_CLEAR, 0, 0);
          OpenFile(hwnd);
          break;
        case MI_FONT:
          WinSendMsg(hwnd, UM_CLEAR, 0, 0);
          ChgFont(hwnd);
          break;
        case MI_EXIT:
          WinPostMsg(hwnd, WM_QUIT, 0, 0);
          break;
        default:
          break;
        }
      break;
    case WM_ERASEBACKGROUND:
        return (MRESULT)TRUE;
   }
   return WinDefWindowProc(hwnd, msg, mp1, mp2);
}
/*****************************************************************/
HWND CreateSlider(HWND hwnd)
{
   SLDCDATA  sldcData;
   HWND      hSlider;
   ULONG     ulSliderStyle;
   USHORT    I;
   CHAR      szText[5],
             szFont[15];
   sldcData.cbSize = sizeof(SLDCDATA);
   sldcData.usScale1Increments = 11;      /* 0 - 100 Gallons/Second */
   sldcData.usScale1Spacing    = 40;
   sldcData.usScale2Increments = 0;
   sldcData.usScale2Spacing    = 0;
   ulSliderStyle = SLS_HORIZONTAL | SLS_BOTTOM | SLS_BUTTONSLEFT |
                   SLS_RIBBONSTRIP | SLS_OWNERDRAW;
   hSlider = WinCreateWindow(hwnd, WC_SLIDER, "", ulSliderStyle,
                             30, 100, 500, 100, hwnd, HWND_TOP,
```

Figure 7.7. Version 2.0 controls and dialogs: C source file. Continues.

```
                            ID_SLIDER,&sldcData, 0);
  strcpy(szFont, "14.Tms Rmn");
  WinSetPresParam(hSlider, PP_FONTNAMESIZE, sizeof(szFont),
                  szFont);
  for (I = 40; I <= 360; I+=40)
   WinSendMsg(hSlider, SLM_ADDDETENT, MPFROMSHORT(I), 0);
  WinSendMsg(hSlider, SLM_SETSLIDERINFO,
             MPFROM2SHORT(SMA_SHAFTDIMENSIONS, 0), (MPARAM)50);
  WinSendMsg(hSlider, SLM_SETSLIDERINFO,
             MPFROM2SHORT(SMA_SLIDERARMDIMENSIONS, 0),
             MPFROM2SHORT(25,60));
  strcpy(szText, "0");
  WinSendMsg(hSlider, SLM_SETSCALETEXT, MPFROMSHORT(0), szText);
  strcpy(szText, "100");
  WinSendMsg(hSlider, SLM_SETSCALETEXT, MPFROMSHORT
             (sldcData.usScale1Increments - 1), szText);
  return hSlider;
}
/****************************************************************/
HWND CreateMonitor(HWND hwnd)
{
  SLDCDATA sldcData;
  HWND     hMonitor;
  ULONG    ulSliderStyle;
  USHORT   I;
  CHAR     szText[5],
           szFont[15];
  sldcData.cbSize = sizeof(SLDCDATA);
  sldcData.usScale1Increments = 0;
  sldcData.usScale1Spacing = 0;
  sldcData.usScale2Increments = 7;
                          /* 0 -> 3000 Gallons (500/increment) */
  sldcData.usScale2Spacing = 50;
  ulSliderStyle = SLS_VERTICAL | SLS_READONLY | SLS_RIBBONSTRIP |
                  SLS_OWNERDRAW | SLS_PRIMARYSCALE2;
  hMonitor = WinCreateWindow(hwnd, WC_SLIDER, "", ulSliderStyle,
                             550, 50, 150, 420,
                             hwnd, HWND_TOP, ID_MONITOR, &sldcData,
                             0);
  strcpy(szFont, "14.Tms Rmn");
  WinSetPresParam(hMonitor, PP_FONTNAMESIZE, sizeof(szFont),
szFont);
```

Figure 7.7. Version 2.0 controls and dialogs: C source file. Continues.

```
   WinSendMsg(hMonitor, SLM_SETSLIDERINFO, MPFROM2SHORT
              (SMA_SHAFTDIMENSIONS, 0), (MPARAM)20);
   for (I = 0; I <= sldcData.usScale2Increments; I++)
   {
      _itoa(I*500, szText, 10);
      WinSendMsg(hMonitor, SLM_SETSCALETEXT, MPFROMSHORT(I),
szText);
      WinSendMsg(hMonitor, SLM_SETTICKSIZE, MPFROM2SHORT(I, 8), 0);
   }
   return hMonitor;
}

/****************************************************************/

HWND CreateVSet(HWND hwnd)
{
   VSCDATA   vscData;
   HWND      hVSet;
   ULONG     ulVSetStyle,
             ulColIdx;
   LONG      lWinCol;
   USHORT    usRow,
             usCol;

   vscData.cbSize = sizeof(VSCDATA);
   vscData.usRowCount    = 2;
   vscData.usColumnCount = 8;

   ulVSetStyle = VS_COLORINDEX | VS_BORDER | VS_ITEMBORDER;

   hVSet = WinCreateWindow(hwnd, WC_VALUESET, "", ulVSetStyle,
                           30, 30, 300, 100, hwnd, HWND _ TOP,
                           ID_VSET, &vscData, 0);
   lWinCol = CLR_BACKGROUND;
   WinSetPresParam(hVSet, PP_BACKGROUNDCOLORINDEX,
                   sizeof(lWinCol), &lWinCol);
   ulColIdx = 0;
   for (usRow = 1; usRow <= vscData.usRowCount; usRow++)
    for (usCol _ 1, usCol <_ vscData.usColumnCount; usCol++)
    {
      WinSendMsg(hVSet, VM_SETITEM, MPFROM2SHORT(usRow, usCol),
                 MPFROMLONG(ulColIdx++));
    }
   return hVSet;
}
```

Figure 7.7. Version 2.0 controls and dialogs: C source file. Continues.

```
/****************************************************************/
HWND CreateVSet2(HWND hwnd)
{
  VSCDATA  vscData;
  HWND     hVSet;
  HBITMAP  hbm,
           ahBitmap[4];
  ULONG    ulVSetStyle;
  LONG     lWinCol;
  USHORT   usRow,
           usCol,
           I;

  vscData.cbSize = sizeof(VSCDATA);
  vscData.usRowCount = 2;
  vscData.usColumnCount = 2;

  ulVSetStyle = VS_BITMAP | VS_BORDER | VS_ITEMBORDER |
                VS_SCALEBITMAPS;

  hVSet = WinCreateWindow(hwnd, WC_VALUESET, "", ulVSetStyle, 30,
                          200, 300, 150, hwnd, HWND_TOP, ID_VSET2,
                          &vscData, 0);

  lWinCol = CLR_BACKGROUND;
  WinSetPresParam(hVSet, PP_BACKGROUNDCOLORINDEX,
                  sizeof(lWinCol), &lWinCol);
  for (I = 0; I <= 3; I++)
  {
    hbm = WinGetSysBitmap(HWND_DESKTOP, I+SBMP_SBUPARROW);
    ahBitmap[I] = hbm;
  }
  I = 0;
  for (usRow = 1; usRow <= vscData.usRowCount; usRow++)
   for (usCol = 1; usCol <= vscData.usColumnCount; usCol++)
   {
     WinSendMsg(hVSet, VM_SETITEM, MPFROM2SHORT(usRow, usCol),
                MPFROMLONG(ahBitmap[I++]));
   }
  return hVSet;
}
/****************************************************************/
MRESULT EXPENTRY NbookWndProc(HWND hwnd, ULONG msg, MPARAM mp1,
                              MPARAM mp2)
```

Figure 7.7. Version 2.0 controls and dialogs: C source file. Continues.

```c
{
   PAGESELECTNOTIFY  *pSelectedPage;
   BOOKTEXT BookText;
   HWND     hPage;
   CHAR     szTabText[20],
            *TabText;
   RECTL    rcl;
   SHORT    sItem;
   USHORT   usTabTextLength;
   static   HWND hNotebook;
   static   BOOL fVert = FALSE;

   switch (msg)
     {
      case WM_CREATE:
        hNotebook = CreateNotebook(hwnd);
        if (!hNotebook)
        {
           WinMessageBox(HWND_DESKTOP, hwnd,
                       "Cannot find NAMES.TXT",
                       "Notebook Failure", 0,
                       MB_ERROR | MB_OK | MB_MOVEABLE);
           return (MRESULT)TRUE;          /* Discontinue creation */
        }
        break;
      case WM_SIZE:
       WinQueryWindowRect(hwnd, &rcl);
       WinMapWindowPoints(hwnd, WinQueryWindow(hwnd, QW_PARENT),
                     (PPOINTL)&rcl, 2);
       WinSetWindowPos (hNotebook, 0, rcl.xLeft, rcl.yBottom,
                     rcl.xRight-20, rcl.yTop-20, SWP_SIZE |
                     SWP_MOVE);
       break;

      case WM_CONTROL:
        switch(SHORT1FROMMP(mp1))
        {
           case ID_NOTEBOOK:
             switch(SHORT2FROMMP(mp1))
        {
         case BKN_PAGESELECTED:
           pSelectedPage = (PAGESELECTNOTIFY *)mp2;
           TabText = szTabText;
           BookText.pString = TabText;
```

Figure 7.7. Version 2.0 controls and dialogs: C source file. Continues.

```
                    usTabTextLength = (USHORT)WinSendMsg (hNotebook,
                                    BKM_QUERYTABTEXT, MPFROMLONG
                                    (pSelectedPage->ulPageIdNew),
                                    &BookText);
              if (usTabTextLength == 1)    /* Initial letter only in tab? */
              {
                hPage = (HWND)WinSendMsg(hNotebook,
                                    BKM_QUERYPAGEWINDOWHWND,
                                    MPFROMLONG
                                    (pSelectedPage->ulPageIdNew),
                                    0);
                WinEnableWindowUpdate (WinWindowFromID(hPage,
                                    ID_LISTBOX), FALSE);
                WinSendDlgItemMsg(hPage, ID_LISTBOX, WM_CHAR,
                                    MPFROMSH2CH(KC_CHAR, 0, 0),
                                    MPFROM2SHORT((USHORT)szTabText[0],
                                    0));
                sItem = (SHORT)WinSendDlgItemMsg(hPage, ID_LISTBOX,
                                    LM_QUERYSELECTION, 0, 0);
                WinSendDlgItemMsg(hPage, ID_LISTBOX, LM_SETTOPINDEX,
                                    MPFROMSHORT(sItem), 0);
                WinShowWindow(WinWindowFromID(hPage, ID_LISTBOX),
                                    TRUE);
              }
              break;
            default:
              break;
          }
          break;
        }
        break;

    case WM_BUTTON2DOWN:
    {
       ULONG   ulNotebookStyle;

       fVert = !fVert;

       if (fVert)
         ulNotebookStyle = BKS_BACKPAGESBL | BKS_MAJORTABBOTTOM |
                           BKS_SQUARETABS;
       else
         ulNotebookStyle = BKS_BACKPAGESBR | BKS_MAJORTABRIGHT |
                           BKS_ROUNDEDTABS | BKS_SPIRALBIND;

       WinSetWindowULong(hNotebook, QWL_STYLE, ulNotebookStyle);
```

Figure 7.7. Version 2.0 controls and dialogs: C source file. Continues.

```c
      WinShowWindow(hNotebook, TRUE);
    }
    break;

  case WM_CLOSE:
    WinShowWindow(WinQueryWindow(hwnd, QW_PARENT), FALSE);
    return (MRESULT)FALSE;

  case WM_ERASEBACKGROUND:
     return (MRESULT)TRUE;

  }
  return WinDefWindowProc(hwnd, msg, mp1, mp2);
}
/**************************************************************/
HWND CreateNotebook(HWND hwnd)
{
  HWND    hNotebook,
          hListPage,
          hPage;
  ULONG   ulNotebookStyle,
          ulPageID;
  LONG    lWinCol;
  CHAR    szMinorTab[15],
          szNameAddrBuf[80],
          szFirstName[15],
          szLastName[15],
          szName[30],
          szStreet[30],
          szTown[30],
          szCounty[30],
          szInit[2];
  BYTE    bInit;

  if ((Names = fopen("NAMES.TXT", "r")) == NULL)
    return 0;

  ulNotebookStyle = BKS_BACKPAGESBR | BKS_MAJORTABRIGHT |
                    BKS_ROUNDEDTABS | BKS_SPIRALBIND;
  hNotebook = WinCreateWindow(hwnd, WC_NOTEBOOK, "",
                              ulNotebookStyle, 0, 0, 0, 0, hwnd,
                              HWND_TOP, ID_NOTEBOOK, 0, 0);
  lWinCol = CLR_BACKGROUND;
  WinSetPresParam(hNotebook, PP_BACKGROUNDCOLORINDEX,
                  sizeof(lWinCol), &lWinCol);
```

Figure 7.7. Version 2.0 controls and dialogs: C source file. Continues.

```
WinSendMsg(hNotebook, BKM_SETDIMENSIONS, MPFROM2SHORT(50, 25),
           MPFROMSHORT(BKA_MAJORTAB));
WinSendMsg(hNotebook, BKM_SETDIMENSIONS, MPFROM2SHORT(75, 25),
           MPFROMSHORT(BKA_MINORTAB));
bInit = '0';
szInit[1] = '\0';

hListPage = WinLoadDlg(hNotebook, hNotebook, 0, 0,
                       DLG_LISTPAGE, 0);
while (fgets(szNameAddrBuf, 80, Names))
{
 strcpy(szName, strtok(szNameAddrBuf, ","));
 strcpy(szStreet, strtok(NULL, ","));
 strcpy(szTown, strtok(NULL, ","));
 strcpy(szCounty, strtok(NULL, ","));
                                        /* Extract first and last names */
 strcpy(szFirstName, strtok(szName, " "));
 strcpy(szLastName, strtok(NULL, " "));

 if (bInit != szLastName[0])            /* Change of surname initial */
 {
  bInit = szLastName[0];
  ulPageID = (ULONG)WinSendMsg(hNotebook, BKM_INSERTPAGE, 0,
                              MPFROM2SHORT(BKA_MAJOR |
                              BKA_AUTOPAGESIZE |
                              BKA_STATUSTEXTON,
                              BKA_LAST));
  szInit[0] = bInit;
  WinSendMsg(hNotebook, BKM_SETTABTEXT,
             MPFROMP(ulPageID), MPFROMP(szInit));
  WinSendMsg(hNotebook, BKM_SETSTATUSLINETEXT,
             MPFROMP(ulPageID), MPFROMP("Address Book"));
  WinSendMsg(hNotebook, BKM_SETPAGEWINDOWHWND,
             MPFROMP(ulPageID), MPFROMHWND(hListPage));
 }
 ulPageID = (ULONG)WinSendMsg(hNotebook,
                             BKM_INSERTPAGE, 0,
                             MPFROM2SHORT(BKA_MINOR |
                             BKA_AUTOPAGESIZE, BKA_LAST));
 strcpy(szMinorTab, szFirstName);
 WinSendMsg(hNotebook, BKM_SETTABTEXT, MPFROMP(ulPageID),
            szMinorTab);
 hPage = WinLoadDlg(hNotebook, hNotebook, 0, 0, DLG_PAGE, 0);
```

Figure 7.7. Version 2.0 controls and dialogs: C source file. Continues.

```
  sprintf(szName, "%s %s", szFirstName, szLastName);
  if (szCounty[strlen(szCounty)-1] == '\n')
    szCounty[strlen(szCounty)-1] = '\0';

 WinSetDlgItemText(hPage, ID_NAME, szName);
 WinSetDlgItemText(hPage, ID_ADDR1, szStreet);
 WinSetDlgItemText(hPage, ID_ADDR2, szTown);
 WinSetDlgItemText(hPage, ID_ADDR3, szCounty);
 WinSendMsg(hNotebook, BKM_SETPAGEWINDOWHWND, MPFROMP(ulPageID),
            MPFROMHWND(hPage));
 sprintf(szName, "%s, %s", szLastName, szFirstName);
 WinSendDlgItemMsg(hListPage, ID_LISTBOX, LM_INSERTITEM,
                   MPFROMSHORT(LIT_END), MPFROMP(szName));
 }
 fclose(Names);
 WinShowWindow(hNotebook, TRUE);

 return hNotebook;
}
/****************************************************************/
VOID OpenFile(HWND hwnd)
{
 FILEDLG  OpenDlg;
 CHAR     szText[CCHMAXPATH];
                                       /* Initialize OpenDlg to NULL */
 memset(&OpenDlg, 0, sizeof(FILEDLG));
 OpenDlg.cbSize = sizeof(FILEDLG);   /* Set size                    */
                                     /* Open Dialog and centred     */
 OpenDlg.fl = FDS_OPEN_DIALOG | FDS_CENTER;
                                     /* Dialog title                */
 OpenDlg.pszTitle = "Sample Open Dialog";
 OpenDlg.pszOKButton = "Open";       /* OK button text              */
 OpenDlg.pszIDrive = "D:";           /* Start with the D drive      */
                                     /* Display dialog              */
 WinFileDlg(HWND_DESKTOP, hwnd, &OpenDlg);
 if (OpenDlg.lReturn == DID_OK)
 {                                   /* user pressed "Open"         */
   sprintf(szText, "Selected File:\n%s", OpenDlg.szFullFile);
 }
 else                                /* User cancelled              */
   sprintf(szText, "Open Dialog Cancelled");
 WinMessageBox(HWND_DESKTOP, hwnd, szText, OpenDlg.pszTitle, 0,
               MB_INFORMATION | MB_OK | MB_MOVEABLE);
 return;
```

Figure 7.7. Version 2.0 controls and dialogs: C source file. Continues.

```
}
/****************************************************************/
VOID ChgFont(HWND hwnd)
{
 FONTDLG   FontDlg;
 CHAR      szFamilyName[FACESIZE],
           szText[CCHMAXPATH],
           szPointSize[3];
 USHORT    usPointSize;
 HPS       hps;

 szFamilyName[0] = '\0';                /*Initialize buffer          */
 hps = WinGetPS(hwnd);                  /*Get presentation space     */
                                        /* Initialize FontDlg to NULL */
 memset(&FontDlg, 0, sizeof(FONTDLG));
 FontDlg.fl = FNTS_CENTER;              /* Centre dialog             */
 FontDlg.cbSize = sizeof(FONTDLG);      /* Set size                  */
 FontDlg.hpsScreen = hps;               /*Set presentation space     */
 FontDlg.usFamilyBufLen = FACESIZE;     /*Set buffer length          */
                                        /*Pass pointer to buffer     */
 FontDlg.pszFamilyname = szFamilyName;
                                        /*Dialog title               */
 FontDlg.pszTitle = "Sample Font Dialog";
 FontDlg.clrFore = CLR_RED;             /* Preview foreground colour */
 FontDlg.clrBack = CLR_YELLOW;          /* Preview background colour */
                                        /*Preview text               */
 FontDlg.pszPreview = "aBcDeFgHiJkLmNoPqRsTuVwXyZ";
                                        /*Display dialog             */
 WinFontDlg(HWND_DESKTOP, hwnd, &FontDlg);
 WinReleasePS(hwnd);                    /*Return presentation space  */

 if (FontDlg.lReturn == DID_OK)         /*User pressed OK            */
 {
  sprintf(szText, "Selected Font:\n%u.%s",
          FIXEDINT(FontDlg.fxPointSize),
          FontDlg.fAttrs.szFacename);
 }
 else                                   /*User cancelled             */
   sprintf(szText, "Font Dialog Cancelled");

 WinMessageBox(HWND_DESKTOP, hwnd, szText, FontDlg.pszTitle, 0,
               MB_INFORMATION | MB_OK | MB_MOVEABLE);
 return;
}
```

Figure 7.7. Version 2.0 controls and dialogs: C source file. Concluded.

8
The atom manager and user messages

8.1 The atom manager

8.1.1 What is an atom?

There are two kinds of atoms, string and integer. A string atom is a numerical value which represents a character string. At boot time a system atom table is built, and by using this it is possible to obtain a unique number for a given character string. It can be used by the program developer for such things as unique user message IDs (see Sec. 8.2), and is used by the system for class names. These atoms are called integer atoms (see Sec. 2.4). Integer atoms range in value from 0x0001 to 0xBFFF and string atoms range from 0xC000 to 0xFFFF.

8.1.2 System and private atom tables

To obtain the handle of the system atom table use `WinQuerySystemAtomTable`:

```
HATOMTBL   hSysAtomTable;

hSysAtomTable = WinQuerySystemAtomTable();
```

The system atom table, built at boot time, is accessible by all processes running in your system; if you need to have a private atom table then use `WinCreateAtomTable`:

```
case WM_CREATE:
  hMyAtomTable = WinCreateAtomTable(1024, 0);
  WinAddAtom(hAtomTable, "STRING 1");
  WinAddAtom(hAtomTable, "STRING 2");
  ;
  ;
```

```
    ;
    WinAddAtom(hAtomTable, "STRING n");
    break;
```

This table will only be accessible by the process that created it.

8.2 Unique user messages

In Presentation Manager you can create your own private messages to send either to your own application or to another. The IDs of these messages are `WM_USER+N`, where `WM_USER` is 0x1000 and `N` is greater than or equal to 0. The usual convention for user messages is `UM_xxx` so you would normally define them in your header file as follows:

```
#define  UM_ABORT      WM_USER
#define  UM_FINISHED   WM_USER+1
```

Now, it is fine defining a message, say `WM_USER+1`, for your own private use in your application, but the problems start when an ill-behaved application decides to broadcast its own message to every application running on your system. If this message also has the ID `WM_USER+1` then your application may produce undesirable results, depending on what processing you do with this message. If *all* applications use the atom manager to obtain their message IDs this problem disappears.

The steps you need to take to obtain a unique ID using the atom manager are as follows:

1 Declare a variable of type ATOM to be your message ID.
2 Obtain the handle to the system atom table using `WinQuerySystemAtomTable`.
3 Obtain the ID by calling `WinAddAtom`.
4 You can now check for this ID in your window procedure.

The following example sets up a unique message `um_unique_msg`, and when mouse button 1 is pressed the application sends itself this message:

```
ATOM       um_unique_msg;

/* ------------------------*/
/* In your main procedure... */
/* ------------------------*/

um_unique_msg = WinAddAtom(WinQuerySystemAtomTable(),
                            "UM_UNIQUE_MSG");

while (WinGetMsg(hab, &qmsg, (HWND)NULL, 0, 0))
   WinDispatchMsg(hab, &qmsg);

WinDeleteAtom(WinQuerySystemAtomTable(), um_unique_msg);
```

```
/**************************************************/
/*----------------------------*/
/* and in your window procedure... */
/*----------------------------*/
if (msg == um_unique_msg)
{
  DosBeep(100, 100);
  DosBeep(400, 100);
  DosBeep(700, 100);
  DosBeep(1000, 100);
}
else
{
  switch (msg)
    {
      case WM_BUTTON1DOWN:
        WinSendMsg(hwnd, um_unique_msg, 0, 0);
        break;
      ;
      ;
      ;
    }
}
```

Note that since the message ID is now a *variable* you cannot use it in your `switch` statement. Instead, you must check for it outside the `switch` statement using an `if` statement. On exit the atom is deleted from the table.

8.3 Sample program

This program illustrates the use of the atom manager and user messages. It comprises just a listbox and two pushbuttons (Fig. 8.1). The listbox displays the contents of the system atom table and a private atom table, depending on the state of a flag. Initially, the 'active' table is our private user table. To switch tables a unique user message, `um_unique_msg`, is sent to the window procedure by pressing the `Change Atom Table` pushbutton. The message also causes a series of beeps to be sounded and the listbox to be cleared.

The atom table contents are displayed by pressing the `Display Atoms` button. The table search starts at 0xC000, the lowest possible string atom value, and ends at either 'This is the last string' or 'UM_UNIQUE_MSG', depending on whether the 'active' table is our private table or the system table respectively.

The following listings show the program's header file, Fig. 8.2, resource file, Fig. 8.3, and C source file, Fig. 8.4.

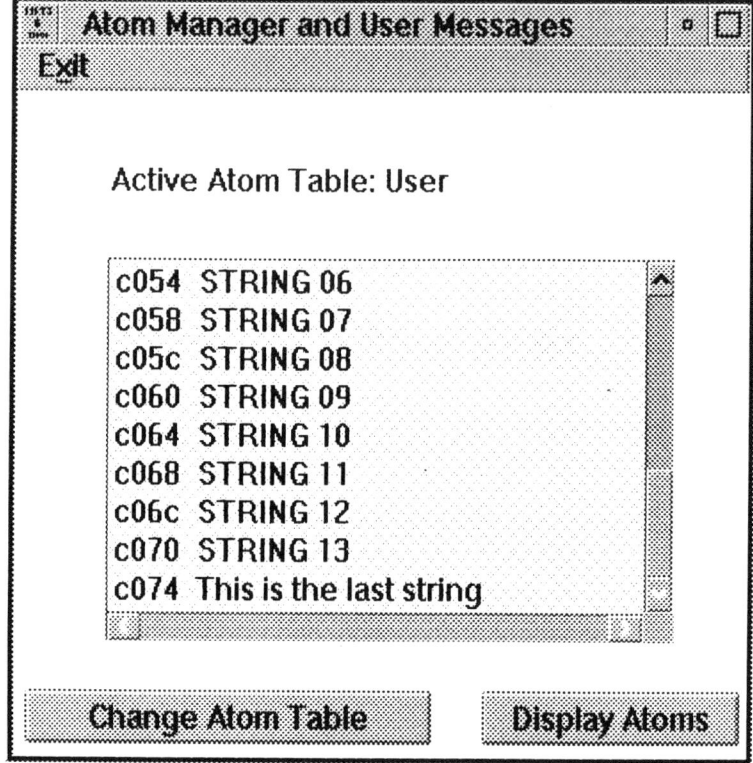

Figure 8.1. Atom manager and user messages output.

#define	ID_MAINWND	200
#define	ID_TITLE	201
#define	IDM_ONE	202
#define	MI_EXIT	203
#define	MI_RESUME	204
#define	ID_LISTBOX	205
#define	ID_BUTTON1	206
#define	ID_BUTTON2	207
#define	ID_TEXT	208

Figure 8.2. Atom manager and user messages: header file.

```
#include <os2.h>
#include "atom.h"

STRINGTABLE PRELOAD
BEGIN
  ID_TITLE, "Atom Manager and User Messages"
END

ICON        ID_MAINWND atom.ico

ACCELTABLE  ID_MAINWND
BEGIN
  VK_F3,    MI_EXIT,         VIRTUALKEY
END

MENU        ID_MAINWND PRELOAD
BEGIN
  SUBMENU "E~xit",                      IDM_ONE
  BEGIN
    MENUITEM "~Exit Program\tF3",  MI_EXIT,    MIS_TEXT
    MENUITEM "~Resume Program",    MI_RESUME,  MIS_TEXT
  END
END
```

Figure 8.3. Atom manager and user messages: resource file.

```
#define   INCL_WINWINDOWMGR
#define   INCL_WINFRAMEMGR
#define   INCL_WINSWITCHLIST
#define   INCL_WINSYS
#define   INCL_WINATOM
#define   INCL_WINLISTBOXES
#define   INCL_WININPUT
#define   INCL_WINSTATICS

#include <os2.h>
#include <string.h>
#include <stdio.h>
#include "atom.h"

MRESULT   EXPENTRY MainWndProc(HWND, ULONG, MPARAM, MPARAM);

ATOM      um_unique_msg;
```

Figure 8.4. Atom manager and user messages: C source file. Continues.

```
/*****************************************************************/
INT main(VOID)
{
  HAB      hab;
  HMQ      hmq;
  HWND     hwndFrame,
           hwndClient;
  QMSG     qmsg;
  ULONG    flFrameFlags;
  CHAR     szTitle[80];
  SWCNTRL  PgmEntry;
  LONG     lX_Left,
           lY_Bot,
           lHeight,
           lWidth,
           lScrHeight,
           lScrWidth;
/*****************************************************************/
  hab = WinInitialize(0);
  hmq = WinCreateMsgQueue(hab, 0);

  WinRegisterClass(hab, "Atom", MainWndProc,
                   CS_SIZEREDRAW, 0);

  WinLoadString(hab, (HMODULE)NULL, ID_TITLE,
                sizeof(szTitle), szTitle);

  flFrameFlags = FCF_TITLEBAR | FCF_SYSMENU | FCF_MENU |
                 FCF_SIZEBORDER | FCF_MINMAX |
                 FCF_ACCELTABLE | FCF_ICON;

  hwndFrame = WinCreateStdWindow(HWND_DESKTOP, 0,
                                 &flFrameFlags, "Atom",
                                 szTitle, 0, (HMODULE)NULL,
                                 ID_MAINWND, &hwndClient);

  lScrWidth  = WinQuerySysValue(HWND_DESKTOP, SV_CXSCREEN);
  lScrHeight = WinQuerySysValue(HWND_DESKTOP, SV_CYSCREEN);

  lWidth  = 400;
  lHeight = 400;
```

Figure 8.4. Atom manager and user messages: C source file. Continues

```
lX_Left = (lScrWidth  - lWidth)  / 2;
lY_Bot  = (lScrHeight - lHeight) / 2;

WinCreateWindow(hwndClient, WC_LISTBOX, NULL,
                WS_VISIBLE | LS_HORZSCROLL, 50, 60, 300,
                200, hwndClient, HWND_TOP,
                ID_LISTBOX, 0, 0);

WinCreateWindow(hwndClient, WC_BUTTON,
                "Change Atom Table", WS_VISIBLE,
                5, 5, 220, 30, hwndClient,
                HWND_TOP, ID_BUTTON1, 0, 0);

WinCreateWindow(hwndClient, WC_BUTTON, "Display Atoms",
                WS_VISIBLE, 250, 5, 140, 30,
                hwndClient, HWND_TOP, ID_BUTTON2, 0, 0);

WinCreateWindow(hwndClient, WC_STATIC,
                "Active Atom Table: User", WS_VISIBLE |
                SS_TEXT, 50, 280, 300, 30, hwndClient,
                HWND_TOP, ID_TEXT, 0, 0);

/*--------------------*/
/* Startup in foreground */
/*--------------------*/

WinSetWindowPos(hwndFrame, 0, lX_Left, lY_Bot, lWidth,
                lHeight, SWP_SIZE | SWP_MOVE | SWP_SHOW |
                SWP_ACTIVATE);

/* ----------------*/
/* Add to window list */
/* ----------------*/

PgmEntry.hwnd           = hwndFrame;
PgmEntry.hwndIcon       = (HWND)NULL;
PgmEntry.hprog          = (HPROGRAM)NULL;
PgmEntry.idProcess      = (PID)NULL;
PgmEntry.idSession      = (ULONG)NULL;
PgmEntry.uchVisibility  = SWL_VISIBLE;
PgmEntry.fbJump         = SWL_JUMPABLE;
strcpy(PgmEntry.szSwtitle, szTitle);

WinAddSwitchEntry(&PgmEntry);
```

Figure 8.4. Atom manager and user messages: C source file. Continues.

```
  um_unique_msg = WinAddAtom(WinQuerySystemAtomTable(),
                             "UM_UNIQUE_MSG");

  while (WinGetMsg(hab, &qmsg, (HWND)NULL, 0, 0))
    WinDispatchMsg(hab, &qmsg);

  /* -------------------------------- */
  /* Remove from window list and clean up */
  /* -------------------------------- */

  WinDeleteAtom(WinQuerySystemAtomTable(), um_unique_msg);
  WinRemoveSwitchEntry(WinQuerySwitchHandle(hwndFrame, 0));
  WinDestroyWindow(hwndFrame);
  WinDestroyMsgQueue(hmq);
  WinTerminate(hab);
  return 0;
}

/*****************************************************************/

MRESULT EXPENTRY MainWndProc(HWND hwnd, ULONG msg, MPARAM mp1,
                             MPARAM mp2)
{
  static HATOMTBL   hMyAtomTable,
                    hSysAtomTable,
                    hAtomTable;
  static USHORT     usAtomStart = 0xC000,
                    usAtomEnd;
  static BOOL       fMyTable = TRUE;

  CHAR       szAtom[256],
             szListEntry[256];
  USHORT     I;

  if (msg == um_unique_msg)
  {
    DosBeep(100, 100);
    DosBeep(400, 100);
    DosBeep(700, 100);
    DosBeep(1000, 100);

    WinSendMsg(WinWindowFromID(hwnd, ID_LISTBOX),
               LM_DELETEALL, 0, 0);
```

Figure 8.4. Atom manager and user messages: C source file. Continues.

```c
    fMyTable = !fMyTable;

    if (fMyTable)
    {
      hAtomTable = hMyAtomTable;
      WinSetWindowText(WinWindowFromID(hwnd, ID_TEXT),
                       "Active Atom Table: User");
    }
    else
    {
      hAtomTable = hSysAtomTable;
      WinSetWindowText(WinWindowFromID(hwnd, ID_TEXT),
                       "Active Atom Table: System");
    }
  }
  else
  {
    switch (msg)
      {
        case WM_CREATE:
          hMyAtomTable = WinCreateAtomTable(1024, 0);
          hSysAtomTable = WinQuerySystemAtomTable();
          hAtomTable = hMyAtomTable;

          WinAddAtom(hAtomTable, "This is the first string");
          WinAddAtom(hAtomTable, "STRING 02");
          WinAddAtom(hAtomTable, "STRING 03");
          WinAddAtom(hAtomTable, "STRING 04");
          WinAddAtom(hAtomTable, "STRING 05");
          WinAddAtom(hAtomTable, "STRING 06");
          WinAddAtom(hAtomTable, "STRING 07");
          WinAddAtom(hAtomTable, "STRING 08");
          WinAddAtom(hAtomTable, "STRING 09");
          WinAddAtom(hAtomTable, "STRING 10");
          WinAddAtom(hAtomTable, "STRING 11");
          WinAddAtom(hAtomTable, "STRING 12");
          WinAddAtom(hAtomTable, "STRING 13");
          WinAddAtom(hAtomTable, "This is the last string");
          break;

        case WM_COMMAND:
```

Figure 8.4. Atom manager and user messages: C source file. Continues.

```
              switch (SHORT1FROMMP(mp1))
                {
                  case ID_BUTTON1:
                    WinSendMsg(hwnd, um_unique_msg, 0, 0);
                    break;
                  case ID_BUTTON2:
                    WinSendMsg(WinWindowFromID(hwnd,
                         ID_LISTBOX), LM_DELETEALL, 0, 0);
                    if (fMyTable)
                      usAtomEnd = (USHORT)WinFindAtom
                        (hAtomTable, "This is the last string");
                    else
                      usAtomEnd = (USHORT)WinFindAtom
                        (hAtomTable, "UM_UNIQUE_MSG");
                    for (I = usAtomStart; I <= usAtomEnd; I++)
                      {
                       if (WinQueryAtomName(hAtomTable,
                              (ATOM)I, szAtom, sizeof(szAtom)))
                         {
                           sprintf(szListEntry, "%x %s", I,
                                 szAtom);
                           WinSendMsg(WinWindowFromID(hwnd,
                                   ID_LISTBOX),
                                   LM_INSERTITEM,
                                   (MPARAM)LIT_END,
                                   szListEntry);
                         }
                      }
                    break;
                  case MI_EXIT:
                    WinPostMsg(hwnd, WM_QUIT, 0, 0);
                    break;
                  default:
                    break;
                }
              break;
            case WM_ERASEBACKGROUND:
              return (MRESULT)TRUE;
          }
    }
  return WinDefWindowProc(hwnd, msg, mp1, mp2);
}
```

Figure 8.4. Atom manager and user messages: C source file. Concluded.

9
Window words and initialization data

Window words are a portion of memory allocated within a window structure. The logical pointer to the window structure is the window handle. `WinQueryWindowULong` and `WinQueryWindowUShort` give access to these sections of the window structure. Presentation Manager predefines several of the window words, for example, the window style, the pointer to the window procedure, and the handle to the message queue associated with the window.

When you register a window class, you can specify how many window words (in bytes), beyond those predefined by Presentation Manager, that you would like allocated for each window of that class, by using the `cbWindowData` parameter in a `WinRegisterClass` call. Once the instance of the class is created, you can access the window words by using `WinQueryWindowULong`, or `WinQueryWindowUShort`, by specifying the window handle returned on `WinCreateWindow` and an index value.

Window words are typically used to point to data that is unique to each instance, or window, of a class. Defining what that data contains is up to you. Usually it is allocated and initialized in the `WM_CREATE` message of your window procedure and accessed whenever your window procedure needs it to process a message.

9.1 Window words for client windows

You will often have multiple windows of the same class and each window may need to store some data, for example a text window may need to store one or more initialization strings. It is a bad idea to put data in global variables, as it makes it difficult to reuse the window class and multitasking may not work. If a global variable is changed while processing one window then it will apply to all other windows of that class, which is probably not what you want.

It is usual to store pointers to data in window words rather than the data itself, as it is more efficient.

The steps you need to take are as follows:

1   When registering the class, you specify how many extra bytes you want. The first non-reserved window word is at offset QWL_USER. However, if your window is likely to be subclassed then you should skip this and start at the next word, so define

    #define QWL_MYWWORD (QWL_USER + 4)

    and use this as the offset instead of QWL_USER, but do not forget to allow for the extra four bytes when you register your window class.

2   When your window processes the WM_CREATE message, use DosAllocMem to allocate memory for your data and use WinSetWindowULong to put the pointer to this memory into the window word after initializing the data.

```
typedef   struct _WINDATA
{
  USHORT  usWinCount;
  CHAR    szWinText[33];
} WINDATA;

WINDATA   *pWinData;
static    PVOID    BaseMem,
                   MemOffset;

case WM_CREATE:
  DosAllocMem(&BaseMem, 4096, PAG_READ | PAG_WRITE |
              PAG_COMMIT);
  DosSubSetMem(BaseMem, DOSSUB_INIT, 4096);
  DosSubAllocMem(BaseMem, &MemOffset, sizeof(WINDATA));
  pWinData = MemOffset;

  pWinData->WinCount = 0;
  strcpy(pWinData->szWinText, "Initial text");
  WinSetWindowULong(hwnd, QWL_USER, (ULONG)pWinData);
  break;
```

Using 16-bit OS/2 we could just call DosAllocSeg to allocate the memory, but we cannot do that in OS/2 V2.0, as each time we allocate memory we get at least 4096 bytes (1 page). This would be an incredible waste of memory, and if all applications running in version 2.0 did this we would soon be running out of memory, that is, the sum of physical memory and available swap space. Instead, we allocate sufficient memory to begin with and suballocate as required. You should, of course, check the return code from DosSubAllocMem. If it is 311, or ERROR_DOSSUB_NOMEM, then there is insufficient memory remaining, so you need to allocate further pages. An alternative technique would be to allocate sufficient memory at the start and write an exception handler to trap access violations and commit pages as appropriate. Since this is new for version 2.0, a simple exception handler that could be used here is included in Chapter 15.

Window words and initialization data

3. When you wish to retrieve the pointer use `WinQueryWindowULong`:

   ```
   pWinData = (WINDATA *)WinQueryWindowULong(hwnd,
                                             QWL_USER);
   ```

4. Finally, when the window receives a `WM_DESTROY` message use `DosSubFreeMem` to release the storage associated with the window word:

   ```
   case WM_DESTROY:
     pWinData = (WINDATA *)WinQueryWindowULong(hwnd,
                                               QWL_USER);
     DosSubFreeMem(BaseMem, pWinData, sizeof(WINDATA));
     break;
   ```

At first sight this may seem rather complex so, to clarify, look at Sec. 9.4.

9.2 Window words for dialog boxes

Since a dialog box is no more than a frame window, it has, by default, four bytes of instance data at offset `QWL_USER` which can be used to store a pointer, just as for window words for a client window. The only difference is that storage should be allocated in the `WM_INITDLG` case statement rather than the `WM_CREATE` statement.

9.3 Initialization data for dialog boxes

If initialization data is required for a dialog box then it can be passed to the dialog box procedure using the `CreateParams` parameter on the `WinLoadDlg` or `WinDlgBox` call. It can be accessed in the dialog procedure through parameter `mp2`:

```
                /* Define data structure for dialog box */
typedef struct _DLGDATA
{
  CHAR   szEntry1Text[33];
  CHAR   szEntry2Text[33];
  CHAR   szEntry3Text[33];
} DLGDATA;

/*------------------------------*/
/* In your main window procedure... */
/*------------------------------*/

DLGDATA InitData;
```

```
case ID_xxx:                               /* Display dialog box */
  strcpy(InitData.szEntry1Text, "Initial Dlg text 1");
  strcpy(InitData.szEntry2Text, "Initial Dlg text 2");
  strcpy(InitData.szEntry3Text, "Initial Dlg text 3");
  hDlg = WinLoadDlg(HWND_DESKTOP, HWND_DESKTOP, DlgProc,
                    (HMODULE)NULL, DLG_WWORDS, &InitData);
  WinShowWindow(hDlg, TRUE);
  break;

/*--------------------------------*/
/* and in your dialog box procedure...*/
/*--------------------------------*/

DLGDATA *pDlgData;

case WM_INITDLG:
  pDlgData = (DLGDATA *)mp2;
  WinSetWindowText(WinWindowFromID(hwndDlg, ID_ENTRY1),
                   pDlgData->szEntry1Text);
  WinSetWindowText(WinWindowFromID(hwndDlg, ID_ENTRY2),
                   pDlgData->szEntry2Text);
  WinSetWindowText(WinWindowFromID(hwndDlg, ID_ENTRY3),
                   pDlgData->szEntry3Text);
  ;
  ;
  ;
  break;
```

9.4 Sample program

This program is rather more complex than the others in this book, but can be explained diagrammatically by Fig. 9.1. The main client window makes use of two window words, one for its child windows and the other to receive the output from modeless dialog boxes.

The first window word is used to pass initialization data to a child window. The data structure comprises a count of windows and an initial string of text to display in the child's entry field. When a child window is created the count is incremented in both the main client's and child's window word data area and is displayed in the child window. The initialization text is written to the entry field and can be modified. This change can be saved by pressing mouse button 1 (MB 1).

When a dialog box is created, initialization data is passed to it via the mp2 parameter of the WinLoadDlg call and is displayed in its entry fields which may be modified (Fig. 9.2). When the OK button is pressed the window word data area is updated with the new text and a WM_USER message is sent to the main client

Window words and initialization data

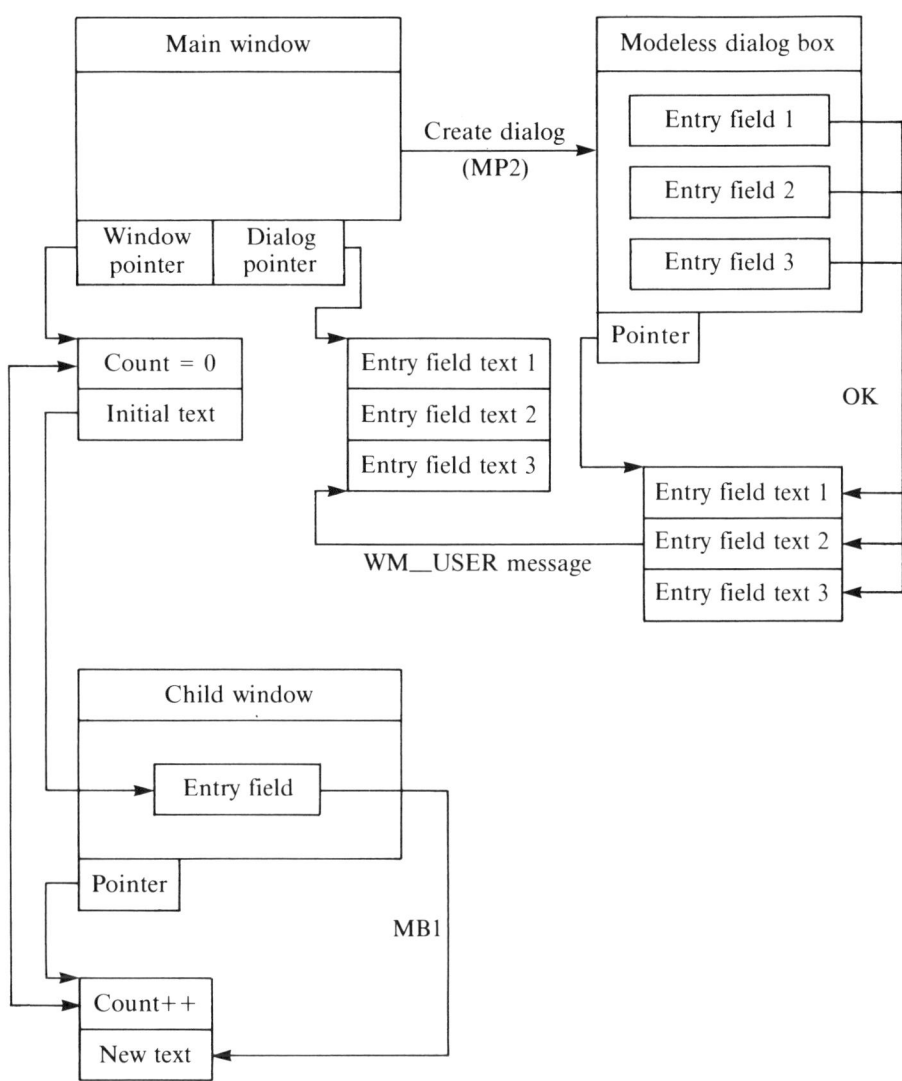

Figure 9.1. Use of window words in the sample program.

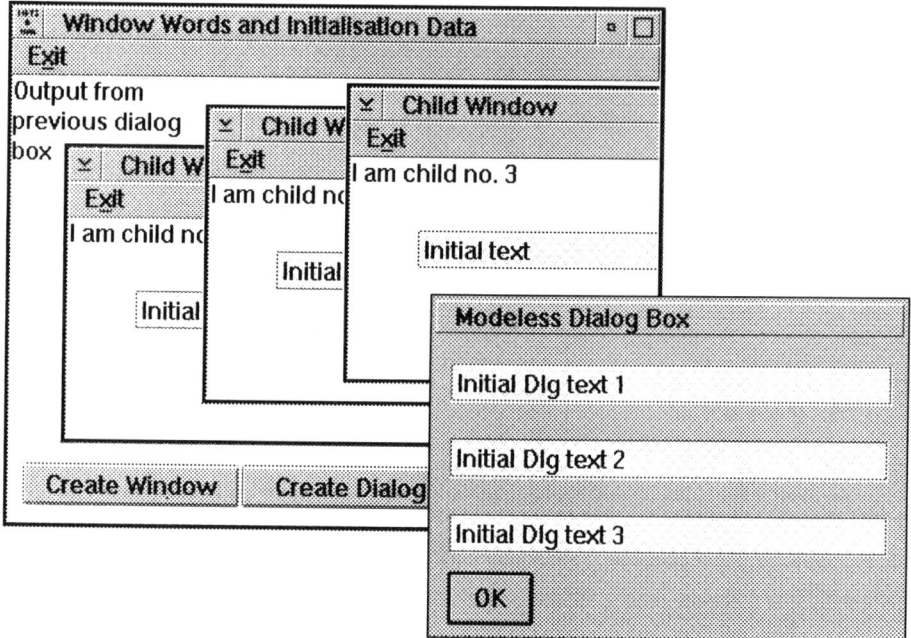

Figure 9.2. Window words and initialization data output.

window. One of the parameters, `mp1`, of this message is the dialog box window handle, so that the main client window can access the dialog box's window word data area and take a copy of it. The client then destroys the dialog box and displays the dialog box's text in the main window.

The main points brought out in this sample are the use of window words to:

- Pass initialization data to multiple child windows
- Retrieve data from dialog boxes

Figure 9.3. takes a closer look at the C source for this program (see page 206).

When we register the window classes we define how many bytes to reserve for window words. In this case we define eight bytes for the main window, since we require two window words; and four bytes for the child windows. The main window comprises just two pushbuttons, one to create a child window and another to create a modeless dialog box.

When the main window is created, we allocate a page of memory (4096 bytes), suballocate it and store pointers to the window word data structures, `WINDATA` and `DLGDATA`, at `QWL_USER` and `QWL_USER+4`, respectively. This is an obvious change from 16-bit OS/2 where we would probably just issue a `DosAllocSeg` for the necessary space on demand, as follows:

```
case WM_CREATE:
  OFFSETOF(pClientWinData) = 0;
  OFFSETOF(pDlgData) = 0;
  DosAllocSeg(sizeof(WINDATA),
              (PSEL)&SELECTOROF(pClientWinData), 0);
  DosAllocSeg(sizeof(DLGDATA),
              (PSEL)&SELECTOROF(pDlgData), 0);
  pClientWinData->usWinCount = 0;
  ;
  ;
  ;
```

If you press the `Create Window` pushbutton, a child window is created, and during this creation process we retrieve the handle of the main client window so that we can get the pointer to its parent's window word data (`WINDATA`) which holds the initialization data. If this is the first child then we allocate a page of memory and initialize it for suballocation. This is to store its child's unique initialization data. As you can see from the code, we limit the number of child windows that can be created. This is because no extra benefit would be gained in allowing an indefinite number to be created in this sample program. In reality, of course, you would check the return code on the `DosSubAllocMem` call for a value of 311, `ERROR_DOSSUB_NOMEM`, and allocate further memory, or write your own exception handler (see Chapter 15). This limit is set to 100, which at first sight implies only 3500 bytes (length of `WINDATA` = 35) are being used. However, 100 is the absolute maximum we can hold in a page of memory. The reason for this is quite straightforward. Whenever we suballocate a memory object, 64 bytes are used for control information; this leaves us 4032 bytes for data in our example. Now, when we actually suballocate memory we always receive an amount divisible by eight, so if we ask for an amount which is not, then it is rounded up to the next eight. Since our `WINDATA` structure is 35 bytes long we are actually allocated 40 bytes. So, 100 windows will require:

`64 + (100 × 40) = 4064 bytes`

So we have wasted a few bytes, but if we were converting this program from 16-bit OS/2, without using suballocation, and just replaced the `DosAllocSeg` with `DosAllocMem`, we could be using as much as *400 kb* of memory. The importance of looking carefully at all your memory management routines when converting to 32-bit cannot be overstressed. The more memory you use, the more paging will affect your and, more importantly, your user's system.

By performing a similar calculation, we can store data sufficient only for 38 dialog boxes. These limits are, of course, more than sufficient for this example. So, when the child window is displayed it shows the text `'I am child no. N'`, where

N increments for each new child window, and the child window's entry field is initialized to 'Initial text'. This text can be changed and saved in the child's window word by pressing mouse button 1. Failure to press it will cause the initial text to be redisplayed if the window is repainted. In a real application, pressing mouse button 1 would *not* normally be the method used to cause the data structure to be updated. It is done here purely for simplicity and convenience.

Finally, as each window is destroyed the space associated with it is freed, and when the last window is destroyed use of the memory pool is ended. Again, this is different from the 16-bit version where we probably did not suballocate:

```
case WM_DESTROY:
   pClientWinData = (WINDATA *)WinQueryWindowULong(hwnd,
                                    QWL_USER);
   DosFreeSeg(SELECTOROF(pClientWinData));
   break;
```

When a dialog box is created, it will contain the text 'Initial Dlg text N', where N is 1, 2 and 3. Changing this text and pressing OK causes the text to be passed back to the client window for display, at which time the dialog box is destroyed and the storage released.

The method used for communicating between the dialog box and the client window is a user message, UM_DLG_DONE, defined as WM_USER.

The following listings show the program's C source file, Fig. 9.3, header file, Fig. 9.4, resource file, Fig. 9.5, and dialog template, Fig. 9.6.

```
#define    INCL_WINWINDOWMGR
#define    INCL_WINFRAMEMGR
#define    INCL_WINSWITCHLIST
#define    INCL_WINSYS
#define    INCL_WINBUTTONS
#define    INCL_WINENTRYFIELDS
#define    INCL_WININPUT
#define    INCL_WINDIALOGS

#include   <os2.h>
#include   <string.h>
#include   <stdio.h>
#include   "wwords.h"

MRESULT EXPENTRY MainWndProc  (HWND, ULONG, MPARAM, MPARAM);
MRESULT EXPENTRY ChildWndProc (HWND, ULONG, MPARAM, MPARAM);
MRESULT EXPENTRY DlgProc      (HWND, ULONG, MPARAM, MPARAM);

typedef struct _WINDATA
{
```

Figure 9.3. Window words and initialization data: C source file. Continues.

```
  USHORT  usWinCount;
  CHAR    szWinText[33];
} WINDATA;

typedef struct _DLGDATA
{
  HWND    hwndClient;
  CHAR    szEntry1Text[33];
  CHAR    szEntry2Text[33];
  CHAR    szEntry3Text[33];
} DLGDATA;

/***************************************************************/

INT main (VOID)
{
  HAB     hab;
  HMQ     hmq;
  HWND    hwndFrame,
          hwndClient;
  QMSG    qmsg;
  ULONG   flFrameFlags;
  CHAR    szTitle[80];
  SWCNTRL PgmEntry;
  LONG    lX_Left,
          lY_Bot,
          lHeight,
          lWidth,
          lScrHeight,
          lScrWidth;

  /***************************************************************/

  hab = WinInitialize(0);
  hmq = WinCreateMsgQueue(hab, 0);

  WinRegisterClass(hab, "Wwords", MainWndProc,
                   CS_SIZEREDRAW, 2*sizeof(ULONG));

  WinRegisterClass(hab, "WwordsChild", ChildWndProc,
                   CS_SIZEREDRAW, sizeof(ULONG));

  WinLoadString(hab, (HMODULE)NULL, ID_TITLE,
                sizeof(szTitle), szTitle);
```

Figure 9.3. Window words and initialization data: C source file. Continues.

```
flFrameFlags = FCF_TITLEBAR    | FCF_SYSMENU | FCF_MENU |
               FCF_SIZEBORDER | FCF_MINMAX  |
               FCF_ACCELTABLE | FCF_ICON    |
               FCF_NOBYTEALIGN;

hwndFrame = WinCreateStdWindow(HWND_DESKTOP, 0,
                              &flFrameFlags, "Wwords",
                              szTitle, 0, (HMODULE)NULL,
                              ID_MAINWND, &hwndClient);

WinCreateWindow(hwndClient, WC_BUTTON, "Create Window",
                WS_VISIBLE | WS_CLIPSIBLINGS |
                BS_PUSHBUTTON, 10, 10, 150, 30,
                hwndClient, HWND_BOTTOM,
                ID_PUSHBTN1, 0, 0);

WinCreateWindow(hwndClient, WC_BUTTON, "Create Dialog",
                WS_VISIBLE | WS_CLIPSIBLINGS |
                BS_PUSHBUTTON, 160, 10, 150, 30,
                hwndClient, HWND_BOTTOM,
                ID_PUSHBTN2, 0, 0);

lScrWidth  = WinQuerySysValue(HWND DESKTOP, SVCXSCREEN);
lScrHeight = WinQuerySysValue(HWND_DESKTOP, SV_CYSCREEN);

lWidth  = 450;
lHeight = 350;

lX_Left = (lScrWidth  - lWidth)  / 2;
lY_Bot  = (lScrHeight - lHeight) / 2;

/*---------------------*/
/* Startup in foreground */
/*---------------------*/

WinSetWindowPos(hwndFrame, 0, lX_Left, lY_Bot, lWidth,
                lHeight, SWP_SIZE | SWP_MOVE | SWP_SHOW |
                SWP_ACTIVATE);

/*----------------- */
/* Add to window list */
/*----------------- */

PgmEntry.hwnd        = hwndFrame;
PgmEntry.hwndIcon    = (HWND)NULL;
PgmEntry.hprog       = (HPROGRAM)NULL;
```

Figure 9.3. Window words and initialization data: C source file. Continues.

```
  PgmEntry.idProcess     = (PID)NULL;
  PgmEntry.idSession     = (ULONG)NULL;
  PgmEntry.uchVisibility = SWL_VISIBLE;
  PgmEntry.fbJump        = SWL_JUMPABLE;
  strcpy(PgmEntry.szSwtitle, szTitle);
  WinAddSwitchEntry(&PgmEntry);

  while (WinGetMsg(hab, &qmsg, (HWND)NULL, 0, 0))
    WinDispatchMsg(hab, &qmsg);

  /* -------------------------------- */
  /* Remove from window list and clean up */
  /* -------------------------------- */

  WinRemoveSwitchEntry(WinQuerySwitchHandle(hwndFrame, 0));
  WinDestroyWindow(hwndFrame);
  WinDestroyMsgQueue(hmq);
  WinTerminate(hab);
  return 0;
}

/*****************************************************************/

MRESULT EXPENTRY MainWndProc(HWND hwnd, ULONG msg,
                             MPARAM mp1, MPARAM mp2)
{
  static ULONG flCFrameFlags = FCF_TITLEBAR | FCF_SYSMENU |
                               FCF_SIZEBORDER | FCF_MENU |
                               FCF_ACCELTABLE;
  HWND     hChildFrame,
           hChildClient,
           hDlg;
  HPS      hps;
  RECTL    rcl;
  WINDATA  *pClientWinData;
  DLGDATA  *pDlgData,
           *pClientDlgData,
           InitData;
  static   PVOID   BaseMem,
                   MemOffset;
  static   LONG    lX = 20,
                             /* Start X position for Child Window */
```

Figure 9.3. Window words and initialization data: C source file. Continues.

```
                        lY = 50;    /* Start Y position for Child Window */
  static    USHORT   usDlgCount = 0;/* Count of dialog boxes              */

  switch (msg)
    {
    case WM_CREATE:
      DosAllocMem(&BaseMem, 4096, PAG_READ | PAG_WRITE |
                  PAG_COMMIT);
      DosSubSetMem(BaseMem, DOSSUB_INIT, 4096);
      DosSubAllocMem(BaseMem, &MemOffset,
                     sizeof(WINDATA));
      pClientWinData = MemOffset;
      DosSubAllocMem(BaseMem, &MemOffset,
                     sizeof(DLGDATA));
      pDlgData = MemOffset;


      pClientWinData->usWinCount = 0;
      strcpy(pClientWinData->szWinText, "Initial text");
      pDlgData->szEntry1Text[0] = '\0';
      pDlgData->szEntry2Text[0] = '\0';
      pDlgData->szEntry3Text[0] = '\0';
      WinSetWindowULong(hwnd, QWL_USER,
                        (ULONG)pClientWinData);
      WinSetWindowULong(hwnd, QWL_USER+4,
                        (ULONG)pDlgData);
      break;


    case WM_DESTROY:
      pClientWinData = (WINDATA *)WinQueryWindowULong
                                  (hwnd, QWL_USER);
      pDlgData = (DLGDATA *)WinQueryWindowULong(hwnd,
                            QWL_USER+4);
      DosSubFreeMem(BaseMem, pClientWinData,
                    sizeof(WINDATA));
      DosSubFreeMem(BaseMem, pDlgData,
                    sizeof(DLGDATA));
      DosSubUnsetMem(BaseMem);
      DosFreeMem(BaseMem);
      break;
```

Figure 9.3. Window words and initialization data: C source file. Continues.

```
case WM_PAINT:
  hps = WinBeginPaint(hwnd, (HPS)NULL, (PRECTL)NULL);
  WinQueryWindowRect(hwnd, &rcl);
  pDlgData = (DLGDATA *)WinQueryWindowULong(hwnd,
                    QWL_USER+4);
  WinDrawText(hps, strlen(pDlgData->szEntry1Text),
          pDlgData->szEntry1Text, &rcl,
          SYSCLR_WINDOWTEXT, SYSCLR_WINDOW,
          DT_LEFT | DT_ERASERECT);
  rcl.yTop -= 20;
  WinDrawText(hps, strlen(pDlgData->szEntry2Text),
          pDlgData->szEntry2Text, &rcl,
          SYSCLR_WINDOWTEXT, SYSCLR_WINDOW,
          DT_LEFT | DT_ERASERECT);
  rcl.yTop -= 20;
  WinDrawText(hps, strlen(pDlgData->szEntry3Text),
          pDlgData->szEntry3Text, &rcl,
          SYSCLR_WINDOWTEXT, SYSCLR_WINDOW,
          DT_LEFT | DT_ERASERECT);
  WinEndPaint(hps);
  break;

case WM_COMMAND:
  switch (SHORT1FROMMP(mp1))
    {
      case ID_PUSHBTN1:
        hChildFrame = WinCreateStdWindow(hwnd, 0,
                    &flCFrameFlags, "WwordsChild",
                    "Child Window", 0,
                    (HMODULE)NULL, ID_CHILDWND,
                    &hChildClient);

        WinCreateWindow(hChildClient, WC_ENTRYFIELD,
                    "", WS_VISIBLE | ES_MARGIN,
                    50, 75, 200, 20,
                    hChildClient, HWND_TOP,
                    ID_ENTRYFLD, 0, 0);

        WinSetWindowPos(hChildFrame, 0, lX, lY, 300,
                    200, SWP_SIZE | SWP_MOVE |
                    SWP_SHOW);
```

Figure 9.3. Window words and initialization data: C source file. Continues.

```
            lX += 10;                        /* Offset the next window */
            lY += 10;
            break;

          case ID_PUSHBTN2:
            if (++usDlgCount <= MAX_DLGBOXES)
            {
              InitData.hwndClient = hwnd;
              strcpy(InitData.szEntry1Text,
                     "Initial Dlg text 1");
              strcpy(InitData.szEntry2Text,
                     "Initial Dlg text 2");
              strcpy(InitData.szEntry3Text,
                     "Initial Dlg text 3");
              hDlg = WinLoadDlg(HWND_DESKTOP,
                                HWND_DESKTOP, DlgProc,
                                0, DLG_WWORDS,
                                &InitData);
              WinShowWindow(hDlg, TRUE);
            }
            else
            {
              WinAlarm(HWND_DESKTOP, WA_WARNING);
              usDlgCount = MAX_DLGBOXES;
            }
            break;

          case MI_EXIT:
            WinPostMsg(hwnd, WM_QUIT, 0, 0);
            break;

          default:
            break;
        }
     break;

  case UM_DLG_DONE:
    pDlgData = (DLGDATA *)WinQueryWindowULong
                              ((HWND)mp1, QWL_USER);
    pClientDlgData = (DLGDATA *)WinQueryWindowULong
                              (hwnd, QWL_USER+4);
    strcpy(pClientDlgData->szEntry1Text,
           pDlgData->szEntry1Text);
```

Figure 9.3. Window words and initialization data: C source file. Continues.

```
            strcpy(pClientDlgData->szEntry2Text,
                pDlgData->szEntry2Text);
            strcpy(pClientDlgData->szEntry3Text,
                pDlgData->szEntry3Text);
            usDlgCount-;                    /* Dialog box being destroyed */
            WinDestroyWindow((HWND)mp1);
            WinInvalidateRect(hwnd, NULL, TRUE);
            break;
        case WM_ERASEBACKGROUND:
            return (MRESULT)TRUE;
        }
    return WinDefWindowProc(hwnd, msg, mp1, mp2);
}

/*************************************************************/

MRESULT EXPENTRY ChildWndProc(HWND hwnd, ULONG msg, MPARAM mp1,
                              MPARAM mp2)
    HWND      hFrame,
              hClient;
    HPS       hps;
    RECTL     rcl;
    CHAR      szText[20];
    WINDATA   *pChildWinData,
              *pClientWinData;
                                /* Count of windows in existence */
    static    USHORT  usWinCount = 0;
    static    PVOID   BaseMem,
                      MemOffset;

    switch (msg)
      {
        case WM_CREATE:
                        /* Get handle of our main client window */
                        /* i.e. grandparent of this window      */
            hFrame = WinQueryWindow(hwnd, QW_PARENT);
            hClient = WinQueryWindow(hFrame, QW_PARENT);
            pClientWinData = (WINDATA *)WinQueryWindowULong
                                    (hClient, QWL_USER);
            if (++usWinCount == 1)
```

Figure 9.3. Window words and initialization data: C source file. Continues.

```
      {                        /* First window going to be created */
        DosAllocMem(&BaseMem, 4096, PAG_READ | PAG_WRITE |
                    PAG_COMMIT);
        DosSubSetMem(BaseMem, DOSSUB_INIT, 4096);
      }

      if (usWinCount > MAX_WINDOWS)
      {                        /* No more windows can be created */
        WinAlarm(HWND_DESKTOP, WA_WARNING);
        usWinCount = MAX_WINDOWS;
        return (MRESULT)TRUE;
      }

      DosSubAllocMem(BaseMem, &MemOffset,
                     sizeof(WINDATA));
      pChildWinData = MemOffset;
      pChildWinData->usWinCount =
                   ++pClientWinData->usWinCount;
      strcpy(pChildWinData->szWinText,
             pClientWinData->szWinText);
      WinSetWindowULong(hwnd, QWL_USER,
                        (ULONG)pChildWinData);
      break;

    case WM_DESTROY:
      pChildWinData = (WINDATA *)WinQueryWindowULong
                                 (hwnd, QWL_USER);
      DosSubFreeMem(BaseMem, pChildWinData,
                    sizeof(WINDATA));

      if (-usWinCount == 0)
                              /* Last window being destroyed? */
      {
        DosSubUnsetMem(BaseMem);
        DosFreeMem(BaseMem);
      }
      break;

    case WM_PAINT:
      hps = WinBeginPaint(hwnd, (HPS)NULL, (PRECTL)NULL);
      pChildWinData = (WINDATA *)WinQueryWindowULong
                                 (hwnd, QWL_USER);
      WinQueryWindowRect(hwnd, &rcl);
```

Figure 9.3. Window words and initialization data: C source file. Continues.

```
            sprintf(szText, "I am child no. %d",
                    pChildWinData->usWinCount);
            WinDrawText(hps, strlen(szText), szText, &rcl,
                        SYSCLR_WINDOWTEXT, SYSCLR_WINDOW,
                        DT_LEFT | DT_ERASERECT);
            WinSetWindowText(WinWindowFromID(hwnd, ID_ENTRYFLD),
                             pChildWinData-> szWinText);
            WinEndPaint(hps);
            break;

        case WM_CLOSE:
            WinDestroyWindow(WinQueryWindow(hwnd, QW_PARENT));
            break;
        case WM_BUTTON1DOWN:
            pChildWinData = (WINDATA *)WinQueryWindowULong
                                       (hwnd, QWL_USER);
            WinQueryWindowText(WinWindowFromID(hwnd,
                               ID_ENTRYFLD), sizeof(
                               pChildWin Data-> szWinText),
                               pChildWinData->szWinText);
            break;

        case WM_COMMAND:
            switch (SHORT1FROMMP(mp1))
              {
                case MI_EXIT:
                    WinDestroyWindow(WinQueryWindow(hwnd,
                                     QW_PARENT));
                    break;


                default:
                    break;
              }
            break;


        case WM_ERASEBACKGROUND:
            return (MRESULT)TRUE;
    }
    return WinDefWindowProc(hwnd, msg, mp1, mp2);
}
```

Figure 9.3. Window words and initialization data: C source file. Continues.

```
MRESULT EXPENTRY DlgProc(HWND hwndDlg, ULONG msg, MPARAM mp1,
                        MPARAM mp2)
{
  DLGDATA *pDlgData;
  static  HWND   hClient;
  static  PVOID  BaseMem,
                 MemOffset;
  static  USHORT usDlgCount = 0;
                          /* Count of dialog boxes in existence */
  switch (msg)
  {
    case WM_INITDLG:
      pDlgData = (DLGDATA *)mp2;
      hClient = pDlgData->hwndClient;
      WinSetWindowText(WinWindowFromID(hwndDlg,
                   ID_ENTRY1), pDlgData-> szEntry1Text);
      WinSetWindowText(WinWindowFromID(hwndDlg,
                   ID_ENTRY2), pDlgData-> szEntry2Text);
      WinSetWindowText(WinWindowFromID(hwndDlg,
                   ID_ENTRY3), pDlgData-> szEntry3Text);

      if (++usDlgCount == 1)
                       /* First dialog box going to be created */
      {
        DosAllocMem(&BaseMem, 4096, PAG_READ | PAG_WRITE |
                   PAG_COMMIT);
        DosSubSetMem(BaseMem, DOSSUB_INIT, 4096);
      }
      DosSubAllocMem(BaseMem, &MemOffset, sizeof
                   (DLGDATA));
      pDlgData = MemOffset;
      WinSetWindowULong(hwndDlg, QWL_USER, (ULONG)
                   pDlgData);
      break;


    case WM_COMMAND:
      switch(SHORT1FROMMP(mp1))
      {
        case ID_OK:
```

Figure 9.3. Window words and initialization data: C source file. Continues.

```
          pDlgData = (DLGDATA *)WinQueryWindowULong
                              (hwndDlg, QWL_USER);
          WinQueryWindowText(WinWindowFromID(hwndDlg,
                         ID_ENTRY1), sizeof(
                         pDlgData-> szEntry1Text),
                         pDlgData->szEntry1Text);
          WinQueryWindowText(WinWindowFromID(hwndDlg,
                         ID_ENTRY2), sizeof(
                         pDlgData-> szEntry2Text),
                         pDlgData-> szEntry2Text);
          WinQueryWindowText(WinWindowFromID(hwndDlg,
                         ID_ENTRY3), sizeof(
                         pDlgData-> szEntry3Text),
                         pDlgData-> szEntry3Text);
          WinPostMsg(hClient, UM_DLG_DONE, (MPARAM)hwndDlg,
                     0);
          break;
        default:
          return FALSE;
      }
      break;

    case WM_DESTROY:
      pDlgData = (DLGDATA *)WinQueryWindowULong(hwndDlg,
                         QWL_USER);
      DosSubFreeMem(BaseMem, pDlgData, sizeof(DLGDATA));
      if (-usDlgCount == 0)
                              /* Last dialog box being destroyed? */
      {
        DosSubUnsetMem(BaseMem);
        DosFreeMem(BaseMem);
      }
      break;


    default:
      return WinDefDlgProc(hwndDlg, msg, mp1, mp2);
  }
  return FALSE;
}
```

Figure 9.3. Window words and initialization data: C source file. Concluded.

```
#define UM_DLG_DONE   WM_USER
#define MAX_WINDOWS   100
#define MAX_DLGBOXES  38
#define ID_MAINWND    200
#define ID_TITLE      201
#define IDM_ONE       202
#define MI_EXIT       203
#define MI_RESUME     204
#define ID_PUSHBTN1   205
#define ID_PUSHBTN2   206
#define ID_CHILDWND   207
#define ID_ENTRYFLD   208
#define DLG_WWORDS    256
#define ID_OK         257
#define ID_ENTRY1     258
#define ID_ENTRY2     259
#define ID_ENTRY3     260
```

Figure 9.4. Window words and initialization data: header file.

```
#include <os2.h>
#include "wwords.h"

STRINGTABLE PRELOAD
BEGIN
  ID_TITLE, "Window Words and Initialization Data"
END

ICON          ID_MAINWND wwords.ico

ACCELTABLE  ID_MAINWND
BEGIN
  VK_F3,    MI_EXIT,        VIRTUALKEY
END

ACCELTABLE  ID_CHILDWND
BEGIN
  VK_F3,    MI_EXIT,        VIRTUALKEY
END

MENU          ID_MAINWND PRELOAD
BEGIN
```

Figure 9.5. Window words and initialization data: resource file. Continues.

```
    SUBMENU    "E~xit",                    IDM_ONE
    BEGIN
      MENUITEM "~Exit Program\tF3",    MI_EXIT,      MIS_TEXT
      MENUITEM "~Resume Program",      MI_RESUME,    MIS_TEXT
    END
END

MENU          ID_CHILDWND PRELOAD
BEGIN
    SUBMENU "E~xit",                     IDM_ONE
    BEGIN
      MENUITEM "~Close Window\tF3",    MI_EXIT,      MIS_TEXT
      MENUITEM "~Resume",              MI_RESUME,    MIS_TEXT
    END
END

rcinclude wwords.dlg
```

Figure 9.5. Window words and initialization data: resource file. Concluded.

```
DLGINCLUDE 1 "WWORDS.H"

DLGTEMPLATE DLG_WWORDS LOADONCALL MOVEABLE DISCARDABLE
BEGIN
    DIALOG "Modeless Dialog Box", DLG_WWORDS, 165, 98, 159, 79,
           FS_NOBYTEALIGN | FS_SCREENALIGN |
           WS_VISIBLE, FCF_TITLEBAR
    BEGIN
        ENTRYFIELD    "", ID_ENTRY1, 7, 62, 147, 8, ES_MARGIN
        ENTRYFIELD    "", ID_ENTRY2, 7, 42, 146, 8, ES_MARGIN
        ENTRYFIELD    "", ID_ENTRY3, 7, 22, 146, 8, ES_MARGIN
        DEFPUSHBUTTON "OK", ID_OK, 5, 2, 29, 14
    END
END
```

Figure 9.6. Window words and initialization data: dialog template.

10
Window enumeration

10.1 What is enumeration?

Enumeration is the process by which you can obtain the window handle of all the child windows of any given parent window handle. If you start with `HWND_DESKTOP` then you can obtain all the main window handles in your system. Similarly, using `HWND_OBJECT` you can obtain all the object window handles.

You would use enumeration if you needed to find the handle of a window running in another process, or even in your own process, so that you could send it a message. The API functions you use for enumeration are `WinBeginEnumWindows`, `WinGetNextWindow` and `WinEndEnumWindows`.

In the following example we search for an object window of class `ThreadsObj` (used later in Fig. 12.4):

```
#define   UM_SUICIDE WM_USER+4

HENUM     hEnum;
HWND      hWin;
CHAR      szClassBuffer[20];

                        /* Start enumerating object windows */
hEnum = WinBeginEnumWindows(HWND_OBJECT);
                        /* Keep going until NULL returned    */
while (hWin = WinGetNextWindow(hEnum))
{
  WinQueryClassName(hWin, sizeof(szClassBuffer),
                    szClassBuffer);
                        /*---------------------------------*/
                        /* If class name is that of our    */
                        /* THREADS program, kill it        */
                        /*---------------------------------*/
```

```
    if (!strcmp(szClassBuffer, "ThreadsObj"))
    {
      WinPostMsg(hWin, UM_SUICIDE, 0, 0);
    }
}
WinEndEnumWindows(hEnum);               /* End enumeration */
```

If we find it, we send it a user message, which in this case is a message to force the thread to exit. There should, of course, be some cooperation between the two processes. We should never send random messages to other processes in the system as this may cause undesired effects.

10.2 Obtaining the handle of a child window

Suppose you need to send a message to a window in another process, a listbox for example. To do this you obviously need the handle of that listbox, and this can be obtained by enumerating the child windows of the desktop, HWND_DESKTOP.

Because only the immediate children of the specified parent window are enumerated, child windows of the child, that is, the grandchildren, are excluded. This means that when we receive a handle we need to check it for a frame window, or for a class name of "#1". If it is a frame window then we get the class name of its client window, and if it is what we are looking for then we can start a second enumeration loop using the client window handle as the parent. We now need to check for a listbox, and this has a class name of "#7". In the following example we search for the listbox in the THREADS program. We know that this application has only one listbox, so as soon as we get a class name of "#7" we have our desired handle and can do just as we please with it. In this case we just change its colour:

```
HENUM   hEnum,
        hEnumC;
HWND    hWin,
        hLbox;
CHAR    szClassBuffer[20];

hEnum = WinBeginEnumWindows(HWND_DESKTOP);
while (hWin = WinGetNextWindow(hEnum))
{
  WinQueryClassName(hWin, sizeof(szClassBuffer),
                    szClassBuffer); /*------------------*/
  if (!strcmp(szClassBuffer, "#1"))  /* Frame?           */
  {                                  /*------------------*/
                                     /* Get class name   */
    WinQueryClassName(WinWindowFromID(hWin, FID_CLIENT),
                      sizeof(szClassBuffer),
```

```
                                szClassBuffer);
                                            /*-----------------*/
                                            /* Our class?     */
                                            /*-----------------*/
      if (!strcmp(szClassBuffer, "Threads"))
      { hEnumC = WinBeginEnumWindows(WinWindowFromID
                                    (hWin, FID_CLIENT));
        while (hLbox = WinGetNextWindow(hEnumC))
        {
          WinQueryClassName(hLbox, sizeof(szClassBuffer),
                        szClassBuffer);
                                            /*-----------------*/
                                            /* Listbox?       */
                                            /*-----------------*/
          if (!strcmp(szClassBuffer, "#7"))
            {
              ChangeCol(hLbox);       /* See sample program */
              break;
            }
        }
        WinEndEnumWindows(hEnumC);
      }
    }
  }
}
WinEndEnumWindows(hEnum);
```

For a list of class names see Sec. 2.4. Alternatively, since we know this application we also know the ID of the listbox (see the header file for the THREADS sample program, Fig. 12.2), therefore we can use this to obtain the window handle directly by using `WinWindowFromID`, thus avoiding the need for the second enumeration loop. However, this may not always be the case, but between consenting applications it is, and so the second enumeration loop becomes:

```
if (!strcmp(szClassBuffer, "Threads"))
{
  hClient = WinWindowFromID(hWin, FID_CLIENT);
  hLbox = WinWindowFromID(hClient, ID_LIST);
}
```

10.3   Sample program

The program in Fig. 11.4 covers both window enumeration and icon handling.

11
Icons

Note: The code in this chapter is relevant for OS/2 version 2.0 only if, in the Workplace Shell, you have opted to display your minimized windows on the desktop. You will find this option in the OS/2 System -> System Setup -> System settings on the Window page. This option applies to all minimized windows in your system, but you can override it by changing it for each window or object. You will find a Window option on every object's Settings notebook. If you have not opted for this then the icons you see on the desktop are *not* minimized applications but workplace objects and have different properties. By default, minimized application windows are hidden. This, of course, does not apply to OS/2 version 1.x.

11.1 Are icons necessary?

It is not always necessary to define an icon for your application. Some applications, for example clocks, may require their window to be painted continually, even when minimized. To do this you must ensure that any drawing your application does can automatically scale itself to the window size, hence the icon will appear to the application to be just a small window.

If you do use this approach, be careful to avoid the FCF_ICON frame creation flag. If you do use it without an icon defined then WinCreateStdWindow will fail. Also, note that if you use FCF_STANDARD you automatically include FCF_ICON.

However, having said that, it is not necessary to have an icon, but it is desirable, although you may not actually use it when your window is minimized. The reason is that when you define an application in Presentation Manager under version 1.x, it will use the icon along with the program title in the group to which it belongs; if you have not defined one, the default icon is used. Under version 2.0, of course, users can supply their own icon.

11.2 Changing icon text

To change the text under an icon for your own application, use `WinSetWindowText` to change the frame title:

```
hwndFrame = WinQueryWindow(hwnd, QW_PARENT);

WinSetWindowText(hwndFrame, "Icon Text");
```

However, if you need to change the text under an icon for another application, you must first obtain the window handle of its frame window. You do this by enumerating the windows on the desktop and checking each window for the `WS_MINIMIZED` style. When you have found the relevant window you can use its handle in the `WinSetWindowText` call:

```
HENUM   hEnum;
HWND    hWin;
CHAR    szTitle[40];

/*------------------------------------------------------*/
/* This code puts the text of all minimized applications */
/* into a listbox                                        */
/*------------------------------------------------------*/

hEnum = WinBeginEnumWindows(HWND_DESKTOP);
while (hWin = WinGetNextWindow(hEnum))
{
  if (WinQueryWindowULong(hWin, QWL_STYLE) & WS_MINIMIZED)
                                            /* Minimized? */
  {
    WinQueryWindowText(hWin, sizeof(szTitle), szTitle);

    WinSendMsg(WinWindowFromID(hwnd, ID_LISTBOX),
               LM_INSERTITEM, MPFROMSHORT(LIT_END),
               MPFROMP(szTitle));
  }
}
WinEndEnumWindows(hEnum);
```

11.3 Hiding icon text

To hide icon text you need the handle of the window that contains the text. It is *not* the frame window handle, although that is the handle you use if you wish to change the text. It is the *next* window in the Z-order that is required. To get this handle you use `WinQueryWindow` with the `QW_NEXT` code. This should return you a handle with the class name of `#32765`. Once you have this you can hide the window using `WinShowWindow`:

```
case ID_HIDE:
  /*--------------------------------------------------------*/
  /* Using the frame handle get the next window in the      */
  /* Z-order, that is the icon text window                  */
  /*--------------------------------------------------------*/
  hIconText = WinQueryWindow(hWin, QW_NEXT);
  WinQueryClassName(hIconText, sizeof(szClassBuffer),
                    szClassBuffer);

                                        /* Icon text window? */
  if (!strcmp(szClassBuffer, "#32765"))
    WinShowWindow(hIconText, FALSE);
  break;
```

In this code it is assumed that hWin, the frame handle of a minimized window, has already been assigned. In fact, in the sample program which illustrates this (see Sec. 11.5), the handles of all the minimized applications are stored in the item handles of a listbox.

11.4 Dynamic update of icon

If you do not require your application continually to update its window while minimized, but would still like to convey a state of change to your user when a certain event happens, then you can do so by 'updating' the icon. You do this by sending the frame a WM_SETICON message followed by a WinInvalidateRect. It does mean, of course, that you have to provide more than one icon. In fact, using this method you could display several icons, one after the other, to achieve a simple animated effect. We do this in the following code, where we display a bouncing ball whenever the window is minimized. To avoid unnecessary timer processing, the timer is not started until the window is about to be minimized and it is stopped again when the window is restored:

```
static   BOOL       fDefIcon = TRUE;
static   HPOINTER   hIcon1,
                    hIcon2;

case WM_CREATE:
  /*----------------------*/
  /* Load our two ball icons */
  /*----------------------*/

  hIcon1 = WinLoadPointer(HWND_DESKTOP, (HMODULE)NULL,
                          ID_ICON1);
  hIcon2 = WinLoadPointer(HWND_DESKTOP, (HMODULE)NULL,
                          ID_ICON2);
```

```
    break;

case WM_MINMAXFRAME:
  if (((PSWP)mp1)->fl & SWP_MINIMIZE)
    WinStartTimer(WinQueryAnchorBlock(hwnd), hwnd, 1, 500);
  else
    if (((PSWP)mp1)->fl & SWP_RESTORE)
      WinStopTimer(WinQueryAnchorBlock(hwnd), hwnd, 1);
  break;

case WM_TIMER:
  /*---------------------------------------------------*/
  /* Every half-second replace the icon to produce a   */
  /* bouncing effect                                   */
  /*---------------------------------------------------*/

  hwndFrame = WinQueryWindow(hwnd, QW_PARENT);

  if (fDefIcon)
    WinSendMsg(hwndFrame, WM_SETICON, (MPARAM)hIcon2, 0);
  else
    WinSendMsg(hwndFrame, WM_SETICON, (MPARAM)hIcon1, 0);

  WinInvalidateRect(hwndFrame, NULL, FALSE);
  fDefIcon = !fDefIcon;
  break;
```

11.5 Sample program

To use all the features in this program you must also run the THREADS sample program (see Chapter 12). Our program demonstrates the use of window enumeration and icon handling. The main window (Fig. 11.1) has six pushbuttons, the first two of which only work if THREADS is also running:

- `Kill Object Thread`   This enumerates all the object windows on your desktop looking for an object class name of `ThreadsObj`. If it finds it then the program sends it a `UM_SUICIDE` message to force the thread to exit. If the thread is not running a message is displayed.
- `Modify Listbox`   This enumerates all the main windows on your desktop to find a window of class `Threads`. If it finds it then the handle of the listbox in the THREADS program is found and the foreground and background colours are changed.
- `List Minimized Apps`   This button displays a list of all minimized applications in the listbox. If one is selected, its name is copied to the entry field below the listbox where it can be modified.

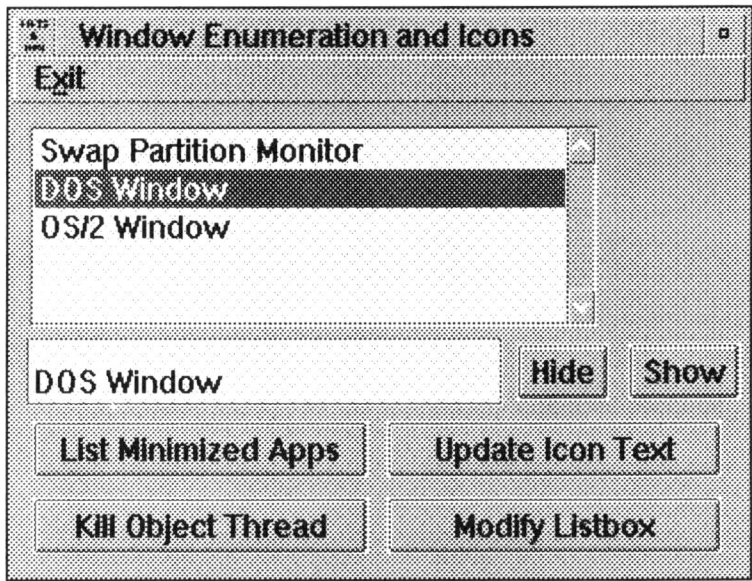

Figure 11.1. Window enumeration and icons output.

With the introduction of the Workplace Shell, a minimized application is not necessarily shown as an icon. You must request that minimized windows are displayed on the desktop. You will find this option in the Settings for the System which you will find in the System Setup folder which, in turn, is in the OS/2 System folder. This option is global and so affects all objects on the desktop. You can override it for an individual window by changing its Settings.

This button will not list anything unless you have requested this option.

- Update Icon Text   After modifying the text, pressing this button causes the text to be changed under the icon.
- Hide   This hides the selected icon text.
- Show   This reshows the selected icon text.

If the main application window is minimized, the icon changes into a bouncing ball. This is done by starting a timer and alternating the display of two icons.

The following listings show the program's header file, Fig. 11.2, resource file, Fig. 11.3, and C source file, Fig. 11.4.

```
#define    ID_MAINWND    200
#define    ID_TITLE      201
#define    IDM_ONE       202
#define    MI_EXIT       203
#define    MI_RESUME     204
#define    ID_KILL       205
#define    ID_MODIFY     206
#define    ID_MIN        207
#define    ID_LISTBOX    208
#define    ID_LIST       209
#define    ID_ENTRY      210
#define    ID_UPDATE     211
#define    ID_HIDE       212
#define    ID_SHOW       213
#define    ID_ICON1      214
#define    ID_ICON2      215
```

Figure 11.2. Window enumeration and icons: header file.

```
#include <os2.h>
#include "enum.h"
STRINGTABLE PRELOAD
BEGIN
  ID_TITLE, "Window Enumeration and Icons"
END

ICON       ID_MAINWND    enum.ico
ICON       ID_ICON1      enum1.ico
ICON       ID_ICON2      enum2.ico

ACCELTABLE ID_MAINWND
BEGIN
  VK_F3, MI_EXIT, VIRTUALKEY
END

MENU       ID_MAINWND PRELOAD
BEGIN
  SUBMENU "E~xit",                        IDM_ONE
  BEGIN
    MENUITEM "~Exit Program\tF3",         MI_EXIT,   MIS_TEXT
    MENUITEM "~Resume Program",           MI_RESUME, MIS_TEXT
  END
END
```

Figure 11.3. Window enumeration and icons: resource file.

```
#define   INCL_WINWINDOWMGR
#define   INCL_WINFRAMEMGR
#define   INCL_WINSWITCHLIST
#define   INCL_WINSYS
#define   INCL_WINBUTTONS
#define   INCL_WINLISTBOXES
#define   INCL_WINENTRYFIELDS
#define   INCL_WINTIMER
#define   INCL_WINPOINTERS
#define   INCL_WINDIALOGS

#define   UM_SUICIDE   WM_USER+4

#include <os2.h>
#include <string.h>
#include <stdlib.h>
#include "enum.h"

MRESULT EXPENTRY MainWndProc(HWND, ULONG, MPARAM, MPARAM);

VOID      ModifyLbox(VOID);
VOID      ChangeCol (HWND);


/**************************************************************/

INT main (VOID)
{
   HAB      hab;
   HMQ      hmq;
   HWND     hwndFrame,
            hwndClient;
   QMSG     qmsg;
   ULONG    flFrameFlags;
   CHAR     szTitle[80];
   SWCNTRL  PgmEntry;
   LONG     lX_Left,
            lY_Dot,
            lHeight,
            lWidth,
            lScrHeight,
            lScrWidth;

   hab = WinInitialize(0);
   hmq = WinCreateMsgQueue(hab, 0);
```

Figure 11.4. Window enumeration and icons: C source file. Continues.

```
WinRegisterClass(hab, "Enum", MainWndProc,
                 CS_SIZEREDRAW, 0);
WinLoadString(hab, (HMODULE)NULL, ID_TITLE,
              sizeof(szTitle), szTitle);


flFrameFlags = FCF_TITLEBAR  | FCF_SYSMENU   | FCF_MENU |
               FCF_DLGBORDER | FCF_MINBUTTON |
               FCF_ACCELTABLE | FCF_ICON;

hwndFrame = WinCreateStdWindow(HWND_DESKTOP, 0,
                               &flFrameFlags, "Enum",
                               szTitle, 0, (HMODULE)NULL,
                               ID_MAINWND, &hwndClient);

lScrWidth  = WinQuerySysValue(HWND_DESKTOP, SV_CXSCREEN);
lScrHeight = WinQuerySysValue(HWND_DESKTOP, SV_CYSCREEN);

lWidth  = 400;
lHeight = 300;

lX_Left = (lScrWidth  - lWidth)  / 2;
lY_Bot  = (lScrHeight - lHeight) / 2;

WinSetWindowPos(hwndFrame, (HWND)NULL, lX_Left, lY_Bot,
                lWidth, lHeight, SWP_SIZE | SWP_MOVE |
                SWP_SHOW | SWP_ACTIVATE);

WinCreateWindow(hwndClient, WC_BUTTON,
                "Kill Object Thread", WS_VISIBLE, 10, 10,
                180, 30, hwndClient, HWND_TOP, ID_KILL, 0, 0);

WinCreateWindow(hwndClient, WC_BUTTON, "Modify Listbox",
                WS_VISIBLE, 200, 10, 180, 30, hwndClient,
                HWND_TOP, ID_MODIFY, 0, 0);

WinCreateWindow(hwndClient, WC_BUTTON,
                "List Minimized Apps", WS_VISIBLE, 10, 50,
                180, 30, hwndClient, HWND_TOP, ID_MIN, 0, 0);

WinCreateWindow(hwndClient, WC_LISTBOX, NULL, WS_VISIBLE,
                10, 130, 300, 100, hwndClient, HWND_BOTTOM,
                ID_LISTBOX, 0, 0);
```

Figure 11.4. Window enumeration and icons: C source file. Continues.

```
  WinCreateWindow(hwndClient, WC_ENTRYFIELD, NULL,
                  WS_VISIBLE | ES_MARGIN, 10, 90, 250, 30,
                  hwndClient, HWND_BOTTOM, ID_ENTRY, 0, 0);

  WinCreateWindow(hwndClient, WC_BUTTON, "Hide",
                  WS_VISIBLE, 270, 90, 50, 30,
                  hwndClient, HWND_TOP, ID_HIDE, 0, 0);

  WinCreateWindow(hwndClient, WC_BUTTON, "Show",
                  WS_VISIBLE, 330, 90, 60, 30, hwndClient,
                  HWND_TOP, ID_SHOW, 0, 0);

  WinCreateWindow(hwndClient, WC_BUTTON,
                  "Update Icon Text", WS_VISIBLE, 200,
                  50, 180, 30, hwndClient, HWND_TOP,
                  ID_UPDATE, 0, 0);

                                         /* Add to window list */
  PgmEntry.hwnd          = hwndFrame;
  PgmEntry.hwndIcon      = (HWND)NULL;
  PgmEntry.hprog         = (HPROGRAM)NULL;
  PgmEntry.idProcess     = (PID)NULL;
  PgmEntry.idSession     = (ULONG)NULL;
  PgmEntry.uchVisibility = SWL_VISIBLE;
  PgmEntry.fbJump        = SWL_JUMPABLE;
  strcpy(PgmEntry.szSwtitle, szTitle);
  WinAddSwitchEntry(&PgmEntry);

  while (WinGetMsg(hab, &qmsg, (HWND)NULL, 0, 0))
    WinDispatchMsg(hab, &qmsg);

  /*---------------------------------*/
  /* Remove from window list and clean up */
  /*---------------------------------*/

  WinRemoveSwitchEntry(WinQuerySwitchHandle(hwndFrame, 0));

  WinDestroyWindow(hwndFrame);
  WinDestroyMsgQueue(hmq);
  WinTerminate(hab);
  return 0;
}
/***********************************************************/
```

Figure 11.4. Window enumeration and icons: C source file. Continues.

```
MRESULT EXPENTRY MainWndProc(HWND hwnd, ULONG msg, MPARAM mp1,
                             MPARAM mp2)
{
  HENUM    hEnum;
  HWND     hWin,
           hFrame,
           hTitle;
  CHAR     szClassBuffer[20],
           szMsgText[30],
           szTitle[40];
  BOOL     fObjFound;

  static   SHORT    sIdx;
  static   HPOINTER hIcon1,
                    hIcon2;
  static   BOOL     fDefIcon = TRUE;

  switch (msg)
    {
      case WM_CREATE:
        hIcon1 = WinLoadPointer(HWND_DESKTOP,
                                (HMODULE)NULL, ID_ICON1);
        hIcon2 = WinLoadPointer(HWND_DESKTOP,
                                (HMODULE)NULL, ID_ICON2);
        break;

      case WM_MINMAXFRAME:
        if (((PSWP)mp1)->fl & SWP_MINIMIZE)
          WinStartTimer(WinQueryAnchorBlock(hwnd),
                        hwnd, 1, 500);
        else
          if (((PSWP)mp1)->fl & SWP_RESTORE)
            WinStopTimer(WinQueryAnchorBlock(hwnd),
                         hwnd, 1);
        break;

      case WM_TIMER:
        hFrame = WinQueryWindow(hwnd, QW_PARENT);

        if (fDefIcon)
          WinSendMsg(hFrame, WM_SETICON, (MPARAM)hIcon2, 0);
```

Figure 11.4. Window enumeration and icons: C source file. Continues.

```
      else
        WinSendMsg(hFrame, WM_SETICON, (MPARAM)hIcon1,
                   0);

      WinInvalidateRect(hFrame, NULL, FALSE);
      fDefIcon = !fDefIcon;
      break;

   case WM_CONTROL:
      switch(SHORT1FROMMP(mp1))
      {
        case ID_LISTBOX:
          switch(SHORT2FROMMP(mp1))
          {
            case LN_SELECT:
              sIdx = (SHORT)WinSendDlgItemMsg(hwnd,
                 ID_LISTBOX, LM_QUERYSELECTION, 0, 0);
              WinSendDlgItemMsg(hwnd, ID_LISTBOX,
                                LM_QUERYITEMTEXT,
                                MPFROM2SHORT (sIdx,
                                sizeof(szTitle)),
                                MPFROMP(szTitle));

              if (sIdx != LIT_NONE)
              WinSetWindowText(WinWindowFromID(hwnd,
                                ID_ENTRY), szTitle);
            break;

            default:
              break;
          }
          break;
      }
      break;

   case WM_COMMAND:
      switch (SHORT1FROMMP(mp1))
        {
          case ID_KILL: /* Kill object thread if running */
            fObjFound = FALSE;
            hEnum = WinBeginEnumWindows(HWND_OBJECT);
```

Figure 11.4. Window enumeration and icons: C source file. Continues.

```
      while (hWin = WinGetNextWindow(hEnum))
      {
        WinQueryClassName(hWin,
          sizeof(szClassBuffer), szClassBuffer);
        if (!strcmp(szClassBuffer, "ThreadsObj"))
        {
          WinPostMsg(hWin, UM_SUICIDE, 0, 0);
          fObjFound = TRUE;
        }
      }

      WinEndEnumWindows(hEnum);

      if (!fObjFound)
      {
        strcpy(szMsgText,
          "Object thread not running");
        DosBeep(1000, 100);
      }
      else
        strcpy(szMsgText, "Object thread killed");

      WinMessageBox(HWND_DESKTOP, hwnd, szMsgText,
         "Window Enumeration Sample Program", 0,
         MB_INFORMATION | MB_OK | MB_MOVEABLE );
      break;

    case ID_MODIFY:
                  /* Modify listbox in THREADS program */
      ModifyLbox();
      break;

    case ID_MIN:          /* List minimized applications */
      WinSendMsg(WinWindowFromID(hwnd,
         ID_LISTBOX), LM_DELETEALL, 0, 0);
      WinSetWindowText(WinWindowFromID(hwnd,
                    ID_ENTRY), "");
      sIdx = 0;
      hEnum = WinBeginEnumWindows(HWND_DESKTOP);
      while (hWin = WinGetNextWindow(hEnum))
```

Figure 11.4. Window enumeration and icons: C source file. Continues.

```
      {
        if (WinQueryWindowULong(hWin, QWL_STYLE) &
                              WS_MINIMIZED)
        {
          WinQueryWindowText(hWin,
              sizeof(szTitle), szTitle);
          WinSendMsg(WinWindowFromID(hwnd,
                     ID_LISTBOX), LM_INSERTITEM,
                     MPFROMSHORT(LIT_END),
                     MPFROMP(szTitle));


          /*--------------------------*/
          /* Save handle for each window */
          /*--------------------------*/

          WinSendMsg(WinWindowFromID(hwnd,
                     ID_LISTBOX),
                     LM_SETITEMHANDLE,
                     MPFROMSHORT(sIdx),
                     MPFROMHWND(hWin));
          sIdx++;
        }
      }
      WinEndEnumWindows(hEnum);
      break;

    case ID_UPDATE:                  /* Change icon text */
      WinQueryWindowText(WinWindowFromID(hwnd,
          ID_ENTRY), sizeof(szTitle), szTitle);

      hWin = (HWND)WinSendMsg(WinWindowFromID
                              (hwnd, ID_LISTBOX),
                              LM_QUERYITEMHANDLE,
                              MPFROMSHORT(sIdx),
                              0);
      WinSetWindowText(hWin, szTitle);
      WinSendMsg(WinWindowFromID(hwnd,
                 ID_LISTBOX), LM_SETITEMTEXT,
                 MPFROMSHORT(sIdx),
                 (MPARAM)szTitle);
      break;
```

Figure 11.4. Window enumeration and icons: C source file. Continues.

```
                    case ID_HIDE:
                    case ID_SHOW:
                      hWin = (HWND)WinSendMsg(WinWindowFromID
                                              (hwnd, ID_LISTBOX),
                                              LM_QUERYITEMHANDLE,
                                              MPFROMSHORT(sIdx),
                                              0);
                      hTitle = WinQueryWindow(hWin, QW_NEXT);
                      WinQueryClassName(hTitle, sizeof
                          (szClassBuffer), szClassBuffer);
                      if (!strcmp(szClassBuffer, "#32765"))
                                                      /* Icon text window? */
                      {
                        if (SHORT1FROMMP(mp1) == ID_HIDE)
                          WinShowWindow(hTitle, FALSE);
                        else
                          WinShowWindow(hTitle, TRUE);
                      }
                      break;

                    case MI_EXIT:
                      WinPostMsg(hwnd, WM_QUIT, 0, 0);
                      break;

                    default:
                      break;
                 }
              break;

       case WM_ERASEBACKGROUND:
          return (MRESULT)TRUE;
       }
       return WinDefWindowProc(hwnd, msg, mp1, mp2);
}

/*******************************************************************/

VOID ModifyLbox(VOID)
{
   HENUM   hEnum,
           hEnumC;
```

Figure 11.4. Window enumeration and icons: C source file. Continues.

```
HWND    hWin,
        hLbox;
CHAR    szClassBuffer[20];
BOOL    fAppFound;

fAppFound = FALSE;
hEnum = WinBeginEnumWindows(HWND_DESKTOP);
while (hWin = WinGetNextWindow(hEnum))
{
  WinQueryClassName(hWin, sizeof(szClassBuffer),
                    szClassBuffer);

  if (!strcmp(szClassBuffer, "#1"))
                                                /* Frame?      */
  {
                                                /* Get class name */
    WinQueryClassName(WinWindowFromID(hWin, FID_CLIENT),
                      sizeof(szClassBuffer),
                      szClassBuffer);

    if (!strcmp(szClassBuffer, "Threads"))
                                                /* Our class?  */
    {

      /*--------------------------------------------*/
      /* If we already know the ID of the listbox we can  */
      /* use it to get the handle directly rather         */
      /* than enumerate.                                  */
      /*                                                  */
      /* ChangeCol(WinWindowFromID(WinWindowFromID        */
      /*           (hWin, FID_CLIENT), ID_LIST));         */
      /*                                                  */
      /*-------------------------------------------- */

      hEnumC = WinBeginEnumWindows(WinWindowFromID(hWin,
                          FID_CLIENT));
      while (hLbox = WinGetNextWindow(hEnumC))
      {
        WinQueryClassName(hLbox, sizeof(szClassBuffer),
                          szClassBuffer);    /*-------------*/
        if (!strcmp(szClassBuffer, "#7"))    /*  Listbox?  */
          {                                  /*-------------*/
```

Figure 11.4. Window enumeration and icons: C source file. Continues.

```
                    ChangeCol(hLbox);
                    fAppFound = TRUE;
                    break;
                  }
              }
              WinEndEnumWindows(hEnumC);
            }
        }
    }
  WinEndEnumWindows(hEnum);
  if (!fAppFound)
  {
    DosBeep(1000, 100);
    WinMessageBox(HWND_DESKTOP, (HWND)NULL,
                  "THREADS not running",
                  "Window Enumeration Sample Program",
                  0, MB_INFORMATION | MB_OK | MB_MOVEABLE );
  }
  return;
}

/************************************************************/

VOID   ChangeCol(HWND hLbox)
{
  LONG   lFColour,
         lBColour;
  static   BOOL fRedBgnd = FALSE;

  if (fRedBgnd)
  {
    lFColour = CLR_RED;
    lBColour = CLR_YELLOW;
  }
  else
  {
    lFColour = CLR_YELLOW;
    lBColour = CLR_RED;
  }
  WinSetPresParam(hLbox, PP_BACKGROUNDCOLORINDEX,
                  sizeof(lBColour), &lBColour);
```

Figure 11.4. Window enumeration and icons: C source file. Continues.

```
  WinSetPresParam(hLbox, PP_FOREGROUNDCOLORINDEX,
                  sizeof(lFColour), &lFColour);
  fRedBgnd = !fRedBgnd;
  return;
}
```

Figure 11.4. Window enumeration and icons: C source file. Concluded.

12
Threads and timers

If you need to do some lengthy processing in your program and you code it directly in your window procedure, performance will suffer as a result. The reason is that in Presentation Manager there is only one system message queue to handle all user input, keyboard and mouse, and until your program completes the processing of its current message and returns control to Presentation Manager, the next message in this queue is held. It is therefore essential that all Presentation Manager programs obey the 'tenth of a second' rule, that is, process the message and return control to Presentation Manager in less than one tenth of a second. So, to overcome this problem for lengthy processing you must start a second thread in which to do it, enabling control to be passed back to Presentation Manager. This technique is used later in this chapter to create a three-minute timer. The thread does nothing but sleep for three minutes and then *posts* a message back to the client window at the end of that period. It then goes back to sleep for a further three minutes.

12.1 Creating a thread

The process for starting a thread in 32-bit OS/2 has been improved and made easier to use. It is now possible to pass a parameter to it, usually a pointer to a parameter block; the system now allocates and deallocates the stack for you and it is possible to create a thread in a suspended state. This obviously means that the parameter list for `DosCreateThread` has changed. It is now:

Pointer to the thread ID (output)
Pointer to the thread routine (input)
Thread argument (input)
Thread flags (input)
Stack size (input)

To start a thread in a suspended state, ensure bit 0 of the thread flags is set to 1. Setting it to 0 will cause the thread to start immediately. If you start a thread in its suspended state then you must call `DosResumeThread` to initiate its execution.

Bear in mind that if you call any C library functions in a secondary thread then you should use `_beginthread` and `_endthread` rather than `DosCreateThread`.

To start a thread in 32-bit:

```
VOID      LTimer(VOID);                    /* Timer thread  */
TID       tidLTimer;                       /* Thread ID     */

/*--------------------*/
/* Create timer thread */
/*--------------------*/

DosCreateThread(&tidLTimer, (PFNTHREAD)LTimer, 0, 0, 4096);
```

and in 16-bit:

```
VOID      LTimer(VOID);                    /* Timer thread    */
TID       tidLTimer;                       /* Thread ID       */
UCHAR     StackLT[4096];                   /* Thread's stack  */

/*--------------------*/
/* Create timer thread */
/*--------------------*/

DosCreateThread((void far *)LTimer, &tidLTimer,
                StackLT+sizeof(StackLT));
```

12.2 Communicating with the main thread

Having started a secondary thread, one of the most important things we will want to do is communicate with the main thread. Now, we have three options open to us when we create a thread:

1. A thread without a message queue
This thread only uses functions which do *not* need a message queue. It is the simplest thread to implement. It can, however, use `WinPostMsg`.

2. A thread with a message queue but without a message processing loop
If you are going to use `WinSendMsg`, or indeed most `Win...` functions, in the thread then you must have a message queue, even though the thread may not process any messages, in which case a message processing loop is not required.

3. A thread with a message queue and a message processing loop
If you need to process messages then you need both a message queue and a message processing loop. If the thread does not have a user interface then you can create an object window and use its window procedure to process the messages; otherwise,

create an ordinary window with controls and use its window procedure in the usual manner.

Let us now look at these in turn.

12.2.1 Thread without a message queue

Section 12.1 showed how to start a thread called `LTimer`. Let us now take a look at this thread. Its sole purpose is to sleep for three minutes, wake up to tell the main thread that three minutes have elapsed and go back to sleep again. To do this, we call `DosSleep`, and on waking call `WinPostMsg` to post back a user message, `UM_THREAD_TIMER`, to the main client window. The window handle for the client is passed to the thread as a parameter. Ensure you use `_System` linkage on the function definition, otherwise the parameter will not be passed.

For a thread with no message queue:

```
VOID   _System LTimer(VOID * parm)
{
  HWND   hwndClient;

  hwndClient = (HWND)parm;
  while (TRUE)
  {
    DosSleep(180000);                      /* Wait for 3 minutes */
    WinPostMsg(hwndClient, UM_THREAD_TIMER, 0, 0);
  }
}
```

This is very simple, but it could just as well have been an extremely complex bit of code taking minutes to execute. If we had put this in our main window procedure then when this code executed, it would have been goodbye to the user interface. Try putting a call to `DosSleep` in your own program's window procedure to see the effect!

12.2.2 Thread with a message queue but without a message processing loop

In the previous example we used `WinPostMsg`, which does not require the presence of a message queue. However, if you use `WinSendMsg`, or indeed most other `Win...` calls, then you *must* create a message queue, that is, you must issue a `WinInitialize` followed by a `WinCreateMsgQueue`. However, it is not necessary to have a message processing loop in the thread unless you intend to create windows in it. Let us now look at a thread with a message queue.

This type of thread will probably be used most often. Consider a client window which contains a listbox filled with data from a database, or some other source. Now, it is quite likely that this could take some time to fill, and so if it was done in the main window procedure then the user interface would suffer performance degradation during this period. To overcome this degradation we must start a thread similar to the following:

```
VOID   ListBox(VOID)
{
  HAB      habThread;
  HMQ      hmqThread;
  habThread = WinInitialize(0);
  hmqThread = WinCreateMsgQueue(habThread, 0);
  WinCancelShutdown(hmqThread, TRUE);
  WinSendMsg(WinWindowFromID(hwndClient, ID_LIST),
             LM_DELETEALL, 0, 0);
  ; /****************************************************/
  ; /* Do some long processing, e.g. fill a listbox from */
  ; /* a database                                        */
  ; /****************************************************/
  WinDestroyMsgQueue(hmqThread);
  WinTerminate(habThread);
  DosExit(0, 0);
}
```

One important point to note for a thread which does not have a message processing loop is that you must call `WinCancelShutdown` after creating your message queue, otherwise if you request shutdown while the thread is running, the system may hang, waiting for your thread to reply to the `WM_QUIT` message it has been sent. This is unlikely in our example, as the thread is not running continually and so shutdown would not normally be requested.

It is assumed that the window handle, `hwndClient`, has already been obtained, by either passing it as a parameter, or, since we have a message queue, using window enumeration. In fact, in the sample program (see Sec. 12.6), window enumeration has been used.

You should note here that if you intend to use a thread of this sort many times in your own program, it is more efficient to start the thread at the beginning in its suspended state and call `DosResumeThread` whenever you need it. Once it completes its processing you can call `DosSuspendThread` to stop it temporarily.

12.2.3 Thread with a message queue and a message processing loop

Sometimes you will have a thread that needs to process window messages, in which case you must supply a window procedure in which to do it, and hence supply a message processing loop. In the following example we have a thread which processes messages but which does not require any interaction with the user. For this type of thread we use an object window, that is, one that can send and receive messages but does not appear on the screen and so cannot have a user interface:

```
VOID ObjThread(VOID)     /* ------------------------------ */
{                        /* Object window thread + window thread */
  HAB     habObj;        /* ------------------------------ */
  HMQ     hmqObj;
  QMSG    qmsg;

  habObj = WinInitialize(0);
  hmqObj = WinCreateMsgQueue(habObj, 0);

  WinRegisterClass(habObj, "ThreadsObj", ObjWndProc, 0, 0);

  WinCreateWindow(HWND_OBJECT, "ThreadsObj", "", 0, 0, 0, 0,
                  0, 0, HWND_BOTTOM, ID_OBJECT, 0, 0);


  while (WinGetMsg(habObj, &qmsg, (HWND)NULL, 0, 0))
    WinDispatchMsg(habObj, &qmsg);

  WinDestroyMsgQueue(hmqObj);
  WinTerminate(habObj);
  DosExit(0, 0);
  return;
}

/******************************************************/

MRESULT EXPENTRY ObjWndProc(HWND hwnd, ULONG msg, MPARAM mp1,
                            MPARAM mp2)
{
  switch (msg)
    {
        /**************************************/
        /* Process window messages as usual   */
        /**************************************/
    }
  return WinDefWindowProc(hwnd, msg, mp1, mp2);
}
```

12.3 Killing a thread (32-bit)

A new function has been added to OS/2 that enables a thread to be killed, DosKillThread. If you use this function, be aware not only that the thread is killed instantly and so cannot perform any clean-up operations, but also that the thread must have been started by the current process. (Personally, I prefer to kill a thread by sending it a suicide message, see Sec. 12.4. At least it is then allowed to tidy its affairs before departing this world, rather than being brutally murdered.) However, there may be occasions when it is perfectly safe to kill a thread and so the introduction of this function will prove useful. The following example assumes that the thread ID has already been assigned:

```
static TID tidLTimer;              /* Thread ID       */

case ID_KILL:
  DosKillThread(tidLTimer);        /* 32-bit only    */
  break;
```

12.4 Killing a thread (16-bit and 32-bit)

Although it is possible to suspend a thread, you cannot kill a thread in 16-bit OS/2. Instead, you must devise some method whereby the thread 'commits suicide', that is, it is forced to issue a `DosExit`. Two methods are possible here:

- By a global variable
- By sending the thread a message

Let us look at the global variable method first. In the following example, while the flag `fThreadActive` is TRUE, whenever the thread awakes from its sleep it will process; if the flag is then set to FALSE in some other thread, after its three-minute sleep it will fall through the loop and exit:

```
VOID LTimer (VOID)                 /* Non-message queue thread */
{
  while (fThreadActive)
  {
  DosSleep(180000);                /* Wait for 3 minutes       */
    if (fThreadActive)
    {
        /*********************/
        /* Do some processing  */
        /*********************/
    }
  }
  DosExit(0, 0);                   /* Kill the thread          */
}
```

If we use the message sending process to kill a thread then that thread must have a message queue and a message processing loop. If we are going to use the window procedure solely to make the thread 'commit suicide', and therefore have no user interface, we can use an object window. When the time comes to kill the thread, we need to obtain the handle of the object window, using enumeration, and then send it a user message, `UM_SUICIDE`. When the thread's window procedure receives this, it posts itself a WM_QUIT message and hence exits:

```
#define UM_SUICIDE  WM_USER+4          /* Define user message */

/*------------------------------------------*/
/* In the main thread's window procedure...  */
/*------------------------------------------*/
case ID_KILL_THREAD:                          /*-------------- */
  WinSendMsg(hwndObject, UM_SUICIDE, 0,0);/* Kill thread  */
  break;                                      /*-------------- */

/***********************************************************/

/*------------------------------------*/
/* In the thread's window procedure...  */
/*------------------------------------*/
case UM_SUICIDE:
  WinPostMsg(hwnd, WM_QUIT, 0, 0);
  break;
```

12.5. Setting a timer for longer than 65 seconds

Using the 16-bit WinStartTimer the time interval is defined in milliseconds as a USHORT, whereas in the 32-bit version it is defined as a ULONG. However, for OS/2 V2.0 it still uses a USHORT internally and will not therefore accept a 32-bit value. This will change when Presentation Manager is fully 32-bit. In the meantime, it obviously restricts you to a time interval of a little over 65 seconds, which is probably all right for most purposes, but occasionally you may need an interval greater than this. Two ways of doing this are:

- WinStartTimer
- DosSleep

Using WinStartTimer define a static variable for the required time period, three minutes in this case, and at a convenient place in your program start a one minute timer. When your window procedure receives a WM_TIMER message, decrement the time period and check for zero. If it is zero then our time is up and we can do the necessary processing and reset the time period:

```
static USHORT usTimePeriod = 3;     /* 3 minute time interval */
WinStartTimer(hab, hwnd, 1, 60000   /* 1 minute timer         */

/***********************************************************/
case WM_TIMER:
  if (--usTimePeriod == 0)                /* 3 minutes elapsed?   */
```

```
{
  DosBeep(100, 100);
  DosBeep(300, 100);
  DosBeep(500, 100);
  DosBeep(700, 100);
  usTimePeriod = 3;
}
break;
```

Using `DosSleep` the time interval is a ULONG and so gives us over 49 days. However, we *must not* use `DosSleep` in our window procedure otherwise performance will suffer, so we start another thread to do the sleeping. When it wakes up, it can send a `WM_USER` message to the client window to trigger the processing, or it may even be possible to do it in the timer thread. This 'thread with no message queue' is covered in Sec. 12.2.1.

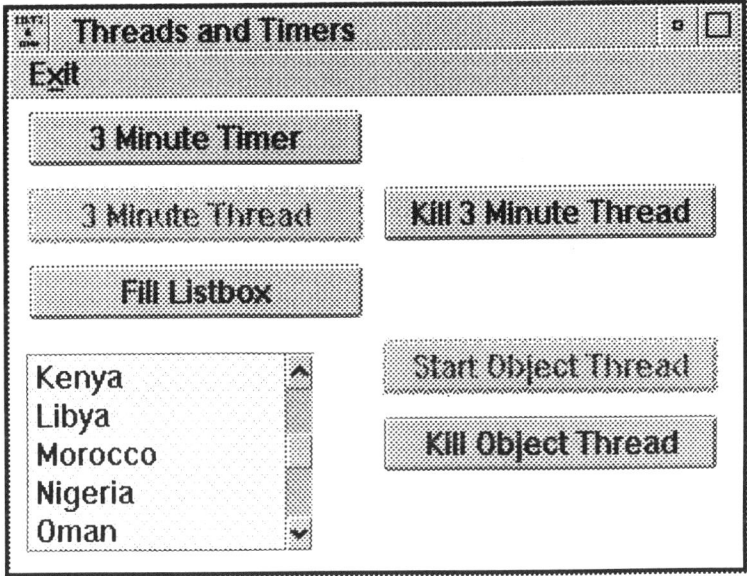

Figure 12.1. Threads and timers output.

12.6 Sample program

This program illustrates the use of multiple threads and timers in a Presentation Manager program. The main window (Fig. 12.1) on startup has four pushbuttons:

- 3 Minute Timer   This causes a timer to start and a series of beeps to sound every three minutes.
- 3 Minute Thread   This starts a thread with no message queue and 'unhides'

another pushbutton which can be used to kill the thread. Again, every three minutes a series of beeps will be heard. Pressing the Kill button causes a Dos-KillThread call to be made, thus ending the thread.

- Fill Listbox This starts another thread which fills the listbox and then ends, it does not continue running. However, since it communicates with the client window using WinSendMsg, this thread requires a message queue. Just to make this a long process 26 items are inserted into a listbox 100 times in the sample program. However, only about 65 groups are inserted, since the listbox limit of 64 kb is reached at this point. When the thread starts, this button is disabled and remains so until the thread completes. Only then can it be pressed again.

Note that the 64 kb listbox limit will not be lifted until the Presentation Manager is fully 32-bit.

- Start Object Thread The last button starts a thread which has both a message queue and a message processing loop. It creates an object window which is used to receive a message telling it to commit suicide. To initiate this message another Kill button is shown. When the thread dies it clears the listbox and sounds a series of beeps.

The following listings show the program's header file, Fig. 12.2, resource file, Fig. 12.3, and C source file, Fig. 12.4.

```
#define   ID_MAINWND    200
#define   ID_TITLE      201
#define   IDM_ONE       202
#define   MI_EXIT       203
#define   MI_RESUME     204
#define   ID_TIMER      205
#define   ID_THREAD     206
#define   ID_KILLER     207
#define   ID_LTHREAD    208
#define   ID_LIST       209
#define   ID_OBJECT     210
#define   ID_OBUTTON    211
#define   ID_KOBUTTON   212
```

Figure 12.2. Threads and timers: header file.

```
#include <os2.h>
#include "threads.h"

STRINGTABLE PRELOAD
BEGIN
  ID_TITLE, "Threads and Timers"
```

Figure 12.3 Threads and timers: resource file. Continues.

```
END
ICON         ID_MAINWND threads.ico

ACCELTABLE   ID_MAINWND
BEGIN
  VK_F3,     MI_EXIT,        VIRTUALKEY
END
MENU         ID_MAINWND PRELOAD
BEGIN
  SUBMENU "E~xit",                        IDM_ONE
  BEGIN
    MENUITEM "~Exit Program\tF3",   MI_EXIT,    MIS_TEXT
    MENUITEM "~Resume Program",     MI_RESUME,  MIS_TEXT
  END
END
```

Figure 12.3. Threads and timers: resource file. Concluded.

```
#define    INCL_WINWINDOWMGR
#define    INCL_WINFRAMEMGR
#define    INCL_WINSWITCHLIST
#define    INCL_WINSYS
#define    INCL_WINTIMER
#define    INCL_WINLISTBOXES
#define    INCL_DOSPROCESS

#define    UM_3_MINUTES_UP              WM_USER
#define    UM_ENABLE_KILL3MIN_BUTTON    WM_USER+1
#define    UM_ENABLE_START3MIN_BUTTON   WM_USER+2
#define    UM_ENABLE_LISTBOX_BUTTON     WM_USER+3
#define    UM_SUICIDE                   WM_USER+4

#include   <os2.h>
#include   <string.h>
#include   <stdio.h>
#include   "threads.h"

MRESULT EXPENTRY MainWndProc(HWND, ULONG, MPARAM, MPARAM);
MRESULT EXPENTRY ObjWndProc (HWND, ULONG, MPARAM, MPARAM);

VOID    _System   LTimer(VOID * ULONG);
VOID              ListBox  (VOID);
VOID              ObjThread(VOID);
HWND              GetClient(VOID);

BOOL    fThreadActive;
```

Figure 12.4 Threads and timers: C source file. Continues.

```
static PSZ szCountry[] = {"Austria", "Belgium", "Canada", "Denmark",
                          "Egypt",   "Finland",  "Greece", "Hungary",
                          "India",   "Japan",    "Kenya",  "Libya",
                          "Morocco", "Nigeria",  "Oman",   "Peru",
                          "Qatar",   "Romania",  "Spain",  "Turkey",
                          "Uruguay", "Venezuela","Wales",
                          "Xanxere", "Yemen",    "Zambia"};
/**************************************************************/
INT main (VOID)
{
  HAB     hab;
  HMQ     hmq;
  HWND    hwndFrame,
          hwndClient;
  QMSG    qmsg;
  ULONG   flFrameFlags;
  CHAR    szTitle[80];
  SWCNTRL PgmEntry;
  LONG    lX_Left,
          lY_Bot,
          lHeight,
          lWidth,
          lScrHeight,
          lScrWidth;
/**************************************************************/
  hab = WinInitialize(0);
  hmq = WinCreateMsgQueue(hab, 0);
  WinRegisterClass(hab, "Threads", MainWndProc, CS_SIZEREDRAW, 0);
  WinLoadString(hab, (HMODULE)NULL, ID_TITLE,
                sizeof(szTitle), szTitle);
  flFrameFlags = FCF_TITLEBAR    | FCF_SYSMENU | FCF_MENU |
                 FCF_SIZEBORDER  | FCF_MINMAX  | FCF_ACCELTABLE|
                 FCF_ICON;
  hwndFrame = WinCreateStdWindow(HWND_DESKTOP, 0, &flFrameFlags,
                                 "Threads", szTitle, 0,
                                 (HMODULE)NULL, ID_MAINWND,
                                 &hwndClient);
  lScrWidth  = WinQuerySysValue(HWND_DESKTOP, SV_CXSCREEN);
  lScrHeight = WinQuerySysValue(HWND_DESKTOP, SV_CYSCREEN);
  lWidth  = 400;
  lHeight = 300;
```

Figure 12.4 Threads and timers: C source file. Continues.

```
lX_Left = (lScrWidth  - lWidth)  / 2;
lY_Bot  = (lScrHeight - lHeight) / 2;
/*----------------------*/
/* Startup in foreground   */
/*----------------------*/

WinSetWindowPos(hwndFrame, 0, lX_Left, lY_Bot, lWidth, lHeight,
            SWP_SIZE | SWP_MOVE | SWP_SHOW | SWP_ACTIVATE);

WinCreateWindow(hwndClient, WC_BUTTON, "3 Minute Timer",
            WS_VISIBLE, 10, 210, 180, 30, hwndClient,
            HWND_TOP, ID_TIMER, 0, 0);

WinCreateWindow(hwndClient, WC_BUTTON, "3 Minute Thread",
            WS_VISIBLE, 10, 170, 180, 30, hwndClient,
            HWND_TOP, ID_THREAD, 0, 0);

WinCreateWindow(hwndClient, WC_BUTTON, "Kill 3 Minute Thread", 0,
            200, 170, 180, 30, hwndClient, HWND_TOP,
            ID_KILLER, 0, 0);

WinCreateWindow(hwndClient, WC_BUTTON, "Fill Listbox",
            WS_VISIBLE, 10, 130, 180, 30, hwndClient,
            HWND_TOP, ID_LTHREAD, 0, 0);
WinCreateWindow(hwndClient, WC_LISTBOX, NULL, WS_VISIBLE,
            10, 10, 150, 100, hwndClient,
            HWND_BOTTOM, ID_LIST, 0, 0);
WinCreateWindow(hwndClient, WC_BUTTON, "Start Object Thread",
            WS_VISIBLE, 200, 90, 180, 30, hwndClient,
            HWND_TOP, ID_OBUTTON, 0, 0);
WinCreateWindow(hwndClient, WC_BUTTON, "Kill Object Thread",
            0, 200, 50, 180, 30, hwndClient,
            HWND_TOP, ID_KOBUTTON, 0, 0);

PgmEntry.hwnd           = hwndFrame;      /*--------------------*/
PgmEntry.hwndIcon       = (HWND)NULL;     /*Add to window list  */
PgmEntry.hprog          = (HPROGRAM)      /*--------------------*/
                          NULL;
PgmEntry.idProc         = (PID)NULL;
PgmEntry.idSession      = (ULONG)NULL;
PgmEntry.uchVisibility  = SWL_VISIBLE;
PgmEntry.fbJump         = SWL_JUMPABLE;
strcpy(PgmEntry.szSwtitle, szTitle);

WinAddSwitchEntry(&PgmEntry);
```

Figure 12.4. Threads and timers: C source file. Continues.

```c
    while (WinGetMsg(hab, &qmsg, (HWND)NULL, 0, 0))
      WinDispatchMsg(hab, &qmsg);

    /*------------------------------------*/
    /* Remove from window list and clean up    */
    /*------------------------------------*/

    WinRemoveSwitchEntry(WinQuerySwitchHandle(hwndFrame, 0));
    WinDestroyWindow(hwndFrame);
    WinDestroyMsgQueue(hmq);
    WinTerminate(hab);
    return 0;
}

/*******************************************************************/
MRESULT EXPENTRY MainWndProc(HWND hwnd, ULONG msg, MPARAM mp1,
                             MPARAM mp2)
{
    HAB      hab;
    HWND     hObject;
    HENUM    hEnum;
    CHAR     szClassBuffer[20];
    BOOL     fObjFound;
    static   USHORT usTimePeriod = 3;      /* 3 minute time interval */
    static   ULONG  ulStackSize = 4096;
    static   TID    tidLTimer,
                    tidLBox,
                    tidObj;

    switch (msg)
      {
        case UM_3_MINUTES_UP:
          DosBeep(1000, 100);
          DosBeep(3000, 100);
          DosBeep(5000, 100);
          DosBeep(7000, 100);
          break;

        case UM_ENABLE_KILL3MIN_BUTTON:
          WinEnableWindow(WinWindowFromID(hwnd, ID_KILLER), TRUE);
          WinShowWindow(WinWindowFromID(hwnd, ID_KILLER), TRUE);
          break;

        case UM_ENABLE_LISTBOX_BUTTON:
          WinEnableWindow(WinWindowFromID(hwnd, ID_LTHREAD), TRUE);
          break;
```

Figure 12.4. Threads and timers: C source file. Continues.

```
      case UM_ENABLE_START3MIN_BUTTON:
        WinEnableWindow(WinWindowFromID(hwnd, ID_THREAD), TRUE);
        WinEnableWindow(WinWindowFromID(hwnd, ID_KILLER), FALSE);
        break;

      case WM_TIMER:
        if (-usTimePeriod == 0)              /* 3 minutes elapsed? */
        {
          DosBeep(100, 100);
          DosBeep(300, 100);
          DosBeep(500, 100);
          DosBeep(700, 100);
          usTimePeriod = 3;
        }
        break;

      case WM_COMMAND:
        switch (SHORT1FROMMP(mp1))
          {
            case ID_TIMER:                   /* Start a timer */
              WinEnableWindow(WinWindowFromID(hwnd, ID_TIMER),
                          FALSE);
              hab = WinQueryAnchorBlock(hwnd);
              WinStartTimer(hab, hwnd, 1, 60000);
              break;

            case ID_THREAD:            /* Start 3 minute timer thread */
              WinEnableWindow(WinWindowFromID(hwnd, ID_THREAD),
                          FALSE);
              fThreadActive = TRUE;
              DosCreateThread(&tidLTimer, (PFNTHREAD)LTimer,
                          (ULONG)hwnd, 0, ulStackSize);
              break;

            case ID_OBUTTON:           /* Start object window thread */
              WinEnableWindow(WinWindowFromID(hwnd, ID_OBUTTON),
                          FALSE);
              DosCreateThread(&tidObj, (PFNTHREAD)ObjThread, 0, 0,
                          ulStackSize);
              break;

            case ID_KOBUTTON:          /* Kill object window thread */
              fObjFound = FALSE;
                                       /* Enumerate object windows  */
                                       /* to find its handle so that */
                                       /* we can send it a message   */
```

Figure 12.4. Threads and timers: C source file. Continues.

```
              hEnum = WinBeginEnumWindows(HWND_OBJECT);
              while (!fObjFound)

              {
                hObject = WinGetNextWindow(hEnum);
                WinQueryClassName(hObject, sizeof(szClassBuffer),
                              szClassBuffer);
                if (!strcmp(szClassBuffer, "ThreadsObj"))
                {
                  fObjFound = TRUE;
                  WinSendMsg(hObject, UM_SUICIDE, 0, 0);
                }
              }
              WinEndEnumWindows(hEnum);
              break;
            case ID_KILLER:                  /* Kill 3 minute thread  */
              WinSendMsg(hwnd, UM_ENABLE_START3MIN_BUTTON, 0, 0);
                                             /*--------------------*/
              DosKillThread(tidLTimer); /* 32-bit only            */
                                             /*--------------------*/
           /* fThreadActive = FALSE; */  /* For 16-bit OS/2 we use */
                                         /* the global flag method */
              break;                         /*--------------------*/

            case ID_LTHREAD:                 /* Start listbox thread  */
              WinEnableWindow(WinWindowFromID(hwnd, ID_LTHREAD),
                              FALSE);
              DosCreateThread(&tidLBox, (PFNTHREAD)ListBox,
                              0, 0, ulStackSize);
              break;

            case MI_EXIT:
              hab = WinQueryAnchorBlock(hwnd);
              WinStopTimer(hab, hwnd, 1);
              WinPostMsg(hwnd, WM_QUIT, 0, 0);
              break;

            default:
              break;
        }
      break;
    case WM_ERASEBACKGROUND:
      return (MRESULT)TRUE;
}
```

Figure 12.4. Threads and timers: C source file. Continues.

```
  return WinDefWindowProc(hwnd, msg, mp1, mp2);
}
/***********************************************************/
VOID    _System LTimer(VOID * parm)    /* Non-message queue thread  */
{
  HWND  hwndClient;

  hwndClient = (HWND)parm;
  WinPostMsg(hwndClient, UM_ENABLE_KILL3MIN_BUTTON, 0, 0);
  while (fThreadActive)
  {
     DosSleep(180000);                 /* Wait for 3 minutes          */
     if (fThreadActive)
       WinPostMsg(hwndClient, UM_3_MINUTES_UP, 0, 0);
  }
  DosBeep(100, 500);                   /*  Will never be executed if */
  DosExit(0, 0);                       /*  DosKillThread used. Will  */
}                                      /*  be killed instantly.      */
/***********************************************************/
VOID  ListBox(VOID)             /* Message queue thread without    */
{                               /* message processing loop         */
  HAB     habThread;
  HMQ     hmqThread;
  HWND    hClient;
  SHORT   I,
          J,
          sCount;
  CHAR    szLBoxLine[20];

  habThread = WinInitialize(0);
  hmqThread = WinCreateMsgQueue(habThread, 0);
  WinCancelShutdown(hmqThread, TRUE);
  hClient = GetClient();
  sCount = 0;
  WinSendMsg(WinWindowFromID(hClient, ID_LIST), LM_DELETEALL,
            0, 0);
  for (J = 0; J < 100; J++)
  {
   for (I = 0; I < 26; I++)
    {
      sCount++;
      sprintf(szLBoxLine, "%d %s", sCount, szCountry[I]);
```

Figure 12.4. Threads and timers: C source file. Continues.

```
      WinSendMsg(WinWindowFromID(hClient, ID_LIST), LM_INSERTITEM,
            MPFROMSHORT(LIT_END), MPFROMP(szLBoxLine)));
    }
  }
  WinDestroyMsgQueue(hmqThread);
  WinTerminate(habThread);
  WinPostMsg(hClient, UM_ENABLE_LISTBOX_BUTTON, 0, 0);
  DosExit(0, 0);
}
/****************************************************************/
VOID   ObjThread(VOID)              /* Thread with a message queue */
{                                   /* and message processing loop */
  HAB      habObj;
  HMQ      hmqObj;
  QMSG     qmsg;

  habObj = WinInitialize(0);
  hmqObj = WinCreateMsgQueue(habObj, 0);

  WinRegisterClass(habObj, "ThreadsObj", ObjWndProc, 0, 0);

  WinCreateWindow(HWND_OBJECT, "ThreadsObj", "", 0, 0, 0, 0, 0, 0,
                  HWND_BOTTOM, ID_OBJECT, 0, 0);

  while (WinGetMsg(habObj, &qmsg, (HWND)NULL, 0, 0))
    WinDispatchMsg(habObj, &qmsg);

  WinDestroyMsgQueue(hmqObj);
  WinTerminate(habObj);
  DosExit(0, 0);
}
/****************************************************************/
MRESULT EXPENTRY ObjWndProc(HWND hwnd, ULONG msg, MPARAM mp1,
                            MPARAM mp2)
{
  SHORT    I;
  static   HWND    hClient;
  switch (msg)
    {
      case WM_CREATE:
        hClient = GetClient();
        WinSendMsg(WinWindowFromID(hClient, ID_LIST),
                   LM_DELETEALL, 0, 0);
        for (I = 0; I < 26; I++)
```

Figure 12.4. Threads and timers: C source file. Continues.

```
            {
              WinSendMsg(WinWindowFromID(hClient, ID_LIST),
                         LM_INSERTITEM, MPFROMSHORT(LIT_END),
                         MPFROMP(szCountry[I]));
            }
            WinEnableWindow(WinWindowFromID(hClient, ID_KOBUTTON),
                            TRUE);
            WinShowWindow(WinWindowFromID(hClient, ID_KOBUTTON),
                          TRUE);
            break;
        case UM_SUICIDE:
            DosBeep(400, 100);
            DosBeep(300, 100);
            DosBeep(200, 100);
            DosBeep(100, 100);
            WinSendMsg(WinWindowFromID(hClient, ID_LIST),
                       LM_DELETEALL, 0, 0);
            WinEnableWindow(WinWindowFromID(hClient, ID_OBUTTON),
                            TRUE);
            WinEnableWindow(WinWindowFromID(hClient, ID_KOBUTTON),
                            FALSE);
            WinPostMsg(hwnd, WM_QUIT, 0, 0);
            break;
    }
    return WinDefWindowProc(hwnd, msg, mp1, mp2);
}
/**************************************************************/
HWND  GetClient(VOID)              /* Get main client window handle */
{
    HENUM hEnum;
    HWND  hWin,
          hClient;
    CHAR  szClassBuffer[20];
    BOOL  fClientFound;

    fClientFound = FALSE;
    hEnum = WinBeginEnumWindows(HWND_DESKTOP);
    while (!fClientFound)
    {
        hWin = WinGetNextWindow(hEnum);
        WinQueryClassName(hWin, sizeof(szClassBuffer),
                          szClassBuffer);
```

Figure 12.4. Threads and timers: C source file. Continues.

```
    if (!strcmp(szClassBuffer, "#1"))
    {
      hClient = WinWindowFromID(hWin, FID_CLIENT);
      WinQueryClassName(hClient, sizeof(szClassBuffer),
                        szClassBuffer);
      if (!strcmp(szClassBuffer, "Threads"))
      {
          fClientFound = TRUE;
      }
    }
  }
  WinEndEnumWindows(hEnum);
  return hClient;
}
```

Figure 12.4. Threads and timers: C source file. Concluded.

13
Menus, task management and shutdown

13.1 Menus and menu bars

13.1.1 Adding items to the system menu

Perhaps one of the most common queries regarding menus is: 'How can I alter the system menu?' Usually, it is for adding an About option, although this is now added as Product Information in the Help pull-down menu. Anyway let us look at how we would answer the query.

The first thing we need to do is to initialize the menu items we intend to insert. Usually, an About... box is inserted as the last option on the menu with a separator to distinguish it from the others. In the following code this definition is the MENUITEM array Item. Following that we have the text associated with these items:

```
VOID    AddMenuItem(HWND hwnd)
{
  HWND          hSysMenu,
                hSysSubMenu;
  MENUITEM      SysMenu;
  SHORT         I,
                sIDSysMenu;
  static MENUITEM  Item[2] = {MIT_END, MIS_SEPARATOR,
                              0, 0, 0, 0,
                              MIT_END, MIS_TEXT,
                              0, ID_ABOUT, 0, 0};
  static CHAR   *Text[2] = {NULL, "~About..."};

  hSysMenu = WinWindowFromID(WinQueryWindow(hwnd,
                             QW_PARENT), FID_SYSMENU);

  sIDSysMenu = SHORT1FROMMR(WinSendMsg(hSysMenu,
```

```
                              MM_ITEMIDFROMPOSITION, 0, 0));
  WinSendMsg(hSysMenu, MM_QUERYITEM,
             MPFROM2SHORT(sIDSysMenu, FALSE),
             MPFROMP(&SysMenu));

  hSysSubMenu = SysMenu.hwndSubMenu;

  for (I = 0; I < 2; I++)
    WinSendMsg(hSysSubMenu, MM_INSERTITEM, MPFROMP(Item+I),
               MPFROMP(Text[I]));
}
```

Having defined our extra menu options we obtain the handle of the system menu by calling `WinWindowFromID` with the identifier `FID_SYSMENU`. However, this is not the handle we ultimately need; what is returned here is the handle of the actual system menu window in the top-left corner of the window. We really need the handle of the submenu, the one which contains all the options. To get this we send the system menu an `MM_ITEMIDFROMPOSITION` message to give us the ID of the actual menu list, and once we have this we can obtain the characteristics of the menu by sending it an `MM_QUERYITEM` message. The important item returned in the `SysMenu` structure is the actual handle of the submenu, armed with this we can insert our items into it by sending the submenu an `MM_INSERTITEM` message.

This code would normally be executed at window creation time, that is, in your `WM_CREATE` case statement, so do not forget that you cannot use `hwndFrame` here if you have defined it as a global variable—a common error, see Sec. 2.1. Clicking on About... will cause a `WM_COMMAND` message to be sent to our window with the low short of `mp1` set to `ID_ABOUT`. On receiving this, we display a message box giving details about the program:

```
case ID_ABOUT:
  WinMessageBox(HWND_DESKTOP, hwnd,
      "Version 1\n31 March 1992\nWritten by Bryan Goodyer",
      "Menus & Task Management Sample Program", 0,
      MB_INFORMATION | MB_OK | MB_MOVEABLE);
  break;
```

This information could, alternatively, be displayed in a dialog box.

13.1.2 Changing a window's menu

There may be times when it is convenient for you to have two or more menus defined in your resource file for a window and, depending on what your user is doing, to switch between them when appropriate. The following resource file has two such menus, the second of which adds an extra option:

```
MENU            ID_MAINWND PRELOAD
BEGIN
  SUBMENU   "E~xit",                  IDM_ONE
  BEGIN
    MENUITEM "~Exit Program\tF3",     MI_EXIT,    MIS_TEXT
    MENUITEM "~Resume Program",       MI_RESUME,  MIS_TEXT
  END
END

MENU            ID_MENU2
BEGIN
  SUBMENU "~Options",                 IDM_TWO
  BEGIN
    MENUITEM "Menu Item ~1",          MI_ITEM1,   MIS_TEXT
    MENUITEM "Menu Item ~2",          MI_ITEM2,   MIS_TEXT
  END
  SUBMENU "E~xit",                    IDM_THREE
  BEGIN
    MENUITEM "~Exit Program\tF3",     MI_EXIT,    MIS_TEXT
    MENUITEM "~Resume Program",       MI_RESUME,  MIS_TEXT
  END
END
```

A quick and easy way to switch the menus is to destroy the current menu and then use `WinLoadMenu` to load the next. You must then follow this with a `WM_UPDATEFRAME` message to force the frame to be redrawn, telling it which frame control has been added, in this case `FCF_MENU`:

```
hwndFrame = WinQueryWindow(hwnd, QW_PARENT);

WinDestroyWindow(WinWindowFromID(hwndFrame, FID_MENU));
WinLoadMenu(hwndFrame, (HMODULE)NULL, ID_MENU2);
WinSendMsg(hwndFrame, WM_UPDATEFRAME, (MPARAM)FCF_MENU, 0);
```

13.1.3 Checking a menu item

Whenever a menu is about to be activated, the system sends your application a `WM_INITMENU` message so that you can make any changes to the submenu before it is displayed. For example, you may need to add a check mark to an item, depending on the current state of the application. The following sample code shows this by setting up a flag, initially `FALSE`, and sending an `MM_SETITEMATTR` message to the menu. Because we are sending the message to the top-level menu rather than the submenu, we must specify `TRUE` to ensure the submenu is searched for the item. To check an item we use the `MIA_CHECKED` attribute. The data associated with this is dependent on the flag, and since it is initially FALSE the item is not checked. However, if we now select the item, the flag changes state and next time the menu is displayed the item will be checked. This also applies to disabling items using the MIA_DISABLED attribute.

With the introduction of OS/2 version 2.0, sending an MM_SETITEMATTR message can be replaced with the macro WinCheckMenuItem, which makes the coding somewhat simpler and easier to read. Both methods are shown in the following code:

```
case WM_INITMENU:
  switch (SHORT1FROMMP(mp1))
  {
    case IDM_TWO:                    /*-------------------------*/
                                     /* Toggle menu item 1 on/off */
                                     /*-------------------------*/

      hwndFrame = WinQueryWindow(hwnd, QW_PARENT);
      hMenu = WinWindowFromID(hwndFrame, FID_MENU);
      WinCheckMenuItem(hMenu, MI_ITEM1, fbChecked);

      /*------------------------------------------------*/
      /*               Alternatively...                 */
      /*                                                */
      /* WinSendMsg(hMenu, MM_SETITEMATTR,              */
      /*            MPFROM2SHORT(MI_ITEM1, TRUE),       */
      /*            MPFROM2SHORT(MIA_CHECKED,           */
      /*            fbChecked ? MIA_CHECKED : 0));      */
      /*------------------------------------------------*/

      break;
  }
  break;

case WM_COMMAND:
  switch (SHORT1FROMMP(mp1))
  {
    case MI_ITEM1:
      fbChecked = (fbChecked ? FALSE : TRUE);
      break;

    ;
    ;
    ;
  }
  break;
```

Two further useful macros are:
- `WinIsMenuItemChecked`

    `fChecked = WinIsMenuItemChecked(hMenu, usMenuID);`
- `WinIsMenuItemEnabled`

    `fEnabled = WinIsMenuItemEnabled(hMenu, usMenuID);`

13.1.4 Deleting items from the system menu

To delete items from an application's system menu you must first obtain its handle and then send it an `MM_DELETEITEM` message. Ensure you use a value of `TRUE` for the `Includesubmenus` flag in the `mp1` parameter. This will cause a search of all the system menu's submenus for the item specified.

To delete the menu items `Size` and `Move` from the system menu use:

```
hwndSysMenu = WinWindowFromID(hwndFrame, FID_SYSMENU);

WinSendMsg(hwndSysMenu, MM_DELETEITEM,
           MPFROM2SHORT(SC_SIZE, TRUE), 0);

WinSendMsg(hwndSysMenu, MM_DELETEITEM,
           MPFROM2SHORT(SC_MOVE, TRUE), 0);
```

13.1.5 Deleting a separator from the system menu

If you want to remove `Close` from the system menu, you will also need to remove the separator following it. To do this, you must first obtain the handle of the system menu submenu, that is, the actual menu displaying the items, and send an `MM_ITEMPOSITIONFROMID` message to obtain the position of `Close` in the menu. You then add one to this to get the position of the separator. Sending an `MM_ITEMIDFROMPOSITION` message for this value gives the actual item ID for the separator, which can now be used in the `MM_DELETEITEM` message. The `Close` option can be deleted in the normal manner, that is, by specifying `(SC_CLOSE, TRUE)` as the first parameter of the `MM_DELETEITEM` message to be sent to the system menu as shown in Sec. 13.1.4 for `Size` and `Move`:

```
VOID DelClose(HWND hwnd) /* Pass in the client window handle */
{
  HWND        hSysMenu,
              hSysSubMenu;
  MENUITEM    SysMenu;
  SHORT       sIDItem,
              sIDSep,
              sIDSysMenu;
```

```
    hSysMenu = WinWindowFromID(WinQueryWindow(hwnd,
                        QW_PARENT), FID_SYSMENU);
    sIDSysMenu = SHORT1FROMMR(WinSendMsg(hSysMenu,
                        MM_ITEMIDFROMPOSITION, 0, 0));
    WinSendMsg(hSysMenu, MM_QUERYITEM,
            MPFROM2SHORT(sIDSysMenu, FALSE),
            MPFROMP(&SysMenu));
    hSysSubMenu = SysMenu.hwndSubMenu;
    sIDItem = SHORT1FROMMR(WinSendMsg(hSysSubMenu,
                        MM_ITEMPOSITIONFROMID,
                        MPFROM2SHORT(SC_CLOSE, FALSE),
                        0));
    if (sIDItem != MIT_ERROR)
    {                                          /*----------------*/
        sIDSep = sIDItem + 1;                  /* Get separator ID */
                                               /*----------------*/
        sIDSep = SHORT1FROMMR(WinSendMsg(hSysSubMenu,
                        MM_ITEMIDFROMPOSITION,
                        MPFROMSHORT(sIDSep), 0));
        WinSendMsg(hSysMenu, MM_DELETEITEM,
                MPFROM2SHORT(SC_CLOSE, TRUE), 0);
        WinSendMsg(hSysSubMenu, MM_DELETEITEM,
                MPFROM2SHORT(sIDSep, FALSE), 0);
    }
}
```

13.1.6 *Disabling/enabling menu bar*

To disable/enable the menu bar, and thus disable/enable all its pull-down menus, use `WinEnableWindow`. Once the menu bar has been disabled no menu option may be selected:

```
/*--------------------*/
/* Disable all menu items */
/*-----------------  ---*/
hwndFrame = WinQueryWindow(hwnd, QW_PARENT);
WinEnableWindow(WinWindowFromID(hwndFrame, FID_MENU),
            FALSE);
/*-----------------  ---*/
/* Enable all menu items */
/*------------- ------*/
```

Menus, task management and shutdown

```
WinEnableWindow(WinWindowFromID(hwndFrame, FID_MENU),
                TRUE);
```

13.1.7 Disabling/enabling items in an application menu

To disable/enable an item in your application menu, you must first obtain its handle and then send it an `MM_SETITEMATTR` message to change the attribute of the item. This would normally be done in your `WM_INITMENU` case statement, depending on the setting of a flag. See also Sec. 13.1.3.

Alternatively, you could use the macro `WinEnableMenuItem` to disable a menu item:

```
hwndFrame = WinQueryWindow(hwnd, QW_PARENT);
hMenu = WinWindowFromID(hwndFrame, FID_MENU);
                                     /*----------------*/
                                     /* Disable item 3 */
                                     /*----------------*/
WinEnableMenuItem(hMenu, MI_ITEM3, FALSE);
```

13.1.8 Disabling/enabling items in the system menu

To disable/enable an item in the system menu, you must first obtain its handle and then send it an `MM_SETITEMATTR` message to change the attribute of the item. However, you can only disable `Close` and `Window list` using this method:

```
/*----------------------*/
/* To disable 'Close'... */
/*----------------------*/

hwndSysMenu = WinWindowFromID(hwndFrame, FID_SYSMENU);

WinSendMsg(hwndSysMenu, MM_SETITEMATTR,
           MPFROM2SHORT(SC_CLOSE, TRUE),
           MPFROM2SHORT(MIA_DISABLED, MIA_DISABLED));

/*----------------------*/
/* To enable 'Close'... */
/*----------------------*/

WinSendMsg(hwndSysMenu, MM_SETITEMATTR,
           MPFROM2SHORT(SC_CLOSE, TRUE),
           MPFROM2SHORT(MIA_DISABLED, 0));
```

Alternatively, you could use the macro `WinEnableMenuItem`, see Sec. 13.1.7.

If you need to disable `Move` then using `WinEnableWindow` to disable the title bar will cause `Move` to be greyed as a result, see Sec. 2.3.1.

Note: There are no such restrictions in *deleting* items from the system menu.

13.1.9 Dismiss `MIA_NODISMISS` menu

If you have a menu in which one or more items are defined with the `MIA_NODISMISS` attribute and you select one of these items, then the menu does not disappear:

```
BEGIN
  MENUITEM "Menu Item ~1", MI_ITEM1, MIS_TEXT
  MENUITEM "Menu Item ~2", MI_ITEM2, MIS_TEXT, MIA_NODISMISS
  MENUITEM "Menu Item ~3", MI_ITEM3, MIS_TEXT
END
```

This may be what you need in your application, but the problem comes when you do want to dismiss it, say by pressing a mouse button. You will not be able to do it by sending an `MM_DISMISSMENU` message as the menu is no longer in menu mode. Instead, you must post `MM_STARTMENUMODE` and `MM_ENDMENUMODE` messages. Notice that the `MM_ENDMENUMODE` message is *posted*. The documentation states that this message should be *sent*. However, the `MM_STARTMENUMODE` message *must be posted*. So if the START was posted, and the END was sent, then the END would be processed first. This is why both must be posted.

To force a menu to dismiss use:

```
case WM_BUTTON1DOWN:
  /*----------------------*/
  /* Force menu to dismiss   */
  /*----------------------*/
  hwndFrame = WinQueryWindow(hwnd, QW_PARENT);
  hMenu = WinWindowFromID(hwndFrame, FID_MENU);
  WinPostMsg(hMenu, MM_STARTMENUMODE, MPFROM2SHORT(FALSE,
             TRUE), (MPARAM)NULL);
  WinPostMsg(hMenu, MM_ENDMENUMODE, MPFROMSHORT(TRUE),
             (MPARAM)NULL);
  ;
  ;
  ;
  break;
```

13.2 Pop-up menus

It can sometimes be useful for your user to be able to pop up a menu by pressing a mouse button, say button 2, rather than have to move to the menu bar and select an item. To do this, you must first define your menu in the usual way in the resource file, and then trap the WM_CREATE/WM_INITDLG, and WM_BUTTON2DOWN messages:

```
MENU ID_MENU2 PRELOAD
BEGIN
   SUBMENU "", ID_OPTIONS2 <=== Include SUBMENU for 16-bit,
                                  it is not required for 32-bit
   BEGIN
     MENUITEM "Menu Item ~1", ID_ITEM1
     MENUITEM "Menu Item ~2", ID_ITEM2
     MENUITEM "Menu Item ~3", ID_ITEM3
     MENUITEM SEPARATOR
     MENUITEM "Menu Item ~4", ID_ITEM4
     MENUITEM "Menu Item ~5", ID_ITEM5
   END
END
```

In OS/2 version 2.0 the use of pop-up menus has been made considerably easier with the introduction of the WinPopupMenu function. Since this function is not available in version 1.x, the code needed to implement pop-up menus for both 16-bit and 32-bit versions is included in the next two sections.

If you are using a pop-up menu in a dialog box, and you have also defined a menu-bar, then ensure you load the pop-up menu *before* the menu bar otherwise you will encounter many problems, and it will not function as desired! Also, you will need to add a case statement for the WM_NEXTMENU message and return NULL from it. Otherwise, if the menu is visible and the user presses button 1 in the dialog box *outside* the menu, your application will hang. Note that this only applies if you are mixing pop-up menus with a menu bar. Section 5.19.1 handles this situation.

13.2.1 16-bit version

In the WM_CREATE/WM_INITDLG case statement you need to obtain the handle of the menu, by using WinLoadMenu, and the menu bar height, by using WinQuerySysValue with a value ID of SV_CYMENU, that is, the height of a single-line menu. This is needed so that you can position the pop-up so that the first menu item lines up with the mouse pointer. Without doing this you will find that the menu items are a menu bar's height below the pointer.

To complete the implementation you need to get the position of the mouse pointer by using either the macro MOUSEMSG or the function WinQueryPointerPos, making sure you adjust the *Y* coordinate by adding the menu bar height to it. Finally you must *post* an MM_STARTMENUMODE message to the menu handle and position the menu using WinSetWindowPos.

You must then add the relevant case statements for the menu items in your `WM_COMMAND` case statement in order to handle the processing of each item:

```
static HWND      hMenu;
static ULONG     ulMenuHt;
POINTL           Pt;

case WM_CREATE:
  hMenu    = WinLoadMenu(hwnd, NULL, ID_MENU);
  ulMenuHt = WinQuerySysValue(HWND_DESKTOP, SV_CYMENU);
  break;

case WM_BUTTON2DOWN:
  Pt.x = MOUSEMSG(&msg)->x;
  Pt.y = MOUSEMSG(&msg)->y + ulMenuHt;
  WinPostMsg(hMenu, MM_STARTMENUMODE, MPFROM2SHORT(TRUE,
             TRUE), NULL);
  WinSetWindowPos(hMenu, HWND_TOP, (SHORT)Pt.x, (SHORT)Pt.y,
             0, 0, SWP_MOVE | SWP_SHOW);
  break;
```

13.2.2 32-bit version

The equivalent 32-bit code, this time for a dialog box, is as follows:

```
case WM_INITDLG:
  hMenu = WinLoadMenu(hwnd, (HMODULE)NULL, ID_MENU);
  break;

case WM_BUTTON2DOWN:
  WinQueryPointerPos(HWND_DESKTOP, &Pt);
  WinMapWindowPoints(HWND_DESKTOP, hwnd, &Pt, 1);
  WinPopupMenu(hwnd, hwnd, hMenu, Pt.x, Pt.y, 0, PU_KEYBOARD |
             PU_MOUSEBUTTON1);
  return (MRESULT)TRUE;
```

See also Sec. 5.19.1.

13.3 Task management

Although the task manager does not exist in OS/2 version 2.0 all the following is still applicable. If you are still using OS/2 version 1.x then where reference is made to the window list, read this as the task list.

13.3.1 Add program title to the window list

If you use the window style FCF_STANDARD, then your program's name will appear in the window list and your title bar, concatenated with any text you may have defined for your application's title bar. For example, if your program was called 'XYZ.EXE' and its title was 'Test Program', then in the window list it would appear as XYZ.EXETest Program.

If you do not want the program's EXE name to appear then do not use the style FCF_TASKLIST, which is one of the styles defined by FCF_STANDARD. Instead, add it to the window list using WinAddSwitchEntry:

```
SWCNTRL  PgmEntry;
static   HWND   hEntry;

PgmEntry.hwnd           = hwndFrame;
PgmEntry.hwndIcon       = (HWND)NULL;
PgmEntry.hprog          = (HPROGRAM)NULL;
PgmEntry.idProcess      = (PID)NULL;
PgmEntry.idSession      = (ULONG)NULL;
PgmEntry.uchVisibility  = SWL_VISIBLE;
PgmEntry.fbJump         = SWL_JUMPABLE;
strcpy(PgmEntry.szSwtitle, Title);

hEntry = WinAddSwitchEntry(&PgmEntry);

while(WinGetMsg(hab, &qmsg, (HWND)NULL, 0, 0))
   WinDispatchMsg(hab, &qmsg);

WinRemoveSwitchEntry(hEntry);
```

On exit from the program's message loop use WinRemoveSwitchEntry to remove the entry. Either declare a static handle, hEntry, or use WinQuerySwitchHandle to get the switch list handle when terminating:

```
WinRemoveSwitchEntry(WinQuerySwitchHandle(hwndFrame, 0));
```

13.3.2 Query/change the program entry in the window list

To change your application's entry in the window list, first use WinQuerySwitchHandle to query the window list for your application, modify the entry and then call WinChangeSwitchEntry to update it. The following code changes the program title and prevents you from jumping to it using the Alt-Esc and Alt-Tab key sequences:

```
SWCNTRL PgmEntry;
HSWITCH hSwl;
```

```
case WM_xxx:
  hSwL = WinQuerySwitchHandle(WinQueryWindow(hwnd,
                              QW_PARENT), 0);
  WinQuerySwitchEntry(hSwL, &PgmEntry);

  PgmEntry.fbJump = SWL_NOTJUMPABLE;
  strcpy(PgmEntry.szSwtitle, "New Title");

  WinChangeSwitchEntry(hSwl, &PgmEntry);
  break;
```

13.3.3 Remove Close *from the window list*

Warning: Undocumented, use with caution.

If you need to remove Close from the window list (32-bit), or disable the End Task button on the task list (16-bit), then use Win16NoShutdown or WinNoShutdown respectively:

```
                /*********************************/
                /* WARNING - UNDOCUMENTED INTERFACE */
                /*********************************/
BOOL   _Far16 _Pascal Win16NoShutdown(USHORT sessionid,
                                      BOOL fNoShutdown);

/*------------------------------------------- */
/*           16-Bit Equivalent              */
/*                                           */
/* BOOL APIENTRY WinNoShutdown(              */
/*            USHORT sessionid,              */
/*            BOOL fNoShutdown);             */
/*------------------------------------------- */

                /* To remove Close from the window list */
Win16NoShutdown(0, TRUE);
                /* To replace Close in the window list  */
Win16NoShutdown(0, FALSE);
```

Think very carefully before using them, and certainly *do not* use them for any software destined for the marketplace! As with all things in OS/2 that are not documented, they are likely to change without notice, or even disappear. If you do use them and they cause problems then you will not be able to obtain support. This also applies to any undocumented API that you may discover by browsing the various OS/2 LIB files.

See also Sec. 13.4.2.

13.3.4 Query the window list

If you need to find out what applications have been added to the window list you can query it by using `WinQuerySwitchList`. This returns a switch list block containing all the current entries. It needs to be called twice, the first time to get the count of entries and the next time to get the entry list. To obtain the count of entries, set the parameters `SwitchEntries` and `DataLength` on the `WinQuerySwitchList` call to `NULL` and `0` respectively. Prior to calling `WinQuerySwitchList` for the second time, you must allocate sufficient memory to hold the returned list. The amount required is obtained by multiplying the size of the switch list block, `sizeof(SWBLOCK)`, by the number of entries returned from the first call:

```
SWCNTRL    swcntrl;
USHORT     usNumTasks,
           usBufSize,
           I;
PSWBLOCK   pswblk;
PVOID      BaseMem;


/*----------------------------------------*/
/* Get number of task entries so that space can be */
/* allocated to store the switch list block        */
/*----------------------------------------*/

usNumTasks = WinQuerySwitchList(hab, NULL, 0);
usBufSize  = sizeof(SWBLOCK) * usNumTasks;
DosAllocMem(&BaseMem, usBufSize, PAG_READ | PAG_WRITE |
            PAG_COMMIT);
pswblk = BaseMem;
WinQuerySwitchList(hab, pswblk, usBufSize);

for (I = 0; I < usNumTasks; I++)
{
  swcntrl = *(PSWCNTRL)((char *)&
  (pswblk[I].aswentry[0].swctl) - sizeof(ULONG)*I);
  ;
  ;
  ;
}
DosFreeMem(BaseMem);
```

The sample program in Chapter 3 makes use of this routine.

13.3.5 Window list options

There are two options of interest:
- `SWL_GRAYED` Use this value for `PgmEntry.uchVisibility` when adding your program to the window list to prohibit switching to it from the window list. In fact, in version 2.0 the entry is removed, whereas in version 1.x it is greyed in the task list.

- `SWL_NOTJUMPABLE` Use this value for `PgmEntry.fbJump` when adding your program to the window list to prohibit switching to it using the `Alt-Esc` key sequence.

13.4 Shutdown

This is an area that has changed significantly under OS/2 version 2.0 with the desktop manager and task list being replaced by the workplace shell and window list respectively. The `Save Desktop` option which was present in OS/2 version 1.x has not been carried forward to version 2.0. Instead, the desktop is automatically saved on system shutdown, when all running applications are sent a `WM_SAVEAPPLICATION` message. Applications can still be closed from the window list but there is no `End Task` button. This has been replaced with a `Close` option on a context menu, displayed by pressing mouse button 2 on the application's entry in the window list. Clicking on this entry causes a `WM_QUIT` message to be posted to the application. At first sight you may think that the only way your users can save the state of your application is to shut down the system, but this is not the case. Whenever your application now receives a `WM_QUIT` message, it also receives a `WM_SAVEAPPLICATION` message, so if you handle this message, every time your program ends it will save its current state.

In all the following sections, window list `Close` is equivalent to the OS/2 V1.x task list `End Task` button.

13.4.1 WM_QUIT message

The `WM_QUIT` message is posted to your application when:

- `Shutdown` is selected from the desktop, in which case all queues receive it.
- `Close` is selected from the window list or the application's system menu.
- The application posts it to itself when exit is requested from its menu bar.

This message always returns `FALSE` and causes your message loop to terminate.

13.4.2 Detecting and preventing/confirming shutdown

Whenever `Close` is selected from the system menu for an application, that application receives a `WM_QUIT` message causing the message loop to end, thus closing the program. However, in this case `mp1` contains the frame handle, but in all other cases it is NULL. It is therefore possible to use this fact either to ignore shutdown completely, or to put up a message box asking for confirmation of closure. To implement this you need to place your message loop in a separate loop (see the following example) and, on exit from the message loop test `mp1`, if it is not NULL then cancel shutdown:

```
while (TRUE)
{
  while (WinGetMsg(hab, &qmsg, (HWND)NULL, 0, 0))
    WinDispatchMsg(hab, &qmsg);

  if (qmsg.mp1 == NULL)    /* Shutdown or window list 'Close' */
    break;
  else                     /* 'Close' from system menu        */
    WinCancelShutdown(hmq, FALSE);
}
```

13.4.3 Shutdown and multiple threads

If you have multiple threads in your application that have their own message queues then ensure that you include a call to `WinCancelShutdown` to prevent the `WM_QUIT` message being sent to it. This is done by specifying a value of `TRUE` for the `CancelAlways` parameter:

```
HAB      habThread;
HMQ      hmqThread;

habThread = WinInitialize(0);
hmqThread = WinCreateMsgQueue(habThread, 0);
WinCancelShutdown(hmqThread, TRUE);
```

If an application's secondary thread has a message queue, it may receive a `WM_QUIT` message after the main thread has processed its `WM_QUIT` message and destroyed itself and the second thread. Presentation Manager will then wait indefinitely for the non-existent thread to return, hence hanging system shutdown. See also Chapter 12.

13.5   Sample program

This program shows the following:

- Starting in background
- Adding/removing from the window list
- Changing the window list
- Querying the window list
- Removing the program's entry from the window list

- Removing Close from the window list for the application
- Disabling Close and Window list in the system menu
- Deleting Size and Move from the system menu
- Prohibiting exit from the window list and system menu
- Adding an About... option to the system menu
- Disabling all menu items

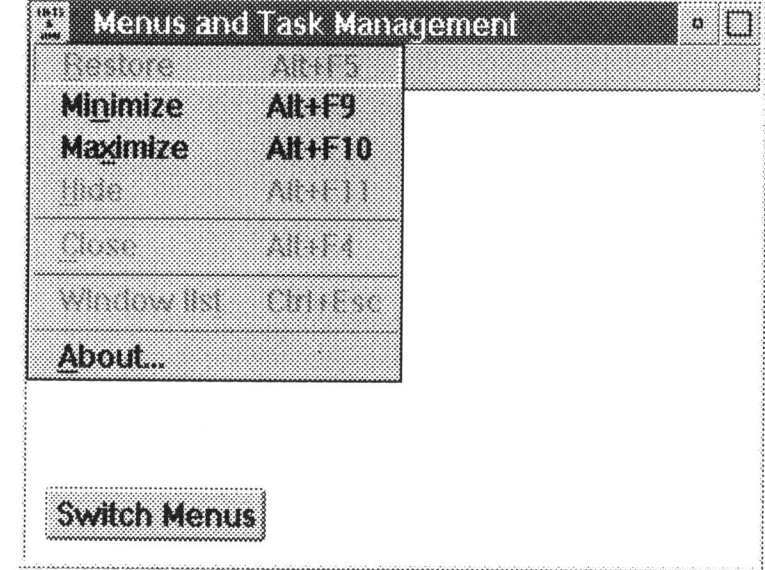

(a)

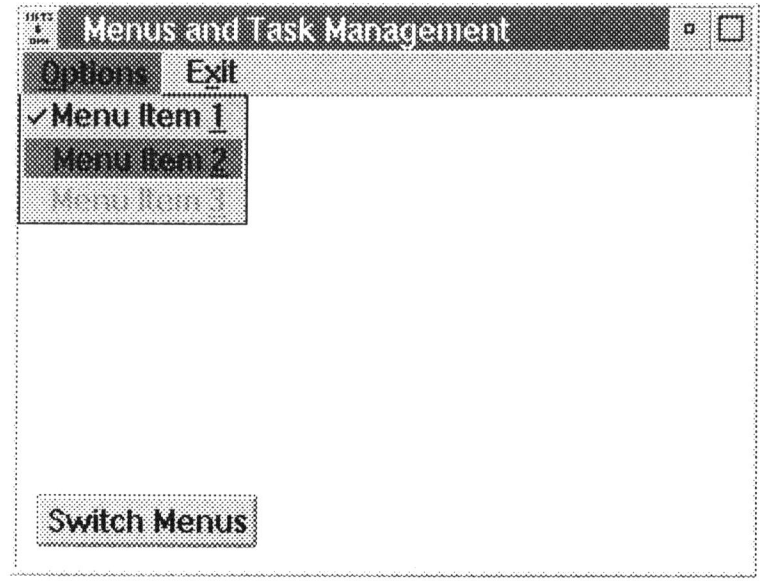

(b)

Figure 13.1. Menus and task management output: (a) system menu, (b) application menu.

- Toggling menu item checked/unchecked
- Deleting Close and its separator from the system menu
- Changing menus

This program starts in the background and as such does not take the focus from you. Initially, Close and Window list in the system menu are greyed out (Fig. 13.1), the menu bar is disabled and Close in the window list for the program is absent.

If you press mouse button 1 in the client area, the menu bar is enabled. Close in the system menu is enabled but will not function. The Close option is also replaced in the window list and, finally, the title is changed in the window list.

If you press mouse button 2 then Close and its separator are deleted from the system menu, and pressing Switch Menus causes a different menu to be loaded. This new menu has two options with three items under Options. The first item can be checked and unchecked, the second has the 'NODISMISS' option and the last is permanently disabled.

The following listings show the program's header file, Fig. 13.2, resource file, Fig. 13.3, and C source file, Fig.13.4.

```
#define    ID_MAINWND    200
#define    ID_TITLE      201
#define    ID_ABOUT      202
#define    MI_EXIT       203
#define    MI_RESUME     204
#define    ID_MENU2      205
#define    MI_ITEM1      206
#define    MI_ITEM2      207
#define    MI_ITEM3      208
#define    ID_SWITCH     209
#define    IDM_ONE       210
#define    IDM_TWO       211
#define    IDM_THREE     212
```

Figure 13.2. Menus and task management: header file.

```
#include <os2.h>
#include "menu.h"

STRINGTABLE PRELOAD
BEGIN
  ID_TITLE, "Menus and Task Management"
END


ICON         ID_MAINWND   menu.ico

ACCELTABLE   ID_MAINWND
BEGIN
  VK_F3,     MI_EXIT,           VIRTUALKEY
END

MENU         ID_MAINWND PRELOAD
BEGIN
  SUBMENU   "E~xit",                   IDM_ONE
  BEGIN
    MENUITEM "~Exit Program\tF3",   MI_EXIT,    MIS_TEXT
    MENUITEM "~Resume Program,      MI_RESUME,  MIS_TEXT
  END
END

MENU         ID_MENU2
BEGIN
  SUBMENU "~Options",            IDM_TWO
  BEGIN
    MENUITEM "Menu Item ~1",   MI_ITEM1,   MIS_TEXT
    MENUITEM "Menu Item ~2",   MI_ITEM2,   MIS_TEXT, MIA_NODISMISS
    MENUITEM "Menu Item ~3",   MI_ITEM3,   MIS_TEXT
  END
  SUBMENU "E~xit",               IDM_THREE
  BEGIN
    MENUITEM "~Exit Program\tF3",  MI_EXIT,    MIS_TEXT
    MENUITEM "~Resume Program",    MI_RESUME,  MIS_TEXT
  END
END
```

Figure 13.3. Menus and task management: resource file.

```c
#define    INCL_WINWINDOWMGR
#define    INCL_WINFRAMEMGR
#define    INCL_WINSWITCHLIST
#define    INCL_WINSYS
#define    INCL_WINMENUS
#define    INCL_WININPUT

#include   <os2.h>
#include   <string.h>
#include   <stdlib.h>
#include   "menu.h"

MRESULT EXPENTRY MainWndProc(HWND, ULONG, MPARAM, MPARAM);
VOID             AddMenuItem(HWND);
VOID             DelClose (HWND);

                                 /*---------------------------*/
                                 /* UNDOCUMENTED              */
                                 /* BE WARNED!                */
                                 /*---------------------------*/
BOOL    _Far16 _Pascal Win16NoShutdown(USHORT, BOOL);

/****************************************************************/

INT main(VOID)
{
   HAB     hab;
   HMQ     hmq;
   HWND    hwndFrame,
           hwndClient,
           hwndSysMenu;
   QMSG    qmsg;
   ULONG   flFrameFlags;
   CHAR    szTitle[80];
   SWCNTRL PgmEntry;
   LONG    lX_Left,
           lY_Bot,
           lHeight,
           lWidth,
           lScrHeight,
           lScrWidth;
/****************************************************************/
```

Figure 13.4. Menus and task management: C source file. Continues.

```
    hab = WinInitialize(0);
    hmq = WinCreateMsgQueue(hab, 0);

    WinRegisterClass(hab, "Menu", MainWndProc,
                  CS_SIZEREDRAW, 0);

    WinLoadString(hab, (HMODULE)NULL, ID_TITLE,
                  sizeof(szTitle), szTitle);

    flFrameFlags = FCF_TITLEBAR   | FCF_SYSMENU | FCF_MENU |
                   FCF_SIZEBORDER | FCF_MINMAX  |
                   FCF_ACCELTABLE | FCF_ICON    |
                   FCF_NOBYTEALIGN;

    hwndFrame = WinCreateStdWindow(HWND_DESKTOP, 0,
                                &flFrameFlags, "Menu",
                                szTitle, 0, (HMODULE)NULL,
                                ID_MAINWND, &hwndClient);

    WinCreateWindow(hwndClient, WC_BUTTON, "Switch Menus",
                  WS_VISIBLE, 10, 10, 120, 30, hwndClient,
                  HWND_TOP, ID_SWITCH, 0, 0);

    lScrWidth  = WinQuerySysValue(HWND_DESKTOP, SV_CXSCREEN);
    lScrHeight = WinQuerySysValue(HWND_DESKTOP, SV_CYSCREEN);

    lWidth  = 400;
    lHeight = 300;

    lX_Left = (lScrWidth  - lWidth)  / 2;
    lY_Bot  = (lScrHeight - lHeight) / 2;
/*--------------------------------------------- */
/* Startup in foreground                        */
/*                                              */
/* WinSetWindowPos(hwndFrame, 0, lX_Left, lY_Bot, */
/*         lWidth, lHeight,SWP_SIZE |            */
/*         SWP_MOVE | SWP_SHOW | SWP_ACTIVATE); */
/*--------------------------------------------- */

/*---------------------*/
/* Startup in background */
/*---------------------*/
```

Figure 13.4. Menus and task management: C source file. Continues.

```
WinSetWindowPos(hwndFrame, HWND_BOTTOM, lX_Left,
            lY_Bot, lWidth, lHeight, SWP_SIZE |
            SWP_MOVE | SWP_SHOW | SWP_ZORDER);

PgmEntry.hwnd          = hwndFrame;
PgmEntry.hwndIcon      = (HWND)NULL;
PgmEntry.hprog         = (HPROGRAM)NULL;
PgmEntry.idProcess     = (PID)NULL;
PgmEntry.idSession     = (ULONG)NULL;
PgmEntry.uchVisibility = SWL_VISIBLE;
PgmEntry.fbJump        = SWL_JUMPABLE;
strcpy(PgmEntry.szSwtitle, szTitle);

WinAddSwitchEntry(&PgmEntry);

                        /*-----------------------------*/
                        /* Remove 'Close' from window list */
                        /*-----------------------------*/
Win16NoShutdown(0, TRUE);

hwndSysMenu = WinWindowFromID(hwndFrame, FID_SYSMENU);

                        /*-----------------------------*/
                        /* Disable 'Close' in system menu  */
                        /*-----------------------------*/

WinSendMsg(hwndSysMenu, MM_SETITEMATTR,
        MPFROM2SHORT(SC_CLOSE, TRUE),
        MPFROM2SHORT(MIA_DISABLED, MIA_DISABLED));

                        /*-----------------------------*/
                        /* Disable 'Window list' in    */
                        /* system menu                 */
                        /*-----------------------------*/

WinSendMsg(hwndSysMenu, MM_SETITEMATTR,
        MPFROM2SHORT(SC_TASKMANAGER, TRUE),
        MPFROM2SHORT(MIA_DISABLED, MIA_DISABLED));

                        /*-----------------------------*/
                        /* Delete 'Size' and 'Move' from */
                        /* system menu                   */
                        /*-----------------------------*/

WinSendMsg(hwndSysMenu, MM_DELETEITEM,
        MPFROM2SHORT(SC_SIZE, TRUE), 0);
```

Figure 13.4. Menus and task management:: C source file. Continues.

```
  WinSendMsg(hwndSysMenu, MM_DELETEITEM,
             MPFROM2SHORT(SC_MOVE, TRUE), 0);

  while (TRUE)
  {
    while (WinGetMsg(hab, &qmsg, (HWND)NULL, 0, 0))
      WinDispatchMsg(hab, &qmsg);

    if (qmsg.mp1 == NULL)
    {
      DosBeep(1000, 200);
      break;
    }
    else
     {
                        /*------------------------------------*/
                        /* Do not allow exit from system menu */
                        /*------------------------------------*/
      DosBeep(100, 200);
      WinCancelShutdown(hmq, FALSE);
     }
  }
                        /*------------------------------------*/
                        /* Remove from window list and        */
                        /* clean up                           */
                        /*------------------------------------*/

  WinRemoveSwitchEntry(WinQuerySwitchHandle (hwndFrame, 0));
  WinDestroyWindow(hwndFrame);
  WinDestroyMsgQueue(hmq);
  WinTerminate(hab);
  return 0;
}
/*****************************************************************/
MRESULT EXPENTRY MainWndProc(HWND hwnd, ULONG msg,
                             MPARAM mp1, MPARAM mp2)
{
  SWCNTRL PgmEntry;
  HWND    hFrame,
          hMenu,
          hSysMenu;
```

Figure 13.4. Menus and task management: C source file. Continues.

```
HSWITCH hSwL;

static BOOL fbSwitched = FALSE,
            fbChecked   = FALSE;

switch (msg)
  {
    case WM_CREATE:
                             /*--------------------------------*/
                             /* Add 'About...' to system menu  */
                             /*--------------------------------*/
      AddMenuItem(hwnd);

      hFrame = WinQueryWindow(hwnd, QW_PARENT);


                                    /*--------------------*/
                                    /* Disable all menu items */
                                    /*--------------------*/


      WinEnableWindow(WinWindowFromID(hFrame, FID_MENU), FALSE);
      break;
    case WM_INITMENU:
      switch (SHORT1FROMMP(mp1))
        {
          case IDM_TWO:

                                    /*------------------------*/
                                    /* Toggle menu item 1 on/off */
                                    /*------------------------*/


            hFrame = WinQueryWindow(hwnd, QW_PARENT);
            hMenu  = WinWindowFromID(hFrame, FID_MENU);
            WinCheckMenuItem(hMenu, MI_ITEM1, fbChecked);

                 /*------------------------------------------*/
                 /*         Alternatively...                 */
                 /*                                          */
                 /* WinSendMsg(hMenu, MM_SETITEMATTR,         */
                 /*            MPFROM2SHORT(MI_ITEM1, TRUE),  */
                 /*            MPFROM2SHORT(MIA_CHECKED,      */
                 /*            fbChecked ? MIA_CHECKED : 0)); */
                 /*------------------------------------------*/
```

Figure 13.4. Menus and task management: C source file. Continues.

```
                                    /*--------------*/
                                    /* Disable item 3 */
                                    /*--------------*/

         WinEnableMenuItem(hMenu, MI_ITEM3, FALSE);
         break;
    }
    break;

  case WM_BUTTON1DOWN:
                              /*-----------------------------*/
                              /* Replace 'Close' in window list */
                              /*-----------------------------*/

    Win16NoShutdown(0, FALSE);

                              /*-----------------------------*/
                              /* Enable 'Close' in system menu  */
                              /*-----------------------------*/

    hSysMenu = WinWindowFromID(WinQueryWindow (hwnd,
            QW_PARENT), FID_SYSMENU);

    WinSendMsg(hSysMenu, MM_SETITEMATTR,
            MPFROM2SHORT(SC_CLOSE, TRUE),
            MPFROM2SHORT(MIA_DISABLED, 0));
                                    /*--------------------*/
                                    /* Enable all menu items */
                                    /*-------------------- */
    hFrame = WinQueryWindow(hwnd, QW_PARENT);
    WinEnableWindow(WinWindowFromID (hFrame, FID_MENU), TRUE);


                                   /*----------------------*/
                                   /* Query window list entry */
                                   /*----------------------*/

    hSwL = WinQuerySwitchHandle(WinQueryWindow(hwnd,
                              QW_PARENT), 0);
    WinQuerySwitchEntry(hSwL, &PgmEntry);

                                   /*----------------------*/
                                   /* Change window list entry */
                                   /*----------------------*/
 /* PgmEntry.uchVisibility = SWL_GRAYED; */
    PgmEntry.fbJump = SWL_NOTJUMPABLE;
```

Figure 13.4. Menus and task management: C source file. Continues.

```c
        strcpy(PgmEntry.szSwtitle,
               "Task Management & Menus");
        WinChangeSwitchEntry(hSwL, &PgmEntry);
        break;

    case WM_BUTTON2DOWN:
                                    /*-------------------------------*/
                                    /* Delete 'Close' and its separator */
                                    /*-------------------------------*/

        DelClose(hwnd);
        break;

    case WM_COMMAND:
      switch (SHORT1FROMMP(mp1))
      {
        case ID_SWITCH:
          hFrame = WinQueryWindow(hwnd, QW_PARENT);
          if (!fbSwitched)                  /*------------ */
                                            /* Switch menus */
          {                                 /*------------ */

             WinDestroyWindow(WinWindowFromID
                          (hFrame, FID_MENU));
             WinLoadMenu(hFrame, (HMODULE)NULL, ID_MENU2);
             WinSendMsg(hFrame, WM_UPDATEFRAME,
                        (MPARAM) FCF_MENU, 0);
             fbSwitched = TRUE;
          }
          else
          {
             WinDestroyWindow(WinWindowFromID
                          (hFrame, FID_MENU));
             WinLoadMenu(hFrame, (HMODULE)NULL, ID_MAINWND);
             WinSendMsg(hFrame, WM_UPDATEFRAME,
                        (MPARAM)FCF_MENU, 0);
              fbSwitched = FALSE;
          }
           break;
        case ID_ABOUT:
                                    /*   ----------------*/
                                    /* Display 'About' box */
                                    /*-------------------*/
```

Figure 13.4. Menus and task management: C source file. Continues.

```
            WinMessageBox(HWND_DESKTOP, hwnd,
                "Version 1\n31 March 1992\ nWritten by Bryan Goodyer",
                "Menus & Task Management Sample Program",
                0,
                MB_INFORMATION | MB_OK |
                MB_MOVEABLE);
            break;

        case MI_ITEM1:
            fbChecked = (fbChecked ? FALSE : TRUE);
            break;

        case MI_ITEM2:
            DosBeep(100, 1000);
            break;

        case MI_EXIT:
            WinPostMsg(hwnd, WM_QUIT, 0, 0);
            break;

        default:
            break;
        }
        break;

    case WM_SAVEAPPLICATION:

                                    /*----------------------------*/
                                    /* Just confirm that this message */
                                    /* is sent when the program ends. */
                                    /*----------------------------*/

        DosBeep(100, 100);
        DosBeep(200, 100);
        DosBeep(300, 100);
        DosBeep(400, 100);
        DosBeep(500, 100);
        return NULL;

    case WM_ERASEBACKGROUND:
        return (MRESULT)TRUE;

    }
    return WinDefWindowProc(hwnd, msg, mp1, mp2);
}
```

Figure 13.4. Menus and task management: C source file. Continues.

```c
/***************************************************************/
VOID   AddMenuItem(HWND hwnd)
{
   HWND           hSysMenu,
                  hSysSubMenu;
   MENUITEM       SysMenu;
   SHORT          I,
                  sIDSysMenu;

   static MENUITEM Item[2] = {MIT_END, MIS_SEPARATOR,
                              0, 0, 0, 0,
                              MIT_END, MIS_TEXT, 0, ID_ABOUT,
                              0, 0};

   static CHAR    *Text[2] = {NULL, "~About..."};

   hSysMenu = WinWindowFromID(WinQueryWindow
              (hwnd, QW_PARENT), FID_SYSMENU);

   sIDSysMenu = SHORT1FROMMR(WinSendMsg(hSysMenu,
                MM_ITEMIDFROMPOSITION, 0, 0));

   WinSendMsg(hSysMenu, MM_QUERYITEM,
              MPFROM2SHORT(sIDSysMenu, FALSE),
              MPFROMP(&SysMenu));

   hSysSubMenu = SysMenu.hwndSubMenu;

   for (I = 0; I < 2; I++)
     WinSendMsg(hSysSubMenu, MM_INSERTITEM, MPFROMP(Item+I),
                MPFROMP(Text[I]));
}


VOID   DelClose(HWND hwnd)
{
   HWND           hSysMenu,
                  hSysSubMenu;

   MENUITEM       SysMenu;
   SHORT          sIDItem,
                  sIDSep,
                  sIDSysMenu;


   hSysMenu = WinWindowFromID(WinQueryWindow
              (hwnd, QW_PARENT), FID_SYSMENU);
```

Figure 13.4. Menus and task management: C source file.

```
  sIDSysMenu = SHORT1FROMMR(WinSendMsg(hSysMenu,
              MM_ITEMIDFROMPOSITION, 0, 0));

  WinSendMsg(hSysMenu, MM_QUERYITEM,
             MPFROM2SHORT(sIDSysMenu, FALSE),
             MPFROMP(&SysMenu));
  hSysSubMenu = SysMenu.hwndSubMenu;

  sIDItem = SHORT1FROMMR(WinSendMsg(hSysSubMenu,
                                    MM_ITEMPOSITIONFROMID,
                                    MPFROM2SHORT
                                    (SC_CLOSE, FALSE), 0));

  if (sIDItem != MIT_ERROR)
  {                                              /*----------------*/
    sIDSep = sIDItem + 1;                        /* Get separator ID */
                                                 /*----------------*/
    sIDSep = SHORT1FROMMR(WinSendMsg(hSysSubMenu,
                                     MM_ITEMIDFROMPOSITION,
                                     MPFROMSHORT(sIDSep), 0));

    WinSendMsg(hSysMenu, MM_DELETEITEM,
               MPFROM2SHORT(SC_CLOSE, TRUE), 0);

    WinSendMsg(hSysSubMenu, MM_DELETEITEM,
               MPFROM2SHORT(sIDSep, FALSE), 0);
  }
}
```

Figure 13.4. Menus and task management: C source file. Concluded.

14
A sample application

14.1 A program to monitor the swap file partition

The swap file, SWAPPER.DAT, by default installed on your boot drive in the directory \OS2\SYSTEM, is the file OS/2 uses when it runs out of physical memory when a request for more memory is received. For example, this request could occur when you start another application, or when a running program reads in a data file. Under DOS you would receive an error message indicating that there is not enough memory. However, under OS/2 this is not necessarily the case. If there is space on the partition on which the swap file is installed then it will be expanded to hold any pages (segments in 16-bit OS/2) that have not been used recently so that the memory request can be satisfied. These swapped pages will be read into memory again if, and when, required. If, however, space runs out on the swap partition then you will receive message SYS1477 as follows:

```
SYS1477: Warning! The partition containing the
SWAPPER.DAT file is full. You may lose data.

Do not ignore this message! Select Display help below
for an explanation and possible recovery actions.

EXPLANATION: The system requires additional virtual memory,
but cannot expand the size of the swapfile to satisfy this
request.
ACTION: Reduce the virtual memory requirement by closing
applications, or increase the amount of available space on
the partition by deleting unwanted files.
```

Now, one major advantage of OS/2 version 2.0 over version 1.x is its ability to shrink the swap file if any pages are no longer required, for example when closing an application that has pages swapped out. In version 1.x the only way to reduce the size of the swap file is to restart the system. The size to which this file can expand is obviously important since, together with the physical memory in your system, it governs how much memory you can use in total. It is therefore advantageous to install your swap file in a partition which has a large amount of free space. To change its location you need to change the following statement:

```
SWAPPATH=C:\OS2\SYSTEM 2048 3072
```

in your CONFIG.SYS to point to the new location. The two figures, 2048 and 3072, are the minimum free space, in kilobytes, allowed on the partition before OS/2 issues a warning, and its initial size, respectively. These may be different on your system. Note that you will *not* receive a warning if an application writes data to the partition and causes the free space to fall below this value; you will only receive it if the swap file needs to increase, by which time it may be too late.

It would be useful if we could monitor the state of this file and the partition on which it resides and receive advance warning of an impending 'out of memory' situation. This program, SWAPMON, does just that, and uses many of the techniques mentioned in this book, including threads, timers, slider controls, interthread communication, enumeration and much more.

14.2 Program summary

The program comprises two windows, one in which to display the partition statistics:

- Swap file location
- Partition size
- Total space used
- Swap file size
- Free space

and the other to display a read-only slider representing the space used on the partition as a percentage of the partition size. Figure 14.1 shows the two windows in their default state. Both are sizeable, and the statistics window can be minimized or hidden. In order to save valuable space on the screen, the two important statistics, free space and swap size, are displayed at the bottom so that they can still be viewed when the window height is reduced. The title bars of both windows can also be removed to reduce space further.

The background colour and font of each window can be changed by dragging the selected colour or font from its respective palette, which can be found in the System Setup folder, and dropping onto the relevant window. In addition, the colour of all attributes can be changed using a colour change dialog.

Each window has its own pop-up menu, rather than a menu bar, with the main window's pop-up menu having the following options:

- Gauge   Displays or hides the slider. It is hidden by default.
- Keep on Top   Keeps the statistics on top of all other windows.

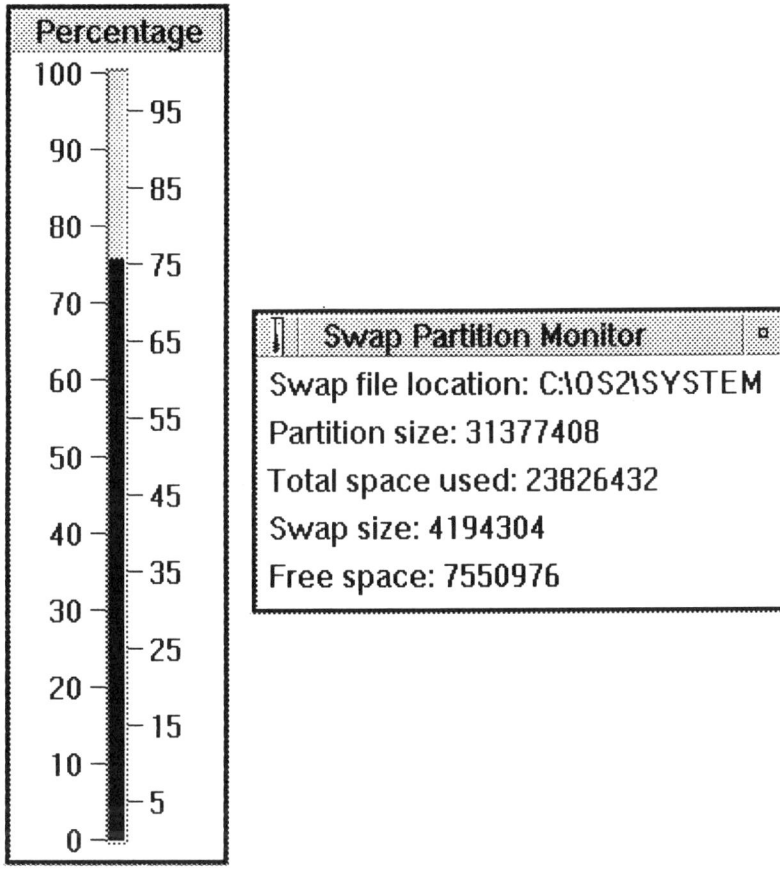

Figure 14.1. Swap partition monitor (default windows).

- Sound   Sounds a series of ascending notes when the swap file increases and a descending series when it shrinks.
- Colour   Displays a dialog box from which you can change the colours of both windows.
- Title Bar   Toggles the title bar on and off.

The gauge's pop-up menu has the following options:

- Vertical   Shows a vertical gauge.
- Horizontal   Shows a horizontal gauge.
- Keep on Top   Keeps the gauge on top of all other windows.
- Title Bar   Toggles the title bar on and off.

Both menus are activated by pressing mouse button 2 when the mouse pointer is over the relevant window. Figure 14.2 shows one of many possible configurations.
   While the program is running, a secondary thread looks at the swap partition

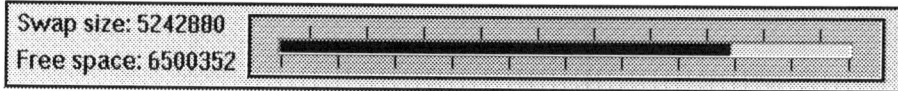

Figure 14.2. Swap partition monitor (possible configuration).

every second and if anything has changed it communicates the data back to the main window procedure for display. If it detects that the free space has fallen below a predetermined danger level, 3 Mb in this case, a dialog box is displayed with a suitable warning. This dialog box has no user interface and so cannot be dismissed; it remains on the desktop until the free space rises above the limit, when the program automatically destroys it.

The program is written as 12 separate modules:

- SWAPMON.C   The main procedure.
- GETSTATS.C   Thread to retrieve the partition statistics.
- GAUGEWND.C   Window procedure for the gauge.
- SLIDER.C   Creates the slider control.
- SUBCLASS.C   Two subclass procedures, one to enable the gauge window to be sized smaller than the default, and the other to subclass the slider control in order to trap the WM_BUTTON2DOWN and WM_PRESPARAMCHANGED messages.
- MAINWND.C   Statistics window procedure.
- DLGWND.C   Colour change dialog box procedure.
- CHNGCOL.C   Procedure to perform the actual colour change.
- STRTORGB.C   Converts a string of three numbers to an RGB structure.
- RGBTOSTR.C   Converts an RGB structure back to a string of three numbers.
- STRTOLNG.C   Converts a string of three numbers to a LONG value.
- GAUGEFRM.C   Obtains the handle of the gauge window's frame.

Let us now look at each module in detail.

14.2.1 SWAPMON.C

This is the main routine. We register two window classes, one for the main, or statistics, window and the other to contain the slider, or gauge. We then create both windows invisibly, start our second thread to monitor the partition and add the program to the window list. Because we want our options saved from one invocation to another, we save all the details in the OS2.INI file, so when the program next starts it can retrieve the relevant data. At this point we need to restore the previously saved size and position of the main window, but if this is the first time the program has run then we default the size and centralize it on the desktop; otherwise we just show it.

Having successfully retrieved the previously saved state of our statistics window, we start the message processing loop and continue until a WM_QUIT message is received, when we clean up and terminate. SWAPMON.C is listed in Fig. 14.3.

```
#define    INCL_DOSPROCESS
#define    INCL_WINSYS
#define    INCL_WINFRAMEMGR
#define    INCL_WINWINDOWMGR
#define    INCL_WINSHELLDATA
#define    INCL_WINSWITCHLIST

#define    STACKSIZE 4096

#include <os2.h>
#include <string.h>
#include <stdlib.h>
#include "swapmon.h"

MRESULT EXPENTRY MainWndProc  (HWND, ULONG, MPARAM, MPARAM);
MRESULT EXPENTRY GaugeWndProc (HWND, ULONG, MPARAM, MPARAM);
MRESULT EXPENTRY SubFrameProc (HWND, ULONG, MPARAM, MPARAM);
VOID    _System  GetStats     (VOID * ULONG);

PFNWP   OldFrameProc;
                              /*--------- Global Variables -------*/
                              /* Application name used in INI file   */
                              /* Application title from RC file      */
                              /*-------------------------------------*/
CHAR    szAppName[] = "SwapMonitor",
        szTitle[40];


/***************************************************************/


INT main (void)
{
  HAB      hab;
  HMQ      hmq;

  HWND     hwndFrame,
           hwndClient,
           hGaugeFrame,
           hGaugeClient;
  QMSG     qmsg;
  ULONG    flFrameFlags;
  CHAR     szSTitle[40];
  SWCNTRL  PgmEntry;
```

Figure 14.3. Swap partition monitor: SWAPMON.C. Continues.

```
    LONG    lX_Left,
            lY_Bot,
            lHeight,
            lWidth,
            lScrHeight,
            lScrWidth;
    TID     tidStats;


/***************************************************************/

    hab = WinInitialize(0);
    hmq = WinCreateMsgQueue(hab, 0);

    WinRegisterClass(hab, "SwapMon", MainWndProc,
                CS_SIZEREDRAW, 0);
    WinRegisterClass(hab, "SwapGauge", GaugeWndProc,
                CS_SIZEREDRAW, 0);

    WinLoadString(hab, (HMODULE)NULL, ID_TITLE,
                sizeof(szTitle), szTitle);
    WinLoadString(hab, (HMODULE)NULL, ID_STITLE,
                sizeof(szSTitle), szSTitle);

    flFrameFlags = FCF_TITLEBAR | FCF_SIZEBORDER |
                FCF_NOBYTEALIGN;

    hGaugeFrame = WinCreateStdWindow(HWND_DESKTOP, 0,
                                    &flFrameFlags,
                                    "SwapGauge", szSTitle,
                                    0, (HMODULE)NULL,
                                    ID_SLIDERWND,
                                    &hGaugeClient);

    OldFrameProc = WinSubclassWindow(hGaugeFrame,
                (PFNWP)SubFrameProc);

    flFrameFlags = FCF_TITLEBAR | FCF_SYSMENU | FCF_MINBUTTON |
                FCF_ICON | FCF_SIZEBORDER | FCF_ACCELTABLE |
                FCF_NOBYTEALIGN;

    hwndFrame = WinCreateStdWindow(HWND_DESKTOP, 0,
                                    &flFrameFlags,
                                    "SwapMon", szTitle,
                                    0, (HMODULE)NULL,
                                    ID_MAINWND, &hwndClient);
```

Figure 14.3. Swap partition monitor: SWAPMON.C. Continues.

```
DosCreateThread(&tidStats, (PFNTHREAD)GetStats,
                (ULONG)hwndClient, 0, STACKSIZE);
                                        /*------------------*/
                                        /* Add to window list */
                                        /*------------------*/
PgmEntry.hwnd          = hwndFrame;
PgmEntry.hwndIcon      = (HWND)NULL;
PgmEntry.hprog         = (HPROGRAM)NULL;
PgmEntry.idProcess     = (PID)NULL;
PgmEntry.idSession     = (ULONG)NULL;
PgmEntry.uchVisibility = SWL_VISIBLE;
PgmEntry.fbJump        = SWL_JUMPABLE;
strcpy(PgmEntry.szSwtitle, szTitle);

WinAddSwitchEntry(&PgmEntry);
if (!WinRestoreWindowPos(szAppName, "StatsSizePos",
                         hwndFrame))
  {                                     /*------------------*/
                                        /* Set default size and */
                                        /* position and     */
                                        /* centralize window  /
                                        /*------------------*/
   lScrWidth  = WinQuerySysValue(HWND_DESKTOP, SV_CXSCREEN);

   lScrHeight = WinQuerySysValue(HWND_DESKTOP, SV_CYSCREEN);

   lWidth     = DEFAULT_WIN_X;
   lHeight    = DEFAULT_WIN_Y;
   lX_Left = (lScrWidth - lWidth) / 2;
   lY_Bot = (lScrHeight - lHeight) / 2;
   WinSetWindowPos(hwndFrame, 0, lX_Left, lY_Bot, lWidth,
                   lHeight, SWP_SIZE | SWP_MOVE |
                   SWP_SHOW | SWP_ACTIVATE);
  }
else
   WinShowWindow(hwndFrame, TRUE);

while (WinGetMsg(hab, &qmsg, (HWND)NULL, 0, 0))
   WinDispatchMsg(hab, &qmsg);
                          /*----------------------------------*/
                          /* Remove from window list and clean up */
                          /*----------------------------------*/
```

Figure 14.3. Swap partition monitor: SWAPMONC.C. Continues.

```
    WinRemoveSwitchEntry(WinQuerySwitchHandle(hwndFrame, 0));
    WinDestroyWindow(hwndFrame);
    WinDestroyWindow(hGaugeFrame);
    WinDestroyMsgQueue(hmq);
    WinTerminate(hab);
    return 0;
}
```

Figure 14.3. Swap partition monitor: SWAPMON.C. Concluded.

14.2.2 GETSTATS.C

This is the monitor thread. Its first task is to find SWAPPER.DAT. Now there are at least two ways this can be done. The first is to scan the CONFIG.SYS and search for the `SWAPPATH` statement; the other is to use the `DPATH` environment variable. The `SET DPATH` statement in your CONFIG.SYS defines which directories a program should search when looking for a data file, and to do this the program uses `DosSearchPath`. The latter method has been used in Fig. 14.4 (not enough use has been made of this useful facility in the past). The only disadvantage of this method, however, is that if you subsequently move the swap file then you must ensure that the `DPATH` statement contains the drive and directory of its new location and that you remove the old SWAPPER.DAT. By default, the `DPATH` already contains the path to SWAPPER.DAT.

To make use of the `DPATH`, we call `DosSearchPath`, and if SWAPPER.DAT is not found we post a user message, UM_NOSWAPPER, back to our main client window and exit the thread. Note here that we have passed the client window handle as a parameter to this thread, a new feature of the `DosCreateThread` function, and because we are using `WinPostMsg` rather than `WinSendMsg` we do *not* need a message queue. Assuming this is successful, we take the first byte of the returned path name to the file, which is the drive letter, and convert it to the drive number. Now, because the ASCII decimal number for A is 65, we subtract 64 from it giving us 1 for drive A, etc. We use this value in a call to `DosQueryFSInfo` to retrieve the drive statistics for our swap partition. We then post another user message, UM_SWAPPER_FOUND, back to our main window procedure, passing the path name of our swap file and the partition size as parameters `mp1` and `mp2` respectively. Having done this bit of initialization, the monitor thread can get down to work in an endless loop. All it does is call `DosFindFirst` to retrieve the swap file size and then call `DosQueryFSInfo` again to get the drive statistics.

If the free space has fallen below our limit, we post a UM_DANGER message back to the main window procedure with the `mp1` parameter set to 1. If the space is now above the limit and we were below it, we post another UM_DANGER message with `mp1` set to 0 to signal that everything is all right again.

A sample application

If there are no danger signs and the statistics have changed, that is, the free space has changed, we post a UM_STATS_CHANGED message, passing the swap file size and free space as parameters.

The thread then goes to sleep for a second before repeating the entire process. Note here that because we are not in a message processing loop we can quite happily use DosSleep. If we had wanted to put this processing in our main window procedure then we would have created a one-second timer and done this processing in the WM_TIMER case statement, thus eliminating the endless loop and DosSleep.

```
#define INCL_DOSMISC
#define INCL_DOSFILEMGR
#define INCL_DOSPROCESS
#define INCL_WINMESSAGEMGR

#include <os2.h>
#include "swapmon.h"


/****************************************************************/

VOID   _System GetStats(VOID * parm)
{                                        /* Get partition statistics */
   HWND         hwndClient;
   CHAR         szPathName[CCHMAXPATH];
   FSALLOCATE   DriveInfo;
   FILEFINDBUF3 InfoBuf;
   BYTE         bDrive;
   ULONG        ulPartSize,
                ulSwapSize,
                ulFreeSpace,
                ulPrevFreeSpace,
                ulAttrib,
                cSearch;
   HDIR         hdir;
   BOOL         fDangerPosted;

   hwndClient    = (HWND)parm;
   fDangerPosted = FALSE;

   if (DosSearchPath(3, "DPATH", "SWAPPER.DAT",
                     szPathName, sizeof(szPathName)))
```

Figure 14.4. Swap partition monitor: GETSTATS.C. Continues.

```c
  {
    WinPostMsg(hwndClient, UM_NOSWAPPER, 0, 0);
    DosExit(0, 0);
  }
  bDrive = szPathName[0] - 64;   /* Convert to drive number, A=1 etc */

  DosQueryFSInfo((ULONG)bDrive, 1, &DriveInfo,
                 sizeof(DriveInfo));

  ulPartSize = DriveInfo.cSectorUnit * DriveInfo.cUnit *
               DriveInfo.cbSector;
  WinPostMsg(hwndClient, UM_SWAPPER_FOUND,
             (CHAR *)(szPathName),
             MPFROMLONG(ulPartSize));

  hdir     = HDIR_SYSTEM;
  ulAttrib = 0;
  cSearch  = 1;
  ulPrevFreeSpace = 0;

  while (TRUE)
  {
    DosFindFirst(szPathName, &hdir, ulAttrib, &InfoBuf,
                 sizeof(InfoBuf), &cSearch, FIL_STANDARD);
    ulSwapSize = InfoBuf.cbFile;

    DosQueryFSInfo((ULONG)bDrive, 1, &DriveInfo,
                   sizeof(DriveInfo));
    ulFreeSpace = DriveInfo.cSectorUnit *
                  DriveInfo.cUnitAvail  *
                  DriveInfo.cbSector;

    if (ulFreeSpace <= DANGER_LEVEL && !fDangerPosted)
    {
      WinPostMsg(hwndClient, UM_DANGER, MPFROMSHORT(1), 0);
      fDangerPosted = TRUE;
    }

    if (fDangerPosted)
    {
      if (ulFreeSpace > DANGER_LEVEL)
      {
        WinPostMsg(hwndClient, UM_DANGER, 0, 0);
        fDangerPosted = FALSE;
      }
    }
```

Figure 14.4. Swap partition monitor: GETSTATS.C. Continues.

```
    if (ulFreeSpace != ulPrevFreeSpace)
    {
      ulPrevFreeSpace = ulFreeSpace;
      WinPostMsg(hwndClient, UM_STATS_CHANGED,
                 MPFROMLONG(ulSwapSize),
                 MPFROMLONG(ulFreeSpace));
    }
    DosSleep(1000);                          /* Wait for 1 second */
  }
}
```

Figure 14.4. Swap partition monitor: GETSTATS.C. Concluded.

14.2.3 GAUGEWND.C

This is the window procedure for the gauge window. It contains just one control, a read-only slider, and that control fills the entire client area of the window. When the gauge window is being created, we create the slider control by calling `Create-Slider` which returns a handle to it, `hSlider`. At this point we also save the frame handle of the gauge window which we will need several times during the processing of this procedure. We also need to read the profile to ascertain the previous state of the application. At this time we need to know the slider bar colour, whether it should remain on top of all other windows and whether the title bar should be visible. The default values for these are, black, not on top and a visible title bar, respectively. We convert the string for the bar colour to a LONG value using `StrToLong`, since it is stored as RGB values rather than pure colours.

At this point we do not know if the gauge is going to be visible or not, and we will not know until the statistics window is created, when we will receive a `UM_SHOW` or `UM_HIDE` message. Assuming the gauge is to be visible, we will receive a `UM_SHOW` message and so we obtain the gauge's attitude, vertical or horizontal, and display it using the previously saved size and position. Do not forget that when we use `WinStoreWindowPos` the window's presentation parameters are also saved, so if we previously dragged a different font, or colour, to the gauge window then this will also be restored. We now need to determine whether the window should remain on top and if the title bar is required. The flags `fTop` and `fTitle` tell us this, so to ensure the window is displayed in its correct state we simulate the user pressing the menu items. For this reason we temporarily reverse the state of these flags in order for the menu processing to act accordingly. If the window is to be hidden then we also turn off the timer, if it was on, since there is no point in having it running if there is no window visible.

This does mean, of course, that if you request the gauge at some later time, you will also need to select the Keep on Top option again.

To ensure the slider control always occupies the entire gauge client window, we trap the WM_SIZE message and resize it accordingly.

Because we have made it possible to change the colour of the slider shaft, or indicator strip as we will call it, we must make the slider ownerdraw and draw the shaft ourselves. We do this in the WM_DRAWITEM message. Its colour is already stored in lBarColour and is initially black. Whenever the colour dialog box is selected from the main window's pop-up menu, and the indicator strip's colour is changed, a UM_NEWBAR message is posted to this procedure with the new colour stored in mp1, so all we need to do here is invalidate the slider to cause a repaint, and hence a WM_DRAWITEM to be sent. We also take advantage of the WM_DRAWITEM message to paint the gauge background. Its colour is stored in lBgndCol, and is initially white. Like the strip colour above, a message is posted here whenever the colour is changed, this time it is a UM_NEWGBGND message.

We now have the four menu options to deal with. Whenever a menu item is selected, a WM_COMMAND message is sent with the low **SHORT** of mp1 set to the menu item's identity. The four options we have are: Vertical (**MI_VERT**), Horizontal (**MI_HORIZ**), Keep on Top (**MI_TOP**), and toggle the Title Bar on and off (**MI_TITLEBAR**). But before we can select an item the menu must be displayed. The problem here is that we do not yet have the window handle of this menu since it is loaded in the slider's subclassed procedure, SubSlider-Proc in **SUBCLASS.C**. To overcome this, SubSliderProc sends us a UM_PASSHWND user message the first time mouse button 2 is pressed, with the handle stored in the mp1 parameter. We also use this message to check, or enable, the menu items as appropriate.

If we press Vertical we disable it from the menu and enable Horizontal and then change the slider's style from SLS_HORIZONTAL to SLS_VERTICAL. We do this by calling WinSetWindowULong. We also save the current attitude (vertical) in the profile and either redisplay the window in its previous position or use the default, depending on whether the program has been run before or not. We do similar processing for the pressing of the Horizontal menu item. If we select Keep on Top then we toggle the check mark and start, or stop, a one-second timer, and so every second we call WinSetWindowPos to put the window back on top. Notice that we do not activate the window as this would indeed cause problems. Similarly, if we press Title Bar then we toggle it on and off. To turn the title bar off we just set its parent to HWND_OBJECT, and to turn it on again reset its parentage to the gauge frame window. We must, however, send the frame a WM_UPDATEFRAME message to activate the change and tell it what controls have been modified. For this window it is just the title bar.

Finally, whenever the application is closed, the window receives a UM_SAVEAPP message, sent from the main window procedure, so that the window's current size, position, presentation parameters, Z-order and title bar state can be saved. GAUGEWND.C is listed in Fig. 14.5.

```
#define   INCL_GPIBITMAPS
#define   INCL_GPILOGCOLORTABLE
#define   INCL_WINFRAMEMGR
#define   INCL_WININPUT
#define   INCL_WINMENUS
#define   INCL_WINSHELLDATA
#define   INCL_WINSTDSLIDER
#define   INCL_WINSYS
#define   INCL_WINTIMER
#define   INCL_WINWINDOWMGR

#include <os2.h>
#include <string.h>
#include <stdlib.h>
#include "swapmon.h"

LONG    StrToLong     (PSZ);
HWND    CreateSlider(HWND);

CHAR    szAppName[];

/***************************************************************/

MRESULT EXPENTRY GaugeWndProc(HWND hwnd, ULONG msg,
                              MPARAM mp1, MPARAM mp2)
{
  static HWND hSlider,
              hGaugeFrame,
              hTitleBar,
              hMenu;
  static LONG lBarColour,
              lBgndCol;
  static CHAR szAtt[2];  /* Gauge attitude - vertical/horizontal */

  static BOOL fTop = FALSE,
              fTitle = TRUE;
  CHAR        szCols[12],     /* Indicator strip colours, RGB */
              szTop[2],       /* Keep gauge on top?           */
              szTitleBar[2];  /* Title bar visibility         */
```

Figure 14.5. Swap partition monitor: GAUGEWND.C. Continues.

```
   POWNERITEM  pOwner;
   RECTL       rcl;

   switch (msg)
     {

     case WM_CREATE:
       hSlider = CreateSlider(hwnd);
       hGaugeFrame = WinQueryWindow(hwnd, QW_PARENT);
       hTitleBar = WinWindowFromID(hGaugeFrame,
                              FID_TITLEBAR);
       PrfQueryProfileString(HINI_PROFILE, szAppName,
               "GaugeBar", "0 0 0", szCols, 12);
       PrfQueryProfileString(HINI_PROFILE, szAppName,
               "GaugeTop", "N", szTop, 2);
       PrfQueryProfileString(HINI_PROFILE, szAppName,
               "GaugeTitleBar", "Y",
               szTitleBar, 2);
       lBarColour = StrToLong(szCols);

       if (szTop[0] == 'Y')
         fTop = TRUE;                         /* Keep on top         */

       if (szTitleBar[0] == 'N')
         fTitle = FALSE;                      /* Invisible title bar */
       break;

     case UM_SHOW:
       PrfQueryProfileString(HINI_PROFILE, szAppName,
                        "GaugeAtt", "V",
                        szAtt, 2);
       if (szAtt[0] == 'V')
       {
         if (!WinRestoreWindowPos(szAppName,
             "GaugeVSizePos", hGaugeFrame))
           WinSetWindowPos(hGaugeFrame, 0, 0, 0,
                           DEFAULT_VERT_X,
                           DEFAULT_VERT_Y,
                           SWP_SIZE | SWP_MOVE);
       }
       else
       {
         if (!WinRestoreWindowPos(szAppName,
             "GaugeHSizePos", hGaugeFrame))
```

Figure 14.5. Swap partition monitor: GAUGEWND.C. Continues.

```
            WinSetWindowPos(hGaugeFrame, 0, 0, 0,
                          DEFAULT_HORIZ_X,
                          DEFAULT_HORIZ_Y, SWP_SIZE | SWP_MOVE);
      }
      WinShowWindow(hGaugeFrame, TRUE);
      if (fTop)
      {
        fTop = FALSE;
                        /* Will be set back to TRUE in MI_TOP */
        WinSendMsg(hwnd, WM_COMMAND,
                   MPFROMSHORT (MI_TOP), 0);
      }
      if (!fTitle)
      {
        fTitle = TRUE;
                    /* Will be set back to FALSE in MI_TITLEBAR */
                    /* Simulate menu select                     */
        WinSendMsg(hwnd, WM_COMMAND,
                   MPFROMSHORT(MI_TITLEBAR), 0);
                                        /* Simulate menu select */
      }
      break;

    case UM_HIDE:
      WinShowWindow(hGaugeFrame, FALSE);
          /* Switch off timer, no point having it if not visible */
      if (fTop)
         WinPostMsg(hwnd, WM_COMMAND,
                    MPFROMSHORT (MI_TOP), 0);
      break;

    case WM_SIZE:
      WinQueryWindowRect(hwnd, &rcl);
      WinSetWindowPos(hSlider, HWND_TOP, 0, 0,
                      rcl.xRight, rcl.yTop, SWP_SIZE |
                      SWP_MOVE | SWP_SHOW | SWP_ZORDER);
      break;

    case UM_NEWBAR:
      lBarColour = LONGFROMMP(mp1);
      WinInvalidateRect(hSlider, NULL, FALSE);
      break;
```

Figure 14.5. Swap partition monitor: GAUGEWND.C. Continues.

```
case UM_NEWGBGND:
  lBgndCol = LONGFROMMP(mp1);
  WinInvalidateRect(hSlider, NULL, FALSE);
  break;

case WM_DRAWITEM:
  pOwner = (POWNERITEM)mp2;
  if (pOwner->idItem == SDA_RIBBONSTRIP)
  {
    GpiCreateLogColorTable(pOwner->hps, LCOL_RESET,
                    LCOLF_RGB, 0, 0, NULL);
    WinFillRect(pOwner->hps, &pOwner->rclItem,
             lBarColour);
    return (MRESULT)TRUE;
  }
  if (pOwner->idItem == SDA_BACKGROUND)
  {
    GpiCreateLogColorTable(pOwner->hps, LCOL_RESET,
                    LCOLF_RGB, 0, 0, NULL);
    WinFillRect(pOwner->hps, &pOwner->rclItem,
             lBgndCol);
    return (MRESULT)TRUE;
  }
  return (MRESULT)FALSE;

case UM_PASSHWND:
  hMenu = HWNDFROMMP(mp1);
  WinCheckMenuItem(hMenu, MI_TOP, fTop);
  WinCheckMenuItem(hMenu, MI_TITLEBAR, fTitle);
  if (szAtt[0] == 'V')
    WinEnableMenuItem(hMenu, MI_VERT, FALSE);
  else
    WinEnableMenuItem(hMenu, MI_HORIZ, FALSE);
  break;

case WM_COMMAND:
  switch (SHORT1FROMMP(mp1))
    {
      case MI_VERT:
        if (szAtt[0] == 'H')
                              /* Changing from horizontal */
          {
```

Figure 14.5. Swap partition monitor: GAUGEWND.C. Continues.

```
              WinStoreWindowPos(szAppName,
                              "GaugeHSizePos",
                              hGaugeFrame);
              WinEnableMenuItem(hMenu, MI_VERT, FALSE);
              WinEnableMenuItem(hMenu, MI_HORIZ, TRUE);
              strcpy(szAtt, "V");
              PrfWriteProfileString(HINI_PROFILE,
                              szAppName,
                              "GaugeAtt",
                              szAtt);
              WinSetWindowULong(hSlider, QWL_STYLE,
                              WinQueryWindowULong
                              (hSlider, QWL_STYLE) &
                              ~SLS_HORIZONTAL);
              WinSetWindowULong(hSlider, QWL_STYLE,
                              WinQueryWindowULong
                              (hSlider, QWL_STYLE)
                              | SLS_VERTICAL);
           }
           if (!WinRestoreWindowPos(szAppName,
                              "GaugeVSizePos",
                              hGaugeFrame))
              WinSetWindowPos(hGaugeFrame, HWND_TOP,
                              0, 0, DEFAULT_VERT_X,
                              DEFAULT_VERT_Y,
                              SWP_SIZE | SWP_MOVE |
                              SWP_SHOW | SWP_ZORDER);
           else
              WinSetWindowPos(hGaugeFrame,
                              HWND_TOP, 0, 0, 0, 0,
                              SWP_SHOW | SWP_ZORDER);
           break;


        case MI_HORIZ:
           if (szAtt[0] == 'V')
                              /* Changing from vertical */
           {
              WinStoreWindowPos(szAppName, "Gauge VSizePos",
                              hGaugeFrame);
              WinEnableMenuItem(hMenu, MI_VERT, TRUE);
              WinEnableMenuItem(hMenu, MI_HORIZ, FALSE);
```

Figure 14.5. Swap partition monitor: GAUGEWND.C. Continues.

```
                  strcpy(szAtt, "H");
                  PrfWriteProfileString(HINI_PROFILE,
                                  szAppName,
                                  "GaugeAtt",
                                  szAtt);
                  WinSetWindowULong(hSlider, QWL_STYLE,
                                  WinQueryWindowULong
                                  (hSlider, QWL_STYLE)
                                  & ~SLS_VERTICAL);
                  WinSetWindowULong(hSlider, QWL_STYLE,
                                  WinQueryWindowULong
                                  (hSlider, QWL_STYLE)
                                  | SLS_HORIZONTAL);
                }
                if (!WinRestoreWindowPos(szAppName,
                                  "GaugeHSizePos",
                                  hGaugeFrame))
                  WinSetWindowPos(hGaugeFrame, HWND_TOP,
                                  0, 0, DEFAULT_HORIZ_X,
                                  DEFAULT_HORIZ_Y,
                                  SWP_SIZE | SWP_MOVE |
                                  SWP_SHOW | SWP_ZORDER);
                else
                  WinSetWindowPos(hGaugeFrame, HWND_TOP,
                                  0, 0, 0, 0, SWP_SHOW |
                                  SWP_ZORDER);
                break;

            case MI_TOP:
                fTop = !fTop;
                WinCheckMenuItem(hMenu, MI_TOP, fTop);
                if (fTop)
                  WinStartTimer(WinQueryAnchorBlock(hwnd),
                                  WinWindowFromID
                                  (hGaugeFrame, FID_CLIENT),
                                  2, 1000);
                else
                  WinStopTimer(WinQueryAnchorBlock(hwnd),
                                  WinWindowFromID
                                  (hGaugeFrame, FID_CLIENT), 2);
                break;

            case MI_TITLEBAR:
```

Figure 14.5. Swap partition monitor: GAUGEWND.C. Continues.

```
                fTitle = !fTitle;
                WinCheckMenuItem(hMenu, MI_TITLEBAR, fTitle);

                if (!fTitle)
                   WinSetParent(hTitleBar, HWND_OBJECT, FALSE);

                else
                   WinSetParent(hTitleBar, hGaugeFrame, FALSE);

                WinSendMsg(hGaugeFrame, WM_UPDATEFRAME,
                           MPFROMLONG(FCF_TITLEBAR), 0);
                break;

             default:
                break;
          }
       break;
    case WM_TIMER:
       WinSetWindowPos(hGaugeFrame, HWND_TOP, 0, 0, 0, 0,
                       SWP_ZORDER);
       break;

    case UM_SAVEAPP:
       if (szAtt[0] == 'V')
          WinStoreWindowPos(szAppName,
                            "GaugeVSizePos",
                            hGaugeFrame);
       else
          WinStoreWindowPos(szAppName,
                            "GaugeHSizePos",
                            hGaugeFrame);

       if (fTop)
          PrfWriteProfileString(HINI_PROFILE, szAppName,
                                "GaugeTop", "Y");
       else
          PrfWriteProfileString(HINI_PROFILE, szAppName,
                                "GaugeTop", "N");

       if (fTitle)
          PrfWriteProfileString(HINI_PROFILE, szAppName,
                                "GaugeTitleBar", "Y");
```

Figure 14.5. Swap partition monitor: C GAUGEWND.C. Continues.

```
            else
               PrfWriteProfileString(HINI_PROFILE, szAppName,
                                     "GaugeTitleBar", "N");
            break;

      }
   return WinDefWindowProc(hwnd, msg, mp1, mp2);
}
```

Figure 14.5. Swap partition monitor: GAUGEWND.C. Concluded.

14.2.4 SLIDER.C

This procedure (Fig. 14.6) creates the slider. It uses both scales, 0 to 100 for scale 2 (left/bottom) and 5 to 95 for scale 1 (right/top). To show both scales we first paint the left-hand scale and then remove the SLS_PRIMARYSCALE2 style and paint the right-hand scale. The main problem here is that the slider occupies the entire client area of the gauge window and we need to trap the WM_BUTTON2DOWN message so that we can make the menu pop up. Now the slider control itself traps this message, so, in order to use it we need to subclass the control, see Sec. 14.2.5. We also set the foreground colour using WinSetPresParam and the background colour by posting a UM_NEWGBGND message back to the gauge window procedure.

```
#define   INCL_WININPUT
#define   INCL_WINSHELLDATA
#define   INCL_WINSTDSLIDER
#define   INCL_WINSYS
#define   INCL_WINWINDOWMGR

#include <os2.h>
#include <stdlib.h>
#include "swapmon.h"

MRESULT EXPENTRY SubSliderProc(HWND, ULONG, MPARAM, MPARAM);
LONG    StrToLong(PSZ);

PFNWP   OldSliderProc;

CHAR    szAppName[];

/**************************************************************/
```

Figure 14.6. Swap partition monitor: SLIDER.C. Continues.

A sample application

```
HWND CreateSlider(HWND hwnd)
{
  SLDCDATA   sldcData;
  HWND       hSlider;
  ULONG      ulSliderStyle;
  LONG       lBgndCol,
             lForeCol;
  USHORT     I;
  CHAR       szText[5],
             szCols[12],
             szAtt[2];

  sldcData.cbSize = sizeof(SLDCDATA);
                              /* 0 -> 100% in increments of 5  */
  sldcData.usScale1Increments = 21;
  sldcData.usScale1Spacing = SCALE_SPACING / 2;
                              /* 0 -> 100% in increments of 10 */
  sldcData.usScale2Increments = 11;
  sldcData.usScale2Spacing = SCALE_SPACING;
  PrfQueryProfileString(HINI_PROFILE, szAppName,
                        "GaugeAtt", "V", szAtt, 2);
  if (szAtt[0] == 'V')
    ulSliderStyle = SLS_VERTICAL | SLS_READONLY |
                    SLS_RIBBONSTRIP | SLS_OWNERDRAW |
                    SLS_PRIMARYSCALE2 | SLS_OWNERDRAW;
  else
    ulSliderStyle = SLS_HORIZONTAL | SLS_READONLY |
                    SLS_RIBBONSTRIP | SLS_OWNERDRAW |
                    SLS_PRIMARYSCALE2 | SLS_OWNERDRAW;

  hSlider = WinCreateWindow(hwnd, WC_SLIDER, "",
                            ulSliderStyle, 0, 0, 0, 0,
                            hwnd, HWND_TOP, ID_SLIDER,
                            &sldcData, 0);

  OldSliderProc = WinSubclassWindow(hSlider,
                                    (PFNWP)SubSliderProc);

  PrfQueryProfileString(HINI_PROFILE, szAppName,
                        "GaugeBgnd", "255 255 255",
                        szCols, 12);
  lBgndCol = StrToLong(szCols);
  WinPostMsg(hwnd, UM_NEWGBGND, MPFROMLONG(lBgndCol), 0);
```

Figure 14.6. Swap partition monitor: SLIDER.C. Continues.

```
  PrfQueryProfileString(HINI_PROFILE, szAppName,
                  "GaugeFgnd", "0 0 0",
                  szCols, 12);
  lForeCol = StrToLong(szCols);
  WinSetPresParam(hSlider, PP_FOREGROUNDCOLOR,
                  sizeof(lForeCol), &lForeCol);
  for (I = 0; I <= sldcData.usScale2Increments; I++)
  {
    _itoa(I*10, szText, 10);
    WinSendMsg(hSlider, SLM_SETSCALETEXT, MPFROMSHORT(I),
             szText);
    WinSendMsg(hSlider, SLM_SETTICKSIZE, MPFROM2SHORT(I,
             8), 0);
  }
  WinSetWindowULong(hSlider, QWL_STYLE,
                  WinQueryWindowULong(hSlider,
                  QWL_STYLE) & ~SLS_PRIMARYSCALE2);
  for (I = 1; I <= sldcData.usScale1Increments; I+=2)
  {
    _itoa(I*5, szText, 10);
    WinSendMsg(hSlider, SLM_SETSCALETEXT, MPFROMSHORT(I),
             szText);
    WinSendMsg(hSlider, SLM_SETTICKSIZE, MPFROM2SHORT(I,
             8), 0);
  }
  return hSlider;
}
```

Figure 14.6. Swap partition monitor: SLIDER.C. Concluded.

14.2.5 *SUBCLASS.C*

This module contains two subclassed procedures: `SubFrameProc` and `SubSliderProc` (Fig. 14.7). The first of these does no more than allow the gauge window frame to be reduced to 15 pels wide and 25 pels high. The other procedure is necessary so that we can trap the `WM_BUTTON2DOWN` and `WM_PRESPARAMCHANGED` messages.

When mouse button 2 is pressed we obtain the gauge frame window handle and, if this is the first press, load the pop-up menu, making the gauge client window the owner, and pass its handle to the gauge window procedure using the `UM_PASSHWND` message. We do this so that the menu requests can be processed in the gauge window procedure. All that needs to be done now is to find the mouse pointer position whenever the button is pressed, map it to our gauge and pop up the menu. Note here that we use `PU_HCONSTRAIN` and `PU_VCONSTRAIN` so that the menu does not disappear off the desktop.

A sample application

We trap the WM_PRESPARAMCHANGED message so that we can save the new background colour and font if they are changed by dragging them from the colour and font palettes. If the colour is changed we need to query the new colour using WinQueryPresParam, post it back to the gauge window procedure and then convert it to RGB values so that it can be written to the profile. We store it just in case the colour is changed using the colour change dialog, in which case we want the latest colour to be reflected for the gauge background. If the font is changed then we again need to query it so that we can set it for the gauge client window. This is to ensure that the pop-up menu inherits the same font. As with the colour, we save the new font in the profile by using WinStoreWindowPos.

```
#define    INCL_GPIBITMAPS
#define    INCL_WINFRAMEMGR
#define    INCL_WININPUT
#define    INCL_WINMENUS
#define    INCL_WINPOINTERS
#define    INCL_WINSHELLDATA
#define    INCL_WINSTDSLIDER
#define    INCL_WINSYS
#define    INCL_WINTRACKRECT
#define    INCL_WINWINDOWMGR

#include <os2.h>
#include <string.h>
#include <math.h>
#include "swapmon.h"

HWND       GetGaugeFrame (VOID);
PSZ        RGBToStr      (RGB);

PFNWP      OldFrameProc;
PFNWP      OldSliderProc;

CHAR       szAppName[];

/******************************************************************/

MRESULT EXPENTRY SubFrameProc(HWND hwnd, ULONG msg, MPARAM mp1,
                              MPARAM mp2)
{
  PTRACKINFO ptrack;

  switch(msg)
  {
    case WM_QUERYTRACKINFO:
```

Figure 14.7. Swap partition monitor: SUBCLASS.C. Continues.

```
      /*------------------------------------------*/
      /* Invoke the default frame window procedure first  */
      /* in order to update the tracking rectangle        */
      /* to the new position                              */
      /*------------------------------------------*/
      OldFrameProc(hwnd, msg, mp1, mp2);

      ptrack = (PTRACKINFO)mp2;
      ptrack->ptlMinTrackSize.x = 15;
      ptrack->ptlMinTrackSize.y = 25;

      return((MRESULT)TRUE);
   }
   return OldFrameProc(hwnd, msg, mp1, mp2);
}
/***************************************************************/
MRESULT EXPENTRY SubSliderProc(HWND hwnd, ULONG msg, MPARAM mp1,
                               MPARAM mp2)
{
   static BOOL fFirstPress = TRUE;
   static HWND hMenu;

   HWND    hGaugeFrame;
   POINTL  pt;
   double  temp;
   RGB     rgb;
   LONG    lBgndCol;
   CHAR    szCols[12],
           szAtt[2],
           szFont[50];

   switch(msg)
   {
     case WM_BUTTON2DOWN:
       hGaugeFrame = GetGaugeFrame();
       if (fFirstPress)
       {
         hMenu = WinLoadMenu(WinWindowFromID(hGaugeFrame,
                             FID_CLIENT), (HMODULE)NULL,
                             ID_SLDRMENU);
         WinSendMsg(WinWindowFromID(hGaugeFrame,
                             FID_CLIENT), UM_PASSHWND,
                             MPFROMHWND(hMenu), 0);
```

Figure 14.7. Swap partition monitor: SUBCLASS.C. Continues.

```
      fFirstPress = FALSE;
   }
   WinQueryPointerPos(HWND_DESKTOP, &pt);
   WinMapWindowPoints(HWND_DESKTOP, hwnd, &pt, 1);
   WinPopupMenu(hwnd, WinWindowFromID(hGaugeFrame,
               FID_CLIENT), hMenu, pt.x, pt.y, 0,
               PU_HCONSTRAIN | PU_VCONSTRAIN |
               PU_KEYBOARD | PU_MOUSEBUTTON1);
   return (MRESULT)TRUE;

case WM_PRESPARAMCHANGED:
   hGaugeFrame = GetGaugeFrame();
   if ((ULONG)mp1 == PP_BACKGROUNDCOLOR)
   {
      WinQueryPresParam(hwnd, PP_BACKGROUNDCOLOR, 0,
                        NULL, sizeof(lBgndCol),
                        &lBgndCol, 0);
      WinPostMsg(WinWindowFromID(hGaugeFrame,
                 FID_CLIENT), UM_NEWGBGND,
                 MPFROMLONG(lBgndCol), 0);
      rgb.bRed = lBgndCol/65536;
      temp = fmod((double)lBgndCol, 65536.00);
      rgb.bGreen = temp/256;
      rgb.bBlue = fmod((double)temp, 256.00);
      strcpy(szCols, RGBToStr(rgb));
      PrfWriteProfileString(HINI_PROFILE, szAppName,
                        "GaugeBgnd", szCols);
   }
   if ((ULONG)mp1 == PP_FONTNAMESIZE)
   {
      WinQueryPresParam(hwnd, PP_FONTNAMESIZE, 0, NULL,
                        sizeof(szFont), &szFont, 0);
                        /* Change font for pop-up menu */
      WinSetPresParam(WinWindowFromID(hGaugeFrame,
                 FID_CLIENT), PP_FONTNAMESIZE,
                 sizeof(szFont), &szFont);
      PrfQueryProfileString(HINI_PROFILE, szAppName,
                        "GaugeAtt", "V",
                        szAtt, 2);
      if (szAtt[0] == 'V')
         WinStoreWindowPos(szAppName, "GaugeVSizePos",
                        hGaugeFrame);
```

Figure 14.7. Swap partition monitor: SUBCLASS.C. Continues.

```
        else
           WinStoreWindowPos(szAppName, "GaugeHSizePos",
                             hGaugeFrame);
      }
      break;
   }
   return OldSliderProc(hwnd, msg, mp1, mp2);
}
```

Figure 14.7. Swap partition monitor: SUBCLASS.C. Concluded.

14.2.6 MAINWND.C

This is the main window procedure (Fig. 14.8). It displays the partition statistics and, like the gauge window, has its own pop-up menu. So, during its creation we load the menu, retrieve all the window handles we will be using and read in the previously saved state from the profile. Note that the slider window handle is obtained directly from the gauge client. We then check if the gauge window was previously displayed or not and reverse the state of the fGauge flag prior to posting the MI_SLIDER message to simulate the menu selection. We also initialize the state of the statistics window in a similar way.

The UM_NOSWAPPER message handles the situation where the program cannot find the swap file. It is posted by the GetStats thread. If this happens then we put up a message box and post ourselves a WM_QUIT message to force termination. Assuming the swap file has been found then GetStats posts a UM_SWAPPER_FOUND message with the mp1 and mp2 parameters set to the swap file's path name and the partition size respectively.

Whenever any event occurs that causes the free space on the swap partition to change, GetStats posts a UM_STATS_CHANGED message. The parameters on this message are the current swap size and total free space available. We are now able to calculate the total space used by all files on the partition and invalidate the window to cause a repaint, and hence display the values. We also need to update the position of the indicator strip on the gauge, so we must calculate its new length as a percentage of the partition size. With 40 pels representing 10 per cent, 0 to 100 per cent gives us a total length of 400 pels, therefore the value we need is:

```
(Total Used Space * SCALE_SPACING * 10.00) / Partition Size
```

Note that we use double precision to minimize rounding errors. All we do then is send an SLM_SETSLIDERINFO message to the slider and, if sound has been requested, sound a series of notes according to whether it is an increase or decrease in swap size.

The `WM_PAINT` message does nothing but clear the window using the latest background colour, set the foreground colour and write the text to the window.

The next two user messages, `UM_NEWBGND` and `UM_NEWFGND`, are posted from the `ChangeColour` procedure in response to the statistics window colours being changed.

The final user message, `UM_DANGER`, is posted by the `GetStats` thread whenever the free space falls below the danger limit, set to 3 Mb, or when, after falling below the limit, the free space rises again because of files being removed or the swap file being reduced in size. When the limit is reached we put up a dialog box, `DLG_DANGER`, which remains on the desktop until the free space rises above the limit again, when the dialog box is destroyed. Note that we do not have a dialog box procedure for this since there is no user interface. The only action that can be performed is move.

As in SLIDER.C, we use mouse button 2 to activate the pop-up menu. This menu contains five options as mentioned earlier. Selecting `Gauge` will toggle the gauge window on or off; `Keep on Top` will force the statistics window to remain in view at all times; `Sound` will cause a series of notes to be sounded when the free space changes; `Colour` will bring up a dialog box, `DLG_COLOURS`, which can be used to change the colours of both windows; and finally, `Title Bar` will toggle the title bar on and off.

When the program is terminated we make use of the `WM_SAVEAPPLICATION` message to save the current state of the statistics window, and to inform the gauge window that the application is closing and that it must save its state.

Finally, when the background colour is changed by dragging a colour from the colour palette, we convert it to RGB values, store it in the profile and force a repaint by invalidating the window. We do not need to worry about the font changing here, other than to invalidate the window, since it will automatically be saved when we issue a `WinStoreWindowPos`. The reason we need to query it for the gauge window is because the pop-up menu is not owned by the slider but by the gauge client, and when dropping a font onto this window it is the slider control itself that is affected, leaving the old font in the pop-up menu.

```
#define    INCL_GPIBITMAPS
#define    INCL_GPILOGCOLORTABLE
#define    INCL_WINFRAMEMGR
#define    INCL_WININPUT
#define    INCL_WINMENUS
#define    INCL_WINPOINTERS
#define    INCL_WINSHELLDATA
#define    INCL_WINSTDSLIDER
```

Figure 14.8. Swap partition monitor: MAINWND.C. Continues.

```
#define   INCL_WINSYS
#define   INCL_WINTIMER
#define   INCL_WINWINDOWMGR

#include <os2.h>
#include <string.h>
#include <stdio.h>
#include <math.h>
#include "swapmon.h"

MRESULT EXPENTRY ColourDlgProc(HWND, ULONG, MPARAM, MPARAM);
HWND      GetGaugeFrame       (VOID);
LONG      StrToLong           (PSZ);
PSZ       RGBToStr            (RGB);

CHAR      szAppName[],
          szTitle[];

/****************************************************************/

MRESULT EXPENTRY MainWndProc(HWND hwnd, ULONG msg, MPARAM mp1,
                             MPARAM mp2)
{
  static  HWND     hMenu,
                   hSlider,
                   hFrame,
                   hTitleBar,
                   hSysMenu,
                   hMin,
                   hGaugeFrame,
                   hDangerDlg;
  static  ULONG    ulPartSize,        /* Partition size          */
                   ulSwapSize,        /* Swapper size            */
                   ulUsedSpace,       /* Space used by all files */
                   ulFreeSpace,       /* Free space              */
                   ulPrevSwapSize = 0;
  static  CHAR     *pszPathName,
                   szPathName[CCHMAXPATH];
  static  BOOL     fSwapperOK = FALSE,
                   fSound     = FALSE,
                   fTop       = FALSE,
                   fTitle     = TRUE,
                   fGauge;
  static  LONG     lBgndCol,
                   lForeCol;
```

Figure 14.8. Swap partition monitor: MAINWND.C. Continues.

```
ULONG              ulUsedLength;
LONG               lX,
                   lY;
double             temp;
RGB                rgb;
USHORT             I;
CHAR               szText[CCHMAXPATH],
                   szGauge[2],
                   szSound[2],
                   szTop[2],
                   szCols[12],
                   szTitleBar[2];
POINTL             pt;
RECTL              rcl;
HPS                hps;

switch (msg)
  {
    case WM_CREATE:
      hMenu = WinLoadMenu(hwnd, (HMODULE)NULL, ID_MENU);
      hFrame = WinQueryWindow(hwnd, QW_PARENT);
      hGaugeFrame = GetGaugeFrame();
      hSlider = WinWindowFromID(WinWindowFromID
                               (hGaugeFrame,
                                FID_CLIENT), ID_SLIDER);
      hTitleBar = WinWindowFromID(hFrame, FID_TITLEBAR);
      hSysMenu = WinWindowFromID(hFrame, FID_SYSMENU);
      hMin = WinWindowFromID(hFrame, FID_MINMAX);
      PrfQueryProfileString(HINI_PROFILE, szAppName,
                            "StatsBgnd",
                            "255 255 255",
                            szCols, 12);
      lBgndCol = StrToLong(szCols);
      PrfQueryProfileString(HINI_PROFILE, szAppName,
                            "StatsFgnd",
                            "0 0 0", szCols, 12);
      lForcCol = StrToLong(szCols);
      PrfQueryProfileString(HINI_PROFILE, szAppName,
                            "StatsTop", "N",
                            szTop, 2);
      PrfQueryProfileString(HINI_PROFILE, szAppName,
                            "Sound", "N",
                            szSound, 2);
```

Figure 14.8. Swap partition monitor: MAINWND.C. Continues.

```
            PrfQueryProfileString(HINI_PROFILE, szAppName,
                            "Gauge", "N",
                            szGauge, 2);
            PrfQueryProfileString(HINI_PROFILE, szAppName,
                            "StatsTitleBar", "Y",
                            szTitleBar, 2);

            if (szGauge[0] == 'Y')
              fGauge = FALSE;
            else                    /* Will be set correctly in MI_SLIDER */
              fGauge = TRUE;
                                    /* Now simulate menu select           */
            WinPostMsg(hwnd, WM_COMMAND, MPFROMSHORT
                      (MI_SLIDER), 0);

            if (szTop[0] == 'Y')
              WinPostMsg(hwnd, WM_COMMAND, MPFROMSHORT
                        (MI_TOP), 0);
            if (szSound[0] == 'Y')
              WinPostMsg(hwnd, WM_COMMAND, MPFROMSHORT
                        (MI_SOUND), 0);
            if (szTitleBar[0] == 'N')
              WinPostMsg(hwnd, WM_COMMAND, MPFROMSHORT
                        (MI_TITLEBAR), 0);
            else
              WinCheckMenuItem(hMenu, MI_TITLEBAR, fTitle);
            break;

          case UM_NOSWAPPER:
            DosBeep(1000, 100);
            WinMessageBox(HWND_DESKTOP, hwnd,
                          "Unable to find SWAPPER.DAT",
                          szTitle,
                          0, MB_ICONHAND | MB_OK | MB_MOVEABLE );
            WinPostMsg(hwnd, WM_QUIT, 0, 0);
            break;

          case UM_SWAPPER_FOUND:
            fSwapperOK = TRUE;
            pszPathName = (PSZ)(mp1);
            for (I = 0; I <= CCHMAXPATH; I++)
            {
```

Figure 14.8. Swap partition monitor: MAINWND.C. Continues.

```
      szPathName[I] = *pszPathName++;
      if (szPathName[I] == '\0')
        break;
    }
    ulPartSize = LONGFROMMP(mp2);
    break;

  case UM_STATS_CHANGED:
    ulSwapSize  = LONGFROMMP(mp1);
    ulFreeSpace = LONGFROMMP(mp2);
    ulUsedSpace = ulPartSize - ulFreeSpace;
    WinInvalidateRect(hwnd, NULL, FALSE);

    ulUsedLength = (double)(ulUsedSpace
                    * SCALE_SPACING * 10.00)/ulPartSize;
    WinSendMsg(hSlider, SLM_SETSLIDERINFO,
               MPFROM2SHORT(SMA_SLIDERARMPOSITION,
               SMA_RANGEVALUE),
               (MPARAM)ulUsedLength);

    if (fSound && ulPrevSwapSize != 0)
    {
      if (ulSwapSize > ulPrevSwapSize)
      {
        DosBeep(1000, 50);
        DosBeep(1100, 50);
        DosBeep(1200, 50);
        DosBeep(1300, 50);
        DosBeep(1400, 50);
      }
      if (ulSwapSize < ulPrevSwapSize)
      {
        DosBeep(1400, 50);
        DosBeep(1300, 50);
        DosBeep(1200, 50);
        DosBeep(1100, 50);
        DosBeep(1000, 50);
      }
    }
    ulPrevSwapSize = ulSwapSize;
    break;

  case WM_PAINT:
    hps = WinBeginPaint(hwnd, (HPS)NULL, &rcl);
```

Figure 14.8. Swap partition monitor: MAINWND.C. Continues.

```c
            GpiCreateLogColorTable(hps, LCOL_RESET, LCOLF_RGB,
                            0, 0, NULL);
            GpiSetColor(hps, lForeCol);
            WinFillRect(hps, &rcl, lBgndCol);

            sprintf(szText, "%s %s", "Swap file location:",
                    szPathName);
            pt.x = 5;
            pt.y = 110;
            GpiCharStringAt(hps, &pt, strlen(szText)-12,
                            szText);

            sprintf(szText, "%s %u", "Partition size:",
                    ulPartSize);
            pt.x = 5;
            pt.y = 85;
            GpiCharStringAt(hps, &pt, strlen(szText), szText);
            sprintf(szText, "%s %u", "Total space used:",
                    ulUsedSpace);
            pt.x = 5;
            pt.y = 60;
            GpiCharStringAt(hps, &pt, strlen(szText), szText);

            sprintf(szText, "%s %u", "Swap size:",
                    ulSwapSize);
            pt.x = 5;
            pt.y = 35;
            GpiCharStringAt(hps, &pt, strlen(szText), szText);

            sprintf(szText, "%s %u", "Free space:",
                    ulFreeSpace);
            pt.x = 5;
            pt.y = 10;
            GpiCharStringAt(hps, &pt, strlen(szText), szText);

            WinEndPaint(hps);

            break;

        case UM_NEWBGND:
            lBgndCol = LONGFROMMP(mp1);
            WinInvalidateRect(hwnd, NULL, FALSE);
            break;
```

Figure 14.8. Swap partition monitor: MAINWND.C. Continues.

A sample application

```
case UM_NEWFGND:
  lForeCol = LONGFROMMP(mp1);
  WinInvalidateRect(hwnd, NULL, FALSE);
  break;

case UM_DANGER:
  if (mp1)
  {
    for (I=0; I<=5; I++)                    /* Sound alarm */
    {
      DosBeep(1000, 50);
      DosBeep(1500, 50);
    }
    hDangerDlg = WinLoadDlg(HWND_DESKTOP,
                            HWND_DESKTOP,
                            (PFNWP)NULL,
                            (HMODULE)NULL,
                            DLG_DANGER, 0);
    WinQueryWindowRect(hDangerDlg, &rcl);
    lX = (WinQuerySysValue(HWND_DESKTOP,
            SV_CXSCREEN) - rcl.xRight) / 2;
    lY = (WinQuerySysValue(HWND_DESKTOP,
            SV_CYSCREEN) - rcl.yTop)  / 2;
    WinSetWindowPos(hDangerDlg, HWND_TOP, lX, lY,
                    0, 0, SWP_MOVE | SWP_SHOW);
  }
  else
    WinDestroyWindow(hDangerDlg);
  break;

case WM_BUTTON2DOWN:
  WinQueryPointerPos(HWND_DESKTOP, &pt);
  WinMapWindowPoints(HWND_DESKTOP, hwnd, &pt, 1);
  WinPopupMenu(hwnd, hwnd, hMenu, pt.x, pt.y, 0,
               PU_HCONSTRAIN | PU_VCONSTRAIN |
               PU_KEYBOARD | PU_MOUSEBUTTON1);
  return (MRESULT)TRUE;

case WM_SAVEAPPLICATION:
  if (fSwapperOK)
  {
```

Figure 14.8. Swap partition monitor: MAINWND.C. Continues.

```c
            WinSendMsg(WinWindowFromID(hGaugeFrame,
                    FID_CLIENT), UM_SAVEAPP, 0, 0);
            WinStoreWindowPos(szAppName, "StatsSizePos",
                            WinQueryWindow(hwnd,
                            QW_PARENT));
            if (WinIsMenuItemChecked(hMenu, MI_SLIDER))
              PrfWriteProfileString(HINI_PROFILE, szAppName,
                                "Gauge", "Y");
            else
              PrfWriteProfileString(HINI_PROFILE, szAppName,
                                "Gauge", "N");
            if (WinIsMenuItemChecked(hMenu, MI_TOP))
              PrfWriteProfileString(HINI_PROFILE, szAppName,
                                "StatsTop", "Y");
            else
              PrfWriteProfileString(HINI_PROFILE, szAppName,
                                "StatsTop", "N");

            if (WinIsMenuItemChecked(hMenu, MI_SOUND))
              PrfWriteProfileString(HINI_PROFILE, szAppName,
                                "Sound", "Y");
            else
              PrfWriteProfileString(HINI_PROFILE, szAppName,
                                "Sound", "N");

            if (WinIsMenuItemChecked(hMenu, MI_TITLEBAR))
              PrfWriteProfileString(HINI_PROFILE, szAppName,
                                "StatsTitleBar", "Y");
            else
              PrfWriteProfileString(HINI_PROFILE, szAppName,
                                "StatsTitleBar", "N");
          }
          break;

     case WM_TIMER:
        WinSetWindowPos(WinQueryWindow(hwnd, QW_PARENT),
                    HWND_TOP, 0, 0, 0, 0, SWP_ZORDER);
        break;

     case WM_COMMAND:
        switch (SHORT1FROMMP(mp1))
          {
            case MI_SLIDER:
```

Figure 14.8. Swap partition monitor: MAINWND.C. Continues.

A sample application 321

```
        fGauge = !fGauge;
        WinCheckMenuItem(hMenu, MI_SLIDER, fGauge);
        if (fGauge)
          WinSendMsg(WinWindowFromID(hGaugeFrame,
                     FID_CLIENT), UM_SHOW, 0, 0);
        else
          WinSendMsg(WinWindowFromID(hGaugeFrame,
                     FID_CLIENT), UM_HIDE, 0, 0);
        break;

    case MI_TOP:
        fTop = !fTop;
        WinCheckMenuItem(hMenu, MI_TOP, fTop);
        if (fTop)
          WinStartTimer(WinQueryAnchorBlock (hwnd),
                        hwnd, 1, 1000);
        else
          WinStopTimer(WinQueryAnchorBlock(hwnd),
                       hwnd, 1);
        break;

    case MI_SOUND:
        fSound = !fSound;
        WinCheckMenuItem(hMenu, MI_SOUND, fSound);
        break;

    case MI_TITLEBAR:
        fTitle = !fTitle;
        WinCheckMenuItem(hMenu, MI_TITLEBAR, fTitle);

        if (!fTitle)
        {
          WinSetParent(hTitleBar, HWND_OBJECT, FALSE);

          WinSetParent(hSysMenu, HWND_OBJECT, FALSE);

          WinSetParent(hMin, HWND_OBJECT, FALSE);
        }
        else
        {
          WinSetParent(hTitleBar, hFrame, FALSE);
          WinSetParent(hSysMenu, hFrame, FALSE);
```

Figure 14.8. Swap partition monitor: MAINWND.C. Continues.

```c
                    WinSetParent(hMin, hFrame, FALSE);
                 }
                 WinSendMsg(hFrame, WM_UPDATEFRAME,
                            MPFROMLONG(FCF_TITLEBAR |
                            FCF_SYSMENU | FCF_MINMAX), 0);
                 break;

              case MI_COLOUR:
                 WinDlgBox(HWND_DESKTOP, hwnd, ColourDlgProc,
                           (HMODULE)NULL, DLG_COLOURS, 0);
                 break;

              case MI_EXIT:
                 WinPostMsg(hwnd, WM_QUIT, 0, 0);
                 break;

              default:
                 break;
           }
        break;

     case WM_PRESPARAMCHANGED:
        if ((ULONG)mp1 == PP_BACKGROUNDCOLOR)
        {
           WinQueryPresParam(hwnd, PP_BACKGROUNDCOLOR, 0,
                             NULL, sizeof(lBgndCol),
                             &lBgndCol, 0);
           rgb.bRed = lBgndCol/65536;
           temp = fmod((double)lBgndCol, 65536.00);
           rgb.bGreen = temp/256;
           rgb.bBlue = fmod((double)temp, 256.00);
           strcpy(szCols, RGBToStr(rgb));
           PrfWriteProfileString(HINI_PROFILE, szAppName,
                                 "StatsBgnd", szCols);
        }
        WinInvalidateRect(hwnd, NULL, FALSE);
        break;

     case WM_ERASEBACKGROUND:
        return (MRESULT)TRUE;
   }
   return WinDefWindowProc(hwnd, msg, mp1, mp2);
}
```

Figure 14.8. Swap partition monitor: MAINWND.C. Concluded.

14.2.7 *DLGWND.C*

This is the dialog box procedure, `ColourDlgProc`, used to change the foreground and background colours of the statistics and gauge windows, and the colour of the indicator strip (Fig. 14.9). During initialization we obtain the handles of the gauge frame window and the slider control. We then set up the dialog box by filling the listbox and initializing the colour sliders, one each for the red, green and blue components. We read the profile to get the current colours, or if this is the first time the program has run, default them as follows: white for the window background colours and black for the remainder. Finally, we centralize the dialog box and show it.

Whenever a slider is changed or an entry in the listbox is selected, a `WM_CONTROL` message is sent with the low SHORT of `mp1` set to the control identity. Let us first consider what happens when you select an item in the listbox. The high SHORT of `mp1` will contain `LN_SELECT`, so when we receive this, we obtain the index of the selected item and set the sliders to the appropriate values. The array of structures, `argb`, contains these values since they were obtained during the initialization process: `argb[0]` refers to the statistics background; `argb[1]` to the statistics foreground; `argb[2]` to the gauge background; `argb[3]` to the gauge foreground; and `argb[4]` to the indicator strip.

For each slider we trap the `SLN_CHANGE` and `SLN_SLIDERTRACK` messages, update the value displayed to the right of the slider and, according to which listbox item is selected, call `ChangeColour` to effect the actual colour change. Note that if we are changing the statistics window (index values 0 or 1) we pass a NULL handle to `ChangeColour`. This ensures `ChangeColour` posts the relevant colour change message to the current thread's message queue, so our main window procedure will pick it up and process it.

Finally, when the dialog box is dismissed, all the colour settings are updated in the profile.

```
#define    INCL_GPIBITMAPS
#define    INCL_WINDIALOGS
#define    INCL_WINFRAMEMGR
#define    INCL_WINLISTBOXES
#define    INCL_WINSHELLDATA
#define    INCL_WINSTDSLIDER
#define    INCL_WINSYS
#define    INCL_WINWINDOWMGR

#include <os2.h>
#include <string.h>
#include <stdlib.h>
```

Figure 14.9. Swap partition monitor: DLGWND.C. Continues.

```c
#include "swapmon.h"

HWND    GetGaugeFrame (VOID);
VOID    ChangeColour  (SHORT, HWND, RGB);
RGB     StrToRGB      (PSZ);
PSZ     RGBToStr      (RGB);

CHAR    szAppName[];

/****************************************************************/

MRESULT EXPENTRY ColourDlgProc(HWND hwndDlg, ULONG msg,
                                MPARAM mp1, MPARAM mp2)
{
  static PSZ    szLBoxText[] = {"Statistics Background",
                                "Statistics Foreground",
                                "Gauge Background",
                                "Gauge Foreground",
                                "Indicator Strip"};
  static struct _RGB argb[5];
  static HWND   hSlider,
                hGaugeFrame;
  static SHORT  sIdx;
  LONG          lRed,
                lGreen,
                lBlue,
                lX,
                lY;
  CHAR          szColValue[4],
                szCols[12];
  USHORT        I;
  RECTL         rcl;

  switch (msg)
  {
    case WM_INITDLG:
      hGaugeFrame = GetGaugeFrame();
      hSlider = WinWindowFromID(WinWindowFromID
                                (hGaugeFrame, FID_CLIENT),
                                ID_SLIDER);
      lRed   = CLR_RED;
      lGreen = CLR_GREEN;
      lBlue  = CLR_BLUE;
      WinSetPresParam(WinWindowFromID(hwndDlg, ID_RED),
```

Figure 14.9. Swap partition monitor: DLGWND.C. Continues.

```
                              PP_BACKGROUNDCOLORINDEX,
                              sizeof(lRed), &lRed);
WinSetPresParam(WinWindowFromID(hwndDlg, ID_GREEN),
                              PP_BACKGROUNDCOLORINDEX,
                              sizeof(lGreen), &lGreen);
WinSetPresParam(WinWindowFromID(hwndDlg, ID_BLUE),
                              PP_BACKGROUNDCOLORINDEX,
                              sizeof(lBlue), &lBlue);
for (I = 0; I <= 4; I++)
{
   WinSendDlgItemMsg(hwndDlg, ID_LISTBOX,
                     LM_INSERTITEM,
                     MRFROMSHORT(LIT_END),
                     MRFROMP(szLBoxText[I]));
}
for (I = 16; I <= 256 ; I+=16 )
{
   WinSendDlgItemMsg(hwndDlg, ID_RED,
                     SLM_SETTICKSIZE,
                     MPFROM2SHORT(I, 6), 0);
   WinSendDlgItemMsg(hwndDlg, ID_GREEN,
                     SLM_SETTICKSIZE,
                     MPFROM2SHORT(I, 6), 0);
   WinSendDlgItemMsg(hwndDlg, ID_BLUE,
                     SLM_SETTICKSIZE,
                     MPFROM2SHORT(I, 6), 0);
}
PrfQueryProfileString(HINI_PROFILE, szAppName,
                      "StatsBgnd", "255 255 255",
                      szCols, 12);
argb[0] = StrToRGB(szCols);
PrfQueryProfileString(HINI_PROFILE, szAppName,
                      "StatsFgnd", "0 0 0",
                      szCols, 12);
argb[1] = StrToRGB(szCols);
PrfQueryProfileString(HINI_PROFILE, szAppName,
                      "GaugeBgnd", "255 255 255",
                      szCols, 12);
argb[2] = StrToRGB(szCols);
PrfQueryProfileString(HINI_PROFILE, szAppName,
                      "GaugeFgnd", "0 0 0",
                      szCols, 12);
```

Figure 14.9. Swap partition monitor: DLGWND.C. Continues.

```
            argb[3] = StrToRGB(szCols);
            PrfQueryProfileString(HINI_PROFILE, szAppName,
                            "GaugeBar", "0 0 0",
                            szCols, 12);
            argb[4] = StrToRGB(szCols);


            WinSendDlgItemMsg(hwndDlg, ID_LISTBOX,
                        LM_SELECTITEM, MRFROMSHORT(0),
                        (MPARAM)TRUE);
            WinQueryWindowRect(hwndDlg, &rcl);
            lX = (WinQuerySysValue(HWND_DESKTOP, SV_CXSCREEN) -
                rcl.xRight) / 2;
            lY = (WinQuerySysValue(HWND_DESKTOP, SV_CYSCREEN) -
                rcl.yTop)   / 2;
            WinSetWindowPos(hwndDlg, 0, lX, lY, 0, 0, SWP_MOVE |
                        SWP_SHOW);
            break;


        case WM_CONTROL:
          switch(SHORT1FROMMP(mp1))
          {
            case ID_LISTBOX:
              switch(SHORT2FROMMP(mp1))
              {
                case LN_SELECT:
                  sIdx = (SHORT)WinSendDlgItemMsg(hwndDlg,
                            ID_LISTBOX, LM_QUERYSELECTION,
                            0, 0);
                  WinSendDlgItemMsg(hwndDlg, ID_RED,
                                SLM_SETSLIDERINFO,
                                MPFROM2SHORT
                                (SMA_SLIDERARMPOSITION,
                                SMA_RANGEVALUE),
                                (MPARAM)argb[sIdx].bRed);
                  WinSendDlgItemMsg(hwndDlg, ID_GREEN,
                                SLM_SETSLIDERINFO,
                                MPFROM2SHORT
                                (SMA_SLIDERARMPOSITION,
                                SMA_RANGEVALUE),
                                (MPARAM)argb[sIdx].bGreen);
```

Figure 14.9. Swap partition monitor: DLGWND.C. Continues.

```
              WinSendDlgItemMsg(hwndDlg, ID_BLUE,
                                SLM_SETSLIDERINFO,
                                MPFROM2SHORT
                                (SMA_SLIDERARMPOSITION,
                                SMA_RANGEVALUE),
                                (MPARAM)argb[sIdx].bBlue);
            break;


        default:
          break;
      }
      break;


  case ID_RED:
    switch(SHORT2FROMMP(mp1))
    {
      case SLN_CHANGE:
      case SLN_SLIDERTRACK:
        lRed = LONGFROMMP(mp2);
        _ltoa(lRed, szColValue, 10);
        WinSetDlgItemText(hwndDlg, ID_RVALUE,
                          szColValue);
        argb[sIdx].bRed = (BYTE)lRed;
                        /* Changing statistics colours */
        if (sIdx == 0 || sIdx == 1)
          ChangeColour(sIdx, 0, argb[sIdx]);

                           /* Changing gauge foreground */
        if (sIdx == 3)
          ChangeColour(sIdx, hSlider, argb[sIdx]);

                         /* Changing gauge background/bar */
        if (sIdx == 2 || sIdx == 4)
          ChangeColour(sIdx, hGaugeFrame, argb[sIdx]);
        break;


      default:
        break;
```

Figure 14.9. Swap partition monitor: DLGWND.C. Continues.

```
            }
            break;

        case ID_GREEN:
          switch(SHORT2FROMMP(mp1))
          {
            case SLN_CHANGE:
            case SLN_SLIDERTRACK:
              lGreen = LONGFROMMP(mp2);
              _ltoa(lGreen, szColValue, 10);
              WinSetDlgItemText(hwndDlg, ID_GVALUE,
                              szColValue);
              argb[sIdx].bGreen = (BYTE)lGreen;

              if (sIdx == 0 || sIdx == 1)
                ChangeColour(sIdx, 0, argb[sIdx]);

              if (sIdx == 3)
                ChangeColour(sIdx, hSlider, argb[sIdx]);

              if (sIdx == 2 || sIdx == 4)
                ChangeColour(sIdx, hGaugeFrame, argb[sIdx]);
              break;

            default:
              break;
          }
          break;

        case ID_BLUE:
          switch(SHORT2FROMMP(mp1))
          {
            case SLN_CHANGE:
            case SLN_SLIDERTRACK:
              lBlue = LONGFROMMP(mp2);
              _ltoa(lBlue, szColValue, 10);
              WinSetDlgItemText(hwndDlg, ID_BVALUE,
                              szColValue);
              argb[sIdx].bBlue = (BYTE)lBlue;

              if (sIdx == 0 || sIdx == 1)
                ChangeColour(sIdx, 0, argb[sIdx]);
```

Figure 14.9. Swap partition monitor: DLGWND.C. Continues.

```
              if (sIdx == 3)
                ChangeColour(sIdx, hSlider, argb[sIdx]);

              if (sIdx == 2 || sIdx == 4)
                ChangeColour(sIdx, hGaugeFrame, argb[sIdx]);
              break;

            default:
              break;
          }
          break;

      }
      break;

  case WM_COMMAND:
    switch(SHORT1FROMMP(mp1))
    {
      case ID_EXIT:
        strcpy(szCols, RGBToStr(argb[0]));
        PrfWriteProfileString(HINI_PROFILE, szAppName,
                              "StatsBgnd", szCols);
        strcpy(szCols, RGBToStr(argb[1]));
        PrfWriteProfileString(HINI_PROFILE, szAppName,
                              "StatsFgnd", szCols);
        strcpy(szCols, RGBToStr(argb[2]));
        PrfWriteProfileString(HINI_PROFILE, szAppName,
                              "GaugeBgnd", szCols);
        strcpy(szCols, RGBToStr(argb[3]));
        PrfWriteProfileString(HINI_PROFILE, szAppName,
                              "GaugeFgnd", szCols);
        strcpy(szCols, RGBToStr(argb[4]));
        PrfWriteProfileString(HINI_PROFILE, szAppName,
                              "GaugeBar", szCols);
        break;

      default:
        return FALSE;
    }
    WinDismissDlg(hwndDlg, TRUE);
    break;
```

Figure 14.9. Swap partition monitor: DLGWND.C. Continues.

```
      default:
         return WinDefDlgProc(hwndDlg, msg, mp1, mp2);
   }
   return (MRESULT)FALSE;
}
```

Figure 14.9. Swap partition monitor: DLGWND.C. Concluded.

14.2.8 CHNGCOL.C

This is the ChangeColour procedure (Fig. 14.10) and it just converts the RGB values into a LONG and, depending on which component is being changed, either posts a user message or changes the presentation parameters.

```
#define   INCL_GPIBITMAPS
#define   INCL_WINSYS

#include <os2.h>
#include "swapmon.h"
/***************************************************************/
VOID   ChangeColour(SHORT sLBoxIndex, HWND hwnd, RGB rgb)
{
   LONG lColour;

   lColour = rgb.bRed * 65536 + rgb.bGreen * 256 + rgb.bBlue;

   if (sLBoxIndex == 0)                      /* Statistics background */
      WinPostMsg(hwnd, UM_NEWBGND, MPFROMLONG(lColour), 0);

   if (sLBoxIndex == 1)                      /* Statistics foreground */
      WinPostMsg(hwnd, UM_NEWFGND, MPFROMLONG(lColour), 0);

   if (sLBoxIndex == 2)                      /* Gauge background      */
      WinPostMsg(hwnd, UM_NEWGBGND, MPFROMLONG(lColour), 0);

   if (sLBoxIndex == 3)                      /* Gauge foreground      */
      WinSetPresParam(hwnd, PP_FOREGROUNDCOLOR, sizeof(rgb), &rgb);

   if (sLBoxIndex == 4)                      /* Gauge bar             */
      WinPostMsg(hwnd, UM_NEWBAR, MPFROMLONG(lColour), 0);

   return;
}
```

Figure 14.10. Swap partition monitor: CHNGCOL.C.

14.2.9 STRTORGB.C

This procedure converts a string of colour values into an RGB structure (Fig. 14.11).

```c
#define  INCL_GPIBITMAPS

#include <os2.h>
#include <string.h>
#include <stdlib.h>

/*********************************************************/

RGB   StrToRGB(PSZ szColours)
{
  RGB    rgb;
  CHAR   *szRed,
         *szGreen,
         *szBlue;

  szRed   = strtok(szColours, " ");
  szGreen = strtok(NULL, " ");
  szBlue  = strtok(NULL, " "");
  rgb.bRed   = (BYTE)atoi(szRed);
  rgb.bGreen = (BYTE)atoi(szGreen);
  rgb.bBlue  = (BYTE)atoi(szBlue);
  return rgb;
}
```

Figure 14.11. Swap partition monitor: STRTORGB.C.

14.2.10 RGBTOSTR.C

This procedure converts an RGB structure into a string of colour values (Fig. 14.12).

```c
#define  INCL_GPIBITMAPS
#include <os2.h>
#include <stdio.h>
#include <stdlib.h>

/*********************************************************/

PSZ   RGBToStr(RGB rgb)
```

Figure 14.12. Swap partition monitor: RGBTOSTR.C. Continues.

```
{
  CHAR  szString[13],
        szRed[4],
        szGreen[4],
        szBlue[4];

  _itoa((USHORT)rgb.bRed, szRed, 10);
  _itoa((USHORT)rgb.bGreen, szGreen, 10);
  _itoa((USHORT)rgb.bBlue, szBlue, 10);

  sprintf(szString, "%s %s %s", szRed, szGreen, szBlue);

  return szString;
}
```

Figure 14.12. Swap partition monitor: RGBTOSTR.C. Concluded.

14.2.11 *STRTOLNG.C*

This procedure converts a string of colour values into a LONG (Fig. 14.13).

```
#define  INCL_GPIBITMAPS

#include <os2.h>
#include <string.h>
#include <stdlib.h>

/******************************************************************/

LONG   StrToLong(PSZ szColours)
{
  RGB    rgb;
  LONG   lColour;
  CHAR   *szRed,
         *szGreen,
         *szBlue;
  szRed   = strtok(szColours, " ");
  szGreen = strtok(NULL, " ");
  szBlue  = strtok(NULL, " ");
  rgb.bRed   = (BYTE)atoi(szRed);
  rgb.bGreen = (BYTE)atoi(szGreen);
  rgb.bBlue  = (BYTE)atoi(szBlue);

  lColour = rgb.bRed * 65536 + rgb.bGreen * 256 + rgb.bBlue;
  return lColour;
}
```

Figure 14.13. Swap partition monitor: STRTOLNG.C.

14.2.12 GAUGEFRM.C

This is the `GetGaugeFrame` procedure and is used to enumerate the desktop frame windows in order to find the handle of the gauge frame window (Fig. 14.14).

```c
#define   INCL_WINFRAMEMGR
#define   INCL_WINWINDOWMGR

#include <os2.h>
#include <string.h>
#include "swapmon.h"

/****************************************************************/

HWND GetGaugeFrame(VOID)
                              /* Retrieve gauge frame window handle */
{
  HWND      hWin,
            hGaugeFrame;
  HENUM     hEnum;
  CHAR      szClassBuffer[20];

  hEnum = WinBeginEnumWindows(HWND_DESKTOP);
  while (hWin = WinGetNextWindow(hEnum))
  {
    WinQueryClassName(hWin, sizeof(szClassBuffer),
                      szClassBuffer);
    if (!strcmp(szClassBuffer, "#1"))
    {
      WinQueryClassName(WinWindowFromID(hWin, FID_CLIENT),
                        sizeof(szClassBuffer),
                        szClassBuffer);

      if (!strcmp(szClassBuffer, "SwapGauge"))
        hGaugeFrame = hWin;
    }
  }
  WinEndEnumWindows(hEnum);
  return hGaugeFrame;
}
```

Figure 14.14. Swap partition monitor: GAUGEFRM.C.

The following listings for the SWAPMON program complete the total source for the program. They are the header file, Fig. 14.15, the resource file, Fig. 14.16, and the dialog template, Fig. 14.17. Because this program differs from the skeleton program in that it contains many object files, the link control file, Fig. 14.18, the module definition file, Fig. 14.19, and the make file, Fig. 14.20, are also included.

```
#define   UM_NOSWAPPER        WM_USER
#define   UM_SWAPPER_FOUND    WM_USER+1
#define   UM_STATS_CHANGED    WM_USER+2
#define   UM_NEWBGND          WM_USER+3
#define   UM_NEWFGND          WM_USER+4
#define   UM_NEWGBGND         WM_USER+5
#define   UM_NEWBAR           WM_USER+6
#define   UM_PASSHWND         WM_USER+7
#define   UM_DANGER           WM_USER+8
#define   UM_SHOW             WM_USER+9
#define   UM_HIDE             WM_USER+10
#define   UM_SAVEAPP          WM_USER+11

#define   SCALE_SPACING       40
#define   DEFAULT_WIN_X       300
#define   DEFAULT_WIN_Y       180
#define   DEFAULT_VERT_X      120
#define   DEFAULT_VERT_Y      450
#define   DEFAULT_HORIZ_X     450
#define   DEFAULT_HORIZ_Y     120
#define   DANGER_LEVEL        1024 * 1024 * 3

#define   ID_MAINWND          200
#define   ID_TITLE            201
#define   ID_STITLE           202
#define   ID_MENU             203
#define   ID_SLDRMENU         204
#define   ID_SLIDER           205
#define   ID_SLIDERWND        206

#define   MI_EXIT             300
#define   MI_SLIDER           301
#define   MI_SOUND            302
#define   MI_TOP              303
#define   MI_COLOUR           304
#define   MI_HORIZ            305
#define   MI_VERT             306
#define   MI_TITLEBAR         307
```

Figure 14.15. Swap partition monitor: header file. Continues.

```
#define    DLG_COLOURS     400
#define    ID_EXIT         402
#define    ID_LISTBOX      403
#define    ID_RED          404
#define    ID_GREEN        405
#define    ID_BLUE         406
#define    ID_RVALUE       407
#define    ID_GVALUE       408
#define    ID_BVALUE       409
#define    DLG_DANGER      410
```

Figure 14.15. Swap partition monitor: header file. Concluded.

```
#include <os2.h>
#include "swapmon.h"
STRINGTABLE PRELOAD
BEGIN
  ID_TITLE,  "Swap Partition Monitor"
  ID_STITLE, "Percentage Use"
END
ICON        ID_MAINWND    swapmon.ico
ACCELTABLE  ID_MAINWND
BEGIN
  VK_F3,     MI_EXIT,      VIRTUALKEY
END
MENU        ID_MENU PRELOAD
BEGIN
  MENUITEM "~Gauge",         MI_SLIDER,    MIS_TEXT
  MENUITEM "~Keep on Top",   MI_TOP,       MIS_TEXT
  MENUITEM "~Sound",         MI_SOUND,     MIS_TEXT
  MENUITEM "~Colour...",     MI_COLOUR,    MIS_TEXT
  MENUITEM "~Title Bar",     MI_TITLEBAR,  MIS_TEXT
END
MENU        ID_SLDRMENU PRELOAD
BEGIN
  MENUITEM "~Vertical",      MI_VERT,      MIS_TEXT
  MENUITEM "~Horizontal",    MI_HORIZ,     MIS_TEXT
  MENUITEM "~Keep on Top",   MI_TOP,       MIS_TEXT
  MENUITEM "~Title Bar",     MI_TITLEBAR,  MIS_TEXT
END
rcinclude swapmon.dlg
```

Figure 14.16. Swap partition monitor: resource file.

```
DLGINCLUDE 1 "SWAPMON.H"

DLGTEMPLATE DLG_DANGER LOADONCALL MOVEABLE DISCARDABLE
BEGIN
  DIALOG "Swap Partition Monitor", DLG_DANGER, 23, 19, 148,
         57, FS_SCREENALIGN, FCF_TITLEBAR | FCF_NOBYTEALIGN
         PRESPARAMS PP_BACKGROUNDCOLOR, 0x00000000L
  BEGIN
    CTEXT      "DANGER", 411, 17, 43, 118, 8, DT_VCENTER

               PRESPARAMS PP_FOREGROUNDCOLOR, 0x00FF0000L
    CTEXT      "The free space on your swap",
               413, 4, 25, 140, 8, DT_VCENTER

               PRESPARAMS PP_FOREGROUNDCOLOR, 0x00FF0000L

    CTEXT      "partition has fallen below 3 MB.",
               412, 4, 7, 140, 8, DT_VCENTER

               PRESPARAMS PP_FOREGROUNDCOLOR, 0x00FF0000L
  END
END

DLGTEMPLATE DLG_COLOURS LOADONCALL MOVEABLE DISCARDABLE
BEGIN
  DIALOG "Customize Colours", DLG_COLOURS, 94, 62, 286, 145,
         FS_SCREENALIGN, FCF_TITLEBAR | FCF_NOBYTEALIGN
  BEGIN
    LISTBOX   ID_LISTBOX, 63, 96, 170, 46, WS_GROUP
    CONTROL   "", ID_RED, 47, 71, 202, 19, WC_SLIDER,
              SLS_HORIZONTAL | SLS_CENTER |
              SLS_SNAPTOINCREMENT | SLS_BUTTONSLEFT |
              SLS_RIBBONSTRIP | SLS_HOMELEFT |
              SLS_PRIMARYSCALE1 | WS_TABSTOP |
              WS_VISIBLE
              CTLDATA 12, 0, 256, 0, 0, 0
    CONTROL   "", ID_GREEN, 47, 47, 202, 19, WC_SLIDER,
              SLS_HORIZONTAL | SLS_CENTER |
              SLS_SNAPTOINCREMENT | SLS_BUTTONSLEFT |
              SLS_RIBBONSTRIP | SLS_HOMELEFT |
              SLS_PRIMARYSCALE1 | WS_TABSTOP |
              WS_VISIBLE
              CTLDATA 12, 0, 256, 0, 0, 0
```

Figure 14.17. Swap partition monitor dialog template: Continues.

```
    CONTROL         "", ID_BLUE, 47, 23, 202, 19, WC_SLIDER,
                    SLS_HORIZONTAL | SLS_CENTER |
                    SLS_SNAPTOINCREMENT | SLS_BUTTONSLEFT |
                    SLS_RIBBONSTRIP | SLS_HOMELEFT |
                    SLS_PRIMARYSCALE1 | WS_TABSTOP |
                    WS_VISIBLE
                    CTLDATA 12, 0, 256, 0, 0, 0
    PUSHBUTTON      "Exit", ID_EXIT, 5, 4, 57, 14
    CTEXT           "0", ID_RVALUE, 254, 76, 28, 8,
                    DT_VCENTER | NOT WS_GROUP
    CTEXT           "0", ID_GVALUE, 254, 52, 28, 8,
                    DT_VCENTER | NOT WS_GROUP
    CTEXT           "0", ID_BVALUE, 254, 28, 28, 8,
                    DT_VCENTER | NOT WS_GROUP
    LTEXT           "Red", 411, 4, 76, 20, 8, NOT WS_GROUP
    LTEXT           "Green", 412, 4, 52, 32, 8, NOT WS_GROUP
    LTEXT           "Blue", 413, 4, 28, 20, 8, NOT WS_GROUP
  END
END
```

Figure 14.17. Swap partition: monitor dialog template. Concluded.

```
swapmon mainwnd  getstats subclass gaugewnd slider gaugefrm +
dlgwnd  strtolng strtorgb rgbtostr chngcol /A:16 /E /CO
swapmon.exe
swapmon.map
os2386.lib
swapmon.def
```

Figure 14.18. Swap partition monitor: link control file.

```
NAME         swapmon WINDOWAPI

DESCRIPTION  'Swap Partition Monitor - Written by Bryan Goodyer'

STUB         'OS2STUB.EXE'

DATA         MULTIPLE

STACKSIZE    8192

PROTMODE
```

Figure 14.19. Swap partition monitor: module definition file.

```
all: swapmon.exe

ICC = icc /c /Gm /kb /n50 /Ti

OBJS = swapmon.obj mainwnd.obj subclass.obj getstats.obj\
       gaugewnd.obj slider.obj gaugefrm.obj dlgwnd.obj\
       strtolng.obj strtorgb.obj rgbtostr.obj chngcol.obj

.c.obj:
    $(ICC) $*.c

swapmon.obj: swapmon.c swapmon.h

mainwnd.obj: mainwnd.c swapmon.h

subclass.obj: subclass.c swapmon.h

getstats.obj: getstats.c swapmon.h

gaugewnd.obj: gaugewnd.c swapmon.h

slider.obj: slider.c swapmon.h

gaugefrm.obj: gaugefrm.c swapmon.h

dlgwnd.obj: dlgwnd.c swapmon.h

strtolng.obj: strtolng.c

strtorgb.obj: strtorgb.c

rgbtostr.obj: rgbtostr.c

chngcol.obj: chngcol.c swapmon.h

swapmon.res: swapmon.h swapmon.rc swapmon.ico swapmon.dlg
  rc -r swapmon.rc

swapmon.exe: $(OBJS) swapmon.def swapmon.res
  link386 @swapmon.l
  rc swapmon.res
```

Figure 14.20. Swap partition monitor: make file.

15
A basic exception handler

15.1 Trapping access violations

With the introduction of OS/2 version 2.0 it has become possible to trap access violations by registering your own exception handler. This can be a very useful way of handling large amounts of memory in an application. Consider a text editor, or word processor. When the program starts it does not know how much memory it is going to need to satisfy the user's requirements, so it may just allocate 64 kb, and if that looks like being used up it may allocate another 64 kb and so on. Now in version 2.0 whenever you allocate memory, that memory is not backed up with real memory until you commit it. This means that you can allocate, say, 1 Mb, and only commit one page, that is 4 kb, and only be using 4 kb of real memory but have the remainder reserved for you.

Let us assume then, that you did this. Now, because you have committed the first page you can write into it, assuming you allocated it as read/write, and everything would be fine until you attempted to write into the next page when, under normal circumstances, your program would crash with an access violation. Of course, we would normally be keeping a count of bytes written and commit the next page when necessary, but this is rather cumbersome. What would be convenient here is some mechanism whereby we could automatically have the next page committed to let us continue writing as if nothing had happened. This is where the exception handler comes in—it does just that.

The program listed in Fig. 15.1 registers an exception handler `XCPTHandler` and allocates 64 kb of read/write memory. We then commit the first page and start filling the entire 64 kb with the letter 'Z'. Running the program from the command line will not produce any errors and all 64 kb will have been filled with 'Z'. To see what actually happens you need to run this under the Presentation Manager debugger, IPMD.EXE, see Sec. 15.3. You will notice that every time we access the first byte in the next page the exception handler, listed in Fig. 15.2, takes control. If it is an access violation (which it will be under these circumstances), we obtain the address causing the fault, held in `ExceptionInfo[1]` in the

```
#define   INCL_DOSEXCEPTIONS
#define   INCL_DOSMEMMGR

#include <os2.h>
#include <string.h>

ULONG   XCPTHandler(PEXCEPTIONREPORTRECORD);

INT main(VOID)
{
  EXCEPTIONREGISTRATIONRECORD ExceptionStruct;
  PVOID   BaseMem;
  CHAR    *pData,
          *pChar;
  ULONG   I;

  ExceptionStruct.ExceptionHandler = (_ERR *)&XCPTHandler;
  DosSetExceptionHandler(&ExceptionStruct);

  DosAllocMem(&BaseMem, 65536, PAG_READ | PAG_WRITE);
  DosSetMem(BaseMem, 4096, PAG_DEFAULT | PAG_COMMIT);
  pData = BaseMem;
  pChar = "Z";

  for (I=0; I<65536; I++)
    *pData++ = *pChar;

  DosUnsetExceptionHandler(&ExceptionStruct);
  DosFreeMem(BaseMem);
  return 0;
}
```

Figure 15.1. Exception handler to trap access violations: EXCEPTN.C (main routine).

exception report record, and use this as our base address for the next page to be committed. So, if this page has been allocated then we commit it and continue; if not, we pass the exception on to OS/2 for handling, which will cause our program to terminate. Similarly, any violation other than an access violation will cause our program to be terminated. Try changing the for loop limit from I<65536 to I<=65536 to see the effect of trying to write into the next page after our 64 kb.

There is one point to note here for OS/2 version 2.0, and that is, whenever any memory is allocated, OS/2 returns a pointer aligned on a 64 kb boundary. This is because in version 2.0 all memory is *tiled* by default, and as OS/2 V2.0 is a mixture of 16-bit and 32-bit code internally, a 32-bit API may still require to call 16-bit code, therefore all memory has to be addressable by both 16-bit and 32-bit code. This is also why there is a 512 Mb virtual address space limit; a local descriptor table (LDT) can only hold 8192 descriptors, and as each descriptor can address

```
ULONG    XCPTHandler(PEXCEPTIONREPORTRECORD pXcpt)
{
  PVOID   NextPageBaseAddr;
  ULONG   ulPageSize,
          fulPageAttrs;
  if(pXcpt->ExceptionNum == XCPT_ACCESS_VIOLATION)
  {
    NextPageBaseAddr = (PVOID)pXcpt->ExceptionInfo[1];
    if (NextPageBaseAddr)
    {
      ulPageSize = 4096;
      DosQueryMem(NextPageBaseAddr, &ulPageSize, &fulPageAttrs);
      if ((fulPageAttrs & PAG_FREE) == 0)
      {
        if (DosSetMem(NextPageBaseAddr, ulPageSize, PAG_DEFAULT |
                    PAG_COMMIT) != 0)
          return(XCPT_CONTINUE_SEARCH);
        else
          return(XCPT_CONTINUE_EXECUTION);
      }
    }
  }
                        /* Not an access violation so return it to */
                        /* OS/2 to handle.                         */
  return(XCPT_CONTINUE_SEARCH);
}
```

Figure 15.2. Exception handler to trap access violations: EXCEPTN.C (exception handler).

64 kb, an LDT can address 8K × 64kb, or 512 Mb. These limits can only be lifted when OS/2 is fully 32-bit.

Let us now return to our sample program. If we just allocate 1 byte in our `DosAllocMem` call then we would still be able to access all 64 kb using our exception handler. It would not be until we cross that 64 kb boundary that we would actually crash the program. Even without an exception handler installed, we will still be able to access a complete page of memory since that is the smallest amount that can be allocated, and so long as we do not access beyond that page all will be well. This is something you must remember when coding for 32-bit OS/2, even though you may exceed the bounds of your allocated memory you may not receive an access violation, unlike 16-bit OS/2. It is not until you step over the page boundary that you will receive the page fault. However, when OS/2 is fully 32-bit and memory is no longer necessarily tiled, it is unlikely that you will be able to allocate 1 byte and still access 64 kb, so do not depend on this. Always allocate what you think you will need.

15.2 Trapping guard page exceptions

The same can be achieved by using the guard page technique. A guard page is a special committed page that is used for expand-down memory, as in stacks. The default action on a guard page exception is for the guard page to have its guard attribute removed and the page *below* to be committed and set as a guard page. However, for our purposes we need to expand *upwards* and so we still need to supply our own exception handler to do it. The listing in Fig. 15.3 is the main routine which registers the exception handler and sets the first page of a block of 64 kb of memory as a guard page.

Basically, all we need to do on receipt of a guard page exception (see Fig. 15.4) is to obtain the fault address as before and remove the guard attribute for this page and set the next page as a guard page and continue.

```
#define    INCL_DOSEXCEPTIONS
#define    INCL_DOSMEMMGR

#include   <os2.h>
#include   <string.h>

ULONG   XCPTHandler(PEXCEPTIONREPORTRECORD);

INT main(VOID)
{
  EXCEPTIONREGISTRATIONRECORD ExceptionStruct;
  PVOID    BaseMem;
  CHAR     *pData,
           *pChar;
  ULONG    I;

  ExceptionStruct.ExceptionHandler = (_ERR *)&XCPTHandler;
  DosSetExceptionHandler(&ExceptionStruct);

  DosAllocMem(&BaseMem, 65536, PAG_READ | PAG_WRITE);
  DosSetMem(BaseMem, 4096, PAG_READ | PAG_WRITE | PAG_COMMIT |
            PAG_GUARD);
  pData = BaseMem;
  pChar = "Z";

  for (I=0; I<65536; I++)
    *pData++ = *pChar;

  DosUnsetExceptionHandler(&ExceptionStruct);
  DosFreeMem(BaseMem);
  return 0;
}
```

Figure 15.3. Exception handler to trap guard page exceptions: EXCEPTN2.C (main routine).

```
ULONG   XCPTHandler(PEXCEPTIONREPORTRECORD pXcpt)
{
  PVOID   NextPageBaseAddr;
  ULONG   ulPageSize,
          fulPageAttrs;
  if(pXcpt->ExceptionNum == XCPT_GUARD_PAGE_VIOLATION)
  {
    NextPageBaseAddr = (PVOID)pXcpt->ExceptionInfo[1];
    if (NextPageBaseAddr)
    {
      ulPageSize = 4096;
      DosQueryMem(NextPageBaseAddr, &ulPageSize, &fulPageAttrs);
      if ((fulPageAttrs & PAG_FREE) == 0)
      {
        if (DosSetMem(NextPageBaseAddr, ulPageSize, PAG_DEFAULT)
            != 0)
          return(XCPT_CONTINUE_SEARCH);
        else
        {
          NextPageBaseAddr = (PVOID)(pXcpt->ExceptionInfo[1]
                       + ulPageSize);
          DosSetMem(NextPageBaseAddr, ulPageSize,
                  PAG_READ | PAG_WRITE | PAG_COMMIT | PAG_GUARD);
          return(XCPT_CONTINUE_EXECUTION);
        }
      }
    }
  }
                     /* Not a guard page exception so return it */
                     /* to OS/2 to handle.                      */
  return(XCPT_CONTINUE_SEARCH);
}
```

Figure 15.4. Exception handler to trap guard page exceptions: EXCEPTN2.C (exception handler).

15.3 Running the debugger

As discussed earlier, you will not see anything when running these programs from the command line. In order to appreciate what is happening you must run them using the Presentation Manager debugger, so to get you started follow this sample session:

1. Start the debugger by typing `ipmd exceptn` at an OS/2 command prompt.
2. Set breakpoints by double-clicking on line number 20, the statement containing the `DosAllocMem` call, and line number 41, the first statement in the exception handler.

3 Double-click on the variables `BaseMem` and `NextPageBaseAddr` so that you can monitor their values in the program monitor list.
4 Start running the program by giving the `Source` window the focus and pressing the letter `R`.
5 The debugger will now stop at line 20, so single step by pressing the letter `O`. This will cause the memory to be allocated and a pointer to be returned in `BaseMem`. You will see its value in the program monitor list.
6 Now press `Ctrl-G` and overtype the flat memory address in the `Storage` window using the value returned for `BaseMem`. You will need to use mouse button 1 to move the cursor to the address area. This will now show the memory that has just been allocated to you and will show only `????????`.
7 Give the focus back to the `Source` window and press `R` again to continue. This will give you an `Access Violation` so press Enter and press `R` again. You will now be stopped at line 41 in the exception handler.
8 Single step through to obtain the value `NextPageBaseAddr`. This should be 0x1000 (4 kb) more than your base address. This is because you tried writing into the next page and so raised an exception.
9 Overtype the flat memory address again, this time with the value in `NextPageBaseAddr`, and continue single stepping. The statement at line 50 will cause the next page to be committed and thus initialized with zeros.
10 Press `R` again to continue. You will now see the memory fill with 0x5As and another violation occur when the next page is accessed. This will continue until all 64 kb has been written to, when the program will end.

You should now be able to carry out a similar session with the guard page exception handler, EXCEPTN2.EXE.

Appendix 1
Glossary

A

About
    A message box containing the program's name and version number, and possibly the author and/or copyright information.

Accelerator
    A single keystroke used for fast access to a user's choice.

Accelerator table
    A table containing your accelerator definitions, usually defined in your resource file.

Access violation
    An error caused by a program accessing memory for which it is not authorized.

Active window
    The window which currently has the focus.

ANSI
    American National Standards Institute.

API
    Application programming interface.

ASCII
    American standard code for information interchange.

Atom
    A constant representing a string. This can then be used in place of the string.

Atom table
    A table containing the atoms and their strings.

B

Bitmap
    A graphic image.

Boot
Start the computer by either pressing Ctrl-Alt-Delete or by switching it off and on again.

Buffer
A temporary area of memory.

C

C Set/2
IBM's 32-bit compiler written explicitly for OS/2 version 2.

Checkbox
A box-shaped control that can be used to indicate a choice. A cross is drawn into it when selected, but is empty when not selected.

Checking
Checking a menu item puts a small tick to its left to denote that it has been selected.

Child window
A window positioned relative to another, its parent, and that cannot be moved outside its parent.

Client window
The main body of a window used by the application for displaying or updating data.

Command prompt
Otherwise known as the C prompt. It is the command line as used in a windowed, or full-screen, OS/2 and DOS session.

Computer conferencing
A method of information exchange for any topic, not necessarily just computing. Used mainly for questions and answers or general debate.

CONFIG.SYS
A file in the root directory of your start-up drive that defines your system configuration. This file is vital and should be modified with care. If you accidentally corrupt it you will find a copy in the \OS2\INSTALL directory.

Control
A window used for user input, for example an entry field. It can also be used as output only, for example a read-only slider.

CSD
Corrective service diskette(s). The mechanism IBM uses to distribute software fixes.

CUA
Common user access. An IBM standard designed to ensure computer applications behave consistently.

Cursor
> The screen symbol indicating where keyboard input is to go. In the enhanced editor this is a flashing block or underscore depending whether you are in insert or replace mode.

D

Default procedure
> A window procedure which processes all messages that your window procedure is not interested in. You *must* pass control to this procedure.

Desktop manager
> This is a component of OS/2 version 1.x. It allows the user to organize programs into groups, run them and generally control the running of the desktop.

Developer's toolkit
> A set of tools and files necessary for building a program. It also contains all the technical reference manuals as on-line help files.

Dialog box
> A special frame window that contains one or more controls. Usually created using the dialog box editor.

Dialog box editor
> A special tool provided in the developer's toolkit for the creation of dialog boxes.

DLG file
> Dialog box template file. Its file name has the extension name DLG.

DOS
> Disk operating system. The predecessor of OS/2.

Drag
> Moving an object on the desktop with the help of the mouse.

Drop
> Releasing a dragged object.

E

EA
> Extended attributes. Additional information associated with a file, such as file type or date last accessed. If a file with extended attributes is copied to a diskette, or to any disk partition formatted as a FAT partition, these attributes are stored in the file EA DATA . SF. *Do not erase it* otherwise you may experience problems.

Enhanced editor
> The editor supplied as part of OS/2 version 2.0 in the productivity folder.

Entry field
> A control used for data input.

Enumeration
> The process of searching the desktop for a window handle.

F

FAT
> File allocation table. Used to allocate disk space for a file and compatible with both DOS and OS/2.

Focus
> The window which has the focus is the one about to receive input through either the keyboard or the mouse.

Folder
> A workplace object that contains other objects, just as a 'real world' folder would contain sheets of paper. Depicted on the desktop as an icon in the shape of a pale yellow folder.

Font
> A character set of a particular type and size of typeface.

Frame
> The window encompassing all other parts of an application's window. It is represented on the screen as a border and can usually be used to size a window.

G

GPI
> Graphics programming interface.

Grey
> The term used to indicate that an item is not selectable, for example a greyed menu item.

H

Handle
> An identifier that Presentation Manager uses to identify an object, for example a window.

Header file
> A file containing variable and constant definitions that is included in your program source file using the `#include` statement.

Hello world
> A very basic program that displays the string `Hello World`.

I

Icon
> A small window which represents an object and is usually a picture. It can

be created using the icon editor which is part of OS/2 version 2.0. This editor was only available in the toolkit for OS/2 version 1.x.

Integer
A whole number.

Invalidate
Inform Presentation Manager that a window needs to be painted since it is no longer valid. This could be because another window covering it has been moved away.

K

Kb
Kilobyte (1024 bytes).

KBD
Keyboard.

L

LDT
An internal table, not accessible by applications, that defines the code and data segments for a particular process.

Listbox
A control which shows a scrollable list of selectable items.

M

Main window
The topmost window of an application. Its position is relative to the desktop.

Make
A program, NMAKE.EXE, supplied with the developer's toolkit to aid in the building of a program. Especially useful when you have a program containing many source files, as it causes only those files that have changed since the last compilation to be recompiled.

Maximize
Make a window occupy the entire desktop, or if this is not possible, make it as large as possible.

Mb
Megabyte, or 1 048 576 bytes, that is, 1024 × 1024.

Menu
A window containing a list of choices. A menu can be pulled down from the menu bar or system menu, or popped up by using a mouse button.

Menu bar
The bar beneath the title bar which contains a horizontal list of options.

Minimize
: Make a window as small as possible. This can either be an icon on the desktop or in the minimized window viewer, or invisible.

Minimized window viewer
: A special window in the workplace that holds minimized windows.

MLE
: Multiline entry field. An entry field capable of displaying many lines. The OS/2 system editor uses this control.

Mnemonic
: An underlined letter which appears on a pull-down menu that, when typed, will cause that action to be executed. A mnemonic may also be used to switch window focus. See also tilde.

Modal dialog box
: A dialog box which, when being used, prohibits the user from interacting with its parent window, usually the application's client window. A system modal dialog box prohibits interaction with any other window in the system.

Modeless dialog box
: A dialog box which, when being used, allows interaction with any other window.

MOU
: Mouse.

O

Object window
: A window that has no parent and is not visible but can process messages.

OS/2 (16-bit)
: The initial version of OS/2, that is 1.0 through to 1.3. Requires at least an 80286 processor.

OS/2 (32-bit)
: The latest version of OS/2. Requires at least an 80386 processor.

OS2.INI
: A system file which stores application and system data. This file and OS2SYS.INI are vital, and if corrupted will cause you problems. Like CONFIG.SYS, copies of these files are also installed in your \OS2\INSTALL directory.

OS2SYS.INI
: See OS2.INI.

P

Page
: The minimum amount of memory allocated to a program, 4096 bytes.

Glossary

Pel
> Picture element. The smallest addressable unit on a screen.

Pointer
> The symbol displayed on the screen that is moved by using the mouse, or other pointing device.

Presentation Manager
> This is the graphical user interface introduced with OS/2 version 1.1. It is responsible for allowing multiple applications to run in windows on the desktop.

Process
> A running program and its resources. A process comprises at least one thread.

Pushbutton
> A control that, when pressed, causes an immediate action to take place, for example, cancel an update.

R

Resource file
> A file containing the definition of your program's resources, for example menu and accelerator table definitions.

RGB
> Red–green–blue. Used to express a colour using its three components.

S

Screen
> The monitor display.

Session
> Comprises a virtual screen, keyboard and mouse. A session can run many processes, for example the Presentation Manager session.

Shutdown
> The process which needs to be run before switching off the computer to avoid loss of data, and to ensure the desktop is restored to its previous state next time it is started.

Static field
> A text control; the user cannot enter data into it.

Style
> Property of a window, or control.

System menu
> The pull-down menu at the top-left corner of a window that allows the moving, sizing and closing of that window.

T

Task list
In OS/2 version 1.x, the list showing which programs are currently running. It can be used to switch to the programs or close them.

Thread
A unit of execution. It may be a complete program or just a few statements.

Tilde
The special character, ~, used to define a mnemonic.

Title bar
The bar at the top of a main window containing the program's title. It can be used to move the window around the desktop by dragging it with the mouse.

V

VGA
Video graphics array.

VIO
Video input/output.

W

Window list
The version 2.0 equivalent of the task list.

Window procedure
Code that handles the processing of messages for a window.

Workplace
This is your screen in OS/2 version 2.0. It is similar to a desktop in that it can contain folders, printers, letters, memos or any other object.

Workplace object
This is basically anything that you work with in the workplace, for example a data file or program.

Workplace Shell
This is the OS/2 version 2.0 equivalent of the version 1 Presentation Manager Shell.

Z

Z-order
The 'three-dimensional' ordering of windows. For example, the window with the input focus would be at the top of the Z-order.

Appendix 2
Obtaining accompanying software

Source files, executable programs and three extra chapters (mouse and pointer control, keyboard processing and errors and error processing) are available in machine-readable form for 16-bit or 32-bit OS/2 by sending:

i) a formatted diskette
ii) a cheque for £5.95 sterling
iii) a copy of the form below to

McGraw-Hill Book Company (UK) Ltd
Shoppenhangers Road
Maidenhead, Berks SL6 2QL,
England.

Although every effort has been made to ensure the reliability and accuracy of the disk, the Publisher cannot guarantee that the disk, when used for its intended or any other use, is free from error or defect. You are welcome to use, copy and adapt these programs in any way you please, excepting that the contents of the diskette may not be reproduced without the copyright notice which it is supplied with, nor may it be sold.

Name . . . .
Address . . . .
. . . .
. . . .
. . . .
Telephone . . . .

Important
Please specify whether you require the diskette for 16-bit or 32-bit OS/2. Please note that only the 32-bit diskette contains the sample application to monitor the swap file. This program has been extended since the book was written and now allows the storing of a continuous history of swap file changes.

Index

/EXEPACK, 8
/NOD, 7
_alloca, 16
_beginthread, 241
_ecvt, 16
_endthread, 241
_fcloseall, 16
_fcvt, 16
_gcvt, 16
_itoa, 16
_ltoa, 16
_putenv, 16
_rmtmp, 16
_System linkage, 242
_tzset, 16
_ultoa, 16

About option, 259–260
Active window, 30, 36
Alt-Esc preventing, 32, 46, 269
Alt-Tab preventing, 46, 269
Atom,
  integer, 30, 189
  manager, 189
  string, 189

Bitmap, 67, 69
BKA_*, 154
BKM_*, 153
BKM_QUERYTABTEXT, 160
BKM_SETDIMENSIONS, 155
BKM_SETPAGEWINDOWHWND, 156
BKN_*, 153
BKN_PAGESELECTED, 159
BKS_*, 153
BM_SETDEFAULT, 66
BN_PAINT, 67
BOOKTEXT structure, 160

Broadcasting messages, 190
BS_DEFAULT, 66
BS_USERBUTTON, 67
Button
  default, 66, 67, 102
  push, 66–70, 114
  radio, 70, 114
  user, 67, 102

C source files
  atom manager and user
    messages, 193–198
  Exception handler
    EXCEPTN.C, 340, 341
    EXCEPTN2.C, 342, 343
  General window control, 38
  Listboxes, 127–138
  MLE and radio buttons, 117–124
  Menus and task management, 277–286
  Miscellaneous controls and activities, 105–113
  Skeleton program (16-bit), 3–5
  Skeleton program (32-bit), 11–13
  Swap partition monitor
    CHNGCOL.C, 330
    DLGWND.C, 323–330
    GAUGEFRM.C, 333
    GAUGEWND.C, 299–306
    GETSTATS.C, 295–297
    MAINWND.C, 313–322
    RGBTOSTR.C, 331–332
    SLIDER.C, 306–308
    STRTOLNG.C, 332
    STRTORGB.C, 331
    SUBCLASS.C, 309–312
    SWAPMON.C, 291–294
System modal application
  (16-bit), 53–56

System modal application
    (32-bit), 48–52
Threads and timers, 249–258
Version 2.0 controls and
    dialogs, 171–188
Window enumeration and
    icons, 229–239
Window words and
    initialization data, 206–217
Child window, 221
Class names, 30, 221, 224
Close
    on context menu, 272
    removing from system menu, 263
    removing from window list, 270
CLR_BACKGROUND, 142
Colour
    changing, 57
Comments, 14
Compile options, 6
CONFIG.SYS, 47, 53, 98, 288, 294,
Container, 139
CTEXT statement, 100
CTLDATA, entry field, 71
Ctrl-Esc, preventing, 32, 46
Cursor
    not appearing, 71
    position, 71

DBM_INVERT, 69
DBM_NORMAL, 69
DBM_STRETCH, 69
Debugger, 339
Desktop manager
    save, 32
    shutdown, 32
Dialog box editor, 58, 60, 63, 101
Dialog box
    disabling controls, 65
    focus, 63, 65, 76, 102
    icon, 36, 77, 102
    initialization data, 201
    main window, 60, 101
    menu, 97, 101
    minimizing, 61, 101
    mnemonics, 63, 124
    modeless, 63, 204
    pop-up menu, 101, 267
    position, 63
    retrieving data from, 204
    status bar, 64, 101
    title, 100
    window ID, 65, 102
    window words, 201

Dialogs
    file, 162–165
    font, 165–168
    initializing, 162, 165
    standard, 162
DosAllocMem, 82, 83, 200, 205, 341
DosAllocSeg, 82, 83, 200, 204, 205
DosAsyncTimer, 15
DosBufReset, 15
DosCaseMap, 15
DosChDir, 15
DosChgFilePtr, 15
DosCreateDir, 15
DosCreateThread, 240
DosCwait, 15
DosDeleteDir, 15
DosExit, 15, 245
DosFindFirst, 15
DosFindFirst2, 15
DosFreeMem, 15, 83
DosGetCollate, 15
DosGetCp, 15
DosGetCtryInfo, 15
DosGetDBCSEv, 15
DosGetInfoBlocks, 15
DosGetInfoSeg, 15
DosGetResource, 15
DosGetResource2, 15
DosInsMessage, 15
DosInsertMessage, 15
DosKillThread, 244, 248
DosMapCase, 15
DosMkDir, 15
DosMkDir2, 15
DosNewSize, 15
DosOpen, 15
DosOpen2, 15
DosQCurDir, 15
DosQCurDisk, 15
DosQFHandState, 15
DosQFSAttach, 15
DosQFSInfo, 15
DosQFileInfo, 15
DosQHandType, 15
DosQPathInfo, 15
DosQSysInfo, 15
DosQueryCollate, 15
DosQueryCp, 15
DosQueryCtryInfo, 15
DosQueryCurrentDir, 15
DosQueryCurrentDisk, 15
DosQueryDBCSEnv, 15
DosQueryFHState, 15
DosQueryFSAttach, 15
DosQueryFSInfo, 15, 294

DosQueryFileInfo, 15
DosQueryHType, 15
DosQueryPathInfo, 15
DosQuerySysInfo, 15
DosQVerify, 15
DosQueryVerify, 15
DosResetBuffer, 15
DosResumeThread, 241, 243
DosRmDir, 15
DosSearchPath, 15
DosSelectDisk, 15
DosSetCurrentDir, 15
DosSetDefaultDisk, 15
DosSetFHState, 15
DosSetFHandState, 15
DosSetFilePtr, 15
DosSetFileSize, 15
DosSet priority, 15
DosSetProcCP, 15
DosSetProcessCP, 15
DosSetPrty, 15
DosShutdown, 15
DosSleep, 80, 125, 242, 246, 247, 295
DosStartSession, 46, 56
DosStartTimer, 15
DosStopTimer, 15
DosSubAlloc, 15
DosSubAllocMem, 83, 200, 205
DosSubFree, 15
DosSubFreeMem, 83, 201
DosSubSetMem, 15
DosSubUnset, 15
DosSubUnsetMem, 83
DosSuspendThread, 243
DosTimerAsync, 15
DosTimerStart, 15
DosTimerStop, 15
DosWaitChild, 15
DPATH environment variable, 294
Drag/Drop support for colours
  and fonts, 309
DT_ERASERECT, 31
DT_LEFT, 31
DT_MNEMONIC, 63
DT_WORDBREAK, 100

EM_SETREADONLY, 74
EM_SETSEL, 71
EM_SETTEXTLIMIT, 70
End task button, 270, 272
Entry field
  centralizing text, 100–101
  changing default length, 70
  clearing, 76
  control data, 71
  CTLDATA, 71

cursor, 71
disabling, 65
numeric only, 73, 101
read-only, 74, 102
reading data, 72
subclassing, 73
unreadable, 75, 102
writing data, 75
Enumeration, 30, 87, 220, 224, 243, 333
Errors, common, 17
  SYS1477, 287
ERROR_DOSSUB_NOMEM, 200, 205
ES_UNREADABLE, 75
ES_READONLY, 74
Exception handler, 200, 339

FCF_*, 18
FCF_ICON, 223
FCF_MENU, 261
FCF_MINMAX, 28
FCF_NOBYTEALIGN, 21, 48
FCF_SHELLPOSITION, 18, 19, 33
FCF_STANDARD, 17, 19, 33, 223, 269
FCF_STDNOACCEL, 18
FCF_TASKLIST, 34, 269
FDS_*, 162
FID_MINMAX, 28
FID_SYSMENU, 260
FID_TITLEBAR, 23
File dialog, 162
  Styles, 163
FILEDLG structure, 162–164
Flat memory model, 8
Font
  changing, 58, 114
  dialog, 165
  listbox, 59, 87
  style, 59
FONTDLG structure, 165–168
Frame creation flags, 17–19, 21
Frame ID, 28
Frame window
  handle, 17, 59
  style, 29
FS_DLGBORDER, 29
FS_SIZEBORDER, 29

Global variables, 17, 200, 245
GpiQueryTextBox, 93
Guard page, 342

Hungarian notation, 1
HWND_BOTTOM, 20
HWND_DESKTOP, 24, 220, 224

Index

HWND_OBJECT, 34, 220, 298

ICON statement, 77
Icon
  animated, 225
  changing text, 224
  dialog box, 76
  dynamic update, 225
  hiding text, 224
  minimize/maximize, 28
  standard application, 36
  system, 76
  user, 77

Listbox
  columns, 81, 114
  deleting items, 78
  deselecting items, 78, 124
  flicker, 159
  font, 87
  horizontal scrolling, 92
  inserting items, 77, 124
  item handle, 81, 84, 124, 225
  multiple selection, 78, 79
  non-selectable items, 96
  ownerdraw, 87, 124
  retrieving data, 84
  saving data, 81
  scroll bars, 86
  selecting items, 78, 124
  styles, 85
LIT_END, 77
LIT_FIRST, 79
LIT_NONE, 78, 80
LIT_SORTASCENDING, 77
LIT_SORTDESCENDING, 77
LM_DELETEALL, 78
LM_DELETEITEM, 78
LM_INSERTITEM, 77
LM_QUERYITEMHANDLE, 84
LM_QUERYITEMTEXT, 79
LM_QUERYSELECTION, 79, 80
LM_SELECTITEM, 78
LM_SETITEMHANDLE, 81
LM_SETTOPINDEX, 159
LN_SELECT, 79, 85, 96, 313
Lock parameter, 17
LS_EXTENDEDSEL, 86
LS-MULTIPLESEL, 86
LS_NOADJUSTPOS, 85
LS_NOVERTSCROLL, 86
LS_OWNERDRAW, 88

Memory
  allocation, 82–83, 97
  suballocation, 83, 200

Menu processing, 259
Menu
  bar height, 267
  checking an item, 261
  deleting a separator, 263
  deleting an item, 263
  dialog box, 97, 101
  disabling/enabling an item, 262, 265
  disabling/enabling menu bar, 264
  dismissing, 266
  multiple, 260
  pop-up, 101, 266, 288, 308
  switching, 261
  system, 259, 263, 265
Message
  posting, 35
  sending, 35
  unique ID, 190
MIA_CHECKED, 261
MIA_DISABLED, 262
MIA_NODISMISS, 266
Minimized
  finding minimized applications, 224
  windows on desktop, 223
Minimizing
  dialog box, 61
  window, 26–28
MM_DELETEITEM, 263
MM_DISMISSMENU, 266
MM_ENDMENUMODE, 266
MM_INSERTITEM, 260
MM_ITEMIDFROMPOSITION, 260, 263
MM_ITEMPOSITIONFROMID, 263
MM_QUERYITEM, 260
MM_SETITEMATTR, 261, 265
MM_STARTMENUMODE, 266, 267
MOUSEMSG, 267
MPFROM2SHORT, 71
Multi-line entry field
  clearing, 97
  font, 59
  importing a file, 97–98

Notebook
  associating a window handle with a page, 156
  control, 152
  creating, 154
  description, 139
  inserting pages, 155
  loading, 156
  message attributes, 154

messages, 153
notification codes, 153
size, 159
styles, 153
tab size, 155
tab text, 159–160

Object window, 243, 248
OS2.INI, 33, 36, 290
OWNERITEM structure, 88, 142

PAGESELECTNOTIFY
  structure, 159
PRESPARAMS statement, 57–58
Presentation parameters, 33, 57, 64, 87, 90, 114
PrfQueryProfileData, 33
PrfWriteProfileData, 33
Process ID, 30, 36
Progress indicator, 139
PROTECTONLY, 53
Push button
  default, 66–67, 102
  user, 67, 102
PU_HCONSTRAIN, 308
PU_VCONSTRAIN, 308

QMSG structure, 35
QW_NEXT, 224
QW_PARENT, 17
QWL_STYLE, 27, 66
QWL_USER, 200, 201, 206
QWS_ID, 65
QWS_XRESTORE, 25
QWS_YRESTORE, 25
QWS_CXRESTORE, 25
QWS_CYRESTORE, 25

Radio button initialization, 70, 114

Sample programs
  Atom manager and user messages, 191
  Controls and dialogs (version 2.0), 168
  General window control, 36
  Listboxes, 124
  Menus and task management, 274–286
  MLE and radio buttons, 114
  Miscellaneous controls and activities, 101
  Skeleton, 2, 12–13
  Swap partition monitor, 287–290
  System modal (16-bit), 53–56
  System modal (32-bit), 47–52
  Threads and timers, 247–258

Window enumeration and icons, 226–239
Window words and initialization data, 199
Save desktop option, 32, 272
Saving application state, 32, 272, 290
SBMP_SBUPARROW, 150
SC_CLOSE, 263
Screen resolution, 20–21
SDA_BACKGROUND, 143
SDA_RIBBONSTRIP, 143
SDA_SLIDERARM, 143
SDA_SLIDERSHAFT, 143
SHORT1FROMMP, 79
SHORT2FROMMP, 79
Shutdown, 32, 272
  detecting/preventing, 272
  multiple threads, 273
Skeleton program, 2
SLDCDATA structure, 140
Slider
  control, 140
  control data structure, 140
  creating, 144, 306
  description, 139
  message attributes, 143
  messages, 143
  notification codes, 143
  ownerdraw, 142, 298
  ownerdraw flags, 143
  position, 145
  read-only, 145, 288, 297
  styles, 142
  subclassing, 308
  updating, 146
  user's view, 147
SLM_*, 143
SLM_SETSLIDERINFO, 312
SLN_*, 143
SLN_CHANGE, 146, 323
SLN_SLIDERTRACK, 146, 323
SLS_*, 142
SLS_HORIZONTAL, 298
SLS_PRIMARYSCALE2, 306
SLS_VERTICAL, 298
SMA_*, 143
SPTR_*, 77
STARTDATA structure, 48
Static text
  backslash, 100
  line break, 100, 102
  read-only entry field, 74
  status bar, 64, 101
Styles
  changing, 98

frame, 29
listbox, 85
slider, 308
window, 18, 27
Subclassing
    frame window, 25
    entry field, 73
    slider, 308
SV_CYMENU, 267
SWAPPATH statement, 288
SWAPPER.DAT, 287, 294
SWBLOCK structure, 15
SWCNTRL structure, 16
SWENTRY structure, 15
SWL_GRAYED, 272
SWL_NOTJUMPABLE, 272
SWP structure, 15, 27
SWP_ACTIVATE, 19
SWP_MAXIMIZE, 20
SWP_MINIMIZE, 20, 28, 62–63
SWP_MOVE, 19
SWP_SHOW, 19
SWP_SIZE, 19, 63
SWP_ZORDER, 20, 23
SYS1477 error, 287
System menu
    adding an item, 259
    close, 263, 265, 272
    deleting an item, 263
    deleting a separator, 263
    disabling/enabling an item, 265
    move, 23, 263, 265
    size, 29, 263
System modal, 32, 46

Tab stops,
    adding and removing, 99, 102
Task list, 46, 53
    (see also window list)
Task management, 268
    adding program title to
        window list, 269
    changing program title in
        window list, 269
    querying program title in
        window list, 269
Tenth of a second rule, 240
Text
    changing, 100, 102
Threads
    communicating, 35, 241
    creating, 240
    killing, 244–245
    multiple selection listbox, 80
    shutdown, 272
    starting in a suspended state, 240, 243

without a message queue, 242
with a message queue but
    no message processing
    loop, 242
with a message queue and
    message processing loop, 243
Timer
    longer than 65 seconds, 246
Title bar
    changing, 34, 100
    disabling, 23, 48
    EXE name appearing in, 34
    removing, 34

User messages, 190
USERBUTTON structure, 67

Value set
    attributes, 151
    bitmap, 148, 152
    colour, 147
    control, 147
    control data structure, 147
    creating, 147
    description, 139
    messages, 151
    notification codes, 151
    selecting items, 150–151
    styles, 148
VIA_*, 151
VM_*, 151
VM_QUERYSELECTEDITEM,
    151–152
VM_QUERYITEM, 151
VM_SETITEM, 149
VN_*, 151
VN_SELECT, 150
VS_*, 148
VS_SCALEBITMAPS, 148–149
VSCDATA structure, 147

WC_*, 30
WinAddAtom, 190
WinAddSwitchEntry, 269
WinBeginEnumWindows, 220
WinBeginPaint, 31
WinCancelShutdown, 243, 273
WinChangeSwitchEntry, 269
WinCheckMenuItem, 262
WinCreateAtomTable, 189
WinCreateMsgQueue, 242
WinCreateStdWindow, 2, 17, 19, 223
WinCreateWindow, 199
WinDestroyPointer, 62
WinDestroyWindow, 61, 63, 86
WinDispatchMsg, 35
WinDlgBox, 61, 201

Window
  active, 30, 36
  centralizing, 21
  changing title, 34
  child, 221
  enumeration, 30, 87, 220, 224, 243, 333
  focus, 19
  full-screen, 21
  ID, 65, 102
  initial display, 19
  keeping on top, 23–24
  locking, 14
  maximized, detecting if, 27
  maximizing, detecting when, 26
  maximizing, prohibiting, 28
  menu changing, 260
  minimized, detecting if, 27
  minimizing, 28
  minimizing, detecting when, 26
  minimizing, prohibiting, 28
  minimum size, 25
  movement, 23
  not being displayed, 17
  object, 243, 248
  parent, 17, 24
  position, 19, 21
  prohibiting movement, 23
  prohibiting sizing, 29
  removing title bar, 34
  restoring, detecting when, 26
  restoring to a fixed size or position, 24
  sample program, 36
  saving current state, 32
  size, 19, 25, 28
  starting in the background, 20
  starting maximized, 20
  starting minimized, 20
  subclassing, 23, 25
  system menu, 23
  system modal, 32
  title, 34
  words, 27, 199
Window class, 30
Window list, 46, 48, 265, 272
  adding program title, 269
  changing program title, 269
  options, 272
  querying list, 271
  querying program entry, 269
  removing close, 270
Window style, 18, 27
Window words, 63, 201
WinDrawText, 31

WinEnableMenuItem, 265
WinEnableWindow, 23, 28, 65, 96, 264–265
WinEnableWindowUpdate, 159
WinEndEnumWindows, 220
WinEndPaint, 31
WinEnumDlgItem, 14
WinGetMsg, 35
WinGetNextWindow, 220
WinGetSysBitmap, 148
WinInitialize, 2, 242
WinInvalidateRect, 29, 31, 67, 225
WinIsMenuItemChecked, 263
WinIsMenuItemEnabled, 263
WinLoadDlg, 61, 63, 201, 202
WinLoadMenu, 97, 261, 267
WinLoadPointer, 61, 77
WinLockWindow, 14
WinMapWindowPoints, 28
Win16NoShutdown, 270
WinNoShutdown, 270
WinPopupMenu, 267
WinPostMsg, 35, 241–242, 294
WinProcessDlg, 61
WinQueryActiveWindow, 14, 30
WinQueryAtomName, 30
WinQueryCapture, 14
WinQueryClassName, 30
WinQueryClipbrdOwner, 14
WinQueryClipbrdViewer, 14
WinQueryDlgItemShort, 72
WinQueryDlgItemText, 72
WinQueryFocus, 14
WinQueryPointerPos, 267
WinQuerySwitchHandle, 269
WinQuerySwitchList, 271
WinQuerySysModalWindow, 14
WinQuerySystemAtomTable, 189, 190
WinQuerySysValue, 21, 267
WinQueryWindow, 14, 17, 224
WinQueryWindowLockCount, 14
WinQueryWindowPos, 33
WinQueryWindowProcess, 30
WinQueryWindowRect, 28, 31,
WinQueryWindowText, 63, 72
WinQueryWindowULong, 27, 66, 199, 201
WinQueryWindowUShort, 65, 199
WinRegisterClass, 199
WinRemoveSwitchEntry, 269
WinRestoreWindowPos, 33
WinSendDlgItemMsg, 70
WinSendMsg, 35, 241–242, 248, 294
WinSetDlgItemShort, 14, 75
WinSetDlgItemText, 74, 75, 97, 100

WinSetFocus, 76
WinSetOwner, 24
WinSetPresParam, 57–59, 64, 90, 114, 142, 306
WinSetSysModalWindow, 32, 46, 48
WinSetWindowBits, 29, 67
WinSetWindowPos, 5, 19–22, 28, 62, 63, 267, 298
WinSetWindowText, 34, 64, 74, 75, 97, 100, 101, 224
WinSetWindowULong, 29, 99, 200, 298
WinSetWindowUShort, 14, 24
WinShowWindow, 33, 63, 159, 224
WinStartTimer, 23, 246
WinStopTimer, 24, 32
WinStoreWindowPos, 309
WinSwitchToProgram, 47, 48
WinTerminate, 5
WinWindowFromID, 28, 65, 100, 222, 260
WinWindowFromPoint, 14
WM_ADJUSTWINDOWPOS, 61
WM_BUTTON2DOWN, 267, 306, 308
WM_COMMAND, 5, 35, 260, 268, 298
WM_CONTROL, 67, 68, 70, 146, 150, 159, 323
WM_CREATE, 17–19, 32, 200, 260, 267

WM_DESTROY, 201
WM_DRAWITEM, 88–91, 93, 96, 142, 298
WM_ERASEBACKGROUND, 5
WM_INITDLG, 61, 63–65, 70, 76, 77, 97, 114, 201, 267
WM_INITMENU, 261, 265
WM_MEASUREITEM, 88, 90, 92
WM_MINMAXFRAME, 24, 26, 36
WM_NEXTMENU, 267
WM_PAINT, 31, 36, 312
WM_PRESPARAMCHANGED, 309
WM_QUERYTRACKINFO, 25–26
WM_QUIT, 5, 243, 246, 272–273, 290, 312
WM_SAVEAPPLICATION, 32, 37, 272, 313
WM_SETICON, 61, 77, 225
WM_SIZE, 159
WM_TIMER, 23, 31, 36, 146–147, 246, 295
WM_UPDATEFRAME, 34, 97, 261, 298
WM_USER, 190, 202, 247
Workplace object, 223
Workplace shell, 32, 47, 223, 227
WS_MAXIMIZED, 27
WS_MINIMIZED, 27, 224
WS_VISIBLE, 18, 19